THE TRADE

THE TRADE

MY JOURNEY INTO THE LABYRINTH OF POLITICAL KIDNAPPING

JERE VAN DYK

New York

PublicAffairs, Hachette Book Group, 1290 Avenue of the Americas, New York, NY 10104
www.publicaffairsbooks.com
@Public_Affairs

Printed in the United States of America
First Edition: September 2017
Published by PublicAffairs, an imprint of Perseus Books, LLC, a subsidiary of Hachette Book Group, Inc.

Names have been changed throughout the book for protection.
The publisher is not responsible for websites (or their content) that are not owned by the publisher.

Print book interior design by Linda Mark.

Library of Congress Cataloging-in-Publication Data
Names: Van Dyk, Jere, author. Title: The trade : my journey into the labyrinth of political kidnapping / Jere van Dyk. Description: New York : Public Affairs, an imprint of Perseus Books, LLC, a subsidiary of Hachette Book Group, Inc., 2017. | Includes bibliographical references and index. Identifiers: LCCN 2017017361| ISBN 9781610394314 (hardcover) | ISBN 9781610394321 (ebook) Subjects: LCSH: Van Dyk, Jere—Captivity, 2008. | Political kidnapping—Afghanistan. | Political kidnapping—Middle East. | Journalists—Afghanistan—Biography. | Prisoners—Afghanistan—Biography. | Taliban. Classification: LCC DS371.43.V36 A3 2017 | DDC 364.15/40956—dc23LC record available at https://lccn.loc.gov/2017017361
ISBNs: 978-1-61039-431-4 (HC), 978-1-61039-432-1 (EB)

LSC-C

10 9 8 7 6 5 4 3 2 1

To my brother, Kody

This is the work of ghosts.

You are part of a gigantic picture here.

Contents

Cast of Characters

Professor Rasul Amin: From Kunar Province; studied in Pakistan; Afghan minister of education, later director of Afghanistan Studies Center, considered an independent thinker and Afghan nationalist; had many school friends who worked in the Pakistani government; maintained close ties to Pakistan; uncle of Shahwali Hazrat, author's fixer; relationship with Sameer, a prostitute. Amin died in 2009.

Sameer (pseudonym): A prostitute, hired by Professor Amin; grew up in a Pakistani refugee camp and has links to kidnappers, introducing Shahwali to them. She may have links to the ISI.

(Sami) Sharif: Author's first fixer, arranged through Peter and Hassina Jouvenal; took author into the mountains where Corporal Pat Tillman was killed; later took author to meet the Taliban south of Tora Bora; appears to have been involved in the kidnapping of British documentary filmmaker Sean Langan in March 2008.

Aziz: Sharif's driver, took the author up to Tora Bora and may have been involved in Sean Langan's kidnapping.

Hajji: Aziz's uncle, a drug smuggler turned car smuggler turned human smuggler; in 2007, took author into Mohmand Agency; arranged for author to meet with the Taliban near Tora Bora; in 2008, kidnapped Sean Langan in Bajaur Agency, Tribal Areas of Pakistan, when he was working for Channel 4.

Ahmed: Author's driver, brought to him by Shahwali, but who may have tried to warn and thus save author from kidnappers.

Ahmed Jan: CBS cameraman, author's driver, and friend; came with Fazul to author's release, but overcome with emotion, failed to film it.

Zalgai: Author's fixer and interpreter with Yunus Khalis.

Ehsanullah: Pashtun, longtime Afghan journalist, author's friend, source, and neutral observer.

Yunus Khalis: A famous Afghan mujahideen leader in 1980s, center of mujahideen/Taliban/al-Qaeda nexus, close to bin Laden; in author's view the father or grandfather that bin Laden never had; died in 2006. According to Khalis' guards, former mujahideen, and associates, the author is the only Westerner to visit him after 9/11. Head of the Pakistani-controlled mujahideen political party, Hezb-i-Islami Khalis; the Haqqanis, Mullah Malang, Mirwais Yasini, Abdul Haq, Hajji Abdul Qadir, Hajji Din Mohammad, and Hazrat Ali were all a part of the Khalis faction in 1980s.

Hajji Abdul Qadir: Din Mohammad's older brother, a prominent 1980s mujahideen commander; governor of Nangarhar province and vice president of Afghanistan, killed in 2002 in Kabul, by, apparently, Abdullah and maybe Hajji Zaman, and others, on orders of ISI.

Abdul Haq: Famous mujahideen leader in 1980s jihad against USSR; entered Afghanistan in October 2001 to rally tribes against Taliban, and killed on orders of ISI; quite possibly the man the US, or influential elements within the US government, wanted to be president after 9/11, instead of Hamid Karzai; President Ronald Reagan honored him with a White House dinner. UK prime minister Margaret Thatcher met with him in London.

Hajji Din Mohammad: Pashtun, author's oldest friend in Afghanistan, member of prominent Arsala family; chief negotiator for the Afghan government in talks (currently suspended) with the Taliban; former and current ally of US government; met with President G. H. W. Bush, and three times with President Reagan. Din Mohammad and others warned author repeatedly how dangerous it was to try to find out who was involved in his kidnapping. His brothers Abdul Haq and Hajji Qadir were both killed by Taliban, probably on orders of ISI. His son Izatullah, a poet, was killed with Abdul Haq.

Amrullah Saleh: Tajik, former head of National Directorate of Security (NDS, Afghan intelligence service), plays small but important role in explaining to author what, in his view, happened in his case, i.e., his belief that the author was kidnapped by his so-called friends, mirroring exactly what Din Mohammad, a Pashtun, said.

Mullah Malang: Arranged meeting with author and his kidnappers; famous mujahideen commander during 1980s jihad against USSR; member of parliament; said to be a former and possibly present CIA, Iranian, and ISI asset.

Mirwais Yasini: Pashtun, member of 1980s Hezb-i-Islami Khalis mujahideen political faction; today First Deputy Speaker, Lower House of Parliament; introduced Malang to author; enemy of Feridoun Mohmand, who secured author's release.

Hazrat Ali: Pashai mujahideen commander in 1980s; member of Hezb-i-Islami Khalis faction; allied with Arsala family; hired by CIA to find bin Laden at Tora Bora; said to be one of the men who killed Abdullah's cousin, Khorsheed; after the author's release, Ali's father and other members of his family killed, and his son kidnapped; author believes this is related to his own kidnapping.

Hajji Abdul Zahir, commonly known as Hajji Zahir: Member of parliament, member of the Arsala family; son of Abdul Qadir, nephew to Din Mohammad; hired by the CIA (along with Hazrat Ali and Hajji Zaman) to find bin Laden at Tora Bora; said to have been involved, with Hazrat Ali, in the death of Abdullah's nephew, Khorsheed.

Khorsheed: Close relative of Abdullah; rumored to have been killed by Zahir and Hazrat Ali; as a result, Abdullah took his revenge, killing Zahir's father, Hajji Qadir, a vice president of Afghanistan, in a contract killing in Kabul in July 2002; assassination ordered by the ISI. Abdullah may have pulled the trigger, but Hajji Zaman, said to be an ISI contractor, is said to have been the lead man in the ISI assassination. Zaman is said to have been behind the author's kidnapping, in part, because of author's links to Din Mohammad and the Arsala family.

Feridoun Mohmand: Afghan, member of parliament, chief of the Mohmand tribe, said to be an ISI asset, secured author's release; Mohmand's driver was waved onto the US base in Jalalabad and knew, strangely, exactly where to take the author; Gohar Zaman, former head of Pakistan's Intelligence Bureau, in Dubai for open-heart surgery, had his brother-in-law, Bashir, send ransom money from Pakistan to Mohmand in Kabul; Feridoun Mohmand's convoy was later targeted in a suicide attack; Mohmand may be tied to Michael Semple, and possibly to Gohar Zaman; all three are said to have ties to the ISI.

Sami Yousafzai: Afghan journalist and fixer living in Pakistan; writes for *Newsweek* and Daily Beast, author brought him to CBS, where he has been a consultant.

Daoud Sultanzoy: Tribal leader, former member of parliament, presidential candidate, television host, Ariana Afghan Airlines and later American Airlines pilot; close to President Ghani, warned author that Din Mohammad might hurt him indirectly. Made introduction to Enayat; went to high school with mujahideen anti-Western guerrilla leader Gulbuddin Hekmatyar.

Enayat (pseudonym): Afghan tribal leader from the border region, family links in Miran Shah, a member of parliament, who introduced author to another tribal leader, Arifullah Pashtoon, who brought him together with Ibrahim Haqqani. Pashtoon later claimed that Enayat learned of a 2007 plot by Sirajuddin Haqqani to kidnap the author, and thought to help Sirajuddin and get his share of the ransom money.

Arifullah Pashtoon: leader of the Saberi tribe, from the border region, former chairman, Senate Foreign Relations Committee, Upper House of Parliament, served as intermediary with Haqqanis.

Fazul Rahim: Tajik, one of author's closest friends, worked tirelessly to save him.

Ahmed Shah Amin: freelance journalist, cousin of Fazul Rahim, involved in trying to rescue author; believes that there was a conspiracy in author's release.

Peter Jouvenal: English; businessman and cameraman; covered Afghan-Soviet war for the BBC; filmed CNN bin Laden interview; with his wife, Hassina, owned the Gandamack, a hotel for journalists; he and Hassina introduced the author to Sharif.

The Wahhabi: Shahwali's friend and guide to the Taliban.

The Malik of Ducalam: Plotted to extort money from the author, introducing him to the Trade; sent author across border into Chitral, Pakistan, for first cross-border interview with the Taliban.

Abu Hamza: Taliban commander in Kunar Province; interviewed by author and later may have tried to kidnap him.

Abu Omar: Taliban commander interviewed by author in Chitral, north of the Tribal Areas, Pakistan.

PAKISTAN

Abdullah: Probably an ISI asset; widely rumored to have assassinated, on the orders of the ISI, Hajji Abdul Qadir, a vice president of Afghanistan and Din Mohammad's brother. Underling to Hajji Zaman, probably an ISI asset. Lives in Tribal Areas of Pakistan.

Razi Gul: One of Abdullah's men, one of author's bodyguards, fellow captive, and a captor; he and Sameer are both from Landi Khotal, a town in Khyber Agency, in the Tribal Areas. Sameer apparently introduced Gul to Shahwali.

Gulob: Main jailer who lives, it seems, in Landi Khotal, along with Razi Gul and Abdullah; he, like Razi Gul, is part of Abdullah's gang.

Samad: Author's bodyguard who was also a captive and is part of Abdullah's clan (married, the author believes, to Abdullah's sister) and his gang. He claimed to be involved in a war with the Arsala family. He lives, probably, in Mohmand Agency, Pakistan.

Abdul Wali: Head of the Taliban in Mohmand Agency; ISI asset; Gulob claimed that they were under Abdul Wali.

Hajji Zaman: Probable ISI asset, former 1980s mujahideen commander; hired by the CIA in 2001 to capture or kill bin Laden in Tora Bora. He allegedly just pocketed the money the US paid him to fight al-Qaeda. Lead figure in author's kidnapping. Abdullah worked for him. According to Din Mohammad, Zaman killed his brother Hajji Qadir, widely believed to be on the orders of the ISI. Zaman was killed in 2010, maybe by the Arsala family.

Gohar Zaman: Pashtun, former Pakistani police officer; former head of Intelligence Bureau, the Pakistan police intelligence agency, one of seven Pakistani intelligence agencies; hired by Kroll Inc., which CBS hired, to assist in author's release; Zaman is still linked, it seems, to ISI and MI6.

Ibrahim Haqqani: Diplomatic and political head of the Haqqani Network, lead negotiator for the Taliban in peace talks (currently stalled); according to Ibrahim, his nephew, Sirajuddin Haqqani, is the caliph (spiritual leader) of the Islamic Emirate of Afghanistan; he is also military leader of the Taliban. Ibrahim is said to have direct ties to the chairman of the joint chiefs of staff of the Pakistani army, and to the ISI. Author lived with Ibrahim and his older brother, Jalaluddin Haqqani, founder of the Haqqani Network, as a freelance journalist during Afghan-Soviet war in Afghanistan.

Mahmud Mohmand (pseudonym): Lawyer, tribal chief from Mohmand Agency, invited by the US to study US court system. Michael Semple introduced Mohmand to the author, who then met Mohmand in New York City; Mohmand asked the author if he was kidnapped by the Pakistani government or the Taliban (the first man to introduce this possibility to the author); close ties to US embassy in Pakistan; represents Shakil Afridi, Pakistani doctor hired by CIA to help identify bin Laden's presence in Abbottabad, Pakistan; brought up the names Shah Sab, now with ISIS, and Abdul Wali, head of Taliban in Mohmand, to the author, just as author's captors did.

Shahwali Hazrat: Author's fixer who betrayed him to his kidnappers; worked for his uncle Rasul Amin in Afghanistan Study Center's library before becoming a schoolteacher. FBI wanted to take the author back to Afghanistan to help FBI take him to Guantanamo, or, if he resisted, to kill him. Lives in Peshawar, Pakistan.

Nafay Hamid (pseudonym): Worked tirelessly to help author; served as interpreter in author's 2015 meeting with Ibrahim Haqqani.

Mugaddir Khan: Driver, author's friend, Pashto tutor, and part of the group set up at Michael Semple's farm to rescue author.

WASHINGTON / NEW YORK / UK / GERMANY

Rosanne Klass: Strong conservative, author's friend, prominent American expert on Afghanistan during 1980s Afghan-Soviet war; introduced author to Rasul Amin, minister of education, and who indirectly led him into the labyrinth of political kidnapping.

Bob and John (pseudonyms): FBI agents who were part of author's rescue team and one of whom tried to get the author to return to Afghanistan to capture or kill Shahwali.

Bill (pseudonym): Victim Specialist, FBI, who pressured author to see Rochelle.

Michael Semple: Irish, Muslim, linguist, scholar, MI6 contact, former Oxfam, EU, and UN official at the Bonn Conference in 2001, and in Afghanistan, one of world's premier experts on Afghanistan, married to the daughter of a Pakistani general, considered by CBS as the man who saved author's life.

Bryn Padrig: (pseudonym): English, author was told that he brought money into Pakistan, part of ad hoc group who brought in Sami Yousafzai and Michael Semple to work on author's case.

Rochelle (pseudonym): A psychiatrist imposed on author by FBI; author left her in 2009.

Thomas Ruttig: German scholar from former East Germany, cofounder and codirector of Afghanistan Analysts Network, close to Michael Semple; worked on 2004 UN kidnapping case.

Behroz Khan: Pashtun, Pakistani journalist in Peshawar; today with Voice of America (VOA) in Washington, DC, introduced author to Sami Yousafzai and to Pakistani ambassador Asif Durrani.

Asif Durrani: Currently Pakistani ambassador to the United Arab Emirates; according to Professor Amin, Durrani blackballed author's visa application.

John Solecki: American, and author's friend, UNHCR official, kidnapped in Baluchistan Province, Pakistan, by a secular Baluch guerrilla organization in 2009.

David Rohde: American, and author's friend, former *New York Times* reporter, kidnapped by Haqqani Network in 2008, and from which he escaped. Today, online editor for *The New Yorker*.

Tahir Luddin: Afghan fixer, worked with David Rohde and escaped with him in Pakistan.

Lisa Monaco: Homeland Security adviser and chief counterterrorism adviser to President Obama.

Jennifer Easterly: Senior director for counterterrorism, White House.

Jason Amerine: Special Forces officer tasked to rescue Abdul Haq; sent to protect Hamid Karzai, future president of Afghanistan; tasked to set up a special unit in the Pentagon to rescue Sgt. Bowe Bergdahl, American Caitlan Coleman, her two children, her husband Canadian Joshua Boyle, and American Paul Overby, all believed being held by the Haqqani Network.

David McCraw: assistant legal counsel and now vice president, *New York Times*.

Author's Note and Acknowledgments

On February 16, 2008, a warm, sunny morning, I left Jalalabad, Afghanistan, and crossed into the Tribal Areas of Pakistan, off-limits to foreigners, and hiked up into the mountains of Mohmand Agency, where, at dusk, I was kidnapped. I wrote about the experience in *Captive*. This book uses the story of why I went, some of what I couldn't write about earlier, some of what happened afterward, and the story of my return to find out the truth, to paint a picture not so much of the experience of being kidnapped but to map the dark labyrinth of the geopolitics of kidnapping.

A great many people, directly and indirectly through their support, helped me to write this book, principal among them my brother, Kody Van Dyk, who in 1973 dropped out of his first year at the University of Washington and flew to Europe, where I had been studying and running track, and where I bought an old Volkswagen that we drove across Asia to Afghanistan; and who forty-two years later called me every day in February 2016 when I lay in the Manhattan VA hospital after complications from open-heart surgery, and volunteered to come from his home in Idaho to take care of me. We both want to thank our parents, mainly our mother, who agreed to let him join me long ago on our trip. The world was romantic then, and the road east was open, and the sky was clear.

It is darker now.

Much of the research in this book, both recent and not so recent, has depended on one person recommending me to speak to another. There is a kind of chain—and I've come to believe that a book set in a lawless region that investigates illegality could not have been written any other way. There is no completely reliable source, no ultimate validation of a single truth, no all-persuasive authority. Instead I have talked to everyone caught up in the shadows of the business of kidnapping, and all that it represents. I have had to listen to people telling me things I know cannot be wholly true, but may nonetheless be revealing for unintended reasons. The chain includes the late senator Henry "Scoop" Jackson; Afghans in exile in the suburbs of Washington, DC, seeking help; the Australian photojournalist Jim Sheldon, who gave me the name of his driver, Munchi, in Peshawar, Pakistan, who took me to meet Yunus Khalis and Din Mohammad, who introduced me to Jalaluddin Haqqani, today the patriarch of the feared Haqqani Network, through whom I met his brother, Ibrahim.

After reading her op-ed in the *New York Times* I met and became friends with Rosanne Klass; she told me to look up her friend, Professor Rasul Amin, minister of education, in the new interim government in Afghanistan, through whom I met his nephew, Shahwali, who betrayed me. Rosanne Klass said to me once that it takes a long time, but once you get a feel for Afghanistan, you know when something isn't right. She had a point.

In 2008, after I was released, I didn't believe the little that my rescue team or the FBI told me about my kidnapping. I didn't feel that they were lying, only that they didn't know the truth. I knew almost nothing, beyond that which happened in my cell, but slowly, over the next five years, I began to learn a few things about what happened on the outside. I was not ready to return to South Asia until in 2013 I created an opportunity—with the help of others, particularly Richard Perle, with whom I served in the 1970s on the staff of Senator Jackson—to travel to the Middle East to research a book on the links between the Haqqani Network and jihadist groups there.

And so I was drawn again into the intrigue of Afghanistan and Pakistan. They are not transparent countries. In my experience, there is a subterranean world that an outsider cannot penetrate. Things are rarely what they seem to be. You must go slowly, carefully, and always remember Kipling, who wrote, "Here lies a fool who tried to hustle the East." You must go as if walking through a jungle at night, watching each step. You must always, above all, trust your instincts. This seems obvious, but I, in my ambition, in my rush to cross the mountains, to go where others had not and could not go, got kidnapped because I had not heeded the warnings that surrounded me.

Finally, and for many people this is difficult to understand and easy to mock, because of my upbringing and my experiences, I have had no choice but to go beyond instinct and to trust, sometimes, that I am being led. Call it God's will, kismet, or providence if you wish. Inshallah, "God willing," men say in Arabic. Deus Vult, "God wills it," the Crusaders said in their war against Islam. "God willing," we said in our Plymouth Brethren assembly when I was a boy. Afghanistan and Pakistan are religious countries, where men are mostly aware of the power of God. Religion is the most powerful force in that world. I understand religious fundamentalism, this new phenomenon in Afghanistan, the tension between God and mammon, what it gives to and demands from a man.

This book is about what I call the Trade, the growing international business of political kidnappings, according to the US Treasury the most lucrative source of income, outside of state sponsorship, for illegal groups. But it's more than about money. It is about my attempt, yes, to find the answer to two questions which have haunted me for nine years: Who kidnapped me, and why? But also, it is a search for redemption, a religious term. The only way I could find the answers was to go, as I always have, from one man to the next day. It is a dangerous, sinuous route.

⁘ ⁘ ⁘

I AM ALIVE today thanks to many people, including the team of colleagues who set in motion the events that led to my release. Secondly, I wish to thank Michael Semple, leader of the council formed at his farm outside of Islamabad, a group who worked tirelessly to prevent what Semple called "a second Daniel Pearl."

I would like to thank David Rohde, my cousins George and Stephen Van Dyk and Mark Woodcock, who came to visit me in the hospital after my surgery in 2016; and Alex Strick van Linchtofen, who sent me books and offered to come from the Netherlands to cook for me; my cousin Lois Chapman; Peter Lewis in Los Angeles; Ellen Rust Weintraub in Zurich; military analyst and Ret. Col. Jeff McCausland; and especially Kimberly Sue Goad, who took care of me; Maxemillian Corkum, especially, and Tom Campbell, Bill and Carol Gilbert, Cathy Congdon, John and Diane Marks, and Jane Hawthorne, friends since our youth in the Plymouth Brethren community in Portland, Oregon; Kristin Mulhivill, David and Sue Perry, Chris Jenkins and Clara Miller, Steve Owen, Arthur and Sherry Hill; Grace Kiley, for her help after my second operation; Aden Hayes, whom I met at Ft. Eustis, Virginia, now of Madrid; and Richard Reticki, of Camp King, in Obersurel, Germany, now of Oakland, California; Geoff Hollister, former teammate at the University of Oregon, who came to New York with his wife Wendy, when he was dying of colon cancer, to say good-bye. To teammates Mike Crunican, Bill Norris, Dave Wilborn, Bob Williams, Wade Bell, Gary Lineburg, and Gordon Payne; to my high school teammates Louis Benedict, Bob Mayes, and Mike Olin. To Laura Besserman, Linda Buss, Toni Henderson, Barbara Olsen, and Susan Monti, for the dinner they gave me in our hometown; to Ron and Michele Thompson; to Susan Hall, Randy Wulff, Susie Hirsch, Linda Sanchez, Rita Nellis, Terry Memovich, and Dennis Zoet; and especially to Jack Higgins, the best track coach I ever had; and to all my friends in Vancouver, Seattle, Portland, and San Francisco who came to hear me talk there; to Kirk and Betsy Hall, in Boise, Gary Major in Gooding, Idaho, Denny Earhart in Henderson, Nevada, and especially my sister, M'Lyss Fruhling, all of whom welcomed me home, giving me the strength to go back.

To Dovid Efune, editor at the *Algemeiner*, who inadvertently sent me on a journey to find the truth about the death of Daniel Pearl, which led me on a journey of my own that I didn't expect.

At the Carnegie Council for Ethics and International Affairs, I want to thank Joel Rosenthal, president, who gave me a luncheon; Joanne Myers, director of public affairs programs; Melissa Semeniuk; Richard Haas, president at the Council on Foreign Relations; and James M. Lindsay, senior vice president and director of the David Rockefeller Studies Program, who from 2013 to 2015 took me on as an adjunct senior fellow, giving me the opportunity to study the Haqqani Network in the greater Middle East, which propelled me back to Afghanistan. I want to thank Dr. Vartan Gregorian, President of the Carnegie Corporation, for help to complete this book and another project.

A great many people helped me in Afghanistan, but unfortunately, because of the danger to them, I must keep their names secret. I can publicly thank Hajji Din Mohammad, chief negotiator in the peace talks; Daoud Sultanzoy; Arifullah Pashton, former chairman of the Afghan Senate Foreign Relations Committee; Abdul Rahim, mujahideen spokesman in the 1980s and later ambassador to the US; and especially Fazul Rahim, who risked his life to save mine, and with him Ahmed Jan, Ahmed Shah Amin, and Feridoun Mohmand.

In Pakistan, I want to give a special and lasting thanks to Nafay Hamid for visiting me on a freezing February morning in the hospital in New York, for courageously translating for me with the leadership of the Haqqani Network, for her friendship, guidance, and perseverance; I want to thank Gohar Zaman, Behroz Khan, and Sami Yousafzai.

I wish to thank Lisa Monaco, US Homeland Security adviser and chief counterterrorism adviser to President Obama, and Jennifer Easterly, special assistant on the National Security Council on Counterterrorism; President Barack Obama and Vice President Joe Biden for their work to create a new US policy to help American hostages and their families; members, past and present, of the Fusion Cell, overseen by the Federal Bureau of Investigation, who coordinate efforts among US government agencies to bring hostages home being held today, from Latin America to Asia; and those at the FBI and the State

Department who called my brother and sister when I was being held to give them encouragement.

I am humbly grateful to Dr. Eugene A. Grossi, cardiac surgeon at NYU School of Medicine and the Manhattan VA Hospital, who, with his team, gave me a third chance at life, and who said after my surgery that I had a strong heart, which gave me hope when I needed it most; to my friend Dr. Rosemary Gambetta, and Dr. Alison F. Ward, Dr. Stelios Wilson, and Dr. Shivani Singh; NPs Kathleen Woods, Mary Keary, and Vanessa Dutchin; nurses Mike Cruz, Syeda J. Funes, Carol Rohdes, Trang Hoang, Sam Wu, Noel Chua, Amy Mui, Mary Rodriguez, Joel Dolar, Elaine Francis; patient escort Emil Bellucci and Marabel Durate; occupational therapists Pam Brady and Roxanne Disla; Maribel Edelman, RDSC; Dr. Muriel T. Cruz, RN, MSN, Ed. D; Nina Gabin, PT, DPT, cardiac rehabilitation therapist, and my confidant; and Phillip Payne, fellow rehab patient, former sergeant, Company A, First of the 22nd, Fourth Division, Pleku, Vietnam, who told me to buy new clothes, meaning to look to the future, my friend. To Dr. Michael Kramer, of the Manhattan VA PTSD clinic.

A special thanks to Dr. Anna Scasso, of Albisola, Italy, whom I have known since 1977 and to whom I turned for advice, comfort, information, and second opinions, and to her extended family.

My agent, Michal V. Carlisle, brought me to Clive Priddle at PublicAffairs, who in August 2013 listened patiently as I explained what I wanted to do, and gave me a book contract. Clive also waited for me to return from my travels, listened to me explain what I had learned, and helped me conceive this book, and again waited when I had my heart operations. Through it all he has worked diligently, meeting with me even on weekends, and, like Michael Carlisle, came to support me when I was convalescing. Thanks also to managing editor Melissa Raymond and copy editor Bill Warhop.

❖ ❖ ❖

I wish to salute the memory of Daniel Pearl, Nicholas Berg, Piotr Stańczak, Linda Norgrove, Jim Foley, Steven Sotloff, David Haines,

Alan Henning, Peter Kassig, Kayla Mueller, Luke Somers, and Warren Weinstein.

Also, in Afghanistan, Ajmal Naqshbandi and Sayed Agha; and South Koreans Bae Hyeong-gyu and Shim Seong-min; and in the Philippines, Martin Burnham.

And I want to acknowledge their families who bear the burden of their loss: Judea and Ruth Pearl, Michael and Susan Berg, John and Diane Foley, Art and Shirley Sotloff, Carl and Marsha Mueller, Ed and Paula Kassig, Paula Somers and Jordan Somers, Elaine Weinstein, and Gracia Burnham.

Finally, I have a special kinship with a small group of Americans who have survived the experience of kidnapping: David Rohde, John Solecki, Jessica Buchanan, Roxana Saberi, Michael Scott Moore, Theo Padnos, Yeganeh Salehi, and Jason Rezaian, and those who are still being held.

Jere Van Dyk
Islamabad, Pakistan
April 4, 2017

PART ONE

" You know how things work around here.

Just takes a little longer, usually. "

—NAFAY HAMID

Chapter 1

The White House

June 24, 2015

We sat talking quietly in the large white room at elegant, dark hardwood desks placed together in a square on an inlaid, multicolored wood floor. There was a white folder in front of each of us that read "THE WHITE HOUSE." Inside were papers and a document with the gold Seal of the President of the United States and below that "EXECUTIVE ORDER" and the words "HOSTAGE RECOVERY ACTIVITIES."

Army Lieutenant General Bennet Sacolick sat on my right, and next to him Jen Easterly, special assistant to the president and senior director for counterterrorism. Next to her was the name card for Susan Rice, the national security adviser. She wasn't there. Next to her seat were two more empty chairs. A few minutes passed and two Secret Service agents in dark suits appeared in the doorway. They stood to the side and the room was silent. A tall, slim, energetic-looking man appeared, filling the doorway.

We rose and stood behind our chairs. Slowly President Barack Obama made his way around the room, shaking hands with each person while a photographer took pictures. He lingered before Paula Somers and Jordan Somers, whose son and brother Luke, thirty-three, was killed by al-Qaeda in a SEAL rescue attempt in Yemen in December 2014; and then with Carl and Marsha Mueller, whose daughter Kayla, twenty-six, was killed in a bomb attack in Syria in February 2015; and then with Art and Shirley Sotloff, whose son Steven, thirty-one, was beheaded by ISIS in September 2014; and then with Ed and Paula Kassig, whose son Peter, twenty-six, who became Abdul Rahman, was beheaded by ISIS in November 2014; and then with Diane and John Foley, whose son Jim, forty, was beheaded by ISIS in August 2014. He came around and approached me. He looked at me with a tinge of kindness, his eyes far away. "Hi, Jere, good to see you," he said as we shook hands. A Secret Service agent, his coat unbuttoned, watched closely.

The President touched General Sacolick on the arm and walked to his chair. We sat down and Vice President Joe Biden walked in through the opposite doorway. I stood up to shake hands, but he smiled and told me to sit down, patted me on the shoulder, and sat next to the president. Lisa Monaco, US Homeland Security adviser, sat on the president's right, the vice president on his left, a few inches back.

The room was silent as we waited. "Good morning," said the president, his voice soft and assured. It carried easily around the room. He slowly turned a few pages of a briefing book, barely glancing down. "Thank you for being here." Behind him were the American flag and the president's flag. He looked around the room.

"I am a father and a husband as well as the president. If something happened to one of my daughters, I would do everything I could, regardless of the circumstances, to get her back. I take full responsibility for the actions that I have ordered. I am heartbroken at what many of you have had to suffer. It gnaws at me. I have met with some of you individually and talked with you and have listened to you." He looked around the room as he talked. I stopped writing. There was death and suffering and anger and heartbreak in this room.

He looked back at Vice President Biden. "Joe," he asked, "is there anything you want to say?"

I found myself remembering one of my first days in the Senate as an aide to Senator Henry Jackson from Washington State, where I was born. I was in my twenties. I was walking down a hallway in the Capitol and I saw an energetic, handsome young man in a khaki suit sitting at the head of a table with men around him—Senator Biden. Two years before, his wife and daughter had been killed in a car accident. I encountered him again on the train from Washington, DC, to New York. He was going home to Delaware to be with his two sons, who survived the accident. He smiled and said hello to my sister. I liked him because of this.

Biden's hair was thin now and white, and he looked closely at a small pad of paper in his hand as he took notes. His older son, Beau, had just died. "I agree with everything the president has said. We have lunch privately once a week, just the two of us. You don't know how many times your names have come up when we are alone. We really focus on this. It is a top priority."

A retired FBI agent said that my kidnapping had been part of the president's daily intelligence briefing. It was hard to imagine that the government cared about me. There were people in the room who felt the government never cared.

President Obama continued. "I know that you have taken part in our hostage policy review over the past number of months. I have read the reports." I remembered the letters and e-mails and my long phone conversation with US officials, four months ago, and my own anger. The president continued to turn the pages of his large briefing book. He had long, thin, elegant hands, and a calm, commanding voice. "I know you have some things you'd like to say. Let me open it up and give you a chance to talk."

A dozen people raised their hands. "John," he said, looking at John Foley. The room was silent.

⁘ ⁘ ⁘

THE FIRST TIME I saw Afghanistan was in 1973. I was going to buy a car and drive across Asia, and I'd asked my parents—devout Plymouth Brethren in Washington State—if Kody, my younger brother, could join me. We drove an old Volkswagen from Germany to Herat, down to Kandahar on a road built by the Soviet Union, and then north, on a highway built by the US government. As we approached Kabul, in a valley shining in the sun, I shouted, "Shangri-La!" I was excited.

We found a hotel and parked on the empty street. Kabul was a small city then, with a population of no more than two hundred thousand; people called it the Paris of the East. It was a mix of little shops where men sat on carpets and invited you in for tea, modern buildings, mosques, outdoor cafes, a discotheque, and nine movie theaters. Many women dressed like Europeans; some were veiled. The streets were crowded, and many men carried rifles. There was dirt and poverty, the smells of hashish, wood-burning stoves, and sewage, and a deep, winding bazaar. The Kabul River flowed through the city. Foreigners dressed in whites when they played tennis at the Intercontinental Hotel. I loved going to the bakery on Chicken Street, with its old screen door and hot apple turnovers, which reminded me of a grocery store near my home when I was a little boy. We played flag football on Thanksgiving at the US Embassy, the Peace Corps against the Marine Corps guards: I was the quarterback on the Peace Corps team, and Kody was my end.

There were five thousand hippies in Kabul then, smoking hashish and sitting in the sun listening to rock and roll. At dusk the police, in turbans, with rifles on their backs, patrolled the streets on horses, their hooves echoing in the night. During the day, long camel caravans came through the streets, the women and girls dressed in colorful dresses and silver jewelry, not one of them veiled; turbaned men walked briskly, and the bells on the camel's necks tinkled softly. Then they were gone.

When we ran low on money I sold a pair of jeans to a German for $20, and Kody and I moved to the roof of our hotel until he got sick. I was worried and decided to sell the car and send him home. It was common then to buy a car in Europe, drive it across Asia on the Hippie Trail, stop at modern, vaguely hip caravansaries, sell it for a profit, and fly home. I found a buyer for the car, but learned that the Afghan government would no longer let a foreigner sell his car in Afghanistan. But I could sell it in Pakistan. Unfortunately, Kody's visa was up and the authorities said that they had to put him in jail until I had enough money to get a new one. I rushed down from Kabul through a canyon and pushed the sunroof back; I was worried about Kody, but the police had assured me gently that they would take care of him. It grew warmer and I reached the border. There were cement blocks across the road to keep Afghan tanks from invading the Tribal Areas. I paid a fee and got a visa and I drove around the cement blocks, past (it was literally through) a herd of sheep, and on through the Tribal Areas, whistling in the sun, to Peshawar.

I got the proper papers at the US consulate there, surrounded by yellow flower bushes then, and drove back to the Khyber Pass, where I sold the car to an American schoolteacher, as arranged, before returning to Kabul. I got Kody out of prison and nervously put him, my little brother, on an Australian hippie bus. The driver, in shorts and sandals, said he would take care of him. The bus broke down in Herat and he rode in the back of a truck to Tehran, picked up the deposit in the bank that I left to ensure that I wouldn't sell the car there, took the train to Istanbul, flew to Israel where he saw a homeopathic doctor, then flew to London and home.

Back in Kabul, I bought a full-length wolf coat in the bazaar for $12, and, laughing, said good-bye to Kabul and flew Aeroflot, the cheapest way back to Europe, over the Hindu Kush to Moscow. One night, walking in the snow across a square, I saw a woman glance over and I felt like a man of the world off the Asian steppe. I flew on to Paris, feeling happy, and then home to find Kody sick with jaundice. The next spring, 1974, I became an aide to Senator Henry Jackson in the US Senate.

In December 1979, the Soviet Union invaded Afghanistan and I vowed to return. Using a friend's office in Washington I called the *Washington Post*, the *New York Times*, and every newspaper bureau in Washington. After my twelfth call to the *New York Times* I met with Craig Whitney, the deputy foreign editor, and Bob Semple, the foreign editor; then, after a few days, Craig took me into a room and gave me a check for $500, and a letter of introduction.

I flew to Paris and went to the *Times* bureau, where there was a message that Mike Kaufman, the South Asia correspondent, was in Islamabad. I flew there to meet him. He became my mentor. Mike took me one day with his driver up to Murree, a former British hill station, for lunch, and then we walked outside and over to a ridge and looked west through the trees toward what he called "darkest Afghanistan." All I could see were mountains and forest. It was late afternoon and getting dark.

"Don't worry about the story," he said, "it will come to you." I felt a sigh of relief. A few days later, I put on a seersucker suit and took my small backpack and portable typewriter and went to the train station in Rawalpindi. I stood alone on the entry platform and then traveled in a dusty car, with the windows open, up to Peshawar for the romance of it all. We arrived toward sundown and I walked through empty streets to Dean's, an old British hotel.

The only name I had in Peshawar was Munchi, a driver for Jim Sheldon, an Australian photojournalist, who vouched for his honesty. He gave me two addresses where I could find him. Munchi, a small, thin man with a mustache, introduced himself—the beginning of a friendship, and my first lesson on how I had to work in Afghanistan and Pakistan. The only way forward was for one man to introduce me to another. It was similar in other parts of the world, but in Afghanistan it was essential.

Munchi took me to each of the leaders of the seven mujahideen political parties that were then fighting the Soviet Red Army. I didn't like any of them until we met Yunus Khalis. He was different. I sat on the wood floor with him. He had a long gray beard and wore a bandoleer. He carried a pistol. He had a deep voice and looked to be in his seventies. A younger man sat across from Yunus Khalis. "Who are you and how can we help you?" he asked. I said that I was with the *New York Times* and I wanted to travel with his men into Afghanistan. He talked with Khalis and I watched him write an instruction on a piece of paper and I knew that it contained his approval. I told them where I was staying. The younger man's name was Hajji Din Mohammad and years later he would be at the center of my kidnapping, and of my search to find out who was behind it.

I rejoined Munchi. "Where you like to go next?" he asked.

"Nowhere," I responded. I had found the man I was looking for.

⁂

ONE MORNING SOON afterward a man came and took me to the bazaar to be fitted for baggy pants and a long shirt, called *shalwar kameez*, which I would learn was the national dress of Afghanistan and Pakistan, and I then bought a wool shawl, sandals, and a turban, which he showed me how to wrap. The next morning, three men came, and as we were driving through a crowded street, the car stopped and one man got out as another got in quite without explanation. It was my first experience of intrigue. We left Peshawar and entered open country and continued on a narrow paved road southwest into the Tribal Areas, officially called the Federally Administered Tribal Areas (FATA) of Pakistan, a series of seven "agencies," each for different tribes, that was a buffer zone and a line of defense the size of Massachusetts. They were created by the British—the first in 1879[1] between Afghanistan and British India, of which Peshawar then was a part—to slow the Russians if they invaded.

We drove southwest. I was stuck in the middle in the backseat and couldn't see any signs. I had no idea where we were. We approached two men in khaki uniforms and berets, standing on either side of the road holding a chain between them. My escorts quickly told me how to pronounce the name of the next town in case the soldiers asked. They would repeat this, laughing, as we approached each checkpoint. They were sneaking me into their homeland, where foreigners were not allowed.

We went through many checkpoints, past old adobe British forts, some on hilltops, with whitewashed rocks lining the walkways and the crisp green-and-white Pakistani flag flying in the breeze.

At one checkpoint officials checked the driver's papers and went through our car. They didn't notice that I was a foreigner. We stopped to eat and I had to stay in the car with the driver, keep my head down, and not say a word. My escorts went inside to eat and brought me rice and mutton. When I finished, we drove on, past camels, herds of goats and sheep, electric power lines, donkey carts, and women carrying jugs of water on their heads. It was hot and dusty. When we reached Miran Shah, the capital of North Waziristan, it was hot and flies buzzed around. A man took me to a small shed, where I stayed that night and the next day with three young fighters, flies, mosquitoes, and pine boxes with black lettering, in English, filled with rifles and ammunition. The fighters, in black turbans, cooked rice with a few strands of beef sinew and insisted that I, the guest, take the best parts. We had grapes for dessert, and tea.

The next evening someone knocked on the door and they hid me in a corner, but the newcomer had come for me and escorted me up a rocky hillside to an adobe house. A boy about twelve, whose legs barely reached the pedals, drove me in a small red pickup higher up a rocky track into the mountains. I sat on a plateau with children with unwashed faces staring at me. Night fell and another guide came, and then a man with a rifle, and we walked farther uphill before we turned west. Two searchlights played across the sky. We knelt in the dirt and my guides told me to take off my boots and put on my sandals. I was making too much noise. The Pakistanis could hear me. The lights passed and we walked on. They stopped again after a hundred yards. My two guides took off their sandals and motioned for me to do the same. We walked silently through a dry, rocky riverbed. The rocks cut my feet.

After a few hours, it was safe enough for us to put our sandals back on. The clouds blew away and the moon shone and brilliant white stars covered the sky. We came upon a small white canvas tent, and one guide called and men responded. It was around two o'clock in the morning. We crawled in. There were ten men inside. My guide whispered his message, shook my hand, and both men left. It was cold and my feet hurt and were bloody, but in the shared body heat I fell asleep.

Before dawn, a man woke me, and we walked for an hour until the sun rose. There were mountains behind us, and a man high up on a ridge watching us. There was frost on the ground, desert plants, and sheep grazing. We walked higher and the air was fresh and the land became greener and the sky wider, a crystal pale blue. I wanted to shout. I was in Afghanistan. I felt magnificent, happy to be alive.

That evening we reached a small village. Another guide came overnight and as the sun rose brightly we walked across the high, wide, windy plain of Khost, near where I would walk twenty-six years later, the enemy this time, to find where Corporal Pat Tillman, a former professional football star and the most famous soldier in the US Army, was killed inexplicably. That afternoon we stopped to eat, but I wasn't hungry. My feet were bleeding from walking at night in bare feet, but my guide bounded up rocks like a deer. I shouted at him to slow down and he brought his rifle down and slowly shifted it to his other shoulder—threatening me, I thought, if I shouted at him again. I got the message.

Helicopters appeared. We reached a village that had just been bombed and we had to move on. I bandaged a man's wounds, wondering if he would survive, and he held my hand, his eyes stung with pain. I gave him some painkillers and he gave me a cigarette. I didn't smoke but I took it. I wanted, instinctively, to give him the dignity and pride of being a good host. He was maybe dying but he could still give me something. My guide smiled and took my pack and carried it. Soviet helicopters and MiG fighter jets flew over us. Three days later, we walked through a silent valley, past empty houses and compounds, many of them bombed, and reached the compound of Jalaluddin Haqqani, today the patriarch of the Haqqani Network, the most effective, most lethal of all Taliban-related groups, the closest to al-Qaeda and to the Pakistani army.

I lived with Jalaluddin Haqqani and his men, as well as his younger brother Ibrahim, no more than twenty of us then. For a short time, an Egyptian army major joined us. He was disguised as a journalist, and he didn't like me. Years later, I realized he was one, if not the first, of what men called Afghan-Arabs, the many thousands of foreign fighters who came, sanctioned by the United States and its ally Pakistan, to fight the communists in Afghanistan. A cadre of these young men created al-Qaeda, and Abu Sayyaf in the Philippines, and a multitude of other groups.

I watched Haqqani stand on the roof of his room—separate from others in our compound—cup his hands five times a day, in the rain or snow, before dawn and at night, and call his men to prayer. I watched them place their rifles in front of them, kneel, and bow their heads in the dirt, and I admired their commitment.

Late one Indian summer afternoon Haqqani and I, and other men, raced horses across a high grassy plain, and I laughed in the wind. It was how I wanted it to be. When I was a teenager I used to ride my horse, Chief, fast along the Columbia River in Vancouver, and I dreamed of riding with my chest bare, my hair long, and holding my rifle high, like the Indians I had watched at the Pendleton Round-Up up the river. Haqqani and his men reminded me of them: strong, brave men from the past. I wanted them to be free, to not give in.

The mujahideen saved my life at least three times. Haqqani grabbed my arm and caught me when I tripped at night and started to fall in a stream. He smiled when I practiced using his new, fancy rifle. I didn't feel close to him, but I looked up to him and I trusted him to protect me. I left Haqqani's camp and I went south to Kandahar, away from the mountains and into the desert.

In time, safely back in the United States, I wrote a book about the Afghan war against the Soviets and gave talks and interviews, one in a radio studio where a man who looked like an Afghan, who had been on before me, introduced himself. His name was Zalmay Khalilzad and he taught at Columbia and wanted to get together. He called now and then. Few were interested in Afghanistan beyond the US government, the few journalists who had been there, conservative activists, doctors with Médecins sans Frontières, and politicians for whom the war was a fight against the Soviet Union.

Khalilzad invited me to a meeting at Columbia. There were about ten of us, among them Olivier Roy, the French scholar, and a gray-haired man in a dark suit taking notes, and I knew, instinctively, that this second man worked for the US government, to which Khalilzad seemed to have close ties, and that he was also maybe a US citizen. Khalilzad wanted to start an organization called "Friends of Afghanistan" to promote the cause of the Afghans in the media. Khalilzad and other men talked about this new committee. I was drawn to it. In 1984, I became the director of Friends of Afghanistan. Albert Wohlstetter, the nuclear security analyst, and Zbigniew Brzezinski, Jimmy Carter's national security adviser, both of whom had been academic advisers to Khalilzad, were on the board. I went to Washington and met with people in the State Department and had lunch in the White House, after which a man took Khalilzad and me to his office in the Old Executive Office Building and gave me booklets with "CIA" stamped on the front. I wondered what I was getting into. Khalilzad introduced me to others, some of whom I knew, at the State Department. He took me to a small office that he had there. It appeared that Friends of Afghanistan was under the control of the National Security Council and the State Department. Khalilzad and I and other men met with former secretary of state William Rogers in his office in New York. "The mujahideen are like our founding fathers," said Rogers, looking at me. "They are freedom fighters."

I thought of some of the men I had been with. They were not like George Washington or Thomas Jefferson. They were poor men, with old rifles, torn sandals, who lived on unleavened bread and tea, and who hiked for hours in the mountains, who shivered with fear when helicopters hovered overhead, who, when they were wounded, rode for three days or longer over the mountains or through the desert to a doctor in Pakistan. They were very tough, simple men who always made sure that I ate before them.

In June of 1984 the newly formed Afghan mujahideen government in exile, made up of the seven mujahideen political parties, came to New York, and I, as director of Friends of Afghanistan, was their escort. I rode in a limousine with them and we stopped at the Roosevelt Hotel, owned by Pakistan International Airways, where they were staying. They got out of the car, in their turbans and flowing Afghan clothes, and people stared at these strange, wild men.

We organized a reception at the UN Plaza hotel so that they could meet UN delegates. I stood at the door to welcome them, and UN delegations, when they arrived. I knew that I was being used by the government, but I had signed a contract for one year and would see it through. A solidly built man, about six feet, wearing a light-blue turban and shalwar kameez, appeared at the door and smiled warmly. I hadn't seen him with the other men. "When are you coming back?" he asked. I felt emotion well up. I was amazed that he remembered me. It was Hajji Din Mohammad, who had sat with Yunus Khalis and who sent me to Haqqani. Din Mohammad and I talked and a man took a picture of us. Years later, this picture would become important as I searched for the truth about my kidnapping.

The Iranian delegation came in and rushed to Gulbuddin Hekmatyar, whom I knew from Peshawar and was now the president of the Afghan mujahideen government. The next night I sat with Hekmatyar, a small, soft-spoken, feline man, in his room as he turned down an invitation to meet with President Ronald Reagan. Two months later I received a call from the Committee to Protect Journalists, the New York–based nonprofit organization started in 1981 to defend journalists and freedom of the press. Hekmatyar's political party, Hezb-i-Islami,[2] had issued a statement and a list of ten people. It could not guarantee their safety if they returned to Afghanistan. My name was on the list. It was a death threat.

I was tired of Afghanistan, and of being used by the government. I quit Friends of Afghanistan when my contract was up. *National Geographic* magazine called and sent me on long exploration projects to rough, remote places—and I loved them, looking for danger, seeking the wild, hoping to find something harder than Afghanistan so I could put it behind me, but I never could.

I began to read about Osama bin Laden, who had come to Afghanistan after I left. On September 11, 2001, I woke up early to work on a book I was writing drawn from a *National Geographic* assignment. I had a daytime job working for a private investigative agency on Wall Street. I took the subway downtown. The train moved slowly. I got out at Wall Street and I walked up the stairs and saw people standing in the street staring up. There was no traffic. I thought there was a fire or that someone was threatening to jump. I walked to the corner and saw flames rippling along the side of one of the World Trade Center Buildings. I walked over to the building, stared up, and watched in horror as the building began to crumble.

That evening I went for a walk near my apartment. The city was quiet in a way that it never was, and I could smell residue downtown from the destruction. A woman from my building came up to me. "I'm so glad I've run into you," she said. "Can you come into CBS tomorrow?" She worked at CBS Radio.

"Afghanistan," I thought, "has just come roaring back into my life." The next morning a CBS Radio producer asked me questions about Afghanistan, and CBS put my comments on air. I went home. I would try television. I didn't know anything, went through the phone book, called WABC, which was first in order, and a woman answered. I said that I had worked in Afghanistan for the *New York Times* and had written a book about it. She called back in five minutes and asked me to come over. WABC put me on the air during a special newscast and again that afternoon. I was on WABC every night for a month.

For the next three months, I did commentary on CBS Radio and WABC television, and occasionally the *CBS Evening News*. Eventually CBS wanted to bring their radio correspondent out of Afghanistan and asked me if I would replace her. I had no choice, I had to return. And this is how the Trade, for me, began.

Chapter 2

New York

December 23, 2001

I called Rosanne Klass—once, during the Afghan-Soviet war, one of the most prominent Afghan experts in America—from the airport to tell her I was on my way to Afghanistan.

"Jere, I haven't heard from you in years. What happened to you? It's been ten years since we last saw one another." She paused. "I should be going too," she said softly. "Look up Professor Rasul Amin when you are there," she continued. "President Hamid Karzai has appointed him minister of education. Say hello to him."

I went to see him a week later in Kabul.

Rosanne wanted to be in the thick of things like before but it was different now. The mujahideen, US allies in the Afghan-Soviet war, were gone. She had fought for them and for Afghanistan in the media and in Washington, even in Europe. She was fearless. But the Taliban, intense religious men, in many ways the sons of the mujahideen, were our enemies in 2001.

By the end of her life, Rosanne would become the person I felt closest to in New York. I had first met her in 1980 after I read an op-ed by her in the *New York Times* and called on her at her office, at Freedom House, where she was the director and founder of the Afghanistan Information Center, across the street from Bryant Park. Her desk was piled high with books and papers. She had dark hair combed back and dark intense eyes. She was busy and asked how she could help me. I said that I wanted to go to Afghanistan. She put her glasses up over her forehead and stared at me. Was I tough enough? We talked, and then we went to lunch at a diner on Sixth Avenue and sat at a small greasy table and talked some more. She had gone to Afghanistan in the 1950s and was a school teacher there and had written a book about it, *Land of the High Flags*, which she gave to me and in which she inscribed a note in Dari, the Persian dialect spoken in Afghanistan. She later wrote for the *New York Times.*

She was strongly anticommunist. I had read Solzhenitsyn, knew about Stalin, had been in the army in Germany, and Senator Jackson was one of the strongest anticommunists in the Senate. But I had also been to the Soviet Union twice, once as an athlete and then as a traveler, and had run in track meets in Poland and Czechoslovakia, part of the Soviet Bloc. I didn't hate the communists. I had ridden a troop train from Frankfurt to Berlin and looked at the Soviet soldiers at present arms, bayonets fixed, a sign of respect as we entered the station. They were my age. I had seen the Berlin Wall and gone to East Germany. But I had also lived in Paris when 20 percent of the electorate voted communist, hoping for equality in class-driven France, and I respected the athletes who lived under communism. I liked the people I met there.

"I'll call you when I get back," I told Rosanne.

⁂

I WAS FLYING to the Middle East, the desert, the land of Islam and the Bible, and from there up to Pakistan and then to Afghanistan. I wanted to go out into the desert. Few people understood what it was like to grow up in a Plymouth Brethren community: our quiet Sunday morning service like that of the Amish, the warmth and love of our Assembly, our clan separate from the world. It wasn't until I ventured into the Muslim world, hitchhiking across North Africa after college, and heard men say "Inshallah," or "God willing," as men in our Assembly said, that I recognized a version of the devotion I knew at home.

I wanted to see if the Taliban were like the mujahideen, most of whom were poor, strong, simple, religious men driven mainly to fight the godless invader. Or were they a more rigid, angrier, fiercer force? I wanted to return, too—though I didn't realize it then—to the warmth and the romance and the friendships of before, and to find God, this certainty of my youth.

I refused a glass of wine from the flight attendant. I walked back to the galley and saw a man with a beard standing with his head down, a prayer mat in front of him. I watched him pray, admiring his courage to pray in front of others. He was as devoted as my father. A woman sat in a seat near him holding a child. I returned to my seat, but something told me to go back again, and I walked back to the galley. A woman in an abaya stood in front of the prayer mat, knelt on her knees, touched her forehead to the mat. I stood behind her. I had never seen a Muslim woman prayer before.

They prayed separately from men in mosques, behind lattice wood barriers, by a wall, or up on a mezzanine, where they looked, sitting on the floor in their black wraps, like women covered in darkness. *Mosque* means place of prostration. It could be anywhere, by a stream, or a road, just as a church could be anywhere. *"Where two or three are gathered together in my name, there am I in the midst of them,"* it says in Matthew 18:20. I heard this all the time as a boy.

I couldn't know then that in the future I would be forced to pray, in fear, if I wanted to see the light of day again. Like US servicemen being tortured in the Hanoi Hilton during Vietnam, and American and other Western aid workers and journalists being tortured by the Islamic State, I would seek comfort in faith, whether in Christianity, Islam, or Judaism.

A blond-haired English flight attendant touched my arm. "Please, sir, can you go to the other side of the plane?" She was protecting the woman and her dignity. I walked away, ashamed of my insensitivity, and returned to my seat. The flight attendant urged me to have a chocolate sundae. I said yes, in part to make her happy, and I felt decadent as I ate this rich, worldly food.

I glanced at an Arab across the aisle reading a US magazine. "HOW TO SAVE THE ARAB WORLD," said the headline. Who did we think we were that we, the West—rich, modern, powerful—could think of saving the Arab world, as if we were God? Not everyone wanted to be like us, not those who prayed in the aisles of airplanes, or on prayer mats in the streets of London, Cairo, or Peshawar, or behind their rifles in Afghanistan.

The airport terminal in Abu Dhabi was circular, like a mosque, loud and muggy, and people smoked, ate, drank, and browsed the shops. I went to a duty-free shop, wandering among bottles of alcohol, cigars, cigarettes, chocolate, and packaged food from Europe, all of which represented to me the pursuit of pleasure. I went into another room and stood before a display of French wine and felt warmth seep into me. I picked out a bottle of brandy, two bottles of wine, and cigars for CBS people in Kabul.

I stood in line at a cash register, feeling weak yet part of the world, just another man with cigars and wine in his basket, part of the flow of humanity. I walked to the gate for my flight to Pakistan, and felt better standing among men in skull caps, turbans, and shalwar kameez. We walked quietly into the departure lounge. There was no decadence here, only hard religious certainty.

I wanted to be with the Taliban, not just because I was curious about their faith, but because they represented a chance to do something worthwhile, and because they were an echo of the warmth of the mujahideen and that earlier, exciting time when I lived with them. It was the lure of the wild, which I inherited from my father, the romance of great adventure, to do what others could not, which told me to go into the unknown, always seeking something harder than before.

It was still night when the plane landed in Islamabad. Pakistani soldiers in dark blue sweaters with epaulets, like the British, their former colonial masters, watched the departing passengers closely. They carried automatic rifles, wore black berets and blue pants tucked into their boots. There was something comforting yet eerie about their presence. I felt tension in the air. A jeep, with a soldier glaring at us, standing in the back behind a machine gun, drove around us in a circle. I was back in Asia where I had been so happy twenty years ago. It was cold, Christmas Eve.

The terminal was bigger and more modern now. A man at passport control thumbed through my passport and stamped my visa. I lifted my luggage off the new conveyor belt. Once it had been old, creaky, and exotic. I thought of the alcohol I had bought and wondered if I could get it through customs. It was illegal to bring alcohol into Pakistan, the world's first modern Islamic state, founded in 1947. *Pak* means "pure" in Urdu, the official language, a mixture of Arabic, Hindi, and Pashto—like Pakistan, a mixture of peoples. *Stan* means "land": so land of the pure, the religious pure. To them I would be just another Western infidel.

I offloaded my bags onto another conveyer belt that went through an X-ray machine. This too was new. Customs officers saw the bottles and directed me to a man with a thick black mustache, military ribbons on his uniform, a beret, and a heavy gray jacket. He held a bottle up to the light and asked what it was. I told him that I'd bought it in Abu Dhabi. "I'm a journalist," I said, "going to Afghanistan." I would not argue with customs agents, men I had learned over the years had the power to make my life difficult. They would give in to me if I accepted their authority. I was American; Pakistan and the United States had been allies against communism since the early years of the Cold War. The official handed the bottles back.

Yasmeen, the CBS bureau chief in Pakistan, and her driver came out of the crowd waiting outside and took me to a new black SUV. How modern and comforting and boring this was. Last time I'd found a small taxi. We drove in the dark from the airport in Rawalpindi up a highway to the UN flight office in Islamabad, where I had to check in for my UN flight to Kabul.

I thought of Jalaluddin Haqqani, the mujahideen leader who had given me hospitality at his compound in the mountains in Afghanistan. By October 2001, Haqqani had become the enemy. We were the invader. I remembered Jalaluddin coming over to me when I arrived in his compound and shaking my hand, as another man brought me tea and a plate of honey. In my mind's eye I could still see him standing on a rock ledge at dusk, holding a Qur'an out, looking down at me as his men passed under on their way into battle. It was the word of God and would protect them. Haqqani's men attacked an Afghan army fort with a mortar that night, the only weapon they had besides their rifles, shouting "Allahu Akbar!" every time they dropped a shell into the mortar. It gave them strength to shout "God is great," which traditionally Muslims said when killing an animal for food, and maybe they thought that it directed their shells. Artillery fired back, and we retreated into the night. A shell landed with a thud a few yards away from us but Haqqani's men kept talking and laughing, showing their bravado, and years later I kept shaking my head, wondering why the shell didn't explode.

I realized that I wanted to see Haqqani again. I had heard rumors that after 9/11 the United States had invited him to the US embassy in Islamabad and asked him to come over to the US side. He had been our close ally in the 1980s. He responded that if the US invaded he would go up into the mountains and fight again. Just after the invasion, on October 7, Mullah Muhammad Omar, leader of the Taliban, having refused to hand over Osama bin Laden and with his forces now being decimated by US bombing, announced over the radio that he had appointed Haqqani as his military commander. The US bombed Haqqani's compound. One of his men told me, years later, that they pulled him from the rubble, dazed but well, wondering how the US could find Haqqani but not bin Laden. He was said now to be in the Tribal Areas. I wondered how I could find him. It was this search that would lead me seven years later to a mountain prison in the Tribal Areas, and in 2014 into the dark, brutal world of "the Trade."

❖ ❖ ❖

WHEN THE TALIBAN took power in 1996 only Pakistan, Saudi Arabia, and the United Arab Emirates recognized their government. The

US tried to negotiate an agreement with the Taliban to build a pipeline from Central Asia across Afghanistan. In 1998, US oilmen hosted the Taliban in Houston, but then came 9/11. In the 1980s, all US funding for the war against the Soviet Union in Afghanistan went directly to the Pakistani army, which kept some and distributed the rest among its chosen mujahideen political parties. Why would Pakistan not control the Taliban the same way? After 9/11, Pakistan was considered a dangerous place for Westerners, but I felt more relaxed than I did in New York.

Yasmeen and I talked as we rode in the dark up the highway and into Islamabad. The UN flight to Kabul would leave in two hours. She handed me my ticket as we drove through the quiet city, past walled compounds with houses inside. Islamabad, designed by the Greek architect Constantinos Doxiadis, was founded in 1960 when young Pakistan moved its capital from Karachi—its sprawling business and financial center on the Arabian Sea—seven hundred miles north to the highlands, where it was cooler and where the capital sat on the Grand Trunk Road from the Bay of Bengal, in Bangladesh, to Kabul. It still looked artificial, like an American or European capital in the middle of South Asia. Pakistan had not in the 1960s had the confidence to design its capital. It was like young America having a Frenchman, Pierre L'Enfant, design Washington, DC.

The Supreme Court, the Presidential Palace, and Parliament are all large, stark, white buildings (some of them marble)—symbols of democracy, which the Taliban called a Western religion—with soldiers standing outside their high black iron fences holding their rifles. With its straight roads, square grids, and large houses, the city often felt like an American suburb. There were few people in the streets. There were few sidewalks.

The UN flight office was a white stucco house behind a high wall, protected from the outside world. A white wood pole lay across the entryway. Soldiers raised it, and we drove into the compound. The only way into Afghanistan was on a UN flight. Overland was too dangerous even up the Grand Trunk Road, now largely destroyed in Afghanistan. Four journalists had been killed there a month before,[3] on the same road I had once traveled in my Volkswagen.

The white Fokker jet, with the letters UN painted in blue on the fuselage, flew northwest over brown and green mountainous land. The plane was half filled with seats. The rest was open space for cargo. The US, as the Soviet Union had in the 1980s, controlled the airspace over Afghanistan and only allowed UN, Red Cross, and allied planes into the country. The seats were half filled, too, with journalists, UN employees, and aid workers.

Like them, I wore a parka, sweater, and boots. CBS shared a house with ABC in Kabul. I would use it as a base. I hoped that I hadn't lost my desire to rough it. I looked at the other passengers, many of them going, I assumed, to Afghanistan for the first time, carrying computers and camera gear. There were now only gray jagged mountains below, and gray empty plains. No roads, no trees, no lights, just vast, silent, rugged land. I grew excited. Below was a thin, winding, glacier-green river, like a lifeline: the Kabul River. I would cross it in 2008 and go into the Tribal Areas, hoping to find Haqqani, and get kidnapped; I would cross again at night sitting on a steel plank on a makeshift ferry after I was released. I saw terraced land now, irrigation canals, baked-mud villages, still rugged, inhospitable, and desolate. I could almost feel the dry wind below.

I watched for missiles. In 1981, the mujahideen had begged me, an American, for arms with which to shoot down Russian helicopters. I had watched them tilting forward, firing their rockets. We hid in the bushes and in houses, praying the helicopter gunships wouldn't seek us out. After a battle in Kandahar, an old man, standing under a tree, pleaded with me to stop the helicopters. In 1983, I wrote an op-ed in the *New York Times* passing on his plea. In 1986, they began to arrive. Ten years later, on July 24, 1993, Tim Weiner wrote in the *New York Times* that from 1986 to 1989 the US gave the mujahideen nearly one thousand shoulder-held, heat-seeking anti-aircraft Stinger missiles.[4] On September 25, 2001, Thomas Ricks reported in the *Washington Post*, under the headline "LANDMINES, AGING MISSILES POSE THREAT," that after the Afghan-Soviet war the US started a buy-back program, paying up to $100,000 for each Stinger. All but about two hundred, he wrote, remained in Afghanistan. Years later the US Army fired some of these missiles, and they still worked. Blowback, the CIA called it. As in, *Be careful what you create that it doesn't blow back to hit you*—like helping to create the mujahideen, which led to al-Qaeda, the Taliban, and the Islamic State. According to Joseph Fitchett, reporting in the *New York Times* on September 26, 2001, under the headline "WHAT ABOUT THE TALIBAN'S STINGERS," the CIA had few takers on its offer, and while it estimated that only two hundred or so were left in Afghanistan, in truth only a few had been recovered.[5]

The plane went into a steep descent, the ground rushed up, and we came down between two rust-colored mountain ranges and landed at Bagram Air Base, built by the Soviets, a ramshackle collection of buildings, scrub grass, two runways, and destroyed aircraft. It looked comforting in its destruction.

The land was silent. I walked slowly, breathing in the dry mountain air. I stopped at the edge of the runway. There was a field, another runway, a terminal with a tower whose windows were blown out, and a large hangar with three Chinook helicopters sitting in front of it on the tarmac. Lean, bearded US soldiers in an SUV with tinted windows drove up and watched us. Another soldier, in a wool cap, jeans, and cardigan sweater, wearing a pistol, stood on the runway holding a walkie-talkie. They were in charge now. I looked up at a ridge. The Taliban were up there watching.

A group of US soldiers rode by in a low, open vehicle. Two Afghans put our bags in a row. A soldier came out from the terminal with a German shepherd, which sniffed the bags. I asked the soldier what he was looking for. "It's none of your business," he said. I was a civilian, the enemy. Once it was Alexander, Tamerlane, Babur, the British, the Soviets. Now it was America's turn.

A Russian Mi-24 helicopter appeared over a ridge and came toward us. I tensed, wondering for a second if it was going to attack. Once, they controlled the skies here. People took their bags and left. A man who worked for the UN said that I could ride with him. We set off on a narrow road surrounded by dark, charred fields and adobe houses, one with a machine gun on the roof. Afghans had laid waste to their own country.

We reached the outskirts of Kabul and I grew excited. We drove into Wazir Akbar Khan, the diplomatic enclave. I grabbed my duffel bag and went door to door until I found the CBS-ABC house, where a CBS correspondent, a woman, kindly brought me a cup of tea.

That evening the house filled with men and a few women. There was a scraggly Christmas tree in the corner. I fell asleep in a chair, but someone woke me and I joined twenty people for a dinner of rice, kebabs, potatoes, salad, and vegetables, but I ate little. I didn't know anyone and wasn't hungry. There were bottles of wine, but I didn't drink. I felt separate from everyone there.

Afterward, men smoked and drank Scotch in the living room. I walked outside and looked at the stars. I could smell the faint, familiar odor of wood-burning stoves and sewage. It was comforting.

Chapter 3

Kabul

January 2002

On New Year's Day, the US embassy reopened and threw a party for any American in Kabul. The embassy had lowered its presence in Kabul in 1979, following the kidnapping in January of US ambassador Adolph Dubs from his car by Marxist gunmen, before his death in the Kabul Hotel, now the Serena, at the hands of Afghan security forces under the control of Soviet KGB agents.[6] The embassy officially closed in 1989 after the Soviet withdrawal that February. There were half a dozen bottles of alcohol left over from the 1970s on a table outside on a cold, gray afternoon. One of the diplomats said that she had been there in the 1970s, had fallen in love with Afghanistan, and joined the Foreign Service. She had volunteered to help reopen the embassy. "It's not the same," she said sadly. I walked through the embassy, cold, dusty, and silent. Two marines walked the perimeter. Once Kody and I had played flag football here; people were happy then.

Kabul was quiet and the streets were empty. Uniformed soldiers from the United Front, which the US media incorrectly called for years the Northern Alliance, the multiethnic, Afghanistan-wide, anti-Taliban force, hung around on street corners. There was destruction throughout the city, and piles of rubble. I walked through the city. I needed to find someone to help me begin my work. I asked the CBS interpreters about Rosanne Klass's contact, Abdul Rahim. He would know what was going on beneath the surface and open doors for me, one man leading me to others. He was the mujahideen spokesman and a frequent visitor to New York and Washington. He often spoke on American television. We often had tea and dinner together. When the mujahideen took power in 1992, Abdul Rahim became ambassador to the United States. He had called then and said that I was the only man that he wanted to talk to. We were friends, surely.

By 2002 he had become the minister of communications for the new interim Karzai government. I went to the ministry, at the Kabul Tower, seventeen stories high and the only tall building in Kabul, walked up the wide dark stairs, and found him sitting at the head of a table with his staff. He had a long thick beard and didn't smile. A striking woman with long dark hair, in a black-and-white tweed jacket, her face uncovered, argued with him, and other women joined her. After the meeting ended we went into his office. "I read your book, *In Afghanistan*," he said. "I bought it in Tehran." I didn't know that the Iranians had published it. "This war will last a long time. They will never find Mullah Omar. He can shave his beard and go to Pakistan. His tribe will protect him. Bin Laden cannot hide in a village. A government will protect him."

He meant Pakistan. He would know. He was close to Burhanuddin Rabbani, the former Afghan president. They were both from Badakhshan Province. The US media, following the Bush administration, kept saying that bin Laden was hiding in a cave somewhere along the Afghan-Pakistani border, probably in the Tribal Areas of Pakistan. I believed Rahim.

Rahim gave me a list of people in President Karzai's cabinet, one of whom was Professor Rasul Amin, Rosanne Klass's friend and the interim minister of education, and their phone numbers. I wanted Abdul to laugh like before. "We've had twenty-three years of war," he said. It was time for prayers. He had never worn a beard or talked about praying before. I felt distant from him, and sad; only his voice was unchanged. By giving me the list of people he showed that he was still my friend, that I was still his friend. He encouraged me to dig deep into Afghanistan to help my career. He would help me. I called Rasul Amin and used Rahim's name, and Rosanne's name, and Amin asked me to come to his office.

That night at dinner Bryn Padrig, a CBS producer whom I didn't know, said to others that he heard that Yunus Khalis, the mujahideen leader who had sent me to live with Haqqani, was in Jalalabad. I listened, impressed that he knew him. I had not been certain if he was still alive or not. I wanted to find someone to take me to him—but it might be dangerous. He was close to bin Laden. I would have to be careful, but I knew immediately that I wanted to see him again. I decided to meet Rasul Amin first and go from there.

❖ ❖ ❖

A FEW DAYS later, on a bitterly cold morning, I went to the Ministry of Education to see Professor Amin. He sat in his office by a broken window, in a suit and a sweater, with a heater glowing at his feet. I was almost certain that we had met at Rosanne's apartment but he didn't acknowledge it. He had been a professor in Australia for the last twenty years. President Karzai had called him back to be minister of education. "The country is destroyed. We need new schools, new textbooks, and a new curriculum," he said.

The US had printed math books during the Soviet war in which students read that bullets + rifles = dead Soviet soldiers. The Taliban would later use these same books.

I didn't know it then, but I would learn when I went to see Amin again in 2007 that as a boy he'd gone to school in Pakistan. One of his classmates was Rustam Shah Mohmand, who became a Pakistani diplomat. From 1987–1989 Mohmand was chief commissioner for Afghan refugees, overseeing the refugee camps along the Afghan border. They were funded by the UN High Commission for Refugees and gave shelter to over four million Afghans, providing protection, rations, water, and good positions for those who qualified. The Mujahideen—under the control of the ISI, which controlled the camps—lived in the camps with their families when they weren't fighting in Afghanistan.

Amin, a former history professor at Kabul University, became director of the Writer's Union for a Free Afganistan, in Peshawar, funded by his classmate Rustam Shah Mohmand. Amin's colleague, Professor Syed Bahauddin Majrooh, the former dean of Kabul University's Faculty of Literature, became the director of the Afghanistan Information Center, funded by Mohmand. Amin worked for him before becoming director of the Writer's Union. Majrooh, a kind, rumpled, soft-spoken man, continued to run, with two wives, the Afghanistan Information Center housed in a dusty, rambling office on a quiet dirt street. In 1988 Majrooh published a poll he took of Afghan refugees in which they said that they preferred Zahir Shah, the king of Afghanistan, to the mujahideen. Shortly thereafter, one evening, Majrooh sent his driver to buy food so he could make something to eat. While the driver was gone, a man knocked on the door and shot Majrooh dead when he answered. One rumor was that his driver was involved; another, that a member of his divorced wife's family shot him; and the third and most important rumor, one that I heard, was that Gulbuddin Hekmatyar, the ruthless mujahideen leader who wanted to rule Afghanistan, killed him, either on his own or for the ISI, the Inter-Services Intelligence directorate. ISI backed Hekmatyar and his party, Hezb-i-Islami (to which it provided the most funds), and the other six mujahideen parties that the ISI had created or allowed to function, along with its ally, the US—specifically the CIA—which supplied financial support and materiel.[7]

The US, Pakistan, and Saudi Arabia used the mujahideen as a proxy army to fight the Soviet Union, and the mujahideen leaders, who I called part of the "mullah front" because many were religious men, would use these governments to obtain money and power. These parties had formed the Afghan mujahideen government in exile, backed by

Pakistan and the United States, and it was the same group that I had escorted in New York when Hekmatyar was the president, after which he had issued the death threat against me. Pakistan wanted these parties to rule Afghanistan, not Zahir Shah. Amin, like Majrooh, had a sinecure through Mohmand. This didn't mean much to me at first, but it did when Ehsanullah, an old journalist friend, told me one night, at a Turkish restaurant in Kabul, that there was another organization present in Peshawar, the Afghan Media Resource Center, whose mission was to train Afghans to be journalists to cover the war and send the news to the Muslim world to undermine the Soviet presence there. This was the original reason for the creation of Friends of Afghanistan, where I was the executive director but not the boss. I reported to Khalilzad, but he was never around. This was the world, in Peshawar, in which Majrooh and Rasul Amin came of age and where I believe Amin established his links, through his high school friend Mohmand, to Pakistan.

Boston University won the contract to create the Afghan Media Resource Center. I wasn't at all certain about the Writer's Union or the Afghanistan Information Center, but I felt reasonably sure that the AMRC was a CIA operation in the Cold War against the Soviet Union, and that all three were under the control of the ISI and that Majrooh was killed, like Abdul Haq in 2001, for going off on his own. After Majrooh was killed, his son, Naim Majrooh, took over and ran the Afghan Information Center until the fall of the Taliban. I tried to reach him, but he wouldn't respond.

I ran in the early mornings in Kabul that winter in 2002. The Taliban, whose leaders had fled to Pakistan and whose fighters had taken off their black turbans and returned to their villages, had not yet started to return, and I found a dirt track in a schoolyard. I was afraid of mines. I heard stories of animals and children running in the fields stepping on them. There were mine clearers in the countryside, probing gently with long knives for $7 a day, with stretchers beside them.[8]

I thought back to when I had walked through a mine field in the mountains in November 1981 with Haqqani's men as they escorted me back toward the Tribal Areas. We had two camels leading us as we approached the border. The men knew that Soviet helicopters had come through earlier that day and seeded the mountain passes with small green plastic mines. We followed the footsteps of the man in front of us. Dusk came and we walked slower. I heard an explosion, and another one, and a man cried out softly and others murmured. We passed a camel, and another one, each with a foot blown off, swaying on three legs. I looked at their eyes, but they stared stoically ahead. It grew darker and we walked slowly, staring at clumps of grass. I heard a gurgling scream as a man cut a camel's throat, and then another one. We reached a ridge and the men said that it was clear from there. They stopped to pray and I sat alone praying in gratitude. Haqqani's men had walked in front to protect me. They said good-bye and I hiked down into Pakistan and walked alone to the Yunus Khalis outpost. I only vaguely knew then that the men who guided me and kept me safe were backed by Pakistan and the United States.

I went to the Hotel Intercontinental one night to attend a UN press conference and went to the small bookstore in the lobby and bought Nancy Dupree's books, as Rosanne had asked me to. I thought of old Afghanistan, lunch at the Intercon, watching people play tennis. Nancy and her husband Louis Dupree, America's premier expert on Afghanistan in the last half of the twentieth century, were famous in Afghanistan among foreigners and Afghans for their work and their love of this country. I later saw Nancy and the first thing she said was how much she missed Louis, who died in 1989. "She is our grandmother," an Afghan journalist said to me, speaking, he said, for all Afghans. She would be the last foreigner I talked to before I crossed the border and was kidnapped. I was busy being a correspondent for WABC television and CBS Radio, but I kept thinking of Yunus Khalis and Haqqani. I was wary of who might be around Khalis. I was told that his sons had escorted bin Laden from Tora Bora, the mountain region along the Pakistani border where he had supposedly taken refuge after 9/11 and where Yunus Khalis had a camp. Someone had issued a statement on his behalf calling for jihad against America.

I got to know a fixer who was with us every day named Fazul Rahim. He was in his twenties, a Tajik from the Panjshir Valley north of Kabul.

He was friendly and clearly one of the most capable and energetic of the many fixers in the CBS-ABC house. I said that I wanted a fixer and he introduced me to a new man, called Zalgai, a gentle, witty man from the Shomali Plain north of Kabul who had just come to CBS. We took a taxi on the one road north through the Hindu Kush, stayed in a guesthouse, got stuck in the snow, pushed the car out, and came down into Uzbek country. We reached Mazar-i-Sharif,[9] where it was safe, far from Pashtun country in the south. I realized that I, like everyone, was afraid of the Taliban. We went the next morning to its famous Blue Mosque. We sat on a bench waiting for the fog to lift, watching hundreds of white pigeons and looking at the blue, white, and yellow tiled building shining in the rising sun, as beautiful as a stained-glass window in a cathedral. Men created beauty in their houses of worship, where they went to get away from the world. But the Taliban were opposed to music and any human imagery, considering it the first step to idol worship. They destroyed statues in the Kabul Museum. Like many of the mujahideen before them, the Taliban were opposed to secular education because it took men away from God. We were not so different—when I was a boy, the parents of many of my friends sent them to Christian schools. I later knew of parents who home-schooled their children for the same reason. We only sang a cappella in our Sunday morning service. A piano was too worldly. The walls were bare, but it was comforting and felt true in its austerity. There were only beautiful laminated wood beams that my father had others make when he built our assembly. My mother brought flowers on Saturday nights and arranged them, alone, artistically. They too wanted beauty.

Two days later we returned to Kabul, where we received an announcement that Zalmay Khalilzad, now the US envoy to Afghanistan, would give a press conference. I gave my passport to a marine at the embassy gate. Another marine ran a wand over me and other US journalists and I felt like a foreigner. I watched two marines on their knees poking bayonets in the dirt, looking for mines where once I had played football.

I stood in the back of the room. Khalilzad walked in, in a tie and jacket. He talked about his trips around the country, the partnership that the US was creating with Afghanistan, the gun culture, and his hope that someday Afghanistan would be a normal country, where people would see a soldier or a policeman and would not be afraid. He was reasonably optimistic about the future, but ultimately Afghans would have to decide. "We are willing to try to engage them and to be helpful. We have been extremely pleased with statements by President Karzai." He was talking as an American, but he had come to me eighteen years before, in a radio studio in New York, more as an Afghan than as a naturalized American, because he liked what I had said about Afghanistan. He said that "Afghans would have to rebuild their country." No, I thought, you and I contributed to its destruction when we backed the mujahideen, the fieriest of whom are fighting us today. He had forced the aging Zahir Shah to step aside. Every Afghan I met wanted the king to return, but Pakistan, which backed the Taliban, didn't, nor did the US, which wanted to create a democracy, which the Taliban called a Western religion.

I listened, reflecting on the separate roads we had taken. Years ago, Khalilzad didn't know what to order in a bar, or American slang. Six years later in 2008, I heard conflicting stories about him and my kidnapping.

A journalist with aggression in her voice asked Khalilzad about being an Afghan by birth but working for the United States. "I remember a different Afghanistan," he responded, "as a child in Mazar-i-Sharif. After elementary school we moved here, it was a much nicer place then. I've seen the destruction in my old neighborhood, where we used to play basketball against other schools, and the American International School, all destroyed now. The magnitude of the destruction that one observes is hard." His voice was softer now. "I remember in Mazar-i-Sharif the sea of red poppies in the spring. I am quite perfectly aware of my roots. I am here on a mission for the United States. It has been a defining experience for me."

He began to talk about Iran and returned to his former, political self. For a moment he had been genuine and humble, a man of two countries. Once, he talked bitterly when we were alone about the "white man's burden," and I knew that he had felt the sting of racism and I felt sorry for him. Once the press conference ended he came toward me with a hard look in his eyes, looked past me, and kept going. He was a powerful man now.

Outside in the streets, boys were knocking on car windows, begging. When I first came to Kabul, I loved that I never saw a child beg as I had in other countries. There was a dignity about them. Now, after thirty years of war, little boys begged, ate and fought in the streets, and little girls, who once laughed and carried books, tugged on my arms, begging.

Zalgai and I took a taxi and headed south to Kandahar. I had to file reports for CBS and do interviews with radio affiliates every day. The highway, once smooth and empty, was a crowded, undulating track of dirt and sand. A Kuchi caravan come over a hill, and for a moment I felt young and was excited. They were still here. I watched the women and children walking with their backs straight. The Taliban could never force a nomad woman to wear a veil.

The next day we reached Kandahar and I looked for high adobe barns with holes in the walls where farmers dried grapes for raisins, where I had slept feeling protected by the men around me as artillery pounded in the night, and the trenches where they had fought and the bullets sang around us. It was different now. We were alone. Families worked in the fields among pomegranate orchards. We found a guest-house and I paid the taxi driver and he left. I did interviews on my satellite phone and we went for a walk down a dusty street. We came to an auto repair shop and Zalgai told a mechanic that we needed a driver. A few hours later, a strong-looking turbaned man, about six foot one, came with a car. Zalgai vetted him and we drove through the city. I sat in the back.

"Journ-a-leest," the driver asked, looking in the rear-view mirror.

"*Kha*," I responded, yes.

"Do you know famous American journalist von duck?" His voice was guttural.

"Who?"

"Jerry von duck, an American. He came here fifteen, sixteen years ago and wrote a book on Afghanistan. He filmed parts of Kandahar." He pulled out a paperback book, and handed it to me. It was in Persian, but I saw my photographs.

"I wrote this book." My spine tingled.

He smiled broadly and pulled over. "I bought it in Tehran. It's a wonderful book." He shook my hand and kept shaking it. I leaned back in the seat and felt a deep sense of well-being. The book got mostly good reviews, but didn't sell. "Better that it was called *In North Dakota*," an agent from William Morris said. I gave the book back to the driver. His name was Nematullah Maksoudi. He had underlined passages. He said that he had read it many times. He knew every part of it and kept referring to it. I couldn't get over that what I wrote meant something to an Afghan. He was a soccer coach and a sports announcer.

I said I wanted to go to Mahalajat. I wanted to see the trenches, the wall I climbed over to escape the soldiers coming slowly toward us, the high barn where we later listened to the helicopter roaring above us as I bandaged a wounded man. I thought of the men I had been with. I had a picture of them at home waving good-bye as I sat on a camel leaving to escape south through the desert. They saved my life and I wanted to see them again. I hoped that they were alive.

Maksoudi drove slowly on a bumpy, narrow dirt road. There were trees and adobe houses, children, a canal, and a field of rich green grass. "This isn't Mahalajat," I said quietly.

"Yes, it is," said Maksoudi. "All this was destroyed during the mujahideen time. The houses have been replaced." A US helicopter flew over us. I looked for the trenches, the high barns from that time when we were all together, when the subcommander had stood up and shouted at his men to keep firing, and the commander had motioned for me to get back from the fighting . . . the dust and confusion and the gunfire came back to me. I prayed to God to save me then.

I told this story in a speech in Vancouver, where I grew up, and afterward my father, who had come to hear me, said in disgust that my prayer was a foxhole conversation, meaning not the real thing, and I felt weak and foolish.

"There is a former mujahideen commander who lives around here," said Maksoudi. "We can try to find him. Mullah Malang, the famous mujahideen commander from here, lives in Quetta now." Quetta was south, across the border in Pakistan. I didn't know who Malang was, but in 2007 I would meet him, and because of Maksoudi, I never fully trusted him.

Maksoudi took us to a commander, a thin man with a long black beard and quiet voice, sitting in the shade. We sat with him, in bare feet. "The Soviets destroyed most of Kandahar," he said. "After they left the mujahideen fought one other. Pakistan interfered and helped the Taliban gain power. Mullah Omar and Osama bin Laden took power. Then other mujahideen, with the help of US soldiers, fought the Taliban. Iran is helping Hekmatyar. Pakistan still helps the Taliban. The US is helping us, but we are poor." This was correct, but he politely ignored the tie between Pakistan and the United States.

Zalgai and I took the car north to Herat. Our driver drove fast through the desert, afraid of the men by the road with rifles. This was where in the spring of 1994 Mullah Omar achieved fame, clearing the road of checkpoints set up by former mujahideen who were stealing from and threatening drivers, helping put an end to the chaos, creating the Taliban. We drove down a tree-lined boulevard in Herat, the most elegant of Afghan cities, to the Citadel. Once there had been a small hotel here with a carpet on the dirt floor and a flower in a vase at the reception desk. Now there were auto repair shops. The gentle world of horse-drawn carts, open fires, and roasting kebab was gone. I did radio interviews and went to see Ismail Khan, the mujahideen commander of Herat, with a gray beard now. I mentioned the past. "Ah, the mujahideen," he said, his eyes sparkling. He too glorified that time, when he was young and had something to live for.

I sat by a brick wall one morning and watched a caravan come down the road, women in long, brightly colored dresses walking briskly, one with a small herd of baby black goats around her; a little girl in a gold dress carried one in her arms. Spring was coming and a time of renewal. Once, nomads supplied milk and yogurt to the kings of Afghanistan. Once, it was quiet here.

We flew from Herat back to Kabul. It was late January and the US bombing campaign was over. The Taliban were decimated and US television networks left Afghanistan, but I stayed. The next day the World Food Program called and said that the director was flying around the country and then to Swat, Pakistan, and then back to Kabul and was looking for journalists to go on the flight. I had never been to Swat, heard it was beautiful and wanted to go. It was late afternoon as we were approaching and there was too much cloud cover so we diverted to Islamabad. I went to the CBS bureau. There was a report that a *Wall Street Journal* reporter was missing in Karachi. The next day it snowed in Kabul and the airport was closed. The reporter was still missing. It was eerie. Something was wrong. I volunteered to take a CBS camera crew to Karachi to follow the story. We left that afternoon.

The next day we met a Pakistani journalist named Aamir. He was quick and smart and I hired him as a fixer. I learned that the missing reporter's name was Daniel Pearl. I didn't know him. He had disappeared on January 23. Three days later, his kidnappers sent a ransom demand to journalists: not for money but, strangely, for the US to send Pakistan the F-16 fighter jets it had purchased, but which the US had not delivered. Pearl was killed about ten days later. We learned after he was killed that an Englishman of Pakistani heritage, Ahmed Omar Saeed Sheikh, had orchestrated the kidnapping; the police threatened his relatives and he gave himself up to the ISI, which kept him for a week in Lahore before releasing him to the police. Retired general Perez Musharraf, the president of Pakistan, said that Pearl had come from Mumbai, implying Indian involvement in Pearl's death, and had "made intrusion into the areas which are dangerous and he should have avoided." Moinuddin Haider, the interior minister and former major general, said the same thing, blaming Daniel Pearl for getting killed.

There was nothing more that we could do. The story was over. The crew and I took the hotel bus to the airport. We were approaching the terminal and my phone rang. It was Aamir, our fixer. There was a video of Pearl's death. We had to turn around. We returned to the hotel and learned that every US network, and foreign networks, were trying to get the video. That night, close to midnight, Aamir called again and asked if I wanted to go right now to see it.

I asked Aamir how he knew about the video and he said that he had learned about it from a man in New York. He said that Khalid Sheikh Mohammad, a Kuwaiti member of al-Qaeda, was behind the killing, but that two Yemenis, who were especially militant, had been brought in and had slaughtered Pearl. I was now afraid of Aamir and refused to go with him. He had connections to the jihadist underworld, or to the ISI, or maybe both. I realized that I was standing on the edge of a dark, murky pool, and I didn't want to jump. I called New York and I gave CBS executives the information I had, but said that I didn't want any part of it. I would not help negotiate for it. I wanted Daniel Pearl to be remembered with dignity. I tried to put the video out of my mind.

On March 1, the US Army launched Operation Anaconda, led by the Tenth Mountain Division, in Afghanistan. It was the largest ground attack since Vietnam, against remnants of al-Qaeda. Nick Turner, the cameraman, and George Ioannides, the soundman, and I flew back to Islamabad, and I rushed back to Kabul. The battle was at Shah-i-Kot, where in 1981 I had lived with Haqqani. I remembered entering his compound. I slept on a dirt floor in an adobe room with Ken Guest, a British photojournalist, and later with the Egyptian army major, who came to visit us.

US soldiers of the Tenth Mountain Division out of Fort Drum, New York, later said that it was hard to breathe in the mountains. But they weren't that high. Shah-i-Kot was below the tree line, which is seven thousand feet, and in a valley. I had hiked and run through the mountains around us. The Arabs and Haqqani's men, who were surely at Shah-i-Kot, were fighting for a cause greater than themselves. They had been fighting for thirty years. I admired their courage and I pitied them. The US was extracting revenge for 9/11, sending young men to kill what men in Washington had helped to create. I resolved to find Haqqani, head of what we would soon start to call the Haqqani Network.

We drove down to Gardez, two hours south of Kabul, and I stood in a field with other journalists and looked at the sky, where a B-52 was doing figure eights. We watched plumes of smoke rise from Shah-i-Kot after it dropped its bombs. That evening, I was walking down a dirt street in Gardez and saw Kathy Gannon, of the Associated Press, in a Toyota with Francoise Chipaux of *Le Monde*. Kathy got out and a dozen boys crowded around. We talked and she said that she had driven over the mountains, past Shah-i-Kot, to the border, the first foreigner to do this. I admired her courage. We said good-bye. "Show's over," she said to the crowd, which stood in wonder at this couple hugging in public.

Zalgai, my fixer, and Ahmed Jan, our driver, who also worked for CBS, and I headed east from Gardez on a pitted road. Three armed men came up from a gully and surrounded our car. "Who is that man?" a man in a black turban with a satellite phone asked, looking at me. "He is Uzbek and doesn't speak Pashto," said Zalgai. They wanted a ride, but Zalgai said no. We drove on and I wondered how close we had come to trouble. I looked up at the hills, patches of snow, pine trees, and bombed adobe villages. "I've been here with Haqqani's men. I know these mountains," I thought. The road became a rutted track. We reached the summit of the pass, and I stood in the snow as the wind blew across the mountains. I wondered if the Taliban would shoot me, a foreigner. We had just all but destroyed them at Shah-i-Kot, probably not ten miles away. We drove down the other side of the pass; the ice turned to mud and it grew warm. We passed stone villages sheltered among the trees.

At a checkpoint Afghans were frisking the drivers. On a ridge I saw a muscled man in a brown T-shirt with a beard and a baseball cap, pointing a rifle. He waved me up. "A dangerous place to be traveling alone," he said, watching the road. Two men, like him in their thirties, sat behind him, one reading a paperback, M-4 rifles by their sides. A small fire burned in the center. A red Toyota pickup was behind them with a black tarp over the back. "There is someone watching you higher up," said the soldier. I asked what the road was like. He shook his head. The man with the book asked what I knew about the battle at Shah-i-Kot. I told them what I knew. He asked if I knew how the Detroit Pistons were doing and we relaxed a bit. "I waved you up because I wanted to make sure you're okay, traveling here alone," said the first soldier. He shook his head, as if I was crazy. We wished one another good luck and I left.

Zalgai, Ahmed Jan, and I continued down the rutted dirt road, past scrub trees and villages built into the mountains, like old Indian villages in Arizona and Utah. The road flattened and turned to asphalt and we stopped at a settlement of small wood shops, bought some oranges, and continued. The wind blew and jagged snowy mountains appeared on either side and then in the east a giant white marble mosque appeared with twin minarets made of wood and turquoise. It was Haqqani's new mosque rising over Khost like a cathedral over a village in France or Spain.

We came upon patches of green lawn and white painted buildings and a street crowded with men in dark turbans and shawls. It was sunny and the street was dusty. The mosque was surrounded by a high black iron fence, encompassing a city block. Zalgai and I entered a courtyard. There was a round cement wall three feet high with faucets in the center, for ablutions. Men and boys stood near the mosque, and other boys sat in the courtyard, with books.

"I'm looking for Jalaluddin Haqqani," I said to a man. "I would like to leave a message for him. I lived with him and his men in Shah-i-Kot when I was here as a journalist during the Soviet time." Zalgai translated my request. It was ridiculous what I was doing, but I didn't let that stop me.

"He hasn't been around here in a while," the man responded. "I don't know where he is."

I gave him my e-mail address and he put it in his pocket. I learned years later that I had not been so ridiculous. Ibrahim had been at Shah-i-Kot. The Haqqani village was close by.

Chapter 4

Yunus Khalis

Spring 2002

It was time to find Yunus Khalis. My driver and I drove down from the high plains of Kabul to the heat of Jalalabad. We stopped in front of a small wood-frame house. Zalgai knocked on the door, a young man opened it, and he joined us in the vehicle. His name was Moquium. The four of us drove through a grove of willow trees and wide canals, where it was cool and peaceful, and then out into the sun and up a turning, undulating dirt road into the hills. We came upon a group of men repairing the road and Moquium asked directions. They smiled and a man shouted, pointing the way.

Everyone knew Yunus Khalis, the mujahideen leader, the man whom bin Laden stayed with when he returned from Sudan in 1996 and whom he went to see, it appears, after 9/11 for three days. Father Sheikh he called him—I guessed it was to replace his own father who had died in a plane crash when he was ten. Bin Laden gave a speech to the elders in Jalalabad before he went up to Tora Bora, the mountain region once controlled by Yunus Khalis, the man who sent me on a great adventure that changed my life.

We climbed up the dirt road and jagged, snowy mountains appeared in the east. Tora Bora was up there. We pulled up next to a baked mud compound, with flowers and vines growing over the dark brown walls, and parked under a shady tree. A car drove by up the hill and a man in the car looked over. Three men, one standing and two sitting on a charpoy, a narrow wood cot, in the shade by a guard house, watched us. A dog lay under a small red truck. The men came over as I got out of the car. Flies buzzed around. I was wearing a khaki shirt and pants and was clean shaven. Zalgai told them that we had come to see Yunus Khalis. He was old, they said, and too sick to see visitors—and, although they didn't say it, certainly not a foreigner. I knew him from before, I said. I had lived with his men. I showed them my book with pictures of us.

I stood by the car, trying to look unthreatening. Zalgai and I kept insisting gently, but the men said no. The man who had seen us from the car, and another man, came around the corner. We told them why I had come. They too said no. Back and forth we went. I had never been so insistent. Finally, the man who had been in the car took my card, and the other men followed him into the compound. Zalgai, Ahmed Jan, and Moquium sat on the charpoy in the shade. Minutes passed, and the man who had been in the car came out and said that Khalis would see me but only for a few minutes.

I called to Zalgai, grabbed my notebook and camera. We followed the man into the compound and walked on a stone walkway into another courtyard where two children, seven or eight, played in the grass. We walked on a dirt path to the house. I saw plastic pails and children's sandals. We reached the house, walked up a few steps, and the man took off his shoes. We did the same. No questions, he said, out of respect. I was shaking with excitement. We entered a dark room. A frail, old man wearing a prayer cap lay on his side on a bed.

There he was, so much smaller than before. He had been tall then, with a big chest, and wore a white turban, a bandoleer, and a pistol. Tears came to my eyes. I looked at Khalis lying on the bed. His face was gaunt and his beard gray, but trimmed. I sat on the bed and we shook hands. His were soft and warm, and the calluses were gone. He sat up and I wanted to be alone with him and to talk about the past. I wanted to ask about bin Laden, but mostly I just wanted to be with him. I thanked him for seeing me. He thanked me for coming. I couldn't tell if he recognized me. I barely recognized him.

A boy about four and a girl about five came into the room and climbed onto the bed. He picked up the girl, whom I assumed was his daughter, and kissed her gently on the cheek. His wife, I had been told, was in her early twenties. He had another, older wife, and I heard that she had died.

I tried to speak in Pashto but I forgot almost all the little I knew and had to rely on Zalgai. I told him that I had come twenty years ago, and that he had sent me up into the mountains to be with Jalaluddin Haqqani. He said he appreciated that I and other journalists had come to help them during jihad. I described how he looked then. He nodded. He was sick, his leg was broken, and he hurt all over. He said that he was eighty-four years old. He was younger than my father, but he looked much older.

He took my hand and clasped it to his eyes. He said that he wanted to go to see a doctor in India. Zalgai took a picture of us. I talked about Haqqani, and said how good he had been to me. I hoped Yunus Khalis would talk about him, and that it would lead to a talk about bin Laden. I hoped that he would tell the men with us to arrange for me to see Haqqani.

The man said that we had to go—had been saying it for the last two minutes. I asked if he had a good life. "Oh yes," he said. He had accomplished what he had to do. His war was over. There was an aura of peace about him. After 9/11, there had been a statement in the media in his name calling for jihad against the United States and its allies for invading Afghanistan. I admired him for fighting against great odds for what he thought was right. *"Khoday-pah-mahn,"* I said. "Go with God." We shook hands and I felt the soft warmth of Yunus Khalis's skin, and then we left and walked outside. I knelt to put on my shoes. "You were very lucky," said the man. "He doesn't see anybody. Journalists come here all the time." Again, he said how lucky I was. Moquium, too, kept repeating it.

We drove back up to Kabul. I felt relaxed and more determined now to find Haqqani. I didn't do any reporting about my meeting with Khalis. I only told a few people where I had been. Yunus Khalis, in his generation, was the founding father of jihad in Afghanistan, an icon to the mujahideen and Taliban. That I was the only Westerner to have met him gave me unique standing. Our conversation had not included any great intimacy but the fact that it had happened at all resonated widely.

I returned to New York in mid-April, freelancing but more involved with CBS. One day I was in the newsroom sitting at the Foreign Desk and Marcy McGinnis, the senior vice president, walked in quickly and came over. "I would like you to meet Sophie Roland-Gutterman." She was the foreign editor in the "fishbowl," a small, narrow, glass-enclosed, oval office where the anchor, executive producer, and other editors, like her, prepared the *Evening News*. She seemed shy and had a quiet voice. I learned later that she had started at CNN and had worked in the CBS bureau in London, which covered Europe, the greater Middle East, and South Asia.

On March 20, 2003, the United States invaded Iraq and the CBS bureau chief in London asked a woman in Islamabad to go to Baghdad to run its new bureau and Nafay Hamid took over for her while she was away. I was in New York and flew to Turkey, hoping to go in as a freelancer for CBS into northern Iraq. But men there, unlike the mujahideen in the 1980s, were charging money to take you in, and I rebelled. I got an assignment from *60 Minutes* to go to Afghanistan. I flew to Islamabad to meet the team. Nafay was at the hotel when I arrived. She had a bright, smiling manner and spoke English with an American accent. She had graduated from Pepperdine and seemed more Californian than Pakistani. The *60 Minutes* producers took the UN flight, but I flew Ariana Afghan Airlines—wanting to be closer to Afghanistan— up to Kabul.

It was spring and the jasmine trees were in bloom, chartreuse and bright red. We finished our story and the team left, but I stayed. I wrote to Kody, my brother, asking if he remembered the name of the hotel where we had stayed. He sent the name, the Hilal Hotel, and Zalgai managed to find it. The street, once empty, was filled with cars, bicycles, motorcycles, and donkey carts, and there were shops selling electronic gadgets, televisions, and refrigerators. We climbed the narrow stone stairs to the front desk. Gone were the men sitting around the wood-burning stove. There was a restaurant now and flat-screen televisions on the front wall.

I told the owner that I had stayed there before and wanted to go upstairs. He gave us a key to a room. It was smaller than I remembered, as was the rooftop, where we had moved when we ran low on money. The Kabul River was on one side, the Hindu Kush on another. Was it the same place? We went back outside and I smelled the sewer running by—that was certainly the same. Zalgai took my picture standing in front of the door that led upstairs, where we lived on the peanut butter that Kody bought in Tehran, and where he got jaundice from the lettuce I bought in the bazaar, and I looked at the stars and hoped that God was protecting me.

On May 2, Donald Rumsfeld, US secretary of defense, came and held a press conference with President Karzai in the presidential palace. "We're at a point where we clearly have moved from major combat operations to a period of stability, stabilization, and reconstruction," Rumsfeld said. "The bulk of the country is at peace. Afghans are returning from across the globe. There are nine thousand US troops here. They and coalition forces are dealing with pockets of resistance."

I sat there. The US, with all its money, did not understand that the Taliban had taken off their black turbans and were watching and waiting, their leaders biding time in Pakistan. The Taliban had fought and died to create an Islamic government. God was on their side, and they would not give in.

❖ ❖ ❖

I WAS AT my desk at the CBS house when the phone rang. "Hello, this is George Crile," said the caller. He was in Pakistan and coming up to Kabul the next day. He was a *60 Minutes* producer. I hadn't seen him in twenty years. He was coming with his daughter, Susan, a high school senior. I was impressed that he would bring his daughter to see Afghanistan. He had come to research a story on women's education. I would help him. I wouldn't have to go back to New York.

He was carrying a book around. It was called *Charlie Wilson's War*, and he was the author. It had just been published. I remembered Wilson, a congressman from Texas, who wanted to fight the Russians. "You should meet him," a friend who worked in Congress told me in 1984. "He's doing more than you." I assumed he meant more to help the Afghans. Abdul Rahim, the mujahideen spokesman, had gone to see him on a trip to Washington. "You should meet him, Mr. Jere," he said softly. "He understands."

I began to read George's book on Jalaluddin, Hekmatyar, and Charlie Wilson, who drank hard alcohol, snorted cocaine, traveled with glamorous women, became friends with Pakistani dictator Zia-ul-Haq, and who called Haqqani "goodness personified." I knew relatively well from working in the Senate and as director of Friends of Afghanistan how the government worked; I didn't believe that Wilson, even as chairman of a House subcommittee on defense could secretly appropriate millions of dollars for the mujahideen, work secretly with a renegade CIA agent, and meet with foreign arms dealers, as the book stated, without the knowledge of the leadership of the House of Representatives and the White House. President Reagan and the CIA, under William Casey, wanted to destroy the Soviet Union. I didn't like men like Wilson, who had never seen war, calling loudly for it. But I enjoyed his wild ride.

"There were 58,000 (US) dead in Vietnam and we owe the Russians one," said Wilson. "I have a slight obsession with it because of Vietnam. I thought the Soviets ought to get a dose of it."[10]

Pakistani general Mohammad Yousaf, head of the ISI's Afghan Bureau from 1983 to 1987 and who arranged Wilson's trip into Afghanistan, felt, in dealing with US officials, that the United States was in Afghanistan primarily for revenge against the Soviet Union for backing America's enemies in Vietnam.[11] Then the US invaded in 2001, again out of revenge, this time for 9/11—and it, like the Soviet Union, would become bogged down there. For the Haqqanis, I would learn, there was no difference between the Americans and the Russians. We were all infidel invaders.

Before he left, George gave me his copy of the book and signed it "To my younger brother, Jerry—a brilliant sprinter who has become an inspired long distance runner, until we meet again at home or in some distant clime. George Crile, Kabul, May 2003."

⁜ ⁜ ⁜

A MONTH LATER, back in New York, Marcy McGinnis said that NBC had someone following the hunt for bin Laden and could I do that for CBS? The US didn't know where he was and every journalist and news organization wanted to find him. I began to go to work at 6:00 a.m. and called contacts in South Asia, which was nine hours ahead, Europe, and Washington, and read all that I could about bin Laden. I wrote reports for CBS and over the next year got to know the organization better.

As I thought of bin Laden, I thought of the Egyptian army major that had stayed with us in Afghanistan. He was one of the first of the thousands[12] of young, ardent Muslim men who came from throughout the world to fight the godless communists in Afghanistan. The Arabs felt closest, I heard and read, to Haqqani. If I could get to Haqqani, maybe I could find out where bin Laden was. But I had no idea how to do this, especially from New York.

On October 28, 2004, in an act reminiscent of the chaos in Iraq that was playing out on television worldwide, a group of about seven armed men in military uniforms stopped a UN SUV in Wazir Akbar Khan, the diplomatic enclave in Kabul. They beat the driver, grabbed the three UN employees inside, and drove away.[13] The UN workers were released on November 23. I didn't pay any attention to this story—I was focusing on the hunt for bin Laden—but I should have.

⁜ ⁜ ⁜

IN 2005 I had dinner one night at the Karachi Press Club with Aamir, my fixer when we covered the kidnapping of Daniel Pearl. Afterward, we went outside to have tea in the courtyard. "Be careful here," he warned. "People will say all kinds of things and pretend to be your friend, but they're not. You're not Muslim, and you're a foreigner, and they don't like you; in fact, they hate you, but they will never tell you this. Never forget this."

I never forgot that it had been Aamir who was first to tell me that Khalid Sheikh Mohammad had been with Pearl when he was killed, years before he had proclaimed it at Guantanamo. Aamir introduced me to a Pakistani army colonel named Salman who told me that he had worked for years in Afghanistan and still went there. He gave me his card, which had an address in Virginia. I deduced from this, although he didn't say it, that he was ISI. I felt that he had ties, because of the Virginia address, to US intelligence. We had lunch and he asked me to come to his base. "We can talk better there," he said. I thought of what Aamir said, and declined.

I wanted to learn more from a Pakistani official, someone with authority, about Pakistan's ties to the mujahideen and the Taliban—and Haqqani. Yasmeen, the CBS bureau chief, now back from Baghdad, urged me to go see retired major general Naseerullah Babar, former prime minister Benazir Bhutto's interior minister, in Peshawar and gave me his phone numbers. He was, she said, the father of the mujahideen and the Taliban; he rode with the Taliban when they took Kabul in September 2006, and looted the Kabul Museum.

At his front gate I saw a Buddhist statue on the roof of his garage. "I collect Gandharan art," he said, showing me his artifacts. Gandhara was a kingdom that covered eastern Afghanistan and western Pakistan and lasted for a thousand years until the eleventh century, when Mahmud of Ghazni, a Turk who never lost a battle, raided India seventeen times, looting its Hindu temples and becoming the archetypal Muslim invader. Gandhara produced the Buddhist statues at Bamiyan, which the Taliban, who considered them idols, destroyed with artillery in 2001.

Babar, in his seventies, wore shalwar kameez and a diamond ring, the kind women wear in the West. A servant brought milk tea, a plate of samosas, and cookies. We talked for two afternoons in Peshawar and later in New York, where he was visiting relatives, about how he, in his words, created the mujahideen. "I did my bit," he said, "for Pakistan."

He began in 1973, but the mujahideen began before that. In the 1960s, Burhanuddin Rabbani and other young assistant professors at the Islamic Faculty at Kabul University went on sabbatical to Cairo's al-Azhar University, founded in 988 AD, the oldest, most prestigious Sunni Muslim university in the world, to further their education. This was where they read the works of Sayyid Qutb, the main theorist of the Muslim Brotherhood. Rabbani brought Qutb's books back to Afghanistan and translated them into Dari. Yunus Khalis translated them into Pashto.

In July 1973, Mohammad Daoud Sadar Khan, a Pashtun nationalist, obsessed with the Pashtun lands of the Tribal Areas, now part of Pakistan, overthrew his brother-in-law, King Zahir Shah, and established a replublic. A dozen university students fled to Pakistan. They were led by Gulbuddin Hekmatyar and Ahmed Shah Massoud, under the influence of Professor Rabbani, and were upset at what Rabbani told me in 2007 were the communists around Daoud Khan, whom they called the "Red Prince."

General Babar, as inspector-general the most powerful man then in the North-West Frontier Province, took in those men who in two years would become the leaders of the mujahideen. "I had a code word for each one: the plumber, the electrician, the mason, and so on. I gave them Pakistani passports and put them in the army for training. It was obvious that Hekmatyar, the most dynamic, would be their leader. We realized that we needed a political leader, and so we brought over Rabbani. I needed money and went to the US embassy." If the US provided funds then, it helped to create at the beginning what would become the mujahideen, which led to al-Qaeda, the Taliban, and the Islamic State.

In 1973, Pakistani prime minister Zulfikar Ali Bhutto, concerned about Daoud Khan's calls for Pashtunistan, set up a secret ISI cell on Afghanistan. It was run by General Babar. "We gave them Indian rifles that we captured in our wars with India," he said. In July 1975, the Afghans, who now called themselves the mujahideen, attacked government installations in Afghanistan. "The government killed or captured most of them," said Babar.

But the movement grew. Robert Gates, former director of the CIA, and Zbigniew Brzezinski, NSC adviser to President Carter, have acknowledged[14] that the US began to fund the mujahideen in July 1979. The Haqqanis, Babar said, were not part of the original mujahideen.

On May 15, 2005, Clementina Cantoni, 32, a pretty, smiling woman working for CARE International, was kidnapped on her way to work. The Pope prayed for her. Three weeks later she was released.

In January 2006, I was in Peshawar, staying at Green's Hotel. Behroz Khan came to see me and brought with him Sami Yousafzai, an Afghan journalist living in Peshawar who was working with *Newsweek*. That evening Sami drove us to a restaurant. We got out of the car and a small, skinny man in his twenties, carrying a satchel, brushed hard up against us and walked with us. We sat in the restaurant and I asked Behroz and Sami what that was all about. They both shook their heads. They wouldn't talk about it.

I went a few days later to the US Consulate, surrounded now by barbed wire. The flower bushes were gone. I had tea with the consul general. His assistant, a Pashtun married to an American, asked who I was working with. I said Behroz and he asked that I convey his best wishes. I then mentioned Sami. The assistant seemed to disapprove of my working with Sami.

⁂ ⁂ ⁂

I RETURNED TO New York in March 2006, continued to work for CBS, became a senior fellow at the Carnegie Council, and taught a class on political Islam at night at NYU. On March 21, I read a front-page article in the *New York Times*[15] about Pat Tillman, the Arizona Cardinals football star who joined the army after 9/11, and who had been killed in Afghanistan in 2004. I had read many articles about Tillman, but this one, particularly, caught my attention, and it would lead me, indirectly, to the Haqqanis.

I realized that the truth had not come out. No one, outside of army investigators, had gone into the mountains to investigate Tillman's death. It was Taliban country. I decided to go to find the truth about Tillman. I went to Rome Hartman, the executive producer of *CBS Evening News*, and told him. He supported me and said that I was to report from now on to Sophie Roland-Gutterman, who had just been promoted to foreign editor.

I went out west to see my father and then down to San Jose to see Pat Tillman's father. He gave me the US Army reports on his son's death. I would take them with me up in the mountains.

Jeff McCausland, a military analyst at CBS, urged me to write a monograph for the Strategic Studies Institute, a think tank of the US Army War College, where he had been the dean. I met with the director and got a contract to write on Islamic fundamentalism in South Asia. I could write what I wanted and the institute would not change a word. The way seemed to be opening for me to return to South Asia.

In June, Susan Hall, a high school friend and costume designer in Hollywood, called to say that she was working on a movie on Afghanistan called *Charlie Wilson's War*. A week later, Celia Costas, the executive producer, called and asked if I would meet with Mike Nichols, the director. I knew he had met with one Afghan expert already. She sent me the script to read. I wanted to work on the movie but my father hated Hollywood, and I didn't want to appear decadent to my nephews and nieces. We didn't go to movies when I was a boy. They were too worldly, as they are to the Taliban. I started going to movies as an adult but always felt a bit worldly, this residue from my childhood, when I did. I talked to my brother and sister and they weren't worried. I went one hot July afternoon to Mike Nichols's apartment on Fifth Avenue and we talked about Afghanistan. He raided the refrigerator for lunch and we talked about the script, parts of which I said were wrong. We talked about life and our backgrounds and he talked about what to look for in a woman. I liked him immensely and he hired me to be his Afghanistan consultant.

I didn't know it then, but these two projects would become part of my journey into the labyrinth of my kidnapping.

On July 19, Aamir, in Karachi, sent me an e-mail. "Ur old friend Yunus Khalis died today. . . . His son Anwar ul-Haq has been appointed as his successor." I read his message many times. I thought back to Peshawar, sitting with him on the floor drinking tea, and seeing him again in 2003. Bakhtar, the Afghan government news agency, said on July 25, "President Hamid Karzai expressed his condolences upon hearing about the death of Malawi Mohammad Yunus Khalis. His role in the Afghan struggle against the Soviet Union is preserved in the golden words in the history of Afghanistan."

I finished my semester teaching at NYU and went to Hollywood to work on *Charlie Wilson's War*. There I met Nichols's CIA consultant on the film, Milt Bearden, who was CIA station chief in Pakistan from 1987 to 1989. We had breakfast and he said that he had been given a billion dollars to fight the Soviets in Afghanistan. I asked about Haqqani, whom he had written about and admired as a tough guerrilla leader. He put his head down. "I wish he had come over," he said sadly. The producer said that she wanted to know what games children played in a refugee camp. I had been to these camps but didn't know the games they played, and contacted Sami Yousafzai, who grew up in one. I flew to Pakistan and we went to two camps for the film.

The movie moved to Morocco. I flew to Marrakech, the movie's base, and commuted up into the Atlas Mountains. One afternoon, Milt Bearden and I were standing on a hill with actors and members of the crew in front of two hundred extras in a makeshift refugee camp. Bearden said that they needed men who looked like ISI officers to oversee the camp. He saw to it that they were there and dressed appropriately. He was doing his job, but it was clear that he felt close to the ISI, which angered every Afghan on the set.

I complained to Celia that the Atlas Mountains looked like hills in comparison to Afghanistan. We finished filming and I flew to Kabul. Celia called and asked me to find a helicopter and a cameraman and shoot film in the mountains. I was preparing to do so when Bearden called and said that he was going to his contacts in the Pakistani army and that they would shoot the footage. He had convinced Celia that he could do a better job. It was interesting that he was long retired from the CIA but still close to the Pakistani army. I had met on occasion with retired lieutenant general Hamid Gul, head of the ISI when Bearden was station chief. They worked together. "We had fifty-four thousand foreign fighters, from thirty-eight countries, and we registered everyone," Gul said one day on the phone. "The CIA was very happy."

I had asked Bearden about this over breakfast in Hollywood. "The Pakistanis may have created an Arab brigade after we left, but we did not," he insisted.

After Bearden took over, my time with the movie ended. In Kabul, I moved to a cheaper residence and contacted Fazul Rahim, now in charge of the CBS bureau. He came over immediately with a local phone for me. I said that I wanted to use Sami Yousafzai up in the mountains. He was Pashtun, and Tillman had been killed in Pashtun territory. Fazul, a Tajik, understood. Sami came up from Pakistan to plan the trip. I mentioned the Haqqanis and he knew a man who had been with them. He later came with three men; one was a dull, hulking man, a bodyguard. The former Haqqani man said that he told Sirajuddin, Haqqani's eldest son, that he wanted a raise. He had a family. "Sirajuddin said 'we need younger people,' and so I left." He was now with the National Directorate of Security (NDS), or Afghan intelligence. The man with him had white curly hair and albino skin, and wore a fatigue jacket and running shoes. "I escorted Haqqani to the US embassy in Islamabad," he claimed. Ten years later I would hear the Haqqani side to this famous story.

Sami took me to a store and we bought a packaged shalwar kameez. It would be the first time I had worn Afghan clothes in twenty-five years. It was December and snowing. We left at dawn and stopped in Gardez, two hours south of Kabul. I went for a walk, slipped in the snow, and scraped my hands. A man helped me up, and said gently in Pashto that there was a water faucet across the street where I could clean up. I thanked him and was happy. I had passed as an Afghan. I could still do it. The road was closed but Sami had a friend in Gardez and he let us stay the night. I asked about the Taliban. "They are around here now. They're coming back," he said.

Sami watched me closely. He had been angry at me all day. He was upset when we had to stop the car so I could do an interview using my satellite phone, and I could sense his anger now. "He doesn't like

Americans," he said referring to our host. "You are the invaders now. It is only because of Pashtunwali that you're here." He meant the ancient code of hospitality. "Why aren't you Muslim?" Sami asked. He had talked earlier about an al-Qaeda cemetery where visitors could smell a perfume, but I wouldn't be able to because I was an infidel. He wanted me to pray with him now. I said no.

Two days later the road opened and we drove over the mountains. We got a flat tire and had to stop and Sami was nervous. It was toward sundown and we were in a gorge next to a stream and there were villages around us. "The Taliban come out at night. Don't talk, don't write in your notebook, or use your satellite phone." I looked around slowly. We drove on to Khost and found a hotel where Sami felt safe. It was run by a Pakistani. "What nationality are you?" he asked. "American," I said. He wagged his finger. "No you're not." I would be safe here.

The next morning, we walked down a crowded street to go eat. Our local guide, who Sami had found, grabbed my arm. "Your name will be Gulob. You are an engineer from Kabul and you are here to survey for a road that the government is going to build." We walked up to a second-story restaurant, where it was quiet and safe to eat.

That night I sat in my room, the US Army reports spread out on my cot. Sami came in with a solid man called Mansoor. He was a former Afghan army officer, now an S-2, intelligence officer, for the US Army. He would be my guide in the mountains. We would leave early in the morning. His men would be ready. I felt a pit in my stomach. I had never felt this before. Sami's phone rang and his eyes lit up. He talked but didn't tell me who it was. I felt even more uneasy.

In the morning, we had breakfast and then walked until we came to a dark pickup and a black 4×4 with tinted windows and Mansoor and two men waiting by the road. They hugged me and I felt their rifles beneath their shawls. It was December 14, my birthday. We drove up the highway, turned off onto a dirt road, and crossed a rocky field to a track and began to climb. There were no police here, no soldiers. "We're taking a risk by taking you up into the mountains," said Mansoor. An hour later a truck came toward us and we pulled over. The driver of the truck and the other men inside stared at us.

We kept climbing, passed villages where more men and boys stared, and skirted the edge of a wide canyon with a stream running through it where women were washing clothes. "I've been here before," I said to myself. "Only now I'm the enemy." I had walked through these high plains on my way to Shah-i-Kot in 1981. We came upon two men praying by a stream. "That is the Taliban commander for this area," said Mansoor. "If I wasn't with you, I would arrest him." We reached the canyon where Tillman was killed. "I know the story of the footballer," Mansoor exclaimed. "He was a show soldier."

"We only have half an hour," said Sami. We'd come all this way, and I was paying him and these men for only half an hour? Sami had said the night before that he had been captured, robbed, and threatened by the Taliban in 2005, and was freed a few hours later.

I climbed up the hill where Tillman was standing when he was shot. "We must go," said Sami. "The Taliban are around here." We walked into the canyon. A family appeared and came toward us. The man nodded and he and his wife and daughters kept walking. I waited, turned to watch, and the young women looked back. They had noticed something. It wasn't good. "Gulob," said my guide, smiling, and he put his hand on my shoulder.

Mansoor pointed east. "Haqqani is just over there," he whispered. Pakistan was three miles away. "The Taliban come across the border at night carrying land mines and ammunition, no problem."

I realized at that moment that I wanted to live again in the mountains. I could cross the border, as I had in the 1980s, and go to Haqqani, but I needed men to protect me. I wanted to return to the past. I didn't like being on the outside looking in. I knew this country, I knew these people. I felt closer to them than I did to the West and to the men around me. It was the warmth of the past that I remembered and to which I wanted to return. I understood their struggle against the modern world. It wasn't mine and I was afraid of them now. But I wanted to see them as I had wanted to see Yunus Khalis.

"How far is Shah-i-Kot?" I asked a smiling, wiry guard next to me. He pointed back to where we left the truck. "Just over that mountain, we can go there if you like." I wanted to return to where I had started in 1981. We drove back out to a stream near the highway and the men washed, and prayed. They had all been nervous. But Sami didn't give me time to talk to villagers or compare the army reports to what I saw. I had paid him and I had to pay these gunmen to bring me here, for one half hour. Sami had started out as a sportswriter, and I felt that he wanted to do this story himself.

The next morning Sami said he wanted to leave Khost and go directly across the border to Pakistan, and asked if I would take his things to Kabul. It was dangerous for me to stay there, alone. I had never heard of a fixer leaving someone alone. I pointed out it would not be good for his reputation. He relented and we drove back toward Kabul. He stopped at a stand and bought some Afghan candy for us. I forgave him, but we didn't finish our work. The next morning, he left a note saying he couldn't work with me and he was gone. I felt that he had received a call that night, possibly from *Newsweek*, offering another assignment, and that that was more important to him than what I was paying him to do. I had had dinner at his house, met his sons. As a Pashtun, to invite someone into your home for dinner is to embrace him. But I sensed that there was a part to him that I couldn't reach, and I was wary.

I went to see Peter Jouvenal, a British cameraman who had come also in the early 1980s but stayed on; he married an Afghan and converted to Islam. I knew he was ex-military and he had an air of mystery about him. "There is a lot about me you don't know," he said, in his friendly way. He knew a place in Peshawar where I could get any type of passport. He and his wife owned the Gandamack guesthouse, much favored by journalists. I asked about another fixer. "Sharif," he said. "We'll find him for you," Hassina, his wife, chimed in. I asked Fazul later about Sharif. "Peter introduced us in 2004. He seems okay." I sent a note to Nafay in Islamabad. She had worked with Sharif and liked him.

We met at the Gandamack. Sharif was short, stocky, had a deep voice, and spoke Arabic. His brother cofounded Hezb-i-Islami with Gulbuddin Hekmatyar. Because of this, the communists put him in jail when he was ten for two months. When he was released his family left and they became refugees in Pakistan. "I had nothing to do and wanted a gun," Sharif explained. "I was eleven when I joined the mujahideen, so small that I dragged my rifle in the dirt. The mujahideen took care of me. I carried a rocket launcher with a hundred men behind me. I was a boy. This was freedom."

He had four daughters and two sons. He liked his daughters better than his sons. "You're not a man in Afghanistan unless you have ten children." He smiled. He had four more to go. His brother became bin Laden's director of public relations and was murdered in Dubai in 2002. "If we knew who killed him," he said, "we would kill them." I soon forgot about Sharif's history, until it became a part of mine.

Late in January 2007, Kabul was cold and icy as a laughing Kandahari driver, Sharif, and I drove down to Khost. There, Sharif found Afghans who had been scouts for the US Army and one who had stood next to Tillman when he was killed. We spent hours in the canyon, and over the next four days I finally learned what happened that day in the canyon and how Tillman was killed.

Chapter 5

Family Feuds

I WANTED TO TALK TO THE US SOLDIERS WHO WERE WITH PAT TILL-
man, but to do that I would have to return to the US, and I had to fulfill
my contract to write a monograph for the Army War College. I worked
in Kabul and then flew to India, Kashmir, and to Bangladesh.

On March 3, 2007, I read that fifty-two-year-old Daniele Mastrogiacomo, an Italian correspondent, had been kidnapped in Afghanistan.
It was the first kidnapping of a foreign reporter in the Afghan-Pakistani
theater since Daniel Pearl, the second kidnapping since the UN workers were taken in October 2004.

Sharif, who was close to Ajmal Naqshbandi, a journalist who was
Mastrogiacomo's fixer, later told me the story. Mastrogiacomo, his
driver, Sayed Agha, and Naqshbandi drove from Kabul south to Helmand Province to meet with the Taliban. They were in a restaurant in
Lashkar Gah, the capital, having dinner and waiting for their meeting
when a man, his face partly covered by his turban to disguise himself,
joined them. Naqshbandi didn't know him. He only stayed a short time

and left. They finished and went outside, where men who Naqshbandi didn't know surrounded them and forced them into a car. "We have captured spies," they shouted as they drove away. Sharif thought another group of Taliban, different from those that Mastrogiacomo was going to meet, got word that there was a foreigner there, saw an opportunity, sent a man to confirm it, and grabbed them.

The Taliban demanded that Italy withdraw the 1,800 troops it had stationed in Afghanistan, but the Italian government refused. The Taliban then demanded that the Afghan government release Taliban leaders it was holding. They made a video showing Mastrogiacomo kneeling on the ground, his hands tied, a man holding a rifle to his head, and six feet away a man with a knife pushing Agha, whose hands were also tied, over in the dirt like he was an animal. They beheaded him. The director of Emergency, an Italian hospital in Kabul, contacted the Taliban. The Afghan government freed the Taliban leaders, and on March 19 Mastrogiacomo was released. Everyone in Kabul said that the Italians paid a ransom, but no one knew how much. Three days later the Taliban beheaded Naqshbandi. Afghans were angry that the government negotiated to free a Westerner, but refused to help its own citizens.

I flew to Lahore and Mugaddir Khan, the CBS driver, brought me to Islamabad. Two weeks later, an editor at Times Books in New York sent me an e-mail and said that he wanted to meet when I was back in town. I had met him through Joel Rosenthal, president of the Carnegie Council. I finished my monograph, flew to New York, and we had breakfast in a diner near the Carnegie Council. "The Tribal Areas of Pakistan are like a white space on a map," he said. "The CIA doesn't seem to know where bin Laden is hiding." I knew what was coming and was excited. It was exactly what I had been wanting to do for years and he was giving me a chance. I saw myself hiking in the hot, dusty mountains trying to meet Haqqani or Hekmatyar. They would know about bin Laden. "Write a proposal," the editor said. "Keep your beard."

I went out west to see my father. "Is that you Jere?" he asked, looking at his son with a beard and long hair. He was ninety-three now. He had lived briefly in a rest home, but was only happy in the house that he had had built for his wife, who helped design it, and children. We had a caretaker living with him. He went to the church that he and my mother created for the homeless in Portland, read, and worked in the yard. He sold his four pet sheep. He had already sold part of our land.

"I wish you would stay," my father said. I felt guilty, but I had to leave. I told CBS about my new project. I went to see *A Mighty Heart*, about Daniel Pearl. I watched him sitting in the car on his way to meet the jihadi leader. "He should never have gone alone," I thought. I wondered again and again what he thought when they took out the knife.

On July 19, twenty-three South Korean Christian missionaries were kidnapped while taking a bus from Kabul to Kandahar. At first I asked myself, how could they be so foolish standing out like that after Mastrogiacomo? It was illegal to be a missionary in Afghanistan. There was only one church, in the Italian Embassy. I wondered what the Taliban would do to them. The Koreans refused to eat the food the Taliban gave them, and would only eat food that they felt was clean. One of the kidnappers called Sami Yousafzai. "What do we do?" he asked. "They would only eat 'boxed foot,' cookies and bicuits made in Pakistan." On July 25, the Taliban killed one of the South Korean hostages. Five days later, they killed a second. I cringed quietly. I imagined the Taliban picking each man out and taking him outside and shooting him while the remaining hostages shook in fear. They would pray and sing hymns to give themselves strength.

Again, a team from *60 Minutes* asked me to go to Afghanistan to work on a story. When we finished, I would begin my work for the book in the Tribal Areas.

I asked Sophie if she could help me get a visa for Pakistan. She said no. "I know you want to write this book but you can't say at any time that you work for CBS." If I crossed from Afghanistan illegally through the mountains into Pakistan and got caught, Pakistan would throw me out of the country and could withhold visas from other CBS journalists. Other networks would get visas to go there. CBS would lose viewers. It was a public corporation, with stockholders. I decided that I wouldn't try to get a visa but would instead cross through the mountains into Pakistan. It would be more exciting and interesting. I had done it before.

I left the CBS broadcast center and was walking through Central Park when my phone rang. It was Ana Real, the CBS deputy foreign editor. She was from Nicaragua and her primary focus was Latin America, but part of her job was to arrange visas for camera crews and correspondents. I had stopped by her desk to complain that Sophie would not help me with a visa to Pakistan for my book, and to say good-bye to her and to others on the Foreign Desk. She called and told me to call a man at the Pakistani Consulate, on Sixty-fifth Street, immediately and gave me his number. I thought she had called to help me. I called the consulate and the man told me to come to his office. He wore a gray suit and came around from his desk to shake hands. We had tea but I saw a cold, flinty look behind his smile, and I knew that he was not a Foreign Service officer.

He asked about my plans. I told him I would be going to Afghanistan with *60 Minutes* and wanted to also go to Pakistan. He asked about my background and when I wanted to leave. I talked briefly about the past, always a mistake. Pakistani officials knew that if I had been in Afghanistan in the 1980s and was still involved in Afghanistan, then I was suspect. A prominent producer at CBS said to others that he thought I worked for the CIA. People, I found, glibly threw around those three initials, *CIA*—the romance, to them, of James Bond movies. I explained briefly my background and filled out an application and asked if I could pick up my visa in London. "We have to wait and hear from Islamabad," he replied. It was a way of saying no. He had got the information that he wanted, and it would go in my file. I had been in the consulate many times and knew when a visa was forthcoming. I walked slowly home, dejected. I would find guides and go with them—without CBS backing or a Pakistani visa—over the mountains into Pakistan.

On August 4, I flew to London to do research in the British Museum on the history of the Tribal Areas. Four days later I returned to Kabul. On August 19, the Taliban released two South Korean female hostages. We knew that negotiations were going on. On August 21, four men kidnapped a German aid worker having lunch with her husband in a restaurant in Kabul and demanded a million-dollar ransom. The news spread like wildfire, and foreigners were afraid. It took place in Kabul itself, not in the country. The Kabul police found the men, who were known criminals, within a few hours and the woman was released. The Italians, it seemed, by paying for Mastrogiacomo's intact return, had created a market.

60 Minutes needed a politician for its story, which was on civilian casualties. Fazul knew a member of parliament (MP), Daoud Sultanzoy, and brought him to us to make the introduction. He had lived in the United States and was a former pilot for American Airlines. He had gone to high school with Hekmatyar. Sultanzoy was also a tribal chief and would introduce me to another chief, who would introduce me to yet another chief, who would open, in 2015, the most important door for me of all.

A week later, we finished our work and the crew left. I was anxious to begin work on my own. CBS News wanted some information on drug trafficking and Fazul took me to meet another MP, Mirwais Yasini, who was director of an antinarcotics program. As we sat in his large house in the center of Kabul, he said that in 1981 he had been with Yunus Khalis and had taken Dan Rather, the CBS anchor, into Afghanistan. I felt a kinship to Yasini because of this. I would soon come back to Yasini to seek his help and he would become an important man in my story. In the meantime, I began to go to the Pakistani embassy to apply for a visa. I filled out the application and visited with the press attaché, but he said that he would have to send my application to Pakistan. I knew what that meant. I didn't really need a visa yet, but wanted to go through the motions to keep up a front.

On August 19, the Taliban released two more female Korean hostages. There were rumors that the head of South Korean intelligence was involved directly. On August 29 and 30, the Taliban released the remaining nineteen South Korean hostages.[16] We were happy in Kabul for them. Sophie called and asked if the news was reportable. I couldn't prove it. We soon read that the Korean National Intelligence Service had negotiated secretly, in Pashto, with the Taliban. That was why, to show goodwill, the Taliban released two female hostages. Reuters reported that the Taliban said that South Korea paid $20 million. I heard

$22 million. Kidnapping had long been a tradition among tribes in Afghanistan. The South Koreans had been kidnapped in Ghazni Province, where Sultanzoy was a tribal leader.

Beginning with Mastrogiacomo, and continuing with the UN employees and now the South Koreans, the market value of a foreign hostage was well over a million dollars.[17]

⁙ ⁙ ⁙

BEHROZ KHAN, A Pakistani journalist, came to Kabul on assignment. I said I was having trouble getting a visa for Pakistan. He invited me to a dinner that night at the home of Asif Durrani, the acting Pakistani ambassador. It was strange that Behroz, a Pashtun who said he hated the Pakistani government for its treatment of the Pashtuns, would be invited to and go to dinner in Kabul at the Pakistani embassy.

There were ten of us at a table filled with food and alcohol, with Durrani, solidly built with jet black hair, sitting at the head, laughing, calling for more food, and dominating the room. After dinner, as we were leaving, Behroz asked Durrani if he could help me with a visa. Durrani, who was standing with us, told me to call him.

The next day I called the Pakistani embassy, and Durrani invited me over. We talked for two hours. He asked about my background. I knew it was a mistake, but I mentioned working with Zalmay Khalilzad during the Reagan administration when Pakistan and the US worked closely, hoping that by focusing on this it would help me get a visa. Durrani called for a car and we went to lunch at an Italian restaurant, the only one in Kabul. We returned to the embassy, but still Durrani wanted to talk. "Find out about Khalilzad and the Azizi Bank," he said. I sat there. The Azizi Bank started in 2006 in Kabul. I had heard that friends of Khalilzad, or maybe even Khalilzad himself, were involved in starting a bank in Kabul—or something, but I didn't know anything.[18] Khalilzad and I were not friends, but this was something else. Durrani had just asked me, maybe, to pursue this as a story, but I thought he wanted me to spy on him, possibly in exchange for a visa. I wondered how Behroz could be friends with this man.

That evening I got a call from Ken Guest, the photojournalist and former British Royal Marine I had lived with when I was with Haqqani. He had heard that I was in Kabul. I hadn't seen him in twenty years. Gone was the skinny man with long hair. He was strong-looking, handsome, married, had children, and wore a 9 mm pistol. He and Peter Jouvenal and I spent the evening talking at the Gandamack. Ken asked what I was doing and I told him I planned to be working along the border. "I wouldn't trust anybody," said Ken. "But you know that."

I had dinner with Roshan Khadivi, an American who worked for the United Nations and who had helped the 60 Minutes team. I felt that I could trust her. I said I was going to be working along the border and did she know anyone who could help me. From her I first heard the name of Michael Semple. He was with the UN, and she gave me his numbers and said that he was the only person to call. He knew the languages and the border region. I called him twice, but he didn't call back. I told Fazul my plans. "You might be the one to get to Haqqani," he said. "Stay in touch with me, you understand?"

Ramadan, when the Qur'an was revealed to Mohammad, began September 13 that year. I wanted to fast to draw closer to and understand better the world that I was about to enter. At 3:15 that morning a Gandamack employee knocked on my door and I sat outside on the porch in the dark and ate suhur, the pre-fast meal, in this case an English breakfast of fried eggs, tomatoes, baked beans, and toast. I went back to bed and slept until six. I didn't eat or drink until around 6:00 p.m., when the moon appeared, and then I had iftar with Peter and his wife, Hassina.

I took Sharif to meet Mirwais Yasini, now the deputy speaker of the lower house of parliament, who Fazul had introduced me to and whom I felt I could trust because of his tie to CBS and to Yunus Khalis. I told Yasini what I wanted to do and asked for contacts along the border. No Afghan fixer I met would take me into Pakistan. They all said no, and I saw fear in their eyes. I assumed it was because of the Taliban and al-Qaeda. "It is very dangerous in the Tribal Areas now," Yasini said. "I advise you not to go." He invited us to stay for iftar.

As evening drew near Yasini's backyard filled with politicians and government officials; even a retired US DEA agent was there. At sundown, a call came over the city announcing the sighting of the moon, and we sat with an array of food before us. We began with dates, as Mohammad had, to break the fast. After dinner, the men lined up in two rows and Sharif, who spoke Arabic, led the prayers. I felt awkward sitting with the DEA agent. We were outsiders.

I thanked Yasini for dinner and he invited me to return the following night. I came alone this time, but nothing happened. I returned a third time. Each night there were different men present. The fourth night, he introduced me to a man about six foot three, lean and strong with a gray-black beard. His name was Mullah Malang, a fellow MP. I forgot that Maksoudi, who had read my book, had told me when we were in Mahalajat that Malang, a famous mujahideen commander, was from there. Malang said that he had led seven hundred men, under Yunus Khalis, in Kandahar during the Soviet war. He suggested that we were part of the same family. We would talk more the next day, he said. But then he didn't appear.

Instead he came three nights later, and we sat alone after iftar and I showed him *In Afghanistan* and the pictures of Haqqani, Khalis, and men from Kandahar. He said the men were from Spin Boldak, which was seventy miles away, not Kandahar. I didn't believe him. I had been with them in Mahalajat and walked with them as they carried a dead comrade to their village. They went to the man's home with the body and the women inside began to wail. Malang was from Mahalajat. Why would he lie like this? I began to mistrust him. "Do not tell anyone what you are doing. It is very dangerous," he whispered.

Mullah Malang said that he had a friend, Abdullah, who could help me. He had killed a man and had to flee Afghanistan. He joined the Taliban but wanted to return under a reconciliation program. He needed Malang, a parliamentarian, to help him. It seemed simple enough: since Abdullah needed Malang he wouldn't hurt me. He also, under Pashtunwali, the Pashtun tribal code, was required to protect me, a guest, in his care.

"When you are with Abdullah, talk about the Taliban, their beliefs and their policies," Malang advised. "Tell them you want to explain and show the Taliban to the world. Do not talk about Osama. Go slowly, carefully, talk about how bad the Afghan government is, and only gradually talk about al-Qaeda." I said I knew Gulbuddin Hekmatyar and Jalaluddin Haqqani from before. "Do not talk about them. Abdullah can get to Sirajuddin. Maybe he will take you there."

It was strange that he was comfortable talking about Sirajuddin, Jalaluddin's famous, and powerful, son, but that I was not to mention his father. But I let it go, in part because I was anxious to get going and decided to rely upon Malang. I didn't think it was important to ask who Abdullah had killed or why. I would find out later. I thought that Malang was helping me as a part of Afghan hospitality, which I had experienced many times. I didn't consider that he might want something in return. I would be going where no Westerner had gone in years. If something happened to me, he, a Pashtun, would be shamed, and no Pashtun could tolerate this. I would be protected.

"Tell Abdullah and the other Taliban you meet that you are researching the mujahideen and the Taliban, that you were here before and that you want to learn more about the past, how it evolved and how the Taliban work." Then Malang asked if I could get a South African passport. It was a form of protection. There were South African contractors in Afghanistan but no official military presence. Better a South African than a North American or European passport. Jouvenal knew where I could get an illegal one for $500 in Peshawar.

For three nights for iftar at Yasini's house I sat next to a Hashimi, a former carpet seller in California, now an MP. Hashimi, like Sharif, had once been a member of Hekmatyar's party. I said I wanted to see Hekmatyar again. I knew he would remember that he had threatened to kill me in 1984 if I returned, but we had spent so much time together, in Peshawar and then in New York. "Does he respect you?" Hashimi asked. I nodded and hoped I wasn't deceiving myself. "Why do you want to cross the border? It is dangerous. You are an intellectual. It takes forty years to make an intellectual and here your life is the price of one bullet. Your life is the most precious thing you have.

Thousands die taking a hill which years later people in shorts visit as a tourist site. It's not worth it. If you go to the Tribal Areas, they will kill you like a chicken.

"Don't think for a minute that Afghans like you. They are Muslims. You Americans are infidels. You are not going to Heaven; you are going to Hell. They all smile and say you are their friend but they will turn their back on you and betray you in a minute. I see you with Mullah Malang. He was a famous commander, but I don't think he is a good man."

I didn't want to hear any of this. I assumed that Hashimi and Malang were competing with one another in Parliament. I watched Yasini walking with men on the lawn in front, his hand on their shoulders, talking. It was the Taliban and al-Qaeda now, a new world, but old animosities and rivalries—between Pashtun and Tajik, between religious and secular, between Afghanistan and Pakistan—remained, and now there was war among ambitious upstart guerrilla commanders and tribal chiefs.

⁙ ⁙ ⁙

MALANG, THE FORMER mujahideen commander and MP, called and came to the Gandamack. We sat in wicker chairs on the lawn. I didn't know then that he had also been a Taliban commander. It was the first time he had come to me, apparently with the purpose of putting me at ease with Abdullah. "You can trust Abdullah," said Malang. I was about to enter a very dark tunnel from which I would never completely emerge.

Malang gave me Abdullah's phone numbers and said he would call him for me. I tried for the next two days, but his phones were off. Finally, Abdullah called. "We will meet you in Torkham,"[19] he said, "but I will call you to arrange the time." He spoke in Pashto and it was difficult for me to communicate. He didn't call back. I gave the numbers to Sharif, who reached him three days later.

On September 25, we drove east from Kabul on a dusty plain and down the rocky canyon toward Jalalabad. Sharif's driver Aziz, twenty-eight, swung out into the oncoming lane, passing cars decorated with crepe paper, like a procession for newlyweds. They had actually come from the airport and were taking home a man who been on hajj, or pilgrimage, to Mecca. "People save their whole lives to go," said Sharif. "It cost about twenty thousand dollars." In each car, there seemed to be an old man with a white turban. He could now use *Hajji* as an honorific. "When you return from hajj we believe all your sins are cleansed."

We passed through brown rolling hills and desert, with the Kabul River and willow trees on our left. It was hot and my mouth was dry from fasting. We stopped at a checkpoint and entered Jalalabad. People walked slowly in the heat. We drove down a dirt path through a grove of pine trees to the Spinghar Hotel, checked in, and sat outside under a tree. Sharif called Abdullah, but again his phones were off. By late afternoon we left and drove through the city but had to stop. Cars, rickshaws, horse-drawn carts, and bicyclists waited as if at a starting line. US soldiers stood in the road watching us. They had just defused a car bomb.

That evening we sat on a roof on a kilim, leaning on cushions. Mosquitoes buzzed around, but there was a full moon and a sea of stars. Boys brought trays of fresh lemonade and plates of meat, chicken, rice, vegetables, warm bread, and then fresh yogurt and pomegranate seeds, watermelon, and tea.

I sat next to Hajji, Aziz's uncle, a slim, intense man in his forties with a wispy beard. He wouldn't tell me his name. "I just paid thirty thousand Afghanis [$500] in bribes to bring a new car across from Iran," he said. "I was stopped at many roadblocks. I was kidnapped by bandits. I went to the Taliban court and was freed. There was no crime under the Taliban. Now, I don't know who is in charge."

Hajji was a smuggler. He took his cars to the Pakistani border where men took the engines out, because they were heavy, and donkeys carried them across the mountains to the Tribal Areas. They put the car bodies on two planks between two camels and carried them across. Men reassembled the cars and others drove them as far as China to sell. Hajji asked what I was doing. I told him. He drew slowly on his cigarette.

The third day, Sharif finally got hold of Abdullah. As they talked I watched a car come down the dirt path, pine needles cracking beneath the tires. It was Hajji with another man. Abdullah called again. What did I look like and how far could I walk? I said I could keep up.

"Hajji was one of the biggest drug dealers around," said Sharif. "He had a large quantity of heroin, but someone stole it. He is selling cars now and has contacts in the Tribal Areas." Hajji had a plan. He would drive us to the Afghan border and there raise the chassis and drive into the mountains. Armed men would meet us at the Pakistani border and take us into the Tribal Areas to see a *malik*.[20] We would stay with him one night, and the next day they would bring us back to the border. My job was to go into the Tribal Areas, this no-man's-land for foreigners. This would be a short trip, but a start. Sharif continued: he trusted Aziz and Hajji, and Hajji trusted the other man. Sharif didn't think we'd be kidnapped. Both our lives were on the line. "Journalists sometimes play with fire," he said. "Sometimes the fire surrounds them."

I assumed that Hajji, a businessman, would charge to take me into the Tribal Areas. It made me uneasy that someone would have to pay.

"During jihad," Sharif said, "if we paid for help, and we did, we believed the money would come back to us in Heaven. We died and our children died, but we believed we would see them after Judgment Day. Now, it is all business." The mujahideen had to pay a tribal leader to pass through his territory, to pay a family or a village for food when they stopped to eat, or if they hitched a ride in a truck they would pay for gas. I was told that bin Laden paid tribal leaders so that the Taliban could pass through their territory on the way to Kabul. They were fighting a holy war, and the money would come back to them.

It would cost $1,500 for us to go with Hajji. He needed to pay the gunmen that he was going to hire to guard us in the Tribal Areas. I wasn't sure about Abdullah. I finally said okay to Hajji and felt strong. He needed a few days to prepare.

We went inside the hotel to the lobby, where there was a fan and it was cooler. Sharif saw a man he knew, the malik of Tora Bora, the mountains where bin Laden had gone to after 9/11 and from which he escaped, it was assumed, down into Pakistan. We sat with him. "There were three Afghan forces at Tora Bora," said the malik. "Those led by Hazrat Ali, who was then the commander of Jalalabad; secondly, those led by Hajji Zahir Qadir, son of Hajji Abdul Qadir. Third were those led by Hajji Zaman, commander of Khugiani." It was a district and the name of a tribe, near Tora Bora.

Every name that the malik of Tora Bora just mentioned would play a role, I would learn, even in death, in my kidnapping. I didn't know it then, but he was introducing me, like a playwright, to some of the cast of characters in a byzantine, murky drama.

Abdul Qadir, called Hajji Qadir in honor of his pilgrimage to Mecca, was a famous mujahideen leader, and political leader born in 1951. After the 1979 Soviet invasion of Afghanistan, he joined the mujahideen. He, like his brother Din Mohammad and their younger brother Abdul Haq, who also became famous as a mujahideen leader during the Afghan-Soviet war, were not what became known as extremists but aristocrats, proud members of the famous Arsala family of the Jabbar Khel clan of the large and powerful Ahmadzai tribe in eastern Afghanistan. Their great grandfather, Arsala Khan, was foreign minister before the Second Anglo-Afghan war (1878–1880); another ancestor was a general in the Afghan army that defeated the British at the famous Battle of Maiwand in 1880 in southern Afghanistan, in Helmand Province, where Abdul Haq's father was later the deputy governor.

The three brothers joined Hezb-i-Islami Khalis (the Khalis Islamic Party), one of the most Islamist of the seven mujahideen political parties supported by Pakistan and its allies, the United States, and Saudi Arabia. The leader was Yunus Khalis, who was the three brothers' religious instructor. The Arsala family became the backbone of the Khalis Islamic Party. Din Mohammad was the man I sat with when I met Yunus Khalis and who, three years later—that night in New York at the gathering I hosted as director of Friends of Afghanistan—asked me warmly when I was returning, saying in effect that I was accepted, a member of their brotherhood of mujahideen; because of this, he was the man I felt closest to during that romantic time in the 1980s. He ran the Khalis party and was its representative in the mujahideen government in exile, which was created by Pakistan and the US; he was, I read later, also its liaison to the ISI.

Hajji Zaman, a member of the strong Khugiani tribe, like Yunus Khalis, did not, for some reason, join with Khalis. He joined his competitor, Gulbuddin Hekmatyar, but then left his political party and joined the moderate, royalist National Islamic Front, one of the seven mujahideen parties. I had met some of its fighters and, to me, they were the same—mujahideen up in the mountains, fighting the communist invader. The other mujahideen commander, Hazrat Ali, was a Pashai. It was a different, much smaller, ethnic group, not Pashtun, but strong because they were tightly knit and loyal; spies could not penetrate them. All three men, all from Nangarhar Province, competed with one another, like all men, for money and power. All became famous mujahideen leaders. Years later, I unknowingly walked into this battle and got caught in the middle.

The Soviet Union retreated from Afghanistan in 1989 and the mujahideen government took power in Kabul in 1992. Din Mohammad became deputy prime minister, and Hajji Qadir became governor of Nangarhar Province. In 1994, the Taliban rose in Kandahar, but Hajji Qadir, a moderate and Afghan patriot, like his brothers, saw that they were being taken over by Pakistan and opposed them. On May 18, 1996, Osama bin Laden returned from Sudan to Jalalabad, whose airport was under the control of Jalaluddin Haqqani and went to live near Yunus Khalis. In September 1996, the Taliban took Kabul, after which they turned their sights on Jalalabad. Qadir negotiated its surrender and went to Peshawar, Pakistan, for centuries an Afghan city until the British arrived during their first expedition in 1808[21] and began to push the western border of British India, today Pakistan, west to what would become in 1893 the Durand Line. Qadir opposed the Taliban publicly and the Pakistani government forced him to leave. He went to Germany and traveled between there and Dubai, where his brother, Abdul Haq, also opposed to the Taliban, now lived.

By 1998, Hajji Qadir had returned from Germany to Afghanistan and went north above Kabul to the Panjshir Valley and joined Ahmed Shah Massoud, a Tajik military commander of the United Front, also called the Northern Alliance. He was the most famous guerrilla leader in Afghanistan, leading the last force holding out against the Taliban. Qadir, and Hazrat Ali, became main commanders under Massoud.

On September 9, 2001, two men on Belgian passports, members of al-Qaeda disguised as journalists conducting an interview, assassinated Massoud. Two days later was 9/11.

On October 7, the US invaded Afghanistan. On November 14, Northern Alliance soldiers entered Kabul. On November 19, Hajji Qadir reclaimed the governor's seat in Jalalabad.

On October 21, Abdul Haq went into Afghanistan with a small band, including his nephew, Izatullah, Din Mohammad's son, and another brother, Mohammad Qasim Arsala. Haq opposed the US bombing campaign because he felt that it would kill too many civilians. He thought the Taliban were already fragmented and weak, and that because of his fame—he knew British prime minister Margaret Thatcher, had been honored by President Reagan at a White House dinner, and wanted to be president of Afghanistan—he could rally tribes against the Taliban.

A Taliban force of 350 men came up from Jalalabad, led by the Taliban interior minister Abdul Razak. On October 26, the Taliban surrounded Abdul Haq.

"The ISI helped the Taliban," said the malik of Tora Bora. "A Taliban force came after Abdul Haq and he saw that he had been betrayed."

There are many stories about what happened next, but it appears that one of Haq's men, using a satellite phone, got a message to the CIA, which declined to help or was too slow to help him in time. Secretary of Defense Donald Rumsfeld said that the US sent a missile, but too late.[22] There are many reports that CIA agents famously called Abdul Haq "Hollywood Haq" and "Yesterday's man," following the ISI agenda to denigrate Haq.

On October 21 Haq, who lost a foot to a mine during the Afghan war, was trapped, but refused to plead for his life. "Do not beg," he told one of his men. "Live your life with honor." Razak shot him. The Taliban shot Din Mohammad's son Izatullah and threw him into a well. They let most of the other men go.

Vincent Cannistraro, a former CIA director of counterterrorism, later acknowledged that there was "credible information" that the ISI had betrayed Haq.[23]

A US Special Forces team led by Captain Jason Amerine, stationed in Uzbekistan north of Afghanistan, was preparing to fly in to assist Haq, but by then it was too late. Robert McFarlane, former national security adviser to President Reagan, complained in an op-ed article in the *Wall Street Journal* of "dysfunction within the CIA," which relied upon, even "mimicked its sister agency," the ISI.[24]

"From our estimates, with Abdul Haq dead we had nobody else of any caliber that we could really link up with that could help us with the Pashtun tribes," Amerine explained.[25] That left Hamid Karzai, a royalist and politician. Amerine and his men flew in and linked up with Karzai in southern Afghanistan. I remember Haq, who spoke excellent English, calling me when I was in Quetta in late November 1981, about to cross into Afghanistan, to say that "we," meaning the Khalis faction, can't help you there," meaning in Quetta. Haq wished me well, this man who would be called the Lion of Kabul for his exploits inside Kabul. In December, twenty-five prominent Afghans, among them Hajji Qadir, met under UN auspices in Bonn, Germany, to create a post-Taliban interim government. They chose Hamid Karzai as the interim president. Hajji Qadir became first vice president. Qadir's brother, Din Mohammad, became governor of Kabul.[26] Qadir himself vowed revenge against his other brother's killers—Interior Minister Razak and the ISI.

This brought out into the open a feud between the Arsala family and the ISI, and through my friendship with Hajji Din Mohammad—and earlier, Abdul Haq—I had unknowingly walked into the middle of it. The feud would affect the hunt for bin Laden in Tora Bora because the CIA tasked the Arsala clan, its ally Hazrat Ali (both allies of the US), and their competitor, Hajji Zaman, with finding him in the mountains, and the festering rivalry would claim several other lives. Of those the most consequential to me would be a minor character, Khorsheed, who, I believe, wanted a sinecure as a customs officer, a lucrative position. Unknown to me at the time, he was a relative of Abdullah, the man who was now responsible for my safety in the Tribal Areas.

WHILE WE WERE waiting to hear from Abdullah, Sharif, Aziz, and I drove north, climbing gradually on a new paved road into Kunar Province; the undammed Kunar River rushed by on our right. It got cooler and the leaves were turning yellow in the trees, and families, the women and girls in colored dresses, worked in the fields. We went to a compound of a former governor, who was its leading commander during the Soviet time. We sat in a grape arbor, away from other guests. "We don't know if there is a spy among them," said Sharif.

"The Taliban are all around and you come here like you are walking in Jalalabad," said the former governor. Mullahs were calling over loudspeakers in the villages down in a valley for people to pray. He put his hand on my shoulder. "Why don't you pray? It's not hard." I declined. "The Taliban attacked us two days ago. What is the difference between the mujahideen and the Taliban? The mujahideen rose up from the people. The Taliban are puppets directed by Pakistan."

Against the former governor's advice we drove farther north to Asadabad, the capital of Kunar Province, which would become my base from which I would attempt to cross the border. We met with the governor, Sharif's uncle, a hefty man with thick arms and a wide black beard, who refused to help me cross the border. He didn't want to be responsible if I got captured or killed.

"Al-Qaeda and the Taliban send their people to kill me," said Sharif's uncle. Everything was a production of the ISI. "There were many divisions and some don't even know that they are working for the ISI." He finally arranged for a tribal leader to take me up to the Durand Line. He reminded me that Afghans couldn't make suicide jackets. They weren't smart enough.

The tribal leader, a tall thin man with a wispy beard, took Sharif and me with gunmen up a mountain. He pointed to women, their backs straight, loads of grass and corn stalks piled on their heads. "All our women work so hard," he explained. "We are poor because we have been fighting for thirty years and Pakistan wants to keep the fighting going." Three men came down the road, smiling, exuding happiness, one man carrying a small pan tied to the shawl wrapped around his shoulders. "They are Tablighi Jamaat.[27] They travel from one village to the next inviting people to Islam." They were missionaries who slept in mosques, living off the kindness of villagers. I thought of my Assembly and the missionaries I knew, and who my father helped to support.

We reached the top of a ridge. The wind blew. Two Afghan border guards watched me closely. I saw a paved road winding down the ridge and green, terraced fields in Bajaur Agency, in the Tribal Areas of Pakistan. A hawk circled above us. Crows called in the trees. I didn't know that this place, Nawah Pass, would soon play a role in my kidnapping.

We sat with the Afghan border guards. "These men are all my relatives," said the tribal leader. One man pointed to an outpost fifty yards up the ridge. It was a US base. No one knew what they did there, but they didn't go into Pakistan. I didn't know if they were CIA or Special Forces, but I didn't want to go up there. I wanted to keep my anonymity, and Sharif was on edge. Twenty feet away, two Pakistanis in pressed shalwar kameez—clean shaven with short hair, meaning they were in the army—held walkie-talkies and crouched in the sun. There were other men, with rifles, like them. "ISI," said Sharif. They were listening. An old man with a load on his back walked up a path and into the trees. I wanted to follow him. "The Pakistani militiamen are my relatives," said the tribal leader, "but not the ISI."

"We are few here," said a guard. "They," he nodded at the Pakistanis, "are one hundred. They are worried the US will cross over. They have electric lines along the border, check-posts and military bases." We were sitting on the Durand Line, a ridge twenty yards across. No one knew where the border was.

"What is the Durand Line?" asked the tribal leader. "There is no difference between here and the other side. The real border is between the Punjab, which ends at the eastern bank of the Indus River, and Afghanistan, which we Pashtuns feel begins in the middle of the river."[28] Sharif began to film the soldiers. "Stop, or I'll fire on you," said a soldier.

"If he shoots someone, the revenge killings will go on for years," said the tribal leader. We had to leave before someone found out I was there and attacked us or prepared a bomb down below. The chief put me in a different car, and we raced down the mountain, the dust high behind us. We stopped near the bottom by a hole where a bomb had gone off a week before.

∗ː ∗ː ∗ː

THE NEXT DAY, back in Jalalabad, we sat on plastic chairs in the shade, once again waiting for Abdullah's man. Two guards with rifles crouched by the door under a tree. Sharif kept calling Abdullah, but his phones were still off. A car drove up slowly through the trees and stopped. A bearded, wiry man in his fifties, about five foot ten, walked toward us. I looked at him nonchalantly as he did me. Abdullah was a Talib[29] and so would his man be. He and Sharif talked. I was tired from fasting and wanted to sleep. They kept talking. Sharif turned to me. "He is ready to go today."

My strength returned. So quickly? Could we cross the border?

"Abdullah is ready," the man responded. We would walk three to four hours in the mountains. We'd take food and water. The elderly, the very young, the sick, pregnant women, and travelers could break the fast. We would go for a few days this time, the next time on a longer trip. I looked at him. "Let's go," I said. I was excited about hiking into the mountains, pushing it testing myself against these men. Sharif looked at me, his eyes cold. "No," he said. "You can do it. You can do anything, but I am too fat. I don't want to walk during Ramadan. I won't go." Something was wrong.

"We are ready to go at any time," said Abdullah's man. "We are doing this in friendship. You are Mullah Malang's friend. We will take you across the mountains and protect you." We shook hands and he walked back through the trees. Sharif and I would go instead with Hajji the smuggler. He promised to protect us, but I couldn't go alone. I didn't know him. I didn't trust him and I trusted Sharif because Peter Jouvenal had introduced us.

On October 2, 2007, at 3:15 a.m., I lay awake with a knot in my stomach, the same feeling I had before I went up to where Pat Tillman was killed. I went to the dining room for breakfast. "I talked to my wife last night and she was scared, which makes me nervous," said Sharif. "Ever since Ajmal [Naqshbandi] was beheaded she has been afraid of trips like these. Well, we have to do it." Sharif went to pray. I tried to go back to sleep, but I kept feeling my throat. I went out onto the balcony and listened to the birds, the call to prayer, and people chanting in a mosque. I smelled the fragrance from the flowers, but it only made me lonely.

I was so anxious to go into the Tribal Areas, to be the first to go where no one else would go, that I forgot that two days before, Sharif had refused to go because he said that he was fat and couldn't walk in the mountains. And now he was going. He had looked at me not just with coldness in his eyes, I realized much later, but with fear. I deduced from this that Abdullah's man told him that they were going to kidnap me and demand money for my release and that he would get some of the money; but he knew that they were the Taliban and thought of his friend Ajmal, and said no. But he was willing previously, I realized later, to let me go alone—without a fixer, with men who maybe wanted to kidnap me—into the Tribal Areas.

Just before dawn, Aziz, Sharif, and I drove on the main, paved road east toward the border. A half hour later, Aziz dropped us off by a gas station and Sharif and I sat by the road next to yellow and purple flowers, a grape arbor, and two men lying on rope beds. The sun rose and children walked by carrying school books. Cars and container trucks went by, and donkey carts, and a man leading a string of camels tied to rope around his waist. A little boy walked by singing.

A car pulled up. The smuggler Hajji was driving and Qorie, the man who had come to our hotel with him, sat next to him. We turned off the main road onto a dirt track and drove past dun-colored villages, through a eucalyptus forest, and then high grass, to the Kabul River. We drove the car up onto a metal sheet on top of two small boats, and the ferry slowly crossed the water. We drove down onto the sand and followed a track. The dust was like powder. We came to a stone house with an Afghan flag, and two policemen waved us on. "Pakistan gives everyone in all the villages Pakistani ID cards," said Hajji, "trying to move the Pakistani border into Afghanistan." Red rocky hills rose around us. We came to a grass lean-to with an Afghan flag hanging limply and an old man with bad teeth and a torn shirt standing in the sun. "Be careful of the fighting," he said, pointing east.

"That is the Afghan border," said Hajji. We raced on about two miles, and saw a stone house on a hill marking the Pakistani border. Where were the bodyguards that he had promised? I thought we were going to stop and raise the chassis. I kept quiet. For some reason, instinctively, I trusted them. I was in their hands now. We crossed empty, desolate land with no visible water. We were somewhere in Mohmand Agency, home of the Mohmand tribe, in the Tribal Areas. I watched for the Taliban. We stopped for directions at a village of stone houses with small holes in them, and silence. "People are staring out, wondering, who are we?" said Sharif.

"The only business here is smuggling, guns, and fighting," said Hajji.

We drove on. A car appeared behind us on the undulating dusty road. We passed a cemetery with thin stone markers facing southwest toward Mecca and high flags like I had seen in Tibet and in Indian cemeteries in the American West, hanging in the heat. The car stayed fifty yards behind us. Hajji and Sharif were worried. We came to a trickling stream and stopped. Sharif told me to get out and follow it up into a gully. I got out and walked. I liked the silence. The car stopped behind us and a man, in Western clothes, came walking toward me up the gully. I turned, walked back, and said hello in Pashto, shook his hand and kept going. Another man followed him and I shook hands with him, still in the gully. I was foolish, trying too hard to fit in. We returned to the car. "You are not to say anything to anyone," said Sharif angrily. If someone saw that I was a foreigner we would be at risk.

We passed two men carrying long rifles, with a woman between them. "They are protecting her. Every man here carries a rifle," said Sharif. "He needs to, for protection," said Hajji. Hours passed. There were no electric lines, no stores, no paved roads, no villages, only dust and rolling hills. We entered a canyon and drove for a mile and stopped. High above us was a fortress, like a castle in Germany, of mud and stone. We climbed up a pathway. From on top I could see mountains and heat waves over the desert. It was silent. We were in the Tribal Areas, home of al-Qaeda and the Taliban. We entered a dirt courtyard with a roof extending out from the adobe walls providing shade. Rope cots lined the walls.

A solidly built man, about six foot one with a black and white beard and wearing a turquoise ring, strode out smiling. He asked if I wanted tea. I was fasting. His eyes widened, wondering if his guest was Muslim. It was clear to me that he knew I was coming. His sons were sitting on mountaintops around us fighting over property lines, irrigation, and grazing rights. He knew exactly where his land began and where it ended. They were fighting now only over a few meters. He was malik of four hundred families, which meant up to four thousand people. The Azad, the Mohmand, the Ogarkill were here. Each was a tribe, like Comanche or Apache, hence the name, the Tribal Areas. It was like the Old West.

He had a big *hujra*,[30] where we were sitting, so that anyone, even a stranger, could eat, spend the night, and go on his way. His family had been maliks for over three hundred years. He was Afghan, but his identification was Pakistani. His government—the Karzai government—was weak, but the Taliban were brave. They wanted the old border back at the Indus River. I asked about the fight between the Pakistani army and the Taliban. He laughed. "They say they are against each other, but they are helping one another." Pakistan and the US said that Pakistan had ninety thousand men on the border, and the US media parroted this, but I hadn't seen anyone. He laughed again. "Everyone agrees there is no sign of these soldiers."

I asked about suicide bombers. "I have all the arms and ammunition I need, but I do not know how to make a suicide vest. It is all at a very high level." Could he hide bin Laden? No. The rule of Pashtunwali was that if one family had a problem with another family they could seek refuge in someone's home for one thousand years, but if someone escaped from the government, *panah*, or the right of refuge, did not apply. Osama was too big to be guarded even by forty or fifty men. He was being kept by a government. He meant Pakistan.

Which did he prefer, Afghanistan or Pakistan?

"The people will die from hunger before joining Pakistan," he replied. "You can never ask for a favor once you have fought someone. Never." He was his father now, his grandfather, and his ancestors back through time. "I am Pashtun. When my ancestors lived here, it was Afghanistan. You Americans are playing a double role. You are not honest with the world. You are working with Pakistan."

I sensed this, but couldn't prove it. He showed me a flintlock rifle. "I expelled your uncle with that," said an old man, meaning that I, a Westerner, was British, a foreigner, an infidel. He was proud, like all men in the Tribal Areas, of his tough, warrior heritage. A boy about twelve sat on a carpet. "A man who dies in holy war does not die, but is martyred for Allah," said the old man. It was time for prayers and the malik and his son stood together to begin their prayers. They finished and the malik asked if I wanted to buy the rifle. He handed it to me, but I could never have taken it. He would give it to his son. I wanted my own father's rifle when he died. It was a symbol of manhood, and protection, like a bow and arrow, or a spear. Little girls peaked around a wall watching us, his family. He would protect them. He relied upon his faith for strength.

I felt that we were just beginning to talk, but Hajji said that it was time to leave. It was close to sundown and too dangerous for me to stay for the night. Hajji had promised that we would spend the night, just as he had promised bodyguards. I was upset but had no power over him. Sharif didn't help me. We returned to the car and Hajji drove fast through the canyon. "I know most of the Taliban," said Qorie. "If they stop us I can sort things out." Hajji took a different route back toward the border.

"Qorie is a commander in the Taliban," said Sharif, in English.

"Now he tells me," I thought. Hajji was obliged, under Pashtunwali, to protect me. He would want his money for taking me into the Tribal Areas. I didn't trust him now, but had nowhere to turn. I was dependent upon the three of them for my survival, and Sharif had lied to me. I realized that Hajji, a smuggler, worked with the Taliban. Qorie was part of the Taliban. The malik was probably a smuggler, working with them, part of Hajji's network. The malik said that the Pakistani army worked with the Taliban. They were all together. The US gave billions of dollars to Pakistan to fight the Taliban.

We drove through the desert and came upon three cement buildings. A little girl sat alone on the steps of one building holding a book. A man, about fifty, stood at the door of another building, with children inside, his eyes afraid. It was a school. Hajji asked him directions and he pointed the way. We raced on. Dusk came and we stopped in front of a stone house on a hill with an Afghan flag hanging from a pole, a border post. A lean, muscular man, who looked sixty and held a rifle with one hand against his forearm, stood by the car, questioned us, and waved us on. "The Taliban killed three police there two weeks ago," said Hajji. We drove into the night. There was no track, only a hot, dusty, empty desert. I looked for men with black turbans.

We reached a river, and the men got out and prayed in the sand. I breathed deeply. We were safe now, it appeared, by the Kabul River. We waited for the ferry to take us back across to Afghanistan. I walked along the water. I had a small feeling of accomplishment, but not enough. I had to go deeper into the Tribal Areas to find Haqqani. I wanted more danger, to go with men with black turbans, the Taliban. I needed to find someone else to take me deeper, next time.

Chapter 6

Smugglers and Fixers in the Borderlands

BACK IN KABUL I SOUGHT OUT EHSANULLAH, A WIRY, GRIZZLED OLD journalist friend, who knew everyone and everything. We had green tea and cookies in his office. "You've changed your appearance completely," he smiled. "With your beard and clothes, you look like a real Afghan. But get rid of your American shoes." I asked about Mullah Malang. "He was a famous commander during jihad in Kandahar, but then he became a sort of businessman and a commander and people lost respect for him." I asked what kind of business. "I don't remember but he was among the first to have a new land cruiser, and he stayed in that and the common mujahideen didn't like those who sat in those vehicles." The mujahideen were poor young men, with old rifles and frayed sandals, and they wanted their commanders to be with them on the ground. I asked about Abdullah, who Malang said would take me deep into the Tribal Areas.

"I know Abdullah and that Hazrat Ali killed his cousin, or maybe it was his uncle. I don't think he has the contacts that Malang says. Be careful, and be careful of Yasini. He may be too close to Pakistan. Karzai says so publicly. His family lives openly in Islamabad. Don't listen to Malang. The ISI is everywhere in the Tribal Areas." Yasini was the prominent MP who invited me to iftar at his house in the center of Kabul and who introduced me to Mullah Malang.

I chose to go back to Rosanne Klass's friend Professor Amin, the former minister of education whom I felt I could trust, even though I hadn't seen him since December 2002. Still, the United States and other nations funded what he now called the Afghanistan Study Centre. I found his office, a new two-story house in a new baked-mud compound in Kabul. He was living well with his American money. I rang the bell and a man in jeans with black hair, a big smile, and bright eyes answered. "Where are you from?" he asked. I told him and he smiled. I asked where he was from. "Landi Khotal," he said. "Do you know it?" I did. I asked his name. "Khyber," he responded proudly. Landi Khotal was the railhead on the border in Pakistan just before the Khyber Pass.

Amin, in bare feet, sat on a sofa. I gave him a copy of *In Afghanistan*, which I had promised him. A woman in her twenties, in jeans and a blouse, came in, her face uncovered, smiling and holding a cell phone in each hand. I will call her Sameer. She spoke perfect English and sat down confidently in a chair. I told Amin about my plans to write about the Tribal Areas. "You have crossed the border enough," he said. "The ISI is everywhere. If they find you it won't be good for your health."

I told him about my time with Asif Durrani at the Pakistani embassy, and that I had applied for a visa with the press attaché. He agreed to talk to Durrani. He would think of people to help me along the border, but I must never again cross it, he warned. Sameer rode with me back to the Gandamack, talking as if we were in a taxi in New York. Where did she get this confidence? Who was she? She said that she had grown up in a refugee camp in Pakistan and was the sole provider for her family. I had never met an Afghan woman like her.

"The professor has contacts at the embassy," she said. "He can help you. I know people, too. Maybe I can help you." I didn't pay too much attention to her.

I returned three days later to see Professor Amin. "I think you have been blacklisted by Durrani," he said. Sameer sat close to him on the sofa touching his arms, tickling him, and his face was red as he laughed embarrassedly. I had never seen an Afghan man and woman like this, so intimate in front of a relative stranger. The call sounded to end the day's fast, and the three of us shared iftar.

Sameer offered to introduce me to some people. She later called and said there was a person that she wanted me to me. "He will be good for you," she said. He came to the Gandamack. His name was Shahwali Hazrat, a smiling, pudgy man of medium height, about thirty, with a week's growth of beard and wearing a brown suit. Professor Amin was his uncle. He had worked in the Afghanistan Study Centre's library but was now a schoolteacher. He had seen my book that I had brought to Amin and wanted to translate it into Pashto. He had five children. He wanted to go to Peshawar University but needed $5,000, and the Americans were giving money away. He said that he wanted some of this money to go to school.

His wife and children lived in Peshawar. His parents lived in Kunar Province in Afghanistan. He supported them. Could he cross the mountains into Pakistan? He said no problem. But he had never been a fixer, so how could he cross the border when no one else would? Maybe he knew people. If he was courageous I could teach him to be a fixer. I asked about his family. They lived in darkness. His father was a gatekeeper, but was jobless now. He was illiterate and religious. "He doesn't like that I'm a teacher," said Shahwali. "He thinks I should be a farmer and study the Qur'an. I want an education. I love Shakespeare." He quoted from *The Merchant of Venice*: "'The quality of mercy is not strained / It droppeth as the gentle rain from Heaven' . . . Tell me," he asked, "is Shakespeare's tomb in America? Is the tomb of Jesus in America?"

In retrospect, I wondered if by quoting Shakespeare he wasn't asking for forgiveness for what he was going to do. I asked Fazul, the CBS bureau chief, to find out all he could about him. Fazul knew the owner of the school where Shahwali taught. He seemed to be fine. I had a second meeting with Shahwali. I asked again if he understood how dangerous this was. "Can we have an agreement, sir, that my neck is your neck?" he asked. "If anything happens to me that you will take care of my children." It was strange. He was asking me to support his children if something happened to him. I wondered for a second if I was being set up, but I later realized he was worried about his own life, not mine. I felt he knew that something was going to happen, but I ignored my instincts. I hesitated, and felt uneasy but said yes to make him happy. "Thank you, sir," he said. "We can do all the things you want." I didn't understand until over a year later why he asked me that question. I also realized much later that it was Sameer who introduced us.

Ramadan ended and I was quietly proud that I had fasted very day for a month. I savored the joy of eating during the day again and felt stronger, yet humbled. I knew now what it was like to be hungry.

I went to see Daoud Sultanzoy, the tribal chief and MP I had met through Fazul, and told him that I wanted to cross the border. He called another malik, a fellow MP whom I will call Enayat. The three of us ate kebab with bread and drank green tea while bodyguards paced back and forth in the courtyard. "I will take you to Waziristan," said Enayat. "I will protect you even with the smallest hair on my head." I was excited. Waziristan was the center of al-Qaeda and the Taliban. I hadn't been there since the mujahideen took me down from Peshawar to Miran Shah, the capital.

The next day, Daoud, Enayat, and I drove south onto the open plain under a sky as wide as the American West. Enayat's bodyguards passed us in their car, then fell behind, following this pattern for hours. We approached Khost, near Enayat's tribal land, and I saw the tall twin minarets of Haqqani's mosque dominating the land. Enayat pointed to a small adobe house next to an auto repair shop. "Your friend, Jalaluddin Haqqani, started there."

Enayat's uncle, the district governor, joined us. He wore a black, green, and silver turban, part of which stuck up, like an Indian headdress, to show his bravery and prominence. "You are always identified by your tribe, not by your individuality," said Enayat. He looked at the pictures in my book. "It makes me cry at how our people have suffered. Hekmatyar, Haqqani, and Yunus Khalis were all just fighting for the CIA, British intelligence, and Saudi Arabia. After the Russians invaded, we organized fighters and went to Hamid Gul, head of the ISI, to ask for weapons. 'You're dead because you still remember the Durand Line. We want people who will burn Afghanistan,' he said." Gul wanted Afghans who would destroy their country so that Pakistan could have it, this "strategic depth," a place to which Pakistan could retreat if pushed back by India and not be surrounded. A place through which to connect Pakistan and Sunni Central Asia to recreate the Muslim Mughal Empire. It used the mujahideen, the Haqqanis, and the Taliban in pursuit of this goal.

The next day, another of Enayat's uncles came from Waziristan. We had lunch and went into the desert, with bodyguards, where we could talk. "The tribes have turned against everyone in the Tribal Areas, and each other. The Pakistani army and the Taliban are *ghazi*—men on a holy mission—and if they kill us, the chiefs, which they are doing now, they go to Paradise. They could kidnap you and cut off your head," said Enayat's uncle. No, not me, I thought. I was here before and would be fine, but I reluctantly accepted this. His uncle was truly worried, and thanked me, grateful that he would not have to take me and host me, risking his life for me. Enayat said he would take me, instead, to Kurram Agency, the Tribal Area just north of Waziristan. We drove on rough dusty roads to the border. Enayat's cousin, a gray-bearded man in a white turban who was the district governor, pointed to a hill five hundred yards north with a fort on top. "Pakistan," he whispered. He pointed south to another hill. "Pakistan." The Pakistanis had moved the border west about one hundred yards, but the tribes rebelled and Pakistan moved it back.

We walked east through savannah grass. Two men in their twenties came toward us. I looked for their rifles, but they were unarmed. The governor walked to them. I looked at my cell phone. The service welcomed me to Pakistan. Two Pakistani Frontier Scouts, in khakis and red berets, were two hundred yards south at a border post in a ravine.

"They are watching us," said the governor. "Sadaar, the nearest town, a thousand meters away, is controlled by the Taliban and al-Qaeda. They destroyed televisions there." I walked through the grass. I wanted to go to Sadaar, like a moth to a flame, as if subconsciously seeking martyrdom. "The Frontier Scouts can surround us," Enayat whispered. I reluctantly turned back.

⁘ ⁘ ⁘

Disappointed, I returned to Kabul and went back up north with Shahwali to Kunar Province, his home. I seemed to be living along the border now, spending days traveling north and south and following the Kunar River up and back into Kunar and Nangarhar provinces. We had no plans, but we would improvise, and we did. "Whatever you want, we will do," Shahwali said, his mantra. We were on an isolated, bumpy dirt road. "It would be easy for me to put a bomb in the back of the car," said our driver, brought to us by a friend of Shahwali's, "to stop at a village, go for tea, and boom, the bomb would go off and you would be killed and I could collect the money." This came from out of nowhere. I felt trapped, and vulnerable. We continued north through Taliban country.

We reached a small town called Ducalam in the far north. I walked to a pole that crossed the road. A policeman sat half asleep in a chair. An Afghan flag hung from a shed next to him. The other side of the pole was Pakistan. I wanted to cross, but I was afraid of the police. We went to a café for tea. A small wiry man in his forties, with a creased face, joined us. He was the malik of Ducalam. "I thought you were Nuristani when I saw you in the street," he said. Nuristan, the province of light-skinned people said to descend from Alexander's army, was over a mountain range. China was two hundred miles northeast. We could stay with him.

His brother, a lean, dour man about six foot four, led us into the hills on soft narrow paths through plots of land to a wide stream, beyond which was Pakistan. "You are the first foreigner to come here," he said quietly. "The Pakistani army is in the mountains." It was peaceful and we sat and waited for darkness. "I could get married and settle here," I said. "We wouldn't allow it," he responded. He was honor bound to protect me, but he didn't have to like me.

That night, over dinner in his home, I told the malik that I wanted to cross into Pakistan. "You will be captured or kidnapped," he responded. He knew an ISI officer who had problems and needed money and would talk to me, if I gave him some money. The malik would bring him from Pakistan. It would take time to arrange this. I wouldn't pay the ISI man—that was a bribe—but I told him to go ahead. I had just hired him, one of many men I was hiring along the border. The malik, over the next three weeks, would try to reel me in like a fish.

I was living in a world almost totally cut off from the West, an outsider, at the mercy of my hosts but in Pashtun culture, where a guest was king. I had no protection beyond my belief that these men would protect a guest to preserve their honor, without which they could not live. But at the same time, I was a rich Westerner, a temptation. I checked in with Fazul, my link to the West and my friend. Otherwise I had no one I could talk to. There were men around me, but I was alone, an infidel trying to pass as a Muslim.

We used Asadabad, the provincial capital, as a base. One morning I sat outside our small hotel, having tea and warm bread for breakfast, and an old man stopped at my table. "Prepare for eternity. You must accept Islam," he said, and walked on. He was like men I knew as a boy preaching to me. I knew this world and was comfortable in it.

I asked Shahwali to find a Wahhabi. Bin Laden was a Wahhabi, like most Saudi Arabians, a follower of Muhammad ibn Abd al-Wahhab, an eighteenth-century itinerant revivalist preacher in Arabia who felt that Muslims had lost their way and had to return to the Qur'an to become true Muslims. Wahhabis, whom the British called Hindustani fanatics, had led the war against the British along the Afghan frontier in the nineteenth century. They were stronger in Kunar than in other Afghan provinces.

Shahwali found a friend who was a Wahhabi, a government madrassa teacher. He was a stocky man with a wide black beard, in his thirties. The Wahhabi leafed through my book. He could take me to the Taliban.

I took his picture. Was I going to take it to the Americans? It was insurance. I took pictures of everyone. I was the one who could be kidnapped or killed, I replied. He smiled, nodding. My jailer, Gulob, would later tell me that he and his men were Wahhabis.

The Wahhabi and Ahmed, our driver, took us up past dark villages into the hills. I could feel the pit in my stomach, that warning which told me I was in danger. We walked on a dark path. Two women, like shadows, carrying water, came toward us. I smelled perfume as they passed, and I thought of the West. We entered a village, saw a light in one house, and went to it and waited.

Two hours later, machine gun and rifle fire erupted outside our window, echoing around us, and then I heard artillery. The Americans were somewhere firing back, but I couldn't hear any shells. A man with a rifle entered, circled the room like a cat, out again, returned, shook my hand, and sat across from me. He wore his turban so that it showed only his eyes. His handshake was firm, but his hand was soft. He pointed his rifle low toward me.

His name was Abu Hamza. *Abu* means "father of" in Arabic. It was not a Pashtun name, but a nom de guerre. He wore a padded jacket and an infrared light that looked like a miner's light over his turban. Someone was supporting him for him to have an expensive jacket and a light like this. Who was he fighting? "The foreigners, the infidels." Why was he fighting? "For jihad, like the mujahideen before us." His voice was young, there were no lines in his hands. "Elders support us," he said. He and his men went to Pakistan for training. Sometimes soldiers trained them here. "We know the soldiers are in the army, but they have gray beards like you." I smiled slightly. I was old so he would not kill me.

People supported them because they were fighting for Islam. They got paid based upon the number of operations they ran. He was like an animal ready to spring. "This is a Muslim country and we will fight to the death to expel all foreigners." Was it easy to recruit? There were many men fighting with them, he said, but then he sighed. "It is hard because people are afraid of spies. There are secret ties between the ISI and Pakistan's religious parties." I looked over. Other men stood at the door. "*Taal*," said a small, thin man, about twenty-one and wearing a red and white kaffiyeh. *Taal* means "come" in Arabic. No Afghan wore a kaffiyeh, this Arab headdress, only a turban, a prayer cap, or a felt hat, like his father and grandfather. He was al-Qaeda. The Taliban and al-Qaeda were working together. We left at dawn and watched a US convoy come up the road. It passed us and I was afraid of both sides.

⁘ ⁘ ⁘

A WEEK LATER, Sharif called. The smuggler Hajji, who had taken us last September into Mohmand Agency, had arranged for us to go up into the mountains south of Tora Bora to meet with the Taliban. I called Sophie, not thinking that my phone might be monitored. I was going to see the Taliban and asked if CBS would pay for the footage. She said that a *60 Minutes* correspondent would use it. She was worried, and asked me to call when I was out.

Sharif, Aziz, Hajji, and I drove up into the White Mountains and waited in an adobe village on a high, dusty plain. Our guide, a malik, came and took us up to another village. At sundown, we walked up past a well with women drawing water. They turned away. We kept walking and I looked back and there were women all over the hill, their backs straight, carrying jugs of water on their heads, their black and red shawls flowing like sails in the wind. The malik called the Taliban we were supposed to meet. Men with rifles stood around us. The malik said it was too dangerous with me here, exposed on a hill, but Hajji, who organized this trip, shouted at him. The drug dealer—maybe because of his money, or the network of which he was a part and its ties to distant political leaders, the jobs he created, and the money he brought in to this mountain community—was more powerful than the malik. This, too, was a result of the Soviet war. The Russians bombed the irrigation canals. Poppies require less water than wheat, so farmers switched to poppies. I didn't see then that Hajji was learning about a new form of contraband—kidnapped Westerners.

Eventually, it was just Sharif and me and the gunmen, and we went higher up into the mountains. I heard a buzzing sound, like a lawn-mower engine, in the sky. It was a drone. I imagined Americans sitting in a room watching us. "Everyone knows about the drone," whispered Sharif. We waited. A call came. The Taliban were ready. Sharif said they had Waziri accents. They were from Waziristan. That's where the Haqqanis were.

We walked higher and then took a pickup down into what I called then the valley of death. We met with the Taliban there, while the drone hovered overhead. We waited for the missile to come. I felt like I was with the mujahideen. They carried the same arms, wore the same clothes, poor young religious men fighting the godless invader. The leader said that they, like the mujahideen, received aid, and they fought. He said there was no difference between Punjabis and Pashtun. They were all Muslims. This was more evidence that they were under the control of the Pakistani army, which was traditionally mainly Punjabi,[31] the Pashtuns' lowland enemies. One of the men asked me to become Muslim and to, in effect, join them. I thanked him, but declined. Another man, shivering in the cold, said they would go wherever they were ordered, even Azerbaijan. Their willingness to travel was new. I didn't understand the significance of his statement until later. He said they had blankets and were warm and lived in caves. He invited me to see their training camps another time. A part of me wanted to go with them, but I was afraid they would kidnap me.

It was after midnight, and the drone was gone. I wondered why the US didn't kill us. This, too, would come back to me later. "It is the first interview with the Taliban in the eastern sector," said Sharif. I was drained, and simply so happy that we had survived. As I lay on a cot, shivering by the fire, Aziz said, "I thought we might not see you again." Hajji was silent, staring at the ceiling. I didn't think about why I was doing what I was, but I realized later that seemed to be part of my goal: to come as close to death as possible, to thus, as Churchill said, feel so alive. The next morning, we drove down the mountain and Sharif demanded his money for the trip. We had agreed upon a fee but I hadn't brought it. I was afraid of being robbed. I said I would pay him in Kabul and he could give the money to the others. He glowered at me. I had embarrassed him in front of the malik, but this, too, seemingly unimportant then, became so later.

❖ ❖ ❖

Back at the Gandamack, I counted out the money. Sharif demanded crisp fifty-and one-hundred-dollar bills. I had to use ATMs, a new phenomenon in Kabul, and then go to a bank. "They must be good bills," Sharif insisted, still angry. I didn't like his anger, which was new, or his blatant hunger for money, but I admired his courage. I couldn't have done this without him.

Shahwali called me. I hadn't paid him for our work in Kunar. I met him in Shar-e-Naw Park, where boys played soccer and no one could overhear us. In the 1970s, hippies had lived here, smoking hashish and listening to music. I realized that I was losing Sharif. In addition to his anger about money, he was taking a few days to return my calls. "I will pay you," I told Shahwali, "but you lied. We didn't cross the border." "Yes sir," he replied smiling. He knew that I needed him.

We left the park and went to a café. There was no heat and it was dark and cold, but the tea was hot. He created code words to use on the phone. We discussed the malik of Ducalam and our proposed trip back up north. Time was passing, and I asked Shahwali to meet Abdullah, Mullah Malang's friend, in Pakistan. I gave him Abdullah's phone numbers.

We met three days later in the same cafe. Shahwali gave me a report: "Abdullah selected a spot to meet in Peshawar and came with four men in a nice car and we drove around. The driver called Abdullah an illiterate Talib who cut off people's hands and didn't understand true Islam or how the world worked. Abdullah said he had been in war, had killed men, and understood the world better than he did. Abdullah is a nice man. He will take us, in friendship, into the Tribal Areas. We will never have fewer than twenty bodyguards."

Abdullah wanted money to pave the way. He thought I might be a spy. Shahwali said I was a poor writer and couldn't pay more than $4,000. I refused to pay anything. I called Mullah Malang, but his phone was off. Finally, anxious to move and running out of patience, I gave Shahwali $1,000, part of the advance from the publisher on my book. He sent it by *hawala*,[32] to his brother in Peshawar, who would take the money to Abdullah.

Meanwhile, the Wahhabi was arranging for me to go to a Taliban training camp in the mountains and then with these men into the Tribal Areas. Shahwali had become the broker among Abdullah, the Wahhabi, the malik of Ducalam, and other men, all of whom wanted money, none of whom I trusted. But without them I had nothing. They were part of what I now call "the Trade": the kidnapping business and also a form of war, of settling disputes, and, since 9/11, a growing criminal enterprise. I was losing money, waiting for the right trustworthy person to appear to take me across deep into the Tribal Areas, addicted to the intrigue, the danger, and the mountains, not aware that I was next to be taken.

⁑ ⁑ ⁑

SHAHWALI WENT BACK up to Kunar Province, he said. We met three days later, his eyes tired and watery, in the back of the café, and he slurped his tea like a horse drinking water. It was Christmas and I felt cold and distant from America. Shahwali gave me a new set of clothes as a present. It was kind. Maybe I could trust him. He gave me a report on each of our prospective plans, all of which cost money. I had a strange feeling that I was being surrounded. He then said that Abu Hamza, the Taliban leader I met with, was trying to reach me. "He thinks you are from Nepal and a professor writing a book about the Pashtuns."

Abu Hamza called him on a satellite phone. How did he get such a phone, which was expensive, and how had he got Shahwali's number? Shahwali said that the Wahhabi gave it to him. I refused to see Abu Hamza. I was now worried about his friends, and by extension, Shahwali.

I went to see Fazul. I found him sitting at his desk, smoking a cigarette. "This is your last trip to the north. Too many people know you up there. Go south." I promised to keep calling him. But I ignored his advice. Shahwali and the malik of Ducalam created a plan. I would go to Chitral to meet the Taliban. The malik was mistaken. It was not an ISI officer, but a military intelligence officer who needed money, and he would sneak into Afghanistan to meet with me in Ducalam. The malik would be responsible for the officer's family if anything happened to him in Afghanistan. Shahwali was responsible for the malik's family. Everyone was afraid of being kidnapped. No one trusted anyone, but at the same time, their guarantee that no one would be harmed was their word, and their collateral was a human being.

I kept trying to reach Malang and Abdullah, but their phones were off. I went for a run one evening up on a plateau in Kabul, where the air was cleaner, to relax and think. I would go forward with the malik of Ducalam. He was a tribal leader and would protect me. I was afraid of Abu Hamza, under the control, I felt, of the ISI. I sent Shahwali back to Ducalam. He called the following night from Jalalabad, using our code words. We were on.

I took a taxi down to Jalalabad, the first time I had traveled alone outside of Kabul. I felt vulnerable and was deep in Afghanistan now. I met Shahwali and our driver and we returned in the dark to Ducalam. The malik's brother took us back up into the hills and left us by a cemetery. I looked at the stars. I felt alone, like a speck of sand in the universe. The brother returned. The way was clear and he took us to the malik's home. We had dinner, and the best chicken soup I've ever eaten. The malik's younger brother, nineteen, a polite strapping man, brought in a rifle. The malik gave it to Shahwali. He took out the clip, checked the chamber, and pulled the trigger. He was showing off, but knew what he was doing. Where had he learned that? He was from Kunar, he responded. The malik made a bed of quilts for me and left. The wind blew. The rifle lay on the carpet between Shahwali and me. I wondered if he would shoot me.

We had to stay inside all day. Evening came. We listened as men walked by to the mosque. When it was quiet, the malik's brother came and the two of us left. We walked past a girl next door, about ten and holding an axe on her shoulder, down into the valley to the stream. My guide looked around to see if we were being followed. "Pakistan," he whispered. Finally, after twice meeting the Taliban, twice crossing over briefly into the Tribal Areas, I was going to hike up the mountains—not into buffer zone of the Tribal Areas, but into Pakistan.

We crossed the stream and took a crisscross path up a mountain, entered a village, and came upon a group of boys sitting in the dirt in a circle. They looked up but quickly returned to their conversation. We passed a Pakistani flag hanging from a white pole and walked out into the country, headed east, past a row of stone buildings and a sign that said "ARANADOR FRONTIER SCOUTS." Would they see us? We reached another village and knocked on a wood-slat door. A man opened it and gave us a key. We went next door, unlocked the door, and entered a room with a carpet, cushions, and a light over the door. A baby cried next door and a man and a woman talked quietly. The wind blew. The malik's other, younger brother and Shahwali entered. A half hour later a man entered, his face covered, and sat on his knees. "In the name of God, the compassionate, the merciful, I am Pakistani and as a representative of the Taliban," he began, "I want to present our views."

It was the first time that a Western journalist interviewed a member of the Taliban in his sanctuary in Pakistan. His name was Abu Omar, a nom de guerre. He was twenty-eight. "The Taliban are Afghans. Our goal is to expel the Americans and to impose Islamic law on Afghanistan." He was fighting in Kunar but got hurt and had to return for treatment. They had camps here. Who ran them? "The elders, the ISI, the Istakhabarat." This was Arabic and Pashto for secret agency. His father had sent him to a madrassa to study. From there he was sent to camps where he learned how to use a machine gun and other weapons. He was the leader now of forty men. They got paid for every soldier they killed and for every bomb they planted. They gave money to the families of suicide bombers. He explained the pay structure. Did he work with al-Qaeda? Sometimes. They would fight until they died. The elders had an agenda beyond Afghanistan. What motivated him? "Paradise," he said. The malik's older brother said there was a curfew and we had to go. What did he think of bin Laden? He was working for the sake of Islam in many countries. The older brother told me to stop. And Hekmatyar? He became effusive. "I have met Gulbuddin. Who is this Mullah Omar?" he asked. "We don't even know if he is real." After an hour, Shahwali tried to shake his hand, but he refused and left.

I was afraid that the Taliban were waiting outside. We took a different route back west toward the border. I looked back for Abu Omar and his men. Truck headlights appeared. It looked like an army truck.

I prayed that it would keep on going. It did. I looked up at the stars. No wonder a man working all day in the fields, coming home to an adobe house with a dirt floor, prayed to God. It was his only hope, that God existed and was guiding his life and watching him and his family.

We reached the village, silent in the night, walked through it, and as we approached the edge a man appeared in a green sweater and white turban with cold, staring eyes. He shined a flashlight at us and I knew he was trouble. I stared at him, and he lowered the light and we walked down the mountain. I waited for him to shout. I wore my plastic Chinese shoes and slipped and the malik's younger brother took my arm. Shahwali thrashed through the trees like a wounded animal.

We reached the bottom and walked on rocks across the stream. Shahwali slipped and fell flat in the water. We crossed back into Afghanistan. We walked up a path to our village, climbed up the stairs to the malik's house. The malik opened the door, smiling with relief. I knew when I saw his big smile how dangerous what we just did had been.

The military intelligence officer never appeared. The malik said that he was picked up by the NDS, Afghan intelligence, when he crossed the border. The malik's younger brother drove us immediately out from the village on the rocky dirt road back down to Asadabad.

A mile away a group of Afghans with rifles blocked the road. A small US firebase surrounded by sandbags was by the road. The interrogation started: Who were we? What was I doing here? I gave the senior Afghan my passport and he ordered the three of us to sit on the ground. I felt humiliated as men with rifles stood over us. The Afghan came back and snapped his fingers at me. I followed him inside the base. A sergeant with the National Guard, looking at my passport, glanced at me. "Boy, you really go all in, don't you? We were just reading something you wrote. Would you like to see the captain, would you like some coffee, what can we do for you?" I thanked him, but I couldn't tell him what I was doing. No one would understand. We raced on down the road. An hour later, we stopped by the river and I washed my face and let it dry in the wind. We were far away enough now from the NDS. I went over to the malik's younger brother, who sat on a rock, his eyes filled with tears. His older brother, the malik, had sent another brother to Pakistan as collateral for the military intelligence officer, who was now in the hands of the NDS. The Pakistanis would put his brother, the collateral, in prison. I gave him some money for gas and he raced back up to Ducalam. Another car came along and Shahwali and I hitched a ride back down to Asadabad.

For weeks Shahwali was the intermediary between the malik of Ducalam and me, whom he blamed for his brother being in prison in Pakistan. If Pakistan killed his brother in prison, he would kill Shahwali. I was responsible for Shahwali's children. Shahwali would tell Abu Omar where to find me. Abu Hamza was trying to find me. I was on edge, dealing with hard men in a hard land, little of which was cultivable, where the mean businesses, Hajji said, were guns and smuggling.

⁛ ⁛ ⁛

IN JANUARY 2008, I interviewed President Karzai one evening in his private office. He lamented the loss of Afghan land, specifically the Tribal Areas of Pakistan. He said that Haqqani was dead. I didn't believe him.

Abdullah called Shahwali. He would help me get to Hekmatyar and Haqqani. I had to write letters to them and he would deliver them. If they agreed to see me, we would go to them. I found that I didn't want to write to these killers. I felt close to Haqqani, but he had killed so many people, using suicide bombers now—how could I write a letter, which was intimate? But I finally did, and included a copy of my book, and gave both packets to Shahwali, who delivered them to Abdullah, somewhere, judging by his description, in the mountains near Peshawar.

Ten armed men, he reported, who were with Abdullah looked at my book and said they would take me. I was a real journalist. Again, it was flattery. He told Abdullah that we were putting our heads in Abdullah's hands. How could we trust him? He had joined the Taliban, Abdullah replied, because two powerful men, Hazrat Ali and Hajji Din Mohammad, now with the government and tied to the US, had killed his nephew. He had taken his revenge and could not return to

Afghanistan. He needed Mullah Malang's help. I paid little attention to his story.

Abdullah said we would travel for a few days in the Tribal Areas, return to Afghanistan, and wait for a response to my letters. If there was none, we would go on a longer trip. It was almost identical to what Razi Gul had proposed to Sharif in late September 2007: a few days in, out, and then a longer trip. I thought it was strange, but I was so deep in a world of intrigue and subterfuge that I still thought it was just a trial run. I wasn't too worried, just as I did not pay too much attention to the story about the death of Abdullah's relative and that he had killed a prominent politician in revenge, and was now hiding out in the Tribal Areas. I did not believe that death was cheap here. I remembered walking with men back to their village in 1981 as they carried a dead fighter while his brother cried, and I had listened to the lamentations of the women in his family. I listened to men talk reverently of their former comrades as martyrs, but Afghanistan had become overrun by gun culture. Men killed and were killed, it seemed, all the time.

I had been living along the border off and on now for seven months if I included the time I spent studying Pat Tillman's death, and returning to Kabul was like returning to the West. Yet I still hadn't gone deep into the Tribal Areas. Sharif was working with his friend Sean Langan, a British documentary filmmaker. Sean was staying in the Gandamack. He called me a spy the first time he saw me there and I stayed away from him. It was a reckless thing to say and I was upset. I saw by December 2007 that Sean was working also along the border as if we were in competition. He would be kidnapped after me.

It was late January, bitter cold, snowy and windy. My beard was long now. Shahwali and I huddled in the café. Ehsanullah had given me a list of names of prominent Afghans to interview for my book, indirectly introducing me to them. The last name was Hajji Din Mohammad, the governor of Kabul. The name seemed familiar, but I didn't know who he was. We would see him in an hour.

"I brought one of his books so you would know who he is," whispered Shahwali. He showed me a book, in Pashto, *The Life Story of Yunus Khalis*. I stared at the picture of the author sitting with Hekmatyar and Khalis. It was the man who had sat with Khalis when I met him in 1981, who sent me to live with Haqqani, the same man who stood in the doorway at the UN Plaza Hotel in 1984 and asked when I was returning. I had been trying to find him, this man who meant so much to me, but I had forgotten his name and didn't know anyone whom I thought would know him. I could not know then that he would become the epicenter of my story.

I went back and put on a suit out of respect. We took a taxi to the governor's compound, with its high, dark, thick adobe walls, like a fort. People hunched over in the cold. We waited in a reception area and then entered his office and I recognized him immediately and felt warmth come over me. I wanted to be alone with him. "As soon as you walked in I knew that I knew you," said Din Mohammad. He motioned for me to sit in a chair next to him. "It was 1984," I said. "No," he replied, "1985. We were at the Roosevelt Hotel. Gulbuddin Hekmatyar had refused to meet with President Reagan. I later met with Reagan three times. You called us freedom fighters then." He spoke softly, smiling. "Now you call us warlords." All those years gone by and there we were. I asked about his brothers, Hajji Qadir and Abdul Haq. He had lost both to assassinations. How could he not take revenge?

"My son, Izatullah, was also killed with Abdul Haq," he said softly. How could a man go through this, and go on? "I can sit and cry," he said, "but that is not a solution. I can sit with my rifle and neither is that. My grandfathers died for this country."

I stayed for two hours. A military aide came in to say that men were waiting to see him. "I would like to see you again," I said. He nodded. "I would like to talk about bin Laden," I added. He nodded again. I wished that Shahwali wasn't there. We walked out into the cold.

⁜ ⁜ ⁜

SHAHWALI AND I went to see Hazrat Ali at his home. He was one of the three former mujahideen commanders hired by the CIA to find bin Laden at Tora Bora. A guard took us inside and I saw a treadmill in an empty room. We entered another room with easy chairs, glass coffee tables, and an electric heater. Hazrat Ali hadn't given an interview in two years. He was tired of being asked about the money that the US paid him and why he supposedly let bin Laden get away.

He had fought under Yunus Khalis against the Soviets and was now an MP from Jalalabad. We drank green tea and when I finished he got up and refilled my glass. I gave him my book as my calling card to look at, to establish credibility with him, and he looked at the pictures and at me. "I am thinking," he said, wondering, I think now, who I was and what I was looking for. I couldn't tell him yet. "When the Taliban came to power I stayed in my village, studied them, and decided there was a hand behind them," he began. The "hand" was Pakistan. He, like Hajji Qadir, went north and joined Ahmed Shah Massoud. "We knew that Pakistan and Saudi Arabia were behind them." He meant the Taliban. "There were rumors that the US was also, but there was no proof.

"There were Pakistani soldiers with the Taliban fighting in Mazar-i-Sharif in the north and in Kandahar. I had over three hundred Pakistani prisoners. They didn't wear uniforms, only turbans and shalwar kameez. I asked where they were from. Their relatives, from Pakistan, came for them." He poured more tea. "As far as I have learned Naseerullah Babar was behind this, but he couldn't do it alone. It was the ISI. The Taliban are strong and when they were in power there was peace and stability, but we fought them because they were controlled by Pakistan."

He wouldn't talk about Hajji Qadir. He saw that I had been with Haqqani. He had to do research before he would talk further to me. I would have to come back.

⁎⁎⁎

THE WAHHABI CALLED Shahwali. He had arranged for us to go to a Taliban training camp. Al-Qaeda was there. I was wary, but nothing was happening with Abdullah. Shahwali and I went in a taxi back down to Jalalabad. The news came on the radio. Shahwali listened carefully. Two US journalists were captured trying to sneak into Bajaur Agency with the Taliban. The Pakistani government said in the future all such people would be considered hostages. Who were these journalists? I asked Shahwali. Who took them across and why did they betray them?

Shahwali fell back into the seat. He didn't answer me. I couldn't understand the radio. I asked Shahwali to ask the driver if the announcer said anything more. Shahwali spoke to him, but I couldn't understand him. I felt that Shahwali had made it up, but why? He was saying that Pakistan was involved. I asked him to call the Wahhabi. He would check on this.

He called a friend in Kunar Province. "How did you go to Ducalam?" His friend asked. "Even we cannot go there. It is too dangerous."

Shahwali smiled. "Sir Jere, they asked you to go to these places because no one else would. We will do this together. You said it is your neck as well as mine. That is enough for me."

He smiled, but again he had flattered me instead of answering my question. In Jalalabad, we went to the Khalid Guest House, checked in, and walked up concrete steps to our room. Shahwali was constantly on the phone, talking with the malik of Ducalam, who was demanding now four million Pakistani rupees, the currency along the border, to free his brother and the MI officer. That was nearly $40,000. If we didn't pay him he might send Abu Omar after us. "He could put a gun to my head to learn where you are staying," said Shahwali, trying to frighten me.

I still wanted to talk to the MI officer, but sensed if I returned to Ducalam that the malik would kidnap me. I had nowhere to turn except Din Mohammad, but Malang said I couldn't talk to him about my trip. I didn't want to lose Abdullah. He was my only way into the Tribal Areas. Shahwali sat on his cot while I paced the room, thinking.

Shahwali told me of other friends who could help me. The Wahhabi came to our room to price out our trip to a Taliban training camp. It would cost $5,000. I was on edge and lost my temper. Who did he work for? Who was he really?

He got up and left. Would he hurt me? He was still afraid that I would give his picture to the US Army. I asked Shahwali what we would do if Abdullah took off with my money. Shahwali said he would retaliate by going to Hazrat Ali. He and Hajji Qadir's son, Hajji Zahir, had killed Abdullah's cousin. The Wahhabi returned. We would go to the mountains, but no money would change hands. I asked about bin Laden. The Wahhabi said he was with an "institution" in Pakistan, and that they had used him to fight America.

We left Jalalabad to return to the mountains, where I was happier living in danger. It was sunset and we were quiet as Ahmed drove north along the river, turned up into the mountains, and stopped by the road. The Wahhabi led us in the dark across a field. The soil was plowed and soft and it was hard to see. We crossed a footbridge and Shahwali took my hand until I pulled it away. We walked along a stream. The Wahhabi made a call. We came to a rock and a man appeared and led us into a village, and we climbed up past dark houses watched by men standing in doorways. We entered a plateau where a dozen Taliban surrounded us. I thought I was about to die. They, like other Taliban, carried old Soviet rifles and machine guns, and wore long ammunition belts around their necks; the bullets clanged gently, like wind chimes, in the night. "We've lost so many men," lamented one man, holding a machine gun. I felt sorry for him, an idealistic young guerrilla used by older men. Then, one hundred yards below, a red glowing light appeared just on the other side of the stream. It was the US Army. The Talib placed his machine gun on a rock and got ready. It was suicide. "They are crazy," said the Wahhabi. We ran down the mountain and I didn't know if I would get shot in the front or the back. A man took us into a *hujra*, and I waited for US soldiers to burst into the room.

The Wahhabi said that there was an al-Qaeda fighter with the Taliban and asked if I wanted to go back up to interview him. I said no. He left and I was angry at my cowardice.

⁘ ⁘ ⁘

WE LEFT AT dawn and walked along a river. A girl about ten stood in a clump of trees, watching us. We met Ahmed and drove to the Kunar River and ate bananas and chicken that we had bought the night before, and the Wahhabi and Shahwali laughed and told stories, happy—overjoyed really, like me—to be alive. That afternoon, I sat in our room in Jalalabad writing up my notes. Shahwali went out and rushed thirty minutes later into the room sweating. The Wahhabi had called. People in Bajaur Agency knew that a foreigner, a guide, and a translator were coming from Afghanistan. They would behead the translator and guide and demand millions for the foreigner. Ahmed walked in, smiling. "Hi badcha, how are you?" I liked Ahmed, but he had never walked in so nonchalantly, and smiling, before, or called me *badcha*, which was a slang form of *badash*, which meant king in Pashto and Urdu. It was as if he and Shahwali had planned this scene, like actors in a play. I demanded that we go over every minute of Shahwali's time with Abdullah to find out who among Abdullah's men let the word out that we were coming. Shahwali said that when they were all looking at *In Afghanistan*, someone must have decided to kidnap me. Ahmed slapped the floor in agreement. That was it.

I was alone with Afghans, becoming more confused, more frightened, more uncertain, more paranoid, and more determined to go into the Tribal Areas.

"Study everything," said Ahmed. "Trust is critical. Maybe Abdullah or Malang is going to make a lot of money off you." I didn't think that Ahmed was warning me that I was going to be kidnapped. "Pashtuns are not friends with one another." I didn't realize that Ahmed, the poorest among them, who had driven me again and again up into the mountains, deep into Taliban country up to Ducalam, who had never pressured me for money like the others, was trying to save me. But I was too wrapped up in myself, too deaf in my ambition, to hear his message.

We returned to Kabul. I called Mullah Malang to check again on Abdullah, and Malang agreed to meet. We sat in the back of the Kandahar Restaurant, once the favorite restaurant of the Taliban. It was afternoon and empty and there was no heat. Malang wore a black topcoat, a black wool cap, a scarf, glasses, and a big stone ring, and carried a briefcase.

"There is 'a program' for every American, Canadian, European, and South African, but not for Chinese, Iranians, or, generally, Russians," Malang said. A "program" was a potential plan to kidnap or kill any

Westerner. There were retired American, British, and South African soldiers here, all happy with their high, tax-free salaries. One man told me he was saving for a home in Costa Rica.

Malang advised: "Your trip will be dangerous. There will be al-Qaeda and the Taliban, but Abdullah is a good man. Keep everything secret." What about Din Mohammad? He shook his head. I liked Malang and wanted to trust him. He had a deep, confident laugh. I could see why he was a famous commander. But I felt at home with Din Mohammad.

I said that Abdullah kept asking for money. Malang said that he had become greedy. I was to give him 5,000, 10,000, and 30,000 ($50, $100, and $300) Afghanis at a time. Each would be a thick wad of bills and appear like a lot of money. He opened his briefcase, took out a phone, and showed me a photograph of a Gandharan statue. Did I know of anyone in New York who wanted to buy this? I knew two people in the museum world, one in New York and one in Paris, who might know someone, but this was wrong, selling his country's heritage on the black market. I saw why the mujahideen lost respect for him. I said no.

We walked to the front counter and he called for the check. I paid and we walked out. On Mullah Malang's recommendation, I would go ahead with Abdullah.

⁙ ⁙ ⁙

SHAHWALI CALLED LATE at night. Abdullah Malang had called. It was code for Abdullah. The next morning, I met Shahwali in the café. He hunched over like a Buddha, slurping his tea. Abdullah wanted more money. I shook my head in despair.

"Sir," said Shahwali. "Friendship in America and friendship here are different. Here you kill a friend for money." Shahwali had enemies. If they knew he was working for an American, they would kill him. It was risky to go into the Tribal Areas. If anything happened, Shahwali reminded me, I had promised to take care of his children. I gave him $500. We walked to an ATM and I withdrew another $500. Shahwali called that evening to tell me that Abdullah had received the money. He was ready. I didn't see that I had been lured like a fish onto a hook.

The next morning, Shahwali came for me in a taxi. Steam rose from the engine and spread like vapor over a moor. There was snow piled by the road. We rode east and as we descended it grew warm and it was sunny and the wind blew across the Kabul River and the desert and I thought of the Columbia River in the summer, and home.

We went to the guesthouse and Shahwali found the *jan-i-maz*, the prayer mat, like a small carpet, and prayed. He went to get a haircut and returned, his hair short, his beard trimmed, and wearing a white prayer cap. He looked like a religious student, and he made me nervous. He performed his ablutions and prayed again. Evening came and our driver joined us. The news came on television. The Taliban had kidnapped the Pakistani ambassador to Afghanistan near Landi Khotal. There was a massive search operation underway. "It's all a game," laughed Ahmed. Shahwali prayed again. I asked him to call Abdullah. His phone was off. It was the same the next day.

That night we watched the news again. A Taliban spokesman said they wanted to exchange the ambassador for one of their leaders. The Frontier Scouts and the military had taken him. An analyst said it was all part of the strange game of the ISI. I went to bed at eleven. A few minutes later Mullah Malang called and asked where I was and when I told him he advised me to return to Kabul. My stomach tightened. "The Pakistani army is in the border region hunting for the ambassador. It would be better to go another time."

I asked about Shahwali. "Do not say anything to him. He is inexperienced." I turned on the light. Shahwali looked at me, his face dark and angry. I had never seen that look before. "I am not inexperienced. I've been working with you for two months now." I felt at that moment that Mullah Malang was my friend. He was telling me not to go for a reason. It had nothing to do with the soldiers. I told Shahwali to call Din Mohammad in the morning and tell him that I wanted to go up to Tora Bora and then back to Kabul. "Trust your instincts," I wrote in my notebook. I was desperate to go into Pakistan, and ignored them.

❖ ❖ ❖

On Thursday, February 14, Shahwali and I went to the bazaar and I bought a *maswok*—a stick of clove that served as the toothbrush used by Mohammad—and then we went to a bookstore to buy a Qur'an. I wanted to take one with me, like the maswok, like fasting, to show my interest in Islam, to be close to Islam. It was like a form of protection. Shahwali would not let me touch the Qur'an. I wasn't Muslim and didn't know how to hold it properly. I had to perform ablutions first. I asked if he had called Din Mohammad. He said no. I said to call immediately. He did and said that Din Mohammad said hello. I was two men: one Western, worried about time, this Western obsession; the other Eastern, willing to wait. By saying hello Din Mohammad was saying he would protect me. "He will have his son take us to Tora Bora," said Shahwali. "It's dangerous up there. I don't know if we should go."

Shahwali kept trying to reach Abdullah but his phones were still off. He wanted to walk with me. We found a bench in a park. "On our first night after death God will ask us what did we use our body for, our money and our knowledge? If we were good, we would go to Heaven. If we were bad, we would go to Hell. If we were martyred God would ask if we died for God, or for money. God knew. If you lied, you went to Hell." Why was he preaching like this? It reminded me of when I was a boy. I didn't want to listen. It was an alien religion. It didn't occur to me that he was preaching to himself, preparing for our trip.

We walked through a grove of trees and came to the Mosque of Hajji Qadir. I walked away. I was betraying Din Mohammad by going with his enemies. That night I called my father, now ninety-four. "When are you coming home?" he asked. Was I ever coming home again? Where was I, in Afghanistan? Was it dangerous where I was? I said I was fine. I told Shahwali that I had called my father. "I could tell," he said. I felt good when I hung up. It didn't occur to me that I might subconsciously be saying good-bye.

The next day I went for a walk again through the bazaar, looking to see if people watched me or if I blended in well enough to cross into Pakistan, as always now looking for Abu Hamza, and Abu Omar, afraid that they and their men would come up to me and take me into an alley from which I would just disappear. I went through a gate and into an olive grove on the other side of which was the raised tomb, like that of Napoleon in Paris, and the Mosque of Hajji Qadir. It was Friday and there were hundreds of men sitting outside the crowded mosque and in the olive grove listening to the sermon.

It came time to pray. I tried to join in but felt conspicuous, a charlatan. I left and walked back through the bazaar, then Shahwali called. Abdullah's man had crossed the border and was coming to take us into Pakistan. I walked through a crowd of men next to a cart piled high with cell phones, like vegetables, and reached a road. This was it.

Back at the guesthouse I found the same man whom I had met during Ramadan with Sharif. He introduced himself: Razi Gul. I was relieved to see him, someone I knew. He had come from Landi Khotal. Was the Pakistani army there? He brought his hand up and flicked his wrist as Pashtuns did to dismiss a thought. There were always soldiers around. It was all a game. Malang was misinformed. There was no problem.

Later a rough, bulky man with short hair arrived and, looking at me closely, asked for Shahwali. Razi Gul talked to him. It was Din Mohammad's son's driver, and he had come to take us to Tora Bora instead of the adventure with Abdullah. Suddenly there were men from two warring clans in my room. It didn't occur to me that the driver had rushed there to save me or that Shahwali had lied. I assumed all the men were part of my team.

Shahwali said we would be gone "three to five days, at the most," and that I could go to Tora Bora when I returned. So I told Din Mohammad's driver to go, that I would see him soon.

That night Razi Gul preached to me: "This world is useless. The only thing that counts is the hereafter and Judgment Day. If we do not have enough food in this life, we will have enough there. The heap of a body—the grave—is a house of Heaven or Hell. You need help to cross the border, but after death you will have no mother, brother, sister, or father to help you. You will be alone."

By the time he finished I already felt alone.

Chapter 7

The Trade

Ahmed, Razi Gul, Shahwali, Shahwali's father, whom Shahwali said he had brought to Jalalabad, and I had breakfast. Everyone was relaxed, like we were going on a picnic, and only Shahwali's father, sitting across from me, was quiet, hunched over, a heavy old man eating kebab. I felt sorry for him and wanted to assure him that I would protect his son. They ordered extra kebabs and bread for the trip and the waiters wrapped everything in newspaper. Shahwali told me to give my gear and cell phone to his father, and I did. He came around the table and we shook hands good-bye, and then Shahwali said he was taking his father to a taxi. We finished our tea, and I paid the bill and went to our room. Shahwali came a few minutes later. He had bought a new shirt and took it out of its wrapper and put on a pair of elastic bands, which he had just bought, to give him support on his ankles. He smiled, tapping his legs. He was now ready to climb in the mountains. I smiled at his naïve thoughts, not aware at how naïve I was then myself. We went by separate stairs down to the street.

Ahmed was waiting. I wondered if we were being watched. Ahmed headed west but then made a quick U-turn and we drove toward the Pakistani border. We passed through two checkpoints and the police didn't pay any attention to me. We turned off on the same road that Sami and Hajji and I had taken the previous September, but then we took a different route and the road turned to gravel and then to dirt and ended at a ridge. It was quiet, and we got out of the car. I gave Ahmed my passport as we had agreed at breakfast. I had nothing on me now, no wallet, nothing, except my shoes, that might identify me as a foreigner.

Shahwali told me to pay Ahmed for gas. He was right. I hadn't paid him in a few days. I gave him some money and he came forward, his eyes watery, and hugged me and kissed me on the cheek, and said something I didn't understand. No Afghan had ever kissed me. I think now he was saying good-bye. I thought for years that it was a Judas kiss, but now I think that he was warning me, one last time.

I followed Razi Gul, who carried two plastic bags of food and clothes, as if we were refugees, and then came Shahwali. We climbed and reached a man on a windy bluff holding a rifle. He hugged me. We entered a house and a man gave me water to drink from a pan. We walked out a back door and a driver was waiting. Razi Gul, now armed, was sitting, relaxed now, in the front seat.

We drove up a dusty track into the hills and looked across into a wasteland of dust and rust-red hills and mountains, and then drove down to a river where a man was waiting in a boat with an outboard motor to take us across. We walked through a poppy field, the plants only a few inches high, and approached a mountain when Razi Gul hesitated, unsure which way to go—my first indication, my first fear, that something was up, but I let it go. Samad, who had joined us on the ridge, told him to go forward and we began to climb. That evening before sundown, Samad, a lean, sturdy man in his thirties and in the lead, stopped and sat on a rock, waiting. I had never seen an Afghan stop to rest and thought it strange. We waited for Shahwali and then kept climbing. The land was silent. I asked Razi Gul how long it would be before we reached Abdullah and he said about twenty minutes. We walked down a goat path through a valley, in single file, ten yards apart, like soldiers. I glanced up and saw a tinge of black move behind a rock. I knew it was not an animal and that we were in danger. I stopped.

A dozen men rose behind the ridge, in black turbans, and they came running down the mountain, like Indians, spread out, and I waited to die. They shouted at us to get down but I stayed standing and watched Razi Gul and Samad bend down, but they didn't fire. The leader came up to me and my mouth was dry with fear. He held a walkie-talkie and asked where I came from, and where I was going. I told him in Pashto, but I spoke slowly and mispronounced Peshawar, called "Pek-a-wahr" here, and the leader scoffed. "You are not Pashtun," he said. They led us up the mountain. Razi Gul said he was tired and wanted to sit. One man told him if he did they would behead him.

They sat me down, blindfolded me, and tied my hands behind me. I was like a sheep, in shock, ready to be slaughtered. I thought of my father and my brother and sister. I was certain I was going to die. I waited and heard a man fingering his rifle near my ear. So, this is how it was. I waited in the silence and I felt a breeze. I kept waiting. They pulled me up, untied me, and a man held my hand and took me fast down the mountain. I was blindfolded and stumbled, but I was alive. He pulled me up and we reached flat land and they put me in a car. We drove for an hour, maybe more. Then they pulled me out onto the ground and a man asked if I was Muslim. I recited the Kalima, the profession of faith, to stay alive, but then they pushed me back in, like a sack of potatoes, and now I was truly scared, but strangely calm as I rode alone, and the tires spun in the dirt as we climbed up a mountain and it got cold and I knew then that they were going to kill me, alone, high up on the mountain.

We stopped and they took me out of the car and dogs barked fiercely near my legs and we walked and I felt an adobe wall with my hands. I was led into a room and a man pushed me down onto a cot, and I waited again to die and then a half hour later someone pulled me up and untied my blindfold. A man held a lantern. I saw that Shahwali, Razi Gul, and Samad were with me, and I felt better. I looked at the mud wall behind me, searching for traces of blood. I saw a spike in the dirt floor, and chains tied to it, next to my cot. I was in a Taliban prison, somewhere in the mountains. Rough, bearded men with rifles stood in front of us. A man came in carrying more chains. The men went into the next room and I could hear them talking. "They are eating," said Samad. Two men came in, sat staring at me, and then left. "If they try to kill us, we must kill them," said Razi Gul. "I'll take the shorter one." "I'll take the other one," said Samad. Where, I asked myself, was the safety on a Kalashnikov? We had to kill those men, go next door, and kill the others. It was kill or be killed. I had just changed completely.

⁂ ⁂ ⁂

SIX AND A half weeks later, the commander, who called himself the Maulvi, his chief lieutenant, and Gulob, my main jailer, and three other armed men, their faces half covered, escorted Razi Gul, Samad, Shahwali, and me back out through the same mountains. Other armed men appeared at different times, and then were gone. When we stopped to pray I was thirsty and put my hand in a dark pool and touched my lips. As evening came we reached the same plateau as before and we walked single file, the Maulvi in the lead. I could have rushed him and grabbed his rifle and run, but it would have been suicide. We were going to the exchange. I would be with my wife that night, they said, in Jalalabad. I wasn't married, but had created a wife to whom I had written a ransom letter, sitting on my knees, with gunmen over me. I kept thinking of the suicide bomber that the Maulvi had said would be at the exchange. I walked on, afraid after all the conflicting stories they had told me, the mock executions, the demand for a million dollars and for three of their men from Guantanamo in exchange for me, the suicide recruitment tapes, the threat to sell my kidney, the Maulvi congratulating me on escaping death, that they would shoot me out here in the mountains, with no one around. As night came I grew tired. I didn't know where I was and I stumbled forward, exhausted, my lungs burning, like when I was a boy. We came lower and thrashed through plants as high as my shoulder and I could tell by them, and the soil, which was hard and cracked, that we were near a river.

The Maulvi and Gulob stopped. I put my hands on my knees and Shahwali collapsed in the dirt. I gathered my strength and approached the Maulvi and Gulob. The other men were gone. They stared at me coldly, their faces angry. They were releasing us, but they knew where to find me. The Maulvi glared at me, his eyes gleaming like cat's eyes in the dark, and he said to go. We walked on and I followed Razi Gul and Samad, waiting for the Maulvi and Gulob to shoot me in the back.

We walked through a plowed field and I stumbled in the thick, soft dirt, got up and kept going and fell again, and Shahwali trudged along behind me. We kept going. A light flickered and armed men appeared out of the dark, and a man in white, heavily armed, hugged me gently. We crossed a river in a boat and I again, foolishly, took a sip of water. We reached the far shore where there was a pickup and men waiting. A man gave me a pan of water to drink, but I felt sick now and I knew it was from the dark water in the pool I had sipped that afternoon. I climbed in the back of the pickup and the driver raced on a winding road and we stopped at a camp, and it looked strangely clean and modern with a vaguely pale-yellow building made of corrugated steel. I walked to a charpoy, lay down, and closed my eyes. I felt sick. I opened them and saw Samad sit down on a bench next to a building, among a group of men. He looked at me coldly and he was suddenly small and far away. He was home, this man, who I knew instinctively at that moment had betrayed me, as I was almost certain that he did one night in prison, after which I looked at him in the dark lying on his cot across the room, and I closed my eyes, and saw blood all over him and knew that I wanted to harm him badly. I had never remotely seen that image before in my mind.

I heard Shahwali saying my name quietly and I opened my eyes and he said that Abdullah wanted to talk to me. Abdullah? Was it possible? Why was he here? Where were we? Was this his headquarters? I sat up and a man in his forties, slightly short, bulky, with short dark hair and smiling gently, stood next to me. I asked where he had been. For weeks, I had been waiting for him. He apologized for all the trouble I had been through and said that my people had been trying to capture him. I didn't understand. I realized at that second that a group of men, maybe linked to CBS, had been trying to find me. He said that he had talked to Sirajuddin Haqqani, and I thought of his father Jalaluddin, whose name I had used, hoping that it would keep me alive.

I closed my eyes, feverish and sick now. A man asked if I wanted to eat. I opened my eyes for a second and said no. I watched a line of men walk down a hill for a few more seconds to what, I realized later, was a modern, pale-yellow building. I realized that they were Abdullah's men, but they walked in orderly single file down the hill, and no one carried a rifle, into a building as if it was, I thought strangely, a mess hall. I had never seen such a thing. No one was wearing a turban, and only some seemed to be wearing prayer caps. Only later did this dawn on me. I had never seen Afghans sitting in a row on a bench as Samad and the men next to him sat. They were quiet and reserved. Always men sat on the ground or a carpet or stood around talking. I had never seen Pashtuns in the countryside eat at a table, except at a restaurant, and then only some did. Almost always they sat on a carpet, with a plastic tablecloth in front of them or in a restaurant on a mezza, a raised platform. They may have been real Taliban, I realized later, but they were not like the Maulvi or Gulob or the other hard mountain men with black turbans who had come into our cell. These men were too organized and regimented. This compound was, I feel now, in some way, attached to or part of the military.

Abdullah said they were waiting for a truck to take us. Just after midnight, I learned later, it was time for the official release. The truck arrived and Abdullah, Razi Gul, and other armed men took Shahwali and me down to another part of the river. I wanted to use the bathroom and Razi Gul, wearing his pakhool, or felt hat, and holding his rifle like a normal Afghan guerrilla fighter, escorted me back into the trees. It was the first time we were both alone and I noticed again how light he was on his feet and I knew he was quick and a good fighter and I was suddenly afraid that he could kill me there and then.

A man stood on the bank alone and whistled, and flicked a flashlight on and off. Across the river someone did the same. A pickup appeared and drove down to the water, flashed its lights, and turned them off. A cable above us started to move and the ferry came across slowly. The river was like glass. There were armed men all around me. I wondered what was going to happen. The ferry arrived and Abdullah and a few men, and Razi Gul holding his rifle, and Shahwali and I got on and we rode slowly back across the water. I stood next to Razi Gul and he approached and pulled on my beard. It was intimate and frightening and I knew it was a form of supplication. He was asking me to protect him. He was afraid. Once we crossed the river I had power. I was going to be released.

We reached the opposite shore, Abdullah said good-bye, and Razi Gul and I hugged one another. Shahwali and I stepped down onto the dirt. We were back in Afghanistan. No one else got off the ferry. They were outlaws. We climbed into the pickup and rode on a rough dirt track for an hour, and then I saw a man slowly swinging a lantern and thought it was the Taliban. I wanted to escape, but I was too weak. We stopped and I got out of the truck and felt sick and wanted to lean against the truck, but I couldn't do that. Americans leaned against trucks. I had to stand straight, as a Talib would.

Two men came out of the dark and one of them came up to me and showed me Fazul's CBS ID card and my knees almost buckled. I realized for the first time since I was taken that I was going to live, and that Fazul was involved in the rescue. The man gave me a folded piece of paper. I read it quickly. It was a letter from Fazul. He had given his card to this man. He would take care of me. Fazul was coming for me. I sighed deeply. To this day, every time I think of that moment I become emotional.

A white SUV moved out from beside an adobe house in the dark and came toward us slowly, a dark SUV behind it with rifles sticking out the windows. The white SUV stopped and the man who gave me Fazul's card climbed in the front and I climbed in the backseat. The SUV was new and felt expensive. I glanced at the man who had given me the card. He was thin, refined looking, in tailored Afghan clothes and in his forties. He said hello kindly and gave me a small bottle of water. His driver had a rifle next to him, pointing up. Shahwali was in the other vehicle. The man in the front, I realized later, was called Feridoun, and he, more than anyone, was perhaps responsible for saving my life. I did not know that until I saw Fazul again in Kabul in

2017, and he told me that the moment I reached Feridoun I was finally safe, but not until then. We drove on rough dirt roads in the dark. There was nothing around and I was afraid of the Taliban. I looked back and saw the other SUV behind us and a rifle pointing out the window. Our bodyguards were also afraid. Even then, it seemed, I wasn't safe.

We came to another road and instinctively I questioned whether we were going the right way. A half hour later we stopped and changed directions, but soon the road ended. Who were these men who didn't know where to go? The Taliban were all around here hiding in the forest and could surround us. We turned back and stopped at a crossing and the men got out and talked to those in the vehicle behind them. I got out and, feeling sick, walked in the headlights away where I could be sick, but not too far, afraid of the Taliban. Shahwali came over and up close to me, closer than he had ever stood, and pulled on my beard. It too was intimate. Twice, now, men had pulled my beard. No one had ever done this before. But this time I was angry. I crossed my arms. I wanted to push him away, but I was too weak.

"They have a tape recorder and are questioning me. You must help me," Shahwali pleaded. "I want to ride with you. You said you would protect me."

They, whoever they were, felt he was involved. So did I now. Why else would he be so afraid? When he asked if I would protect him and his children, I never thought it would come to this. What did these men behind us know that I didn't? Was Shahwali really a part of this? Did he betray me, too? I remembered lying on the cot talking with Abdullah. Shahwali was comfortable with him, as if they were friends. I didn't want anyone to see me standing close to Shahwali. I tried to move away, but he pressed closer. He reminded me of the pact, that "your neck is my neck." I would hear these statements a hundred times in the future.

It was time to go. I wanted the men in the other vehicle to take him away from me and to keep interrogating him. I climbed back in the white SUV. Shahwali climbed in with me, and I felt smothered. We rode for another hour, reached a dark village, and I got out and lay on a cot. Men in dark turbans stood around talking. A cell phone rang, the sound of civilization out here in the wild, the first time I had heard one since I was taken. A man brought the phone to me. It was Fazul. Was I okay, he asked? It was so good to hear from him. I said I was fine, my voice breaking. "I will see you in one hour," he said. "Feridoun will take care of you."

The phone rang again and the man brought it to me again. This time it was Bryn Padrig, the CBS producer I had met in Kabul in 2001. I assumed that he was calling from London. He asked if I was hurt or injured. I knew what he was referring to. No, they hadn't tortured me. So many later asked me about torture, afraid of that word, of unrelenting pain, of men having power to do whatever they wanted to you. I was utterly unprepared for Bryn's call. He reminded me that he was English and therefore, he said, didn't cry, but we did, briefly. The phone rang again and it was Michael Semple. I had never talked to him before. "Michael," I asked, "you were involved in this, too?" I was happy to hear his voice, so warm and confident. I remembered asking Roshan Khadivi, my UN friend, for someone she knew who could help me along the border: it was she who had given me Michael's name. I remembered writing to him and that he didn't respond, hurting my pride. I wrote to Roshan, calling him a "so-called Afghan expert." It was this e-mail, he said, that had spurred him to help me. I felt embarrassed and grateful and humbled. I would feel even more so when Bryn would later tell me that Michael saved my life. Nafay, the CBS woman in Pakistan, called, along with a man called Bashir, whom I didn't know. I talked briefly, happy to hear all their voices.

I closed my eyes again. Men began to move and Shahwali said we had to go. We drove on for another hour, past poppy fields up to a man's waist now, past forest and adobe houses. I opened the window to be sick, leaned out and Shahwali grabbed my legs, protecting me as if I was a child, trying to show that he was my friend. Feridoun gave me a box of tissues. "You drank some bad water," he said kindly. We came to another settlement and stopped. There, Fazul came up to me and hugged me and told me I was safe. Behind him was Ahmed Jan, my old driver, holding a camera, smiling warmly, and we hugged one another. Fazul climbed in the SUV with me and gave Shahwali a dirty look. "We think he was involved," he said. I was sitting between them. He asked if I was sick, or injured. I said no. He called my brother, and I talked briefly with one of my nieces, and we both cried. Her parents were at church. Fazul called my sister. She cried and asked how I was. I was fine. "It's been surreal," she said. The FBI, the State Department, and CBS had been calling her. I realized then that the government knew. "We were told not to talk to anyone," she said. She and my brother had not told our father. It would have been too much for him. Again, she asked if I was okay. I didn't want Shahwali with us. The signal cut off. We reached a paved road and Fazul talked on his phone with Jim, an FBI agent. "He's a good man," he said. "We'll meet him soon." Why, I wondered, was he talking to the FBI?

We drove to a US military base and stopped at an intersection. Feridoun got out of the SUV and walked in front of us and was gone. The driver turned to his right and we approached a gate; a soldier pressed a button and a barrier lifted and we drove onto the base. Feridoun's driver, I realized later, strangely, knew exactly where to go. He drove through the base to a garage with a high cyclone fence around it, like a small prison, entered the gate, and we stopped. Two men came to the door. I started to get out and two men grabbed me and lifted me out, helping me.

I walked into a room. It was lit brightly and I sat at a table, Fazul at another table to my left. Shahwali sat at a table across from me, in the corner. "We know all about you," said an American. There was anger in his voice. He had long hair and wore jeans and a pistol. I thought I was a prisoner and waited for the interrogation. I had gone with the Taliban. I wondered if I would go to jail. "Where do you want to go?" he asked repeatedly, "Bagram or Kabul?" I didn't know why he was asking me this. Later I was told that Bagram meant the military, and Kabul the FBI. There were cans of beer and soft drinks on the table. I told him I had drunk some bad water coming out and had been sick for the past few hours. I started to open a soft drink and he told me to drink it slowly. He did care a bit. There was food there, but I couldn't eat. There was a woman there, in her thirties, who said that she was in the navy. She and Shahwali flirted with one another, and I was upset. He had fooled her also. The man with the pistol asked Fazul why he was there, and I said he was the CBS bureau chief, feeling suddenly protective of him. Fazul later told me that the woman told him she had been on the phone with CBS. "I'm CBS," he said. "I've been in the middle of this for weeks." Fazul said she repeated that she had been in direct contact with CBS, implying that she had been involved in my release. "The FBI and the military didn't do anything, but they were all trying to get the glory for saving an American," he said, shaking his head.

You can divide a kidnapping into two parts. All that happens in captivity and—if you are fortunate to survive—all that happens afterward. Afterward had just begun.

PART TWO

"It's an Afghan Casino Royale"

Chapter 8

Back Homeland

Two friendly men with the FBI, whom I will call Bob and John, said they would take Shahwali and me to a doctor and get us something to eat.

Bob drove under bright lights to a checkpoint and then to a row of Humvees and walked into a shed filled with medical supplies. A clock on the wall said 4:00 a.m. Bob took our pictures and I felt like they were mug shots. Back outside, he pointed to a red-brick building. It was a Russian officers' club from the 1980s.

Bob said he had asked the mess hall to open early for me. It was empty and hot and a soldier brought me a large tray of food and nodded, a form of welcome, and I felt grateful I was accepted. I told Shahwali to eat and he took a banana. Fazul sat away from him. I was wide awake now but still not hungry. We walked to another shed that was divided into small rooms, one of which had a narrow cot with new clothes, soap, a toothbrush, news magazines, PowerBars, and my running shoes.

"We wanted you to have everything you needed," said Bob, "and to make you feel at home." Bob asked if I wanted to take a shower. I said no. I didn't say it but I didn't want to leave the mountains. Bob took Shahwali to where the showers were.

I lay on the cot and looked through the magazines, put them down. Daylight came. I still didn't want to take a shower, but I had to appear normal. I walked across the gravel to the latrine and stared at the man in the mirror. My eyes were hollow, my face gaunt, and my hair and beard were wild-looking. What had I become? Not just in prison, but the last year. A part of me liked it. A soldier came in, looked at me, and moved away. I loved the hot water running over me, but felt sad and that I was washing off the mountains. My time with the Taliban and the mujahideen was over.

I sat on my cot, the door open to the hallway, and another open to the outside. A soldier looked in and asked for me.

Shahwali wanted to sit in the sun. Bob and John brought plastic containers of breakfast. I ate some fruit. Fazul joined us. Shahwali said he wanted to go to his family in Peshawar. The doctor, in a uniform with his captain's bars, came over with some medicine. "Boy, you look different," he said, smiling. I looked more American now. Fazul said they thought Shahwali was involved and had refused to talk to him in the SUV. I wondered why the FBI didn't take Shahwali into custody. I would return to Kabul years later, and I asked Fazul. "We weren't sure if he was involved," he replied. "I don't think he got any money. I gave him $200 to make his way home." Fazul said that the FBI interviewed Shahwali a week after my release at the US embassy, and then let him go, and that he would later meet with Shahwali, at Shahwali's request. I asked what they talked about. He said he told him about the FBI meeting.

In 2015 Shahwali tried to friend me on Facebook and I refused. After a year or so he began to call again and send me messages. He kept calling me, asking for help. The NDS was after him, and then the ISI had taken his son into custody and he needed my help. It never ended. He called Fazul. Fazul asked me to tell him to stop. He called again and I got angry and said that the FBI had asked me to come with them to Kabul to take him to Guantanamo and that I had said no, saving him.

I told him to leave me alone. He kept sending messages. I asked how many times he had met with Fazul. Three times, he said.

We left the base and we were met by an SUV waiting by the road. Ahmed Shah Amin, part of CBS and Fazul's cousin, who would later tell me his own version of events, rushed over with my backpack that I had left with Shahwali's father. Fazul was going with Ahmed Shah back to Kabul. They would see me the next day at the embassy.

We drove onto another base crowded with soldiers and vehicles coming and going. Bob pointed to a white plane on the runway and said it was ours. One of our bodyguards, in a black T-shirt and carrying an M-4, introduced himself. I thanked him for coming with us. He said he helped clean out my room in Kabul. "We're glad to have you back," he said. I felt emotional. He said that if I ever wanted to write anything about my experience that a lot people at the Kennedy Special Warfare Center and School at Fort Bragg would like to read it. He gave me his card. Two years later his wife wrote me a letter, with my book, and I was very happy to sign it.

Back in Kabul, two FBI agents took me for pizza. The Taliban had warned me about talking to the government, but I did it anyway. "We're going to get these guys," said the lead agent. Fazul and Ahmed Shah came to the embassy with my mail. I watched them looking at me. Fazul gave me my cell phone. He got it from Shahwali's father. "We tracked him down," he said. "There was a lot that he had to tell you." Other men came to see me, in their late twenties or early thirties, wore jeans, slouched when they walked in, and didn't ask me any questions, just listened. My instincts said CIA. Fazul said he would come back the next day. I felt closer to him than to the men around me.

That evening the acting ambassador asked me if I wanted to talk to him over a stiff drink. I didn't want to tell him that I didn't drink and I was afraid, too, that he would judge me for going with the Taliban. The FBI had a room for me and I slept a few hours, woke before dawn, and went for a walk on the embassy grounds. Afghanistan was outside those walls, but I was afraid of it now.

I met with other men, but only one man, from the Defense Intelligence Agency, seemed to grasp what I had to say and wanted to learn.

A woman in a white dress came in, like an angel. The State Department wanted to issue a statement to the media, and she needed my signature. She put papers down in front of me. I realized that the world would know all about my kidnapping, and that I had been living in the mountains, had crossed into Pakistan—everything I had tried to keep secret for so long: from Pakistan, from other journalists, from the US government, everyone, afraid that I would get caught, and killed or thrown in prison. I signed the paper. Bob began to read it. "I'm no friend of the media," he said, "but shouldn't CBS have the right to announce this?" I didn't know then but a lot had passed between CBS and the FBI.

I wanted to ignore him, but I had to defer to the FBI. I felt darkness come over me and the remaining joy and strength I had felt coming back out through the mountains disappeared. I told the woman that I wanted to think a minute. I called the CBS Bureau in London and asked for Bryn. He was in Islamabad. I realized that he was there because I had been kidnapped, that CBS had set up an operation, which appeared to have included Bryn Padrig, Michael Semple, Fazul, and Nafay. I talked to Jennifer Siebens, the London bureau chief, and thanked her for helping me. I told her about the statement. It was up to me, she said. The State Department wanted to hold a news conference in Washington.

I went back and crossed out my signature that would give the State Department permission to announce my release. I would have to keep everything secret. It made me feel dark and angry. I had just begun a long journey into another world of darkness, and deception.

I called Sophie in New York. "It's so good to hear your voice," she said warmly. Based upon what Bob, the FBI agent, had said about CBS, and on Jennifer's instruction that I should call Sophie, I assumed that she, not the government, was in charge in getting me out of captivity. "I understand that you were in charge," I said, not knowing what that meant. I was upset that I didn't get out myself. I felt weak, like a victim. "Thank you for all that you did for me."

"We'll talk about that when you get back. I'm just happy you're out. Come home safely," Sophie said. I didn't want to go back. I would be under her control and everyone else's now. I said that I wanted to stay and she all but shouted at me. Of course, I was coming back. She had seen before I left what I could not.

I felt warmer and more comfortable in Kabul than I did in New York. I called an Afghan friend in Kabul. She was quiet. "You're still alive," she said softly. "Nancy said that they cleaned out your room at the Gandamack." Nancy was Nancy Dupree, whom I loved, in a way. "She said that they only clean out the rooms of those who died."

Nancy, the last person I talked to before I left with Shahwali and Razi Gul to cross the border, called me in Jalalabad and told me that President Karzai had approved her request that I had taken to him, for land at Kabul University to build a library and study center. The Afghanistan Centre now graces the campus. It will be her legacy and that of her husband, Louis Dupree, who welcomed me and whom I admired, and who represented, like Nancy, the warmth and romance of this ancient land.

⁙ ⁙ ⁙

Bob and John and I stood in the front of the Great Seal of the United States on the embassy wall and people took our picture. There were FBI agents all around, everyone happy. Bob and John and I flew to Dubai, but I was afraid of the Taliban's reach there. We caught our flight to New York and they debriefed me on the plane and said I was fine. Bob said that CBS and maybe others would be at the airport.

The FBI and New York policemen met our flight and escorted me through passport control. Onlookers saw a skinny bearded man struggling to hold up his pants. We entered a room and I sat at a table with a dozen men. A man next to me welcomed me home and said I was safe. I thanked him. A man across from me said that there were messages from the Taliban on my answering machine. They wanted to know if I recognized the voices and if I could tell them what they were saying. They said that Sophie was coming for me, but asked me to go with them instead. I had to go with her. We stood outside waiting. Eventually Sophie came out of a crowd, alone. She gave me a long, warm hug and I hugged her back. We walked away and she called on her phone and we stood by the curb. I was just another man now at the airport waiting for a car.

We rode into the city. She didn't want to talk, she wanted me to recover first. I felt warm but awkward sitting next to her, my boss who had apparently invested so much in getting me out. But I didn't know for sure if she had rescued me. I knew so little, and was haunted by this—and that I had betrayed Din Mohammad by going into the mountains with Abdullah. Sophie said that she had received a call from London and learned that I had been kidnapped and that they had to keep it secret. The FBI came to see her and wanted to know all about me. The Taliban, or whoever they were, had sent a ransom note to my apartment, which the FBI picked up right away.

It was the letter I had written to my make-believe wife. The Taliban had shined a blinding light in my eyes that night, and a man called me a donkey and they demanded $1.5 million and three of their comrades from Guantanamo in exchange for me, but I told them, in despair, that the US would not negotiate, nor would it release prisoners. I thought it was a death sentence. They said later that night that they were lowering the price to $1 million and I was briefly happy. I felt I would live. A man brought out a clean sheet of white paper from inside his shawl and told me to write to my wife and tell her. I decided to make a friend, for purposes of survival, my wife. I wrote to her and referred in the letter, to show that it was from me, to the place where we met. They faxed it to my home. The FBI, which could tell from the fax where it was sent from, later told me that they sent assets to the public call station, but they arrived too late.

Sophie continued. "I called your friend Zalmay Khalilzad, but he would only talk to me through his assistant. I called your friend Elliot Abrams, but he was in Saudi Arabia with Condoleezza Rice. His assistant said he was too busy to help. I called Richard Perle. He called back immediately and told me to get the army involved. He was helpful."

Khalilzad was now the US ambassador to the UN. Elliot Abrams and I had served on Senator Henry Jackson's staff. He was now on the National Security Council to President George W. Bush. Richard Perle also worked for Senator Jackson. He became an assistant secretary of defense under President Reagan, chairman of the Defense Policy Board under President Bush, and was with the American Enterprise Institute, a think tank in Washington.

I later called and wrote to all three men. Only Perle, known as the prince of darkness in Washington for his conservative, hardline politics, would talk to me, and show compassion. Abrams said in an e-mail that he didn't know anything about my kidnapping. Khalilzad didn't respond.

When I met my editor at Times Books after my return, he stared at me, his face reflecting concern but also something else, I thought. He had another meeting. "The FBI came to see me," he said. He wanted me to write about what he called the "fifty days": three days in, forty-five in captivity, and two out. I was to do it immediately. He didn't want me to forget, but more than that I felt he was worried because he had given me a big advance and I got kidnapped. I left feeling cold and angry.

Bryn Padrig called from London to check on me and said, "Michael Semple saved your life." He would say this more than once. I vowed to go to Perth or Johannesburg, the farthest places on the planet, if necessary, to find Semple—the former UN employee who had called me, along with Bryn, the night I crossed back into Afghanistan—and thank him.

A few days after I returned I went down, as I promised I would, to the Federal Building in lower Manhattan to see the FBI. The men were friendly and we sat around a table and I talked and answered their questions. Then an agent across the table who came up from Washington stood up and showed me my ransom letter encased now in a plastic sleeve in a binder. I didn't want to look at it. "Why did you fly to Morocco in 2006?" he asked. I realized that they didn't fully trust me. "I was the Afghan consultant on the movie *Charlie Wilson's War*," I responded, happy to prove that I wasn't the enemy. I told them about the ransom demands and the three men they wanted back from Guantanamo. The lead agent rode with two other agents and I went in an FBI car back to my apartment and the lead agent came upstairs and I looked through my notebook and found the names of the men from Guantanamo and he copied them down in his notebook. I, the kidnap victim, had suddenly become, it appeared, the intermediary in a bigger negotiation.

They took me then to the airport and along the way asked me about Haqqani and Hekmatyar. One agent said that some of Hekmatyar's people were still in Queens but were older now. I thought of Hekmatyar's death threat to me in 1984 and the call I received from the Committee to Protect Journalists asking if I would write an op-ed article in the *New York Times*, and that I, afraid then of his men in Queens, had said no.

I flew to Seattle to see my sister. Her son Luke was returning from visiting his brother, Rory, in college, and would be arriving at the airport about the same time. I should wait for him at the gate. Luke walked off the plane smiling, taller now, a gangling fifteen-year-old, like a nervous colt, and he took my bag and walked with me. It was all I wanted. I got in the back of my sister's SUV and she said hello. I sat quietly while she and Luke talked.

They had horses and I went riding with her husband and one of his friends in a forest north of Seattle and ate by a stream, but I didn't want to rough it anymore. Annaliese, my niece, came home from college and my sister made a big dinner and I ate like a teenager. The next day she told me about the calls from the FBI and the State Department. She couldn't believe that I had been kidnapped. She had to keep quiet. She went for long walks; the fear that I was being tortured, that was the hardest thing. She told herself that if I died that I was doing what I loved. I was sorry that I put her through that.

"Sophie called every day and cried," she said. "She was doing everything she could to help you. We didn't tell Dad. I formed a small prayer group." The next morning, I sat at her dining room table, looking at the evergreens, her lawn, the pond beyond it with a beaver dam, and I began to write. "Why is everything so secret?" she asked. "There has been nothing in the news. Why don't you go on television and talk about your kidnapping?" She told me to call Sophie but when I did she insisted, probably rightly, that I was in no shape to go on television. I would have to keep my story inside of me. I ran through the woods on her property, and cried for the first time. I was home.

I flew to Spokane, rented a car, and drove to Sandpoint, Idaho, to see my brother. He gave me a big hug and I saw pictures of me on his refrigerator. My nieces came rushing downstairs and hugged me too and I cried. I briefly told my story at dinner. "Stockholm Syndrome," said Kody gently. A Dutch doctor who worked in Afghanistan in the 1980s for Médecins sans Frontières had said in 2007 in Kabul, "All the old-timers love the Taliban." Peter Jouvenal had said the same thing: "If my wife would let me, and I didn't have children, I would go hang out with the Taliban." It was the romance of the past.

I was playing one evening with my nephew's dog, Joey. I threw a tennis ball in the snow and he brought it back. My cell phone rang. It was Bill, the FBI agent who sat next to me at the airport in New York and said "welcome home." "Where are you?" he asked. I told him. Joey barked. "Is that a Lab?" How did he know this? It was his FBI training. There was someone he wanted me to see. I will call her Rochelle. I said no.

Sophie gave me the name of a man who worked with journalists who had been traumatized in war. I said I was fine but agreed to call him, for her. He asked if I jumped when I heard a car backfire. It was helicopters that really bothered me. I didn't tell him that I clenched when I got a haircut and the barber took out a razor blade. He talked about emotional stress and said that, like running, I had to get back in shape. I must not be unrealistic about what happened. It was how business was done. I needed calmness and to be grounded. Rochelle called the following evening. She had a warm, melodious voice.

I took the train to Vancouver, Washington, to see my father. I took him to breakfast and offered to pray. He looked at me with surprise, but he didn't eat. After he went to bed early I sat at the dining room table and looked down at the Columbia, with Mt. Hood, in Oregon, to the east and Portland on the south bank, the big city when I was a boy, which my father considered decadent, and which my mother loved.

❖ ❖ ❖

AFTER I RETURNED to New York Shahwali began to call. It was too early to register with me, but I would learn that a kidnapping never ends. Every day it was in the back of my mind, sometimes in small ways, when I read about Afghanistan or Iraq in the news, or in larger ways, when a man questioned my patriotism and hinted that I was a traitor for going with the Taliban, or in serious ways that would come later. Shahwali kept calling, saying that he was in trouble and that my neck was his neck until finally, in anger, I refused to pick up the phone.

I gathered myself to go to the CBS offices for the first time. A friend silently escorted me into the newsroom and as I approached Sophie's office, Terri Stewart, the deputy national editor, hugged me and I broke down. I went into Sophie's office. "I was afraid of this," she said. Bill Felling, the national editor, came in and we shook hands. "Welcome home. I've never had a worse spring, we were all so worried. Sophie went to Mass every night to pray for you."

Bill left and Sophie and I sat there. I felt closer to her than to any other woman in my life. Very few people at CBS knew anything about this, she said. Those who did know kept it quiet. Jeff Fager, the head of *60 Minutes*, wanted to see me. I was in no state, she advised, to go on television, "not yet." I went across the street to Jeff's office. Scott Pelley was there and Bill Owens, the executive editor. I told them a simplified version of the story of my kidnapping and cried briefly, rubbing my hands over my legs. I felt weak, like a child.

"I was trying to get to Jalaluddin Haqqani," I said simply, "because he would know about bin Laden." I explained that every man I met, including my jailer, said that bin Laden was being kept by the Pakistani government. "We have to figure out how to do this," said Fager, meaning how to tell my story. "We have correspondents out there and we can't have them become targets."

"Everyone is going to want to know how you got out," remarked Pelley. I assumed that it was clearly CBS that was responsible. "There are correspondents here who want to do this story. Let us work that out," said Owens. I knew that I had to protect CBS. I sent Jeff Fager a note the next day and said that they didn't have to do the story. I was giving CBS a way out. He didn't respond. Pelley, who kept a list in his desk of all CBS people who had been killed, took me to dinner. I sent a note to Sean McManus, the president of CBS News, and he wrote back to say that he was glad I was out and would see me sometime. I went to Paul Friedman's office, the new senior vice president, part of a new team when Katie Couric was hired as the new anchor. His door was open. He looked up, surprised. "I just want to say thank you," I said. "We didn't do anything," he responded. "It was all Sophie. We just followed her."

I walked away defeated. Only a few friends had cared. I understood, but the US public didn't know or was not interested to know, that the United States was giving billions of dollars to the Pakistani army, which was backing the Taliban and al-Qaeda. "We may be fighting the wrong enemy in the wrong country," Richard Holbrooke, US Special Representative for Afghanistan and Pakistan, told British ambassador Sherard Cowper-Coles,[1] meaning that the US and its allies should be focusing on Pakistan, not fighting the Taliban in Afghanistan. Carlotta Gall, who covered Afghanistan and Pakistan for the *New York Times* from 2002 to 2011, wrote in *The Wrong Enemy*, her book on Afghanistan: "He [Afghan president Hamid Karzai] had long realized that no administration in Washington was going to make Pakistan cease its support for the Taliban. Pakistan continued to ignore U.S. requests that it do more against the militants on its soil, and the United States was evidently not prepared to use greater pressure. Pakistan was, after all, a nuclear-armed country of 180 million Muslims and in the scale of things much more important than much smaller, impoverished, Afghanistan."[2]

Pakistan, in time, would become the center of my search for the truth behind my kidnapping. In the meantime, in 2008, Shahwali still called me, again and again.

I had coffee with Ana Real, the deputy foreign editor, who looked at me, as others did, to see if I was different. "I got my hands dirty," she said, working on my case, but she wouldn't elaborate. I felt that it had to do with money, and wondered why, but I didn't ask. She had sent me to see the man the day I left to begin my trip almost ten months ago, whom I was sure was an ISI agent at the Pakistani consulate. I felt she was simply naïve about who he was, and was trying to help me, but I was upset that she may have compromised me from the start. But I blamed myself, too, for talking to him too much. "Sophie went to Sean McManus and he asked if you were on assignment for CBS." His first concern was the company. Ana said that Sophie then called a wealthy female friend of mine whom I had introduced to Ana, but she, in shock, declined to help. Sophie then called the president of the Carnegie Council, but the Council, too, was unable to help. "Sophie said, 'We're doing this,' and she took over." Ana said that she and Melissa, who worked at the Carnegie Council, had tried to help me. I believed her, but I sensed that my kidnapping was not as simple as people thought.

I ran into Bob Simon, the *60 Minutes* correspondent, on the street outside CBS and told him that I had been kidnapped. He had been captured by Saddam Hussein's men in 1991 and held for forty days, and I wanted to talk to him. He lowered his head and said emotionally, "You never get over it. You never stop thinking about it." He didn't want to talk anymore, and I understood. A kidnapping changes a person in unforeseen ways. It is primal, life or death, and too personal: it reveals a man in his most naked form. Every survivor understands the other. It is a strange brotherhood, but you keep the most important things to yourself or share them only with someone you love and trust.

⁘ ⁘ ⁘

A MONTH AFTER I was released I finally called Rochelle, the therapist, and went to her office. "Come in and sit down," she said warmly. "Can I give you some pills?" It was her first question. A prescription pad lay next to her. I stood there, afraid. She was the FBI and wanted to give me pills. Were they to make me talk or to feel better? I declined her offer but I began to talk to her. I had no one else to talk to. I asked about payment but she wouldn't take money. The Department of Justice provided funds for this, but still she refused the government money. It didn't feel right. I returned the following week, and the week after, and soon she urged me to come twice a week. We talked for two hours each time.

I received an invitation to attend an event in New York for Nancy Dupree, who was giving a talk to raise money for her library. "Don't go," advised Rochelle. "You're not ready." I went anyway and sat in the back. David Rohde of the *New York Times*, whom I became friends with in Afghanistan before I was taken, came in and we sat together. His girlfriend, Kristen, came and sat with us. He knew about my kidnapping. He had sent me a warm e-mail from Kabul after I was released. "You've shaved," said Nancy, and we hugged one another. All the Afghan hands in New York were there, it seemed, but I felt alone and separate and left early, feeling sad, realizing that Rochelle was right.

Bill, the FBI Victim Specialist, called on occasion, and we met for lunch. "Many people get kidnapped and you never hear about them," he said, advising me indirectly to be grateful and to keep quiet. But I felt that there was poison slowly seeping through me.

In May Bryn Padrig called from London. Sean Langan and his fixer Sharif, who had worked for me, had been kidnapped by the Taliban in Pakistan. He asked if I would talk with Sean's producer at Channel 4 to give him some guidance on what to do, and to Sean's ex-wife, Annabel, the mother of their two sons.

Why were they so foolish to keep working on the border after I had been kidnapped? They, too, like so many journalists, thought that they were invulnerable. I told Rochelle about Bryn's call. "You're not ready for this. It could damage you," she said again thoughtfully. But I had to help Sean. His producer called from Channel 4 and said that Sean had a visa for Pakistan and that he and Sharif had driven from Peshawar into the Tribal Areas, reached the house where they were going to stay, when their hosts took them hostage.

How could he drive through the checkpoints in the Tribal Areas? No foreigner could do that unless he had contacts in the Pakistani army. I was impressed. Sean's producer asked how to rescue kidnap victims. He said that Sharif called his son, who called a man in London, who called someone at Channel 4. They called the number back and it went directly to Sharif.

We didn't have any phones in captivity. Who was this intermediary in London? The producer didn't know what to make of it. I thought of the time I sat with Sharif and Razi Gul, and Sharif demanded that I pay him only in crisp fifty-or hundred-dollar bills. Annabel called. She said that she was a former journalist and felt sorry for me that I couldn't talk. She was the first person to express empathy and I liked her warmth and her love for Sean. "He is a soldier," she said, "and when he comes home I am going to do everything I can to be sure that he gets a parade. I am going to get all the publicity I can for him."

On June 21, Sean and Sharif were released. The executive producer of the weekend edition of the *CBS Evening News* asked if I would talk about it on television. I had to say no. Sean called to thank me for talking with Annabel. I read that he had lost five teeth in captivity. "I thought of you when we were in that cell. I would look out the window and wonder how close your cell was to mine," he said kindly. I forgave him for calling me a spy. We were part of a small family now. Sean said that Sharif had a nervous breakdown in captivity. The communists had imprisoned him when he was ten. I asked about Sharif, but Sean said that Sharif had nothing to do with his kidnapping. I kept quiet, but I didn't trust Sharif after my experiences with him. It was strange that his kidnappers allowed him to keep his phone, and that he was in contact while in captivity with someone in London.

I kept returning to what Bryn Padrig had said on the phone. "The FBI didn't do anything. It was Michael Semple who saved your life." I called Michael and he said that he was coming to Washington.

Chapter 9

Michael Semple

SUDDENLY THERE HE WAS, AT THE DUPONT CIRCLE HOTEL (THEN called the Jury's), smiling broadly, a solidly built, sandy-haired man about six foot one with his arms out. He had a good unkempt beard, blue eyes, and he exuded warmth and well-being. Semple had an enthusiasm about him that was infectious. We went for a walk outside. A woman walking toward us stopped and commented on the intensity of our conversation. Semple told her about the importance of Afghanistan, and bringing peace there, and gave her his e-mail address.

I wanted to learn about my kidnapping. I felt the best place to start was with Semple. We hadn't talked since he had called me just after I was released. No one, including Sophie, would talk about my case at CBS. The FBI wouldn't tell me anything. There was a drone over our cell for over a month. I asked Bob, the FBI agent, if it was to watch for me, or to watch the Taliban who were coming and going. "I brought all assets into play," he responded, but did not elaborate. Another time he said, "I had guns pointed at me, trying to save you." I questioned this. If men had guns trained on him, that could only mean that he was out in the countryside along the border looking for me, with other FBI agents and maybe also with US soldiers, facing the Taliban directly, and no one there—FBI agent, US soldier, or Taliban—would have backed down. People would have talked about this. He wouldn't say any more. Bryn Padrig, who reported to Sophie, would not talk. Fazul and Nafay were in Afghanistan and Pakistan. I had nowhere to turn except to Semple.

Semple was Irish, married to a Pakistani, spoke fluent Dari, Pashto, and Urdu, and lived on a farm outside of Islamabad. He didn't have a lot of time to talk, he said, but we would make a start. He had a meeting soon that afternoon at the US Institute of Peace, a federally funded nonpartisan think tank, with people involved in Afghanistan who wanted to hear what he had to report, and the next day with Vice President Cheney's office. All this, on his first visit ever to America, he said. He was an important man.

As we walked, I asked why President Karzai kicked him out of Afghanistan. Every foreigner in the country knew that he had been expelled. He had worked in Afghanistan since the 1990s for NGOs, the EU, and the UN. After 9/11, he was part of the UN team at the Bonn conference. From 2004 to 2008 he was the deputy to the EU's Special Representative for Afghanistan. Yet President Karzai declared Semple and Mervyn Patterson, a British expert on northern Afghanistan, persona non grata; on December 27, 2007, they left the country. Patterson disappeared from public view.

A government spokesman said, "The government of Afghanistan had received reports that the two individuals were involved in activities that were not consistent with their original activities and they were engaged in unauthorized activities."

"Michael was expelled," said the BBC, "for arrogantly behaving like a Great Game–era political officer. An intelligence officer said that Michael 'has the appearance of a man who could have stepped out of 19th Century.'"

I loved this. There were few men like him anymore. I recalled seeing him for the first time, although I didn't know then who it was, dressed in Afghan clothes and walking confidently, unlike other Westerners who wore Western clothes, down a hallway in a diplomat's house last fall at a birthday party for Nancy Dupree. The BBC asked Francis Vendrell, the EU Special Representative in Kabul and Semple's boss, what he was doing at Musa Qala. "Quite honestly, I don't know," he replied.

I asked Lucy Morgan Edwards, an Englishwoman then working for the UN in Kabul and who became a journalist and author, about Semple. "I was told that he was placed in that position by the British government," she said, "and that his paycheck came from London, not the UN." She was implying that he was a spy.

Semple and I kept walking. "Being declared persona non grata has made my life very difficult. I have a contract from Cambridge University Press to write a book on Afghanistan and it is hard to do if I can't be in the country."

"Bryn Padrig said that the FBI didn't do anything but that you saved my life," I said. I embarrassed him and he was quiet. We reached Connecticut Avenue. "I hear that you have a tie to MI6," I said, referring to British intelligence. I had asked this too quickly. He didn't answer. I walked with him to the US Institute of Peace. We agreed to meet back at the hotel and go to dinner. "I've never had sushi," he said. I said that I knew a place in Georgetown. We talked that evening over sushi about Afghanistan. I said how much I liked Hajji Din Mohammad. "He's a wonderful man, isn't he?" he said. This drew me closer to him. We didn't discuss my kidnapping. "We'll meet tomorrow," he said.

The next afternoon, I waited by a Metro station. A car pulled up and a thin, striking South Asian woman in a colorful dress waved me over. A man was driving. Michael was in the backseat. We drove to a white wood-frame house on a quiet street. We had dinner and then Michael and I went to the living room. He opened his laptop. "I learned that you had been spending a lot of time with Mirwais Yasini. That's where I started."

It is where I had started also. I wondered how he knew to start there, but I kept quiet.

Semple continued: "Everyone involved, Fazul, and Nafay, and others just didn't talk about you as their friend, but they loved you. I had never seen anything like that in my experiences in other kidnappings."

I was quiet. I felt unworthy. "We did everything possible to prevent a second Daniel Pearl." I was the next American journalist taken in Pakistan after him. "You have no idea of the ripple effects that come from a kidnapping." I sat there reflecting upon this. "Mullah Malang called Abdullah to his house in Islamabad and grabbed him by the ear and told him to get you out and not harm you. There was a balance of power between the kidnappers and him."

So, Mullah Malang had a house in Pakistan. Why would he, an Afghan, have a house there? Pakistan was the enemy, backing the Taliban. I let it go. Malang was helping me. That's what counted.

I felt that Abdullah was not in control of me, and that another group had taken over, or that other people were directing the Maulvi, the man whom I thought, initially, was in charge, the man who led the attack, the man who interrogated me in captivity and who directed the mock executions, and who said that Abdullah was trying to find me. The Maulvi had congratulated me too many times for escaping death. "You were taken captive by a criminal group, not by the Taliban," insisted Semple. He was saying that the Maulvi and his men were criminals disguised as the Taliban to confuse me.

"Then why did they tell me that I had to convert if I ever wanted to be released; why did they preach to me and tell me to repent for my sins? Why did they force me to pray five times a day?" I asked. I didn't believe that criminals would be so religious.

"It sounds like they played their role very well," Semple replied simply. He felt it was a way to make money. "Both Mullah Malang and I felt that Abdullah could wind it down any time he wanted to."

Semple continued. "I sent someone to Sirajuddin Haqqani to ask if he had you and he said he didn't." I had been laboring to get to Haqqani, yet Michael could get, indirectly it seems, to his son Sirajuddin, the most lethal of all Taliban commanders.

Semple said that there were criminal networks in Peshawar who lived by kidnappings. It was forbidden in Islam, but these networks were patronized by the Taliban. There were sixty-four kidnappings in Peshawar in 2008 already, mostly family members of doctors. Even the son of Hazrat Ali, the powerful commander whom the CIA had hired to capture or kill bin Laden, had been kidnapped. The Trade spared no one. They had negotiated the price down for his son to $60,000.

I knew about this kidnapping. On May 9, five weeks after I was released, gunmen broke into Hazrat Ali's house, killed his father, and kidnapped his wife and children. I wondered if my kidnapping was related.

"An Afghan, even your best friend, is only going to tell you the truth eighty percent of the time," said Semple. "Sean Langan was never in danger. With you the kidnappers were performing a totally unauthorized operation. You were being held in Mohmand Agency. I sent someone to Waziristan and he came back to tell me that Sean and Sharif were in Bajaur Agency. All the systemic information was a characteristic of Sean's group." He meant that Sean and Sharif's kidnappers were part of the kidnapping industry and that Sean and Sharif had been held by criminals in the northern part of the Tribal Areas, above Mohmand Agency. This, too, would become important information in the future.

I asked Semple how he had become involved in my case. "Bryn Padrig contacted me. Fazul, Nafay, and I met at my home. We called it the Islamabad Shura (*shura* means "council"). It was strawberry season. Bryn flew in and we began to task people to do different jobs. Bryn brought in Sami Yousafzai. Gohar Zaman, an old Pakistani policeman, was brought in. Your investigation will not be complete until you talk with him. There is also his brother-in-law, whom he brought in to deal with the kidnappers. We began to identify all the people involved. Who are they answerable to and who can we get to put pressure on them? We got a hold of your phone and went through it.

"I began to deal with the people who set this up," Semple continued. "Abdullah began to emerge as a key figure. Mullah Malang confirmed he was. Fazul went to Shahwali's family in Peshawar and Jalalabad. They said that Shahwali was innocent of any involvement in your kidnapping, and then Fazul came back to them with other information and their story collapsed. He was not innocent. We had multiple lines to Abdullah and found that he—that is, Abdullah—had arranged the phone calls for the kidnappers. All his associates were from Landi Khotal."

I knew then only what Fazul had told me in Feridoun's SUV as we drove to the army base, and that was that they, meaning Fazul and the others who helped get me released, thought that Shahwali was involved. Again I saw Fazul glance at Shahwali once in anger and keep his distance from him. "There is so much I have to tell you," he said, as we sat in the embassy. The FBI was around us. We didn't have any time alone before I had to leave Kabul for Dubai and the US.

Semple said that he found a man who said that Abdullah had fallen in with bad company. Shahwali had whispered to me that Samad, one of my bodyguards who had betrayed me in captivity, was part of Abdullah's clan.

One afternoon, Gulob said that another Taliban commander needed a new kidney and that maybe they would take mine. I imagined them tying me down to a cot before a small, round man came in carrying a leather bag, opened it, and took out a syringe. When I woke up there was a bandage over my stomach and one of my kidneys was gone. "No," I said, when Gulob left, "I will not allow this." I paced the dirt floor of our cell, back and forth, like crazed animal in a cage. "I'm leaving tonight. I am going to escape," I said. There were too many stories in this land of young boys being kidnapped and found dead by a road with their kidneys gone. It was one of the ugliest parts of kidnapping, the illegal worldwide organ trafficking and kidnapping business;[3] indirectly, I would learn, part of the Trade.

Every time the door opened and a guard came in, I looked up to see if I could catch a glimpse outside. I knew, from the direction that we prayed every night, which way was southwest, toward Mecca. I needed to go West through the mountains to Afghanistan. I could run, but how long could I last?

After our last prayer, we were allowed outside for a few minutes in the dark, under a covering, to use a makeshift toilet. Samad was gone for ten minutes, too long. Later, Gulob, our main jailer, came up to me. "If you try to escape, I will come after you like a dog," he said. Samad had told him. In my mind, I saw him that night, in the dark, across the cell, covered with blood. I had never wanted to harm someone, but I did that night. He who told me that his family, meaning Abdullah's family, was at war with Din Mohammad's family, and that they had killed nine people and wounded ten.

Maybe, I thought then, Abdullah and his gang were criminals, as Semple said, which meant that CBS, if it did ransom me, paid money to criminals, not terrorists. Was it more acceptable to pay ransom to criminals than to terrorists? Yes. In the US, no one would think twice about paying ransom to a criminal to save someone's life. The police could later catch the criminal. But this was murkier. A terrorist could strike again. There was a fine line sometimes between criminals and the Taliban. But Malang said that Abdullah was with the Taliban, and Semple had just said that my kidnapping was authorized Taliban activity, implying that the Taliban were involved. He also said that I was held by Abdul Wali, the emir—in other words, the leader—of the Taliban in Mohmand Agency. My jailer, Gulob, said that their leader was Abdul Wali, but I didn't know the truth.

I was cast into a world of mirrors, a labyrinth of lies and misinformation, all designed, I was convinced, to confuse me. I *was* confused. No one else cared, but I did and I needed to figure this out, and it was this journey that would lead me to a conclusion that was more frightening than I ever imagined.

Semple was still talking: Abdullah had a house in Dir, a district north of Peshawar in Mohmand Agency. He was a Mohmand, so Semple had gone to someone senior to him in his tribe to put pressure on him.

It sounded like Abdullah, with his houses and property, was a wealthy man.

Just as I was beginning to wonder if Sean Langan's case and mine were linked, Semple added, "I got Sean and Sharif out. Sharif's driver's uncle and another man were behind it."

Sharif's driver's uncle was Hajji, the smuggler, and the other man was probably Hajji's friend Qorie, the Taliban commander—the same two men who took me, with Sharif, into Mohmand Agency. "I know these men," I told Semple. "I went into Mohmand Agency with Sharif, and the two men, Hajji and Qorie, last September."

I didn't tell Semple that two months after that I'd gone with Hajji, Aziz, and Sharif up into the mountains south of Tora Bora and met with the Taliban. I realized that I had introduced Hajji, a car and drug smuggler, to the world of human smuggling. Perhaps I was responsible for Sean's kidnapping. Channel 4 paid to get Sean and Sharif out. After the news came out, Parliament debated and the British media discussed whether Britain should pay ransom to kidnappers or not. Sean talked about this in an interview.[4] Semple and I agreed that Hajji and Qorie could have taken Sean through the checkpoints in the Tribal Areas. Hajji would have paid off the guards. They were part of his network. He had to take his smuggled cars through there to reach Pakistan proper and China. Years later, Sean would tell me a different version.

"It is a different world now from when the British were here," Semple mused. "Tribal power has been diluted. There is a social revolution going on. Militant networks, linked to mosques, want to turn society upside down and to put militants, and not tribal leaders, in power. They raise money from Karachi to Riyadh. The tribal networks and the militant networks are competing for power. Abdullah, therefore, was not as answerable to his tribe. He owns land now in Nangarhar. If he owned land on his tribe's traditional lands in Mohmand Agency, he would have been answerable to the tribe. We"—and by this Michael meant the CBS team—"nonetheless went to Feridoun, who is from a distinguished Mohmand family, and he exerted pressure on Abdullah."

Feridoun was the man who handed me Fazul's CBS ID card and his letter just after I was released, and who took me, with his driver, to the US Army base in Jalalabad. Sami Yousafzai would tell me in the future that Gohar Zaman had sent the ransom money to Feridoun, not to the Taliban. Gohar Zaman sounded like he was much more than an old policeman, as Semple described him. As he said, my investigation would not be complete until I saw Gohar Zaman. Even then, it would not be complete, but would become even more mysterious.

"It's an Afghan Casino Royale," Semple added, referring to the Ian Fleming novel in which James Bond, in his first mission, must find and then defeat in a card game an arms dealer who finances terrorists, entering a world where no one can trust anyone. I thought I understood, but I didn't; neither did I realize how right Semple was—or that in time I would learn that I didn't know who I could trust at all, and that included people I thought were my friends.

It was getting late. Semple promised to show me his notes the next day. The next morning, we met in a coffee shop by my hotel and he gave me a map he had drawn to show the region where he felt I had been held and the route my kidnappers took leading me in, and the route they took to return me. He didn't seem to have any other notes, at least none that he wanted to share. I wanted more information but I understood, too. He wanted to keep his sources secret. I would be the same way.

⁂ ⁂ ⁂

In August, I went out West to see my father again. I drove up the Columbia Gorge, beyond which the land turned to desert and became for me Indian country. "When you talk to an Indian, ask the name of his tribe," he told me as a boy. "They are proud of their tribe." So too were the Mohmand, the Zadran, the Mesud, and the Waziris, and other Pashtun tribes.

My father went to bed early and I watched the Olympics in Beijing on television. He got up to sip a protein drink, the only thing he ate. I told him to sit and watch the Olympics. They were in China, where he had been after the Philippines. He wasn't interested and went back to bed. He woke up again after ten at night and I was in the kitchen. My father came in, his eyes bright. We stood across from one another. "Do you have to go back there?" he asked. We both knew where "there" was. "No," I said softly. "Can they reach out and grab you here?" he asked. "No," I said. He knew, somehow, that I had gone into the wild. "Good," he said.

My brother and sister and their families came and we had a birthday party for my father when he turned ninety-five. I took him to what he called "the mountain," a mall with a fancy coffee bar where everyone knew him and he could sit and chat with people. We sat at a table. "I was kidnapped by the Taliban," I said. He stared at me and then he looked down. I had to tell him. Two days later, I woke him up early. I had an early flight to go back East. He sat up in bed. "Are you coming back?" he asked softly. I said yes. "Good," he said.

Ten days later Kody called and I flew out to Portland the next morning. As we drove across the Columbia from the airport, he asked, "Are you ready for this?" I sat on the bed in my father's room. There were hymns from our childhood playing on a CD player. My father said he was tired. I said good night and that I would see him tomorrow. "I'm not sure I'll make it through the night," he replied. He said our mother's name, his wife of fifty-three years. His children were home. He died in his sleep.

⁜ ⁜ ⁜

I KEPT SEEING Rochelle. She talked about her family and I felt that I became, in time, the psychiatrist. We met late one afternoon and it stretched into the evening and she brought dinner for us. Twice, at her suggestion, we went to restaurants to hold our sessions there. A pattern was beginning.

Sophie said that CBS had decided it would never broadcast my story. She reiterated that they needed to protect their people, who would be targets if news ever got out. I understood but I felt bitterness now as well as gratitude, not just for the decision, but more than that for the way I was being treated. No one would tell me anything about what had happened on the outside. All I wanted was for someone to tell me the story, and to receive recognition for what I had been doing all those months in the mountains and for being captured by the Taliban, or whoever they were. And I wanted a bit of respect. I felt like I was being shunned. I was extremely fortunate in so many ways, and extremely grateful, so I was upset with myself that I wanted recognition. I felt as if I were trying to promote myself, even though as a boy I had been taught God would punish me for such things. It was better to be humble like my father. Still, it was hard for me to go on as if nothing had happened. I felt like an outsider from the whole world. I wanted people to know. I wanted redemption even though I wasn't sure what that meant, but instead I was forced into silence. Anger, like sludge in a river, slowly seeped into me.

What CBS couldn't say aloud but what CBS people told me was that at the CBS bureau in London Bryn Padrig brought cash to Pakistan as part of the effort to save my life, to prevent a second Daniel Pearl. "What are you going to do if airport security stops you?" a colleague asked. "Tell them the truth," Padrig responded. He landed in Rawalpindi where Nafay arranged for him, I was told, to go directly to the VIP lounge, and there she and Fazul, who had come from Kabul, met him.

It would take me another six years before I could learn what happened after Bryn arrived. It was the beginning of when money met the Trade.

⁂ ⁂ ⁂

ON NOVEMBER 8, 2008, David Rohde of the *New York Times* and Tahir Luddin, his fixer, were in a car south of Kabul going to meet a member of the Taliban, Abu Tayyeb,[5] which, it turns out, was the nom de guerre of Mullah Atiquallah, whose real name, it appears, was Hajji Najubullah.[6] David and Tahir were kidnapped. Two friends in Kabul sent e-mails alerting me. I had to do something. I told Rochelle. "Stay away," she said. "It won't be good for you." I called Craig Whitney, who was the deputy foreign editor at the *Times* when I had first gone as a journalist to Afghanistan, now the assistant managing editor. He took me to lunch and I briefly told him the story. "Forty-five days is a long time," he told me. I told him about the drone. "You are lucky to be alive. CBS has really kept this quiet. We plan to do the same." I went with him back to the paper. "Are you ready?" he asked kindly as we stood outside an office. I met with a small group of people. "The kidnappers are calling David the Red Rooster. What does that mean?" a man asked.

"It means they're not going to kill him," I said. "They called me the Golden Goose. He is worth a lot of money to them." They needed to get Michael Semple involved. I told them what Bryn Padrig had told me about him. "Why is he doing this? What's in it for him?" asked David McCraw, the assistant legal counsel. I hadn't stopped to consider that. "I think he just wants to help people," I responded tamely. "I was told and he told me that he was involved in other kidnappings before mine."

I offered to talk to Kristen Mulvihill, to whom David was now married. Craig called and gave me her number. We agreed to meet at the Carnegie Council. I stood on the sidewalk and she came around the corner and we hugged one another. She needed comfort. I told her about Pashtun tribal codes and tried to convince her that nothing would happen to David. I told her about Michael Semple. "I want to do all I can to give David all the publicity in the world. I want to upgrade his Wikipedia page immediately," said Kristen, showing, like Annabel, Sean Langan's ex-wife, her love.

David's older brother, Lee, came down from New Hampshire. David had been kidnapped and held in Bosnia for ten days in the Bosnian war of independence in 1995. Now Lee, with his contacts, and Kristen prepared their plans to secure David's release. Lee would call Richard Holbrooke, who had negotiated David's freedom in 1995. I thought of my small family in the Northwest, following the government, keeping quiet.

"Sit back," said Craig Whitney to Kristen. "This is going to take a long time." Kristen called and thanked me for introducing her to Michael Semple.

⁜ ⁜ ⁜

KRISTEN LATER TOLD me that after David was kidnapped, the *Times* brought in Clayton Consultants and later the ASIC (American Security International Corporation), where Dewey Clarridge, a well-known former CIA agent, was a consultant. Kristen, on her own, met with Sophie at CBS seeking advice. The *Times* couldn't hire Kroll, the CBS security firm, because it did not have a contract with AIG, the *Times* insurer. The Trade embraced different security companies, some with questionable abilities, tied to insurance companies, all linked to Lloyds of London, all part of the growing international kidnapping and ransom industry. Kristen said, years later, that she wished she could have vetted everyone herself.

The Department of Defense called and asked Kristen if she and her family, and David's family, would approve a raid. Unsure exactly what that meant, she and her family asked a former special forces soldier and family friend, to explain. Again, they talked to the Defense Department.

⁂ ⁂ ⁂

A MONTH LATER Jack Cloonan, a former FBI counterintelligence agent who worked for a British security company, called and asked me to lunch. "I know about drug cartels in South America, but nothing about Pakistan. I need your help. We have no idea where David is being held," he said over his lasagna. General Petraeus said that with a drone they could see, within inches, where someone was, but no one knew where he was. I told him what I could. The *Times* had hired Duane "Dewey" Clarridge, he said, a flamboyant blowhard, in his view, a former CIA agent who had his own firm, reflecting the animosity between the FBI and the CIA. Clarridge claimed that his men had paid off some of the men guarding David. It was possible, but I didn't believe that any Pashtun tied to the Taliban would go against them for money. Clarridge told Fox News[7] that Bowe Bergdahl, the US soldier who had gone AWOL in Paktika Province, was captured by nomads. But Kuchis were isolated, simple people, who only, maybe, carried an old English rifle for protection against bandits or wild animals. I didn't know then that David was being held by the Haqqanis.

Shahwali kept calling, sometimes six or seven times a weekend, reminding me that his neck was my neck and that I promised to protect his children. He never asked for money, but wanted to harass me. He cried once and said that his mother made him go with the Tablighi Jamaat, the worldwide normally apolitical Muslim movement whose mission is to bring Muslims back to the fold of Islam. To me it was an admission of guilt and that his mother wanted him to repent for what he did. I remembered watching the three Tablighi walking down from Nawah Pass, smiling, their eyes filled with joy.

I had lunch with Bill from the FBI again. "Can the Taliban come after me here?" I asked. I was angry at Shahwali calling, forty to fifty times now. He had called my sister at 4:00 a.m. and cried. She felt sorry for him and said he was possibly mentally ill. He called Kody, too, and my sister-in-law was now worried about her children. My captors had taken my notebooks when I was captured, which contained all the numbers of those I felt had some money and could help ransom me. "No, they cannot get you here," said Bill. I asked about Rochelle. "She will take care of you. No one will look after you better."

I felt close to her because I talked to her more than to anyone else. I mentioned in a session that I wanted a piano. A week later she told me that a French woman who lived across the street from her had a baby grand piano and was returning to France and wanted to give it to the right person. Rochelle asked me to come to her home and we went to see the woman. I sat next to Rochelle and the woman asked what was going on. We looked like a couple. I took the piano and was grateful, but felt indebted, and trapped: by her, by the FBI, by CBS, by my publisher, by the Taliban. I had let Rochelle take over my life. I felt, because of my spiritual experience in captivity, that I was being led somewhere.

She wanted me to see a doctor friend of hers in Philadelphia but said that I wasn't strong enough to go alone and that she had to accompany me. When I said no, she said that we needed to go away for my health to a lodge she knew of in upstate New York. I knew it was wrong, but I didn't feel I could say no to her. She knew everything about me. I liked her, felt she had a good heart and was sharp and incisive, and she was the only person I could talk to. She got emotional, talking about her own life, coming into my room, wanting to be close, holding my hand, wanting more—and I felt that I had become the therapist. She said that I was experiencing what she called transference. This scared me.

Bob the FBI agent called from Washington and he and another agent assigned to my case came up to New York and took me to dinner and asked me to go with them back to Afghanistan. "We'll take a prosecuting attorney, find Shahwali and put him in Guantanamo, or, we'll whack him," said Bob. The two agents stared at me, waiting for my answer. Shahwali was harassing me, and I was angry, but I didn't want to go back there, or put Shahwali in prison, or kill him. I couldn't do that. I wasn't even sure what he did. Did he knowingly put himself in that cell for forty-five days, living in fear with the drone over us? He wanted to escape with me to a mosque, where he said we would be safe, but I didn't trust him. Yet Gulob, our jailer, said they were going to bring Shahwali's father in as collateral, and to send Shahwali to Kabul to negotiate our release with Fazul. It was the Trade. But then Gulob said that they didn't trust Shahwali. I didn't know if they were very good actors playing a part, or if they were Taliban, or both.

On December 13, Shahwali called and said he was in trouble. He cried for a good three minutes. He couldn't fake this, could he? He said that he was trapped by the ISI in Peshawar and by the NDS in Afghanistan. Fazul was trying to get to him. The ISI knew, he said, when he crossed the border to Pakistan, where he did not have papers. They might kill him and then I would have to support his children. I didn't believe him, but it was possible that the ISI could arrest him because he had worked for me. I felt an obligation and I didn't want him to die. I told Rochelle about his call. "He is manipulating you," she said. She invited me to her home for Christmas dinner. I felt cut off from other people and said yes.

Shahwali called on Christmas Eve. He may have been indirectly involved, he admitted for the first time, and asked where he should turn himself in. I asked where did his father get the money to buy land when we were in captivity? He said that his brother in Kuwait and his brother in Peshawar who was a carpenter gave the money to him. It was possible. He kept calling and I told Rochelle. She said that she would contact someone in the government and ask that they pick him up. There may be an operation going on tied to David Rohde. I pondered her statement about David. Who was she really, that she had contacts who could do this?

Shahwali sent an e-mail saying he was sorry and that he had gone to see Fazul after I returned to the US. He said that he had taken his father to see Razi Gul so that he would know him. So, I thought, his father and Razi Gul knew one another, but never let on in front of me, at breakfast. Sameer introduced them.

I was dumbfounded. Sameer, the woman who had been with Professor Amin when I went to see him, introduced him to Razi Gul? Was she behind this, a woman who grew up in a refugee camp in Pakistan and who now lived in Kabul? Bob, the FBI agent, wondered about her. I found her full name and phone numbers in my notes, but I had no desire to talk to her.

On February 2, 2009, John Solecki, an American with the UN High Commissioner for Refugees, was kidnapped outside his compound in Quetta, Baluchistan Province, Pakistan. A secular Baluch separatist group killed his driver and took Solecki away. I watched the video of him on television, blindfolded, pleading for help. At least the world knew of him.

On February 3, the *Wall Street Journal* published an article by Judea Pearl, Daniel Pearl's father, titled the "Normalization of Evil." Mr. Pearl wrote of his son's picture hanging on the wall in front of him in his office, and then he wrote, "But I find it hard to look him straight in the eyes and say you did not die in vain." "No," I said, when I read it, "your son did not die in vain. I am alive because of him." I knew that I had to write to the Pearls, but I couldn't do it yet. I didn't have the courage.

On April 4, John Solecki was released. I was thrilled for him.

Every day I thought of David Rohde in captivity. Jack Cloonan called again, and we met for lunch. Cloonan said that the military had ruled out a rescue attempt. The US (with all its assets) and two corporate security firms (one with help from a prominent former CIA agent and his alleged contacts), could not reach David.

They still didn't know where David was. His captors wanted $25 million but they were negotiating that down. "Petraeus said to pay the ransom," he said. I reflected upon this. The commanding general of US, NATO, and other allied forces in Afghanistan was advising them to secretly go against US hostage policy.

My captors had asked my name and my father's name. It was their first question. "The most important question in Afghanistan has always been 'Who was your grandfather?'" Rosanne Klass said. It was the power of the family and the tribe that radical Islam, like communism before it, wanted to destroy, to create a new, more equal world. I gave my name to my captors and said proudly for the first time: Wilmer Jerald Van Dyk. Before, I never liked my name. It was my father's name, yet I was different from him. But as the Maulvi filmed me that night and the man behind me to my right put his rifle to my temple, and as another man put his hand in his shirt to take out the knife, I wanted to be strong for my father. I instinctively pulled my right arm up to fight the man with the knife. They would kill me, but I would fight. It was the worst and proudest moment of my life. I never saw my father back down from anyone.

One Saturday morning when I was twelve, I went with my father in his pickup to the garage where he had his trucks serviced. The owner was his friend. He and his sons, who worked there, were friendly and I liked the roughness of that garage, as I liked my father's shop, where men, who were kind to me, worked skillfully with their hands. He liked men who had calluses on their hands. A part for an engine was late and the owner said it was like "waiting for the second coming of Christ."

"You know that I don't like that kind of talk," my father responded quietly. We finished and walked back to the truck. "Dare to be a Daniel," he said to me. It was the name of a hymn that we sang in our Assembly. We were to be like Daniel in the Lion's Den, to stand alone, for God, against the world, and to not be afraid. It would take me a lifetime to learn about physical courage, in that cell in the mountains, longer still to learn about moral courage.

On June 20 David Rohde and Tahir Luddin escaped from captivity in Pakistan. The news flashed around the world. *CBS Evening News* called and asked if I would go on air to talk about it. I said no. The *New York Times* said that it had not paid a ransom. "Clarridge didn't even know that David had escaped," David McCraw told me later.

David called when he was back in New York. It was dark and he got out of the taxi across the avenue. The light changed and we walked toward each other and hugged one another in the middle. We went to a diner on a corner and he talked for three hours. There were reports that he had been ransomed and he talked to journalists to show that the articles were false. I believed him without hesitation. He was enormously courageous. He knew everything about his kidnapping, it seemed, and there was nothing to hide. He was home and free. He was writing a series of articles for the paper. The next day I told Sophie, my way of showing anger that I had to keep quiet. David was different when he returned, determined. He and Kristen were happily reunited and soon a child was born.

Eight years later I learned that the New York Times moved $2 million to a bank in Afghanistan, which took a fee, and from there a private company took and held it secretly, ready to use it to save David Rohde's life. But Rohde and Tahir Luddin, his fixer, whom he trusted, saved their own lives when Luddin led them in the night to safety. The private company sent the money back. They saved not just themselves, but the New York Times, from the anger of those who preferred that they languish there, and maybe die.

Struggling with my book, and my life in New York, the distance I felt from everyone, my anger bursting on occasion like a geyser, I decided to go back out West. I drove through the nights, feeling freer and stronger, and then along the Columbia and the sun was out and Mt. Hood shining in the distance, welcoming me, and at Portland, Oregon, I crossed the river to Vancouver, Washington, and I was home. I lived in the house, which we hadn't sold yet, that I grew up in, the only place I could finish my book. I got a Washington State driver's license, but I felt lonely. It grew cold and my sister came down from Seattle and we sat by the fireplace and a roaring fire. She was a clinical psychologist. I told her about Rochelle and my sister, in anger, said she was going to call the police. "She is the FBI," I said quietly. A part of me felt like I had been broken.

The rains came and I continued writing and finally finished the book. I saw friends and worked in the yard, pruned trees, cleaned out the paddock where we had kept grain for our horses and my father had created a small shop with a saw and lumber. I looked out over the river, our land below us, now gone, like the West, filled with houses. Eventually, I appreciated that I was living in my father's house. It wasn't my own. I got a cold in that big empty house, and then a cough; it got worse, and a doctor said I had walking pneumonia. I flew back to New York and went to the VA hospital and the doctor said I was getting better but had to go slowly. He saw a reference to my kidnapping in my records. The doctor said that they had a PTSD clinic and did I want to see someone. I said no. "Are you sure?" he asked. I hesitated and changed my mind. I met with the director and broke down twice in half an hour. For the first time, I felt comfortable. He was a man about my age. "It is as if you have been standing still for two years," he said. I was angry at Rochelle, at the FBI, at myself for wasting two years. He arranged for me to see someone. I liked the VA, with veterans from Iraq, Afghanistan, Vietnam, Korea, and World War II, and we all felt a kinship with one another.

Shahwali kept sending e-mails, one to a colleague at the Carnegie Council, trying every way he could to harass me. Sophie asked about him one day and I said that he was still calling. She urged me to go to the FBI and to turn him in. I still didn't want to send him to Guantanamo. "If you want revenge, dig two graves," went the Pashto saying. One for yourself. I had to be careful.

I went to church again. We sang a hymn that I remembered from when I was a boy and again I thought of my mother, and of sitting in my cell and looking up through a hole in the roof and seeing a pale blue sky. There was life outside. And then I thought of the prisoner's chorus from *Fidelio*, as I had in our cell. I was out now, but I had to face another darkness, more insidious, in some ways worse.

❖ ❖ ❖

I PUT ON a front, but I lived in a quiet state of depression. I was mad at my editor, who once observed that because I got kidnapped, I had failed in my original goal to write about the Tribal Areas. Failed. It felt like an accusation. He cut much of my manuscript to focus on my time in captivity. I was mad at my agent, who went along with him. I didn't trust Rochelle. I wanted to go again to the wild, but I had to stay and rewrite the book that my editor wanted, to honor my contract. I felt that CBS didn't know what to do with me. It saved my life, but in turn took it.

"How do I forgive Sophie?" I wrote in my diary. She saved me, but she now controlled me.

Rochelle knew everything about me now, and I felt she was manipulating me. I complained to her that I was ashamed of being ransomed. Colleagues of Solecki's had been kidnapped. He had taken the SERE[8] course, required of UN employees, and knew what to expect. I was a consultant to CBS on a contract, with a salary, but not a full-fledged employee. I never took the course; it was for employees only. His mother and brother came over to Pakistan to work on Solecki's case. The US ambassador came down to Quetta to monitor it. It was in the news. When he got out all his high school classmates contacted him. His whole high school welcomed him home.

His captors said that they were protecting him from the police and the Pakistani government, which wanted him dead to show that they, his kidnappers, were terrorists. He felt like he was in the movie *The Manchurian Candidate*,[9] being brainwashed, but watching as it was being done. The US flew him in a C-130 to Bagram, debriefed him, and flew him home. He was fine now. We didn't talk about being ransomed. It was too delicate to talk about, as if, I felt, it meant going to the heart of what it meant to be a man. We were victims, dependent upon others to pay to save us.

Shahwali kept calling and the Wahhabi was now sending e-mails saying he would take me to Haqqani. I didn't believe him.

John Solecki asked why I couldn't talk. He talked about what he called the "dehumanization of ourselves." Institutions didn't care about us, but individuals did. People thought we were weird now. One night in bed, I saw shadows on the wall and thought a man was standing over my head. I dreamt of a man in a black turban. "Oh, my God," I cried out, and then I saw a man in white holding a rifle.

I went to the CBS Radio office one afternoon to do an interview and I saw Cami McCormick, the Pentagon correspondent. "I am going to Afghanistan," she said excitedly. She was going to embed with the army. I saw darkness, but I kept quiet. "Take a sweater. It gets cold at night," I said. When it came, the news spread quickly. She was in a convoy when it hit an IED. She was in a body cast and all four of her limbs were damaged. A soldier next to her was killed. She was being transferred to a military hospital in Germany. I volunteered to go see her.

I visited her in her room at Walter Reade. The doctors amputated one leg and they were unsure about the other. One of her arms was wired together. I realized again how very fortunate I was. The hospital was filled with wounded men. I was filled with gratitude, but it reminded me of the hospital I was in briefly at Fort Lewis when I was in the army, filled with men my age wounded in Vietnam.

At Rochelle's insistence, I read Gracia Burnham's book, *In the Presence of My Enemies*, about how Gracia and her husband, Martin, Christian missionaries from Kansas, were kidnapped in May 2001 by the Abu Sayyaf group in the Philippines. They spent a desperate year in captivity in the jungle, living on little, always afraid. In February 2002, the George W. Bush administration changed its policy from "no deals at all," to a "case by case consideration, with an openness to ransom if it would bring in some way terrorists to justice."[10] A ransom was paid, but nothing happened. In June 2002, the Philippine army attacked Abu Sayyaf in the jungle. Martin Burnham and Ediborah Yap, a nurse, also a captive, were killed. Gracia Burnham was wounded. She returned later to testify against her captors, and to forgive them, some of whom had become Christians. I felt ashamed that I had complained and could not forgive.

I wrote to Gracia Burnham to tell her that I had read her book and how I admired her, but I felt guilty; her suffering was so much greater. I felt small and ashamed that I had complained. I needed to redeem myself in some way. Again that word, *redemption*, came back to me.

My editor sent me the advanced bound galley for my book, whose cover showed my picture taken by the FBI. I showed it to Sophie. "It looks like you are dead," she said and quickly put it down. I told her that I had written about the amount of money that the Maulvi said they had received for me. She didn't say anything. The Times Books publicist said that she had an agreement with CBS that it would promote the book on all its programs. I was caught between two conglomerates: CBS which didn't want any publicity, and Macmillan, which owned Times Books and clearly hoped the book would become a bestseller.

I told Rochelle about a conversation David Rohde and I had and in our next session she seemed to imply that she had discussed it with a government department. I was angry again, and afraid, but it was the opening I was looking for and I told her I was leaving. I was afraid that she had passed on what I told her.

In the spring of 2010 word was getting out about my book. A man from the Combating Terrorism Center at West Point contacted me and I met with him. He was doing research on what the US now called the Haqqani Network and asked about the Egyptian army officer I had written about in *In Afghanistan*. "We're still trying to find him," said the man from West Point. He meant the US government. I wanted to find the Egyptian, whom I felt, though I had no proof, had become one of the first men in al-Qaeda.

Captive was published in June. My first interview, on C-SPAN, was with a writer from the *New Yorker*. "Are you a Christian?" he asked, leaning forward accusatorially, as if, I felt, mocking me. I said not in the way I was brought up. During my captivity, Gulob said that after the last Muslim prayer at night I could pray on my own, as they did, and I did it for comfort, and one time, for the first time in my life, I felt warmth, like a blanket, and light come over me. It was God, I felt, comforting me. The interview continued back and forth. George Hall, the C-SPAN producer, said it was the best interview he had produced. I was emotionally drained. A colleague saw it and called it an inquisition.

I went to Washington, DC, to promote the book. Ana Real said on the phone that Sophie was walking around the newsroom asking why CBS was not doing anything. I went on a program that aired in the middle of the night, and did radio interviews on ABC, CBS, Fox, NPR, and local stations. Finally, *CBS Evening News* assigned David Martin, the venerable Pentagon reporter, to do a story on me. We met in a hotel. Two publicists were there. I tried to answer David's questions, but I was nervous and couldn't answer him freely and I felt like a politician, crafting an acceptable answer to each question, and he put his notebook down. Mary Walsh, the producer, put her hands on my shoulder and told me to relax. How could I tell the truth? It was CBS. I finally answered each question freely. I trusted David and Mary. David asked at the end, off camera, why I went and I said because my father had been in the Marine Corps in the Pacific and I didn't feel that I measured up. He said that his father had worked for the CIA and he felt the same way. He told Sophie that it was the best interview he had done in twenty-five years. Katie Couric, the CBS anchor, introduced the story on the *Evening News* and said, off camera, "I had no idea. No one told me." CBS had kept my story secret even from her. David did research for a longer piece for CBS News *Sunday Morning*, to find out, he said, the full story, but then CBS told him to stop. I went on other non-CBS television programs and no one, thankfully, asked how I got out.

After my book tour ended, I returned to the newsroom. Sophie asked one day as I passed her desk if I was still receiving my paycheck, and I was worried that she was angry over the book, or because of something I said on television, or that people had come to her, or, as one man said, because I was "too toxic," and that she was threatening to fire me. CBS hardly put me on air anymore.

Chapter 10

The First Daniel Pearl

T HAT O CTOBER, I WENT ON A COLD RAINY NIGHT TO A HOUSE ON lower Fifth Avenue to give a talk at the Deadline Club, the New York chapter of the Society of Professional Journalists. I was sitting in a room gathering my thoughts and the host came in and asked what he should say in his introduction. I gave him some ideas and quoted Michael Semple from the night we met: "We did everything we could to prevent a second Daniel Pearl."

Afterward I sat at a table signing books and a man wearing a yarmulke and a woman came up to me. "Do you think you would have survived if you were Jewish?" the man asked. "I . . . don't know," I responded. I felt uncomfortable. I had never thought of that. "You were the next person after Daniel Pearl and he was Jewish." I was embarrassed. I began to think back to the personal questions that Shahwali asked me in Jalalabad and some of what my captors asked me. Was I Christian or pagan? Did I eat pork? Did I read the Bible? I wondered now if they were trying to find out if I was Jewish. The man's name was Dovid Efune, and he was the editor of *Algemeiner*, a Jewish newspaper.

A week later I gave a talk at the New York Press Association. Gabe Pressman, the New York television reporter, asked if I had been in touch with the Pearls. I was ashamed that I had put it off for two years. I again read the article that Daniel Pearl's father had written in the *Wall Street Journal* in 2009: "*Danny was an optimist, a true believer in the goodness of mankind, yet also a realist. As I look at his picture in front of me I find it hard to look him straight in the eye and say: You did not die in vain.*"

I thought again, "I am alive because of him." I didn't mean it literally, because I didn't know the truth, but I felt it was true, not just because Michael Semple had made the connection, but because I had covered the story of Daniel Pearl in Karachi. He was murdered by al-Qaeda, but I knew that al-Qaeda, composed of foreigners in Afghanistan and Pakistan, did not operate alone; Pakistanis were involved. Everyone knew that, but I felt, again without knowing for certain, that elements of the government, probably the ISI, were behind them. I knew that al-Qaeda and the Taliban worked together.

I had a responsibility to Daniel Pearl, but I didn't know what it was. I nervously wrote to his parents. I mentioned the article in the *Wall Street Journal*. "Your son did not die in vain," I wrote. "I am alive because of your son." I hesitated, then sent my book with the letter.

They wrote back. I put the letter on my desk, afraid to open it and that I had upset them. In fact, they were glad I survived and invited me to come see them the next time I was in Los Angeles. I was relieved, but I still didn't have the courage to face them.

In January 2011, amid snow, Nafay came from Pakistan to New York to visit and told me that she thought that maybe Shahwali's father was behind my kidnapping. "When we went to see him, and told him that his son had been kidnapped, he was unmoved," she said. By "we" she meant part of the CBS team, the Islamabad Shura. I remembered sitting with Shahwali's father, feeling that he was a cold, unemotional man. That was his personality.

It would be impossible for a son, in Pashtun culture, to do anything so dramatic as launch a kidnapping without first telling his father.

Shahwali said that his father lived in darkness and beat him for study-ing English instead of the Qur'an, but after he brought his father to breakfast in Jalalabad before we left to cross the border, I knew that was a lie. They were close. After all, Shahwali told me to give my phone and backpack to him. "We found out where Shahwali lived in Peshawar," said Nafay. I thought of going back, but what would I do if I saw him? One part of me wanted to beat him, and then to learn everything from him. He had called over eighty times now.

Nafay told me that there was a special meeting point. It was the first time she had confirmed there was an exchange. "We all worked so hard to prevent a second Daniel Pearl." She too said it. I could feel myself becoming emotional. "When are you coming back?" she asked. "I will protect you, and Fazul will protect you." She had contacts in the Tribal Areas. She made me more unsettled but excited to find out what really happened.

In July, Michael Semple called. We hadn't talked in more than two years. He wanted me to go to an apartment in New York. I would find two men there from Pakistan. They were on a visit sponsored by the State Department and were returning to Pakistan that night. "Go see them," he said.

If Semple called, it had to be important. I would do whatever he said. The next day, hot and muggy, I went down to Gramercy Park, found the address, and a man on an intercom asked what I wanted. I said that Michael Semple had told me to come there. The door buzzed open and I went down a hallway and knocked on the door. A bulky man in his thirties, about six foot two with a shaved head and wearing a T-shirt and jeans, welcomed me. He asked politely if I wanted tea. There were suitcases on the floor and two men in their forties in a bedroom pack-ing. They joined me in the living room.

"We have been traveling through America, observing your judicial institutions," said one man, formally. He was about six feet, with fair hair, smiling but serious. "We have been here for two weeks and are going home now," said the second man, taller with black hair. "We're from the Tribal Areas."

This was why Semple wanted me to see them. The first man and I sat on the sofa. I gave him my book. "It is a present for you. You can read it on the plane." I wasn't sure why I had brought it.

He looked at the title. "Who kidnapped you, the Taliban or the Pakistani government?" It was his first question. I stared at him. *The government?*

"I thought it was the Taliban, but Michael says it was a criminal group." I was still stunned by his question. "I was traveling along the border trying to get to Haqqani. I know him from the 1980s." I briefly told them the story.

"I know Ibrahim and Khalil," said the second man. He meant two of Jalaluddin's brothers. "I'm from Miran Shah." I couldn't fathom why they were there. We talked about the Haqqanis, the ISI, the Tribal Areas, al-Qaeda, and the Taliban. Soon it was time for me to go; they had a plane to catch. I kept returning to the first question.

I wanted now what I told myself would be one last trip to Afghanistan. I needed to go back for redemption, but I still didn't know what that meant, or what to do to find it.

I continued to see, off and on, Dr. Kramer, my PTSD therapist at the VA. I needed someone to talk to. He was excited one day to go to a conference to see Jonathan Shay, a cutting-edge leader, he said, in his field. Shay worked with Vietnam veterans and was the author of *Achilles in Vietnam: Combat Trauma and the Undoing of Character*. Millions of men went to war, and thousands of people were taken hostage, but only some experienced PTSD. Why? According to Shay and Kramer, who works with veterans from Afghanistan and Iraq, what we call PTSD is not just the result of "a threat to life and limb, but of moral injuries like betrayal," he said. "Torture is mental and physical," Rochelle elaborated one day. "Mental torture lasts longer." Men in Vietnam were betrayed by their officer corps who were safe behind the lines and only cared about their own promotions. They were just punching a time clock. I too felt betrayed by a series of people and I was angry and frustrated.

My sister and her family came to New York for Christmas. She brought me *Unbroken*, about the life of Louis Zamperini, the 1936 US

Olympic 5,000-meter runner who survived in World War II when his plane crashed in the Pacific and he spent weeks in a small boat, and then in a Japanese concentration camp. But what interested me most was the darkness that came over his life following his release. After years of turmoil, Zamperini became a Christian and forgave his captors. I had to forgive, but I was not Zamperini. When I was in captivity I wanted the light, but I didn't know what that meant. I read a book on African exploration[11] and found in it a quote by David Livingstone: "The strangest disease I have seen in this country seems really to be broken heartedness and it attacks free men who have been captured and made slaves."

David Rohde and I met for lunch frequently now, becoming closer, confiding in one another, talking about what we could not discuss with anyone else. It was rare and wonderful. I got to know David McCraw, the assistant legal counsel, and now vice president, for the *New York Times*, whom I had met when he began work on David's case, and became closer to him. He, David, and Kristen had become close during their ordeal; he helped them and we were all part of a small family.

In fall of 2011, Georgetown announced the results of the Pearl Project, a faculty-student project published by the Center for Public Integrity, to find the truth about the death of Daniel Pearl. I read the summary of the 121-page report but there was little mention of the Pakistani government.

In May 2012, a woman from MOST, which I had never heard of but which stood for Muslims on Screen and Television and was linked to the Saban Center for Middle East Policy at the Brookings Institution, asked me to take part in a panel discussion on drone warfare at the Writers Guild in New York. Afterward, the director of MOST invited me to Los Angeles. I realized that it would be a chance for me to meet the Pearls. I wrote to them again. Two days later I received an e-mail from Mrs. Pearl. They were in Israel and would be happy to meet with me when they returned. I felt relieved and nervous at the same time.

In Los Angeles, MOST put me up in a hotel for two days. I didn't know what it wanted, but its director took me to Fox Studios to meet the writers for a program called *Homeland*. We had lunch and I talked, probably too much. The producer asked if my book had been optioned for a movie. While in Hollywood, a reporter for *Time* called to interview me for a story that she was doing on Bowe Bergdahl, the US soldier who disappeared from his unit in 2009 and was being held by the Haqqanis. I knew her from Afghanistan. She asked how long I had been in captivity. I told her. "Oh, that's nothing in comparison to others," she said. I felt belittled. The MOST director took me to see a producer. "We've had enough kidnapping stories," said the producer, a woman of about thirty-five. I realized that they were trying to turn my story into a movie, and again I felt foolish. I thought of a monkey dancing with an organ grinder.

I was to meet the Pearls at the Skirball Cultural Center for lunch. I arrived early and sat in the parking garage. It was May 11, the first anniversary of the death of bin Laden. CBS called and I did radio interviews in a courtyard on my cell phone. I met Narda Zacchino, director of the Daniel Pearl Foundation, outside the restaurant, relieved that she was there. She had been with the *Los Angeles Times* for thirty-one years and then was deputy editor of the *San Francisco Chronicle*. She had coauthored *Boots on the Ground at Dusk*, Mary Tillman's book about her son. I told her that I had gone up into the mountains where Pat Tillman was killed. She wanted me to meet with Mrs. Tillman. Narda and Mary Tillman were looking into whether the government's cover-up of Pat Tillman's death went as high as Vice President Cheney and Secretary of Defense Rumsfeld.

We went into the restaurant. Mrs. Pearl arrived, an elegant, slim, stylish woman, far from the sad older woman I had envisaged. We shook hands. A few minutes later Mr. Pearl came in, medium height, wearing a sport jacket, slacks, and a collared sweater. He had dark, slightly graying hair, wore glasses, and had a short beard. He had an impish way about him as he stood talking to his wife. Their affection for one another was quite clear.

He sat down, ordered a beer, and asked me to have one with him. I never drank alcohol, but I ordered one. We talked for a minute and then he leaned over and looked me in the eye. "Why are you here?" he asked. I wanted to say, "You invited me," but I realized that it was Mrs. Pearl who had probably written the letter. This was painful for them but I was here now and couldn't leave. "I am here because of your son." I couldn't bring myself to say his name.

"You wrote in your article that you feel that your son died in vain. I am alive because of your son," I said gently to everyone now at the table. I knew, without knowing it at all, that he was thinking, "Why did you survive and not my son?" Was it because I wasn't Jewish? I didn't want to talk about that yet.

I told them that when I was released, a man said, "We did everything we could to prevent a second Daniel Pearl." He asked who that man was. I told him about Michael Semple. He nodded. He wanted to know more and we talked.

The waiter came. Mr. Pearl and I ordered salmon and I told the story of my *National Geographic* assignment to write on wild Pacific salmon. His eyes lit up, and I told him where to find the best salmon in the world and we talked happily. It was better to start slowly. It had taken me three years to get up the courage to come see them. It was easier to cross the mountains into Pakistan than to come here.

Mrs. Pearl said that her husband had just been in Dubai where he had given a speech. "He won the Turing Prize this year," she said proudly. The Turing Prize is the Nobel Prize of computer science. Pearl was a professor emeritus at UCLA. I told them the story of my time in Karachi covering the story of their son, and as I talked I realized that I was talking about my links to him.

"Six years later, almost to the day, I was the next person, after your son, taken in Pakistan." I hated using the word *kidnapped*. It was too powerful. I told them how I thought of their son during that time. I told them about the mock executions. "As I sat there, hunched over, it took me a long time to sit up straight and stare at the camera. I thought of your son." I felt emotional talking with them about this, more than I had felt talking about it anywhere else, and I felt weak. I was alive and their son was not. I thought back to when the men stood behind me, wearing sunglasses, holding their rifles, and a man put his hand in his shirt to pull out the knife. "Danny was with you there in that prison, wasn't he?" said Mrs. Pearl. Yes, I said. I hadn't thought of that, but she was right. "He gave me strength."

Dr. Pearl talked of his efforts to promote understanding and to promote the moderates to defeat those who had killed his son. He knew that his son was trying to find the truth, and, I think, to bring Muslims, Christians, and Jews—"The people of the book," some Muslims said—together. Judea Pearl was continuing his son's work.

He talked about Khalid Sheikh Mohammad, who had murdered his son, and it was clear that he had more information. I mentioned the Pearl Project, which concluded that twenty-seven people were involved. "Did you read it?" he asked. He didn't seem to think much of it. I had only read part of it then. I told him about my meeting with the two men from Pakistan in New York, and the first question that one of the men asked me.

On January 27, 2002, a week after Daniel Pearl was taken, a group calling itself the National Movement for the Restoration of Pakistan Sovereignty e-mailed news organizations accusing Pearl of spying for the United States, demanding better treatment of men in Guantanamo, and that the US release the F-16 fighter jets that Pakistan ordered and paid for but which the US had not delivered. Why would a militant group demand F-16s, I asked then, and now? Only a government would want them. Dr. Pearl agreed.

On January 29, 2002, UPI reported, when Daniel Pearl was still alive, "that US intelligence believes the kidnappers are connected to the ISI."

On March 3, 2002, *Dawn*, the most prominent English-language Pakistani newspaper, reported that Secretary of State Colin Powell stated that "no elements of the ISI" were involved in the murder of Daniel Pearl. It appeared that UPI was either wrong or, more likely, that US intelligence knew that it was the ISI, but greater forces in the government, anxious to maintain close ties with Pakistan, its ally since the 1950s in the Cold War against communism and now against a resurgent Russia, didn't want this information to come out.

On March 28, the *Washington Post*, reflecting this thought, said "The ISI is a house of horrors," and that "Seed Sheikh has tales to tell."

On July 16, the *Guardian* wrote: "On January 29, 'a senior Pakistani official,' presumably from the ISI, leaks the fact that Pearl is Jewish to the Pakistani press. This may have been an attempt to ensure the kidnappers would want to murder him, which they do shortly thereafter."

In August, *Vanity Fair* reported that Kamran Khan—the chief investigative reporter for *The News*, who was noted for his close contacts with the ISI—had written, citing a senior Pakistani official, that "some Pakistani security officials . . . are privately searching for answers as to why a Jewish American reporter was exceeding 'his limits' to investigate [a] Pakistani religious group. An India-based Jewish reporter serving a largely Jewish media organization should have known the hazards of exposing himself to radical Islamic groups, particularly those who recently got crushed under American military might." By repeating that Pearl was Jewish, and that the *Wall Street Journal*, owned by Rupert Murdoch, a Protestant, was a largely Jewish organization, the ISI was sending a message to, I felt, the Arabs of al-Qaeda, and Harkat-ul-Mujahideen (the mujahideen movement). Ahmed Omar Saeed Sheikh was a member of that movement.

Vanity Fair continued: "Khan . . . revealed Danny's relationship with Asra Nomani, whom he claimed—falsely—Danny had imported from India to be 'his full time assistant.'"

Nomani is Muslim, born in India. She moved with her family when she was four to the United States, where her father studied for his PhD at Rutgers. She grew up in West Virginia and became a reporter for the *Wall Street Journal* and a friend of Pearl's. She took a leave of absence after 9/11 and moved to Karachi where she wrote for *Salon*, an online magazine. Pearl and his wife stayed in Nomani's house. This was not unusual. In 2007, Kim Barker, with the *Chicago Tribune* (now with the *New York Times*) loaned me her house when I was working in India. Pearl left Nomani's house on January 23, 2002, to go on an interview and never returned. She taught a course at Georgetown, and helped start and direct the Pearl Project in honor of her colleague and friend.

I was told more than once that no journalist in Pakistan working in foreign policy or national security could work for long without the approval of the ISI. I kept wondering why the ISI held Ahmed Omar Seed Sheikh for a week before releasing him to the police. I began to wonder about my own kidnapping.

I read and reread the Pearl Project report titled *The Truth Left Behind: Inside the Killing and Death of Daniel Pearl*. In the summary, called "Key Findings," it does not mention the ISI or any involvement by the Pakistani government. Under a chapter titled "Catching the Mastermind," the authors wrote about Ahmed Omar Saeed Sheikh's possible ties to the ISI, and asked, rhetorically, "Even worse was the ISI involved?" But that was all.

"Danny didn't want to go to Afghanistan," said Dr. Pearl. "He felt it was too dangerous. He didn't have the special training they give journalists." He asked if I had that training. I said no, I was on a contract with CBS, but I was not a regular employee. People asked what I thought of Daniel Pearl. I couldn't judge him, but then said that he should not have gone alone. But then I too went alone. I too didn't see what was going on around me. I had been with the Taliban four times and each time they kept their word. They said that they wouldn't harm me, and they didn't. Until they did.

"My name is Daniel Pearl," he said before he was killed. "I'm a Jewish American from Encino, California, USA. I come from, on my father's side the family is Zionist. My father's Jewish, my mother's Jewish, I'm Jewish. My family follows Judaism. We've made numerous family visits to Israel. Back in the town of Bnei Brak there is a street named after my great grandfather Chaim Pearl who is one of the founders of the town."

"We knew that was a message to us," said Mrs. Pearl. She was quiet. "Why did CBS show that video?" she asked plaintively. She was born in Baghdad. "I went to a French school. Then Israel was created and all Jews were expelled from Iraq." She knew Arabic, learned Hebrew and English, and along the way met Judea. He listened, smiling at her. They talked about their son's statement again. Mrs. Pearl's eyes were warm, remembering how much their son loved them. I kept thinking of him sitting in that room, in handcuffs, wondering if they were going to kill him. "I have never seen the video," I said. "I refused to look at it."

"Why did Dan Rather show it?" Dr. Pearl asked. "How could they do that to Danny's dignity?"

"Yes, how could they do that?" Mrs. Pearl asked. I could see the pain in their eyes.

"He said he did it to show what kind of people they were," Dr. Pearl continued, half answering his own question.

"It was all about money, and ratings, and being first," I said. It was the news business in all its ambition, hardness, and callous disrespect, but it was news: people were drawn to watch it as they once watched hangings. Five years later, as I was writing this book, I thought back to when Aamir called and told me that there was a video of Pearl's killing. I remembered my conversation with CBS executives. I did research and learned that only CBS got the video. I was partially responsible for this. I had helped cause the pain that the Pearls felt.

The Pearl Project states that national security adviser Condoleezza Rice called Marianne Pearl on October 6, 2003, over a year and a half after we knew, to tell her the US felt that Khalid Sheikh Mohammad was involved. Why was the US so slow to find out, or to tell her? I felt, but couldn't prove, that the US and Pakistan were hiding ISI involvement from the public. I remembered that Samad—one of my bodyguards and a fellow captive as well as part of Abdullah's band, or whatever it was—said that Pakistan used the Taliban for its regional goals, and al-Qaeda for its international goals. I was in the hands of the Taliban, or maybe a criminal gang. Daniel Pearl was, in the end, placed in the hands of al-Qaeda.

Mrs. Pearl said that Judea was giving a talk at the Daniel Pearl Magnet School in Van Nuys on artificial intelligence and asked if I wanted to attend. I said yes. Our lunch ended and she got up and walked around the table and hugged me. It was all I could have asked for. I hugged her back gently and kissed her gently on the cheek. I shook hands with Dr. Pearl, but my hand wasn't fully in his and I pushed it forward to shake his hand more fully and he responded, smiled a bit, and turned away. It was hard for him to have me there.

They left and Narda stayed so we could talk about the Pat Tillman story, which she felt was far from over. "I saw Judea's eyes when you were shaking hands. There were tears in them," she said. I hoped that I had done the right thing in coming to see them, but I wasn't sure.

I drove north to Van Nuys and found the school. A reporter and a photographer were there from the *Los Angeles Daily News*. They asked why I was there and I explained. The reporter asked if it was hard always being referred to as a "former hostage. It is as if you are forever known as that." It was true.

We went into the auditorium and Judea Pearl was smiling, sitting in a high director's chair behind a podium. Mrs. Pearl asked me to sit up front next to her. Dr. Pearl nodded hello. Students came in and filled the room. He held a microphone and made a popping sound playfully seeing if it was working properly, the impish, playful side of him. He clicked the remote. A statement appeared on a screen behind him: "Can a computer think?" Below was a photograph of Alan Turing. "It is a mathematical question. How far can you go? Can it truly think?" Dr. Pearl smiled, a professor in his element. He wore black trousers, black shirt, black shoes, and a sport coat. He paced slowly back and forth changing slides. "If, behind a glass wall, there is a machine and you ask it questions and you can't tell by its answers if it is a man or a machine, then it passes the Turing Test." He went off on his lecture. He used a slide to explain how information is passed from one person to another, what he called "the impatient firing squad." I didn't like that phrase.

Mrs. Pearl interrupted, asking him to explain how this was all applicable today. Judea lowered the microphone and looked at her kindly. They spoke in Hebrew. I saw again the love that they had for one another. They had survived the terrible loss of their son, and stayed together, giving one another support. "There are only two states in the world," said Dr. Pearl. "Something is either true or it is false. It is a question of physics. Machines must be able to work with uncertainty."

Mrs. Pearl prodded me to ask, "When are you going to discuss the applications of your work to today?"

"What about Siri?" Narda asked, referring to the artificial personal assistant featured on the Apple iPhone 4S.

"Who is he?" Dr. Pearl joked. It was his mathematical discoveries that led, in great part, to the creation of Siri. He asked a girl to bring up her phone. "Ask it if it knows what three squared is?"

"Nine," Siri replied.

"I love you," said Dr. Pearl.

"I hope you don't say that to all the smartphones," said Siri.

Dr. Pearl smiled. Companies have made millions of dollars off his work. "I don't care about the money," he said later. He loved his work. "I can do today what I could not do yesterday. That is happiness. I do not care about monetary awards. I am proud to be here." He and Ruth came to the school often. The well-known picture of their son, a handsome young man in a light suit, smiling, hangs in the principal's office.

We walked outside. "I wanted to tell you before, but couldn't," I said. "I feel guilty that I survived and your son did not."

"People who survived the Holocaust feel the same way," he said gently. "It is survivor guilt. Put it behind you." We walked slowly down a covered walkway. I wanted more from him, but I didn't know what it was. "It's not physics," he said softly. He couldn't understand why his son was killed.

Mrs. Pearl asked him to get their son's book, and a CD, and bring it from the car. When he was gone, I told her what I just told her husband. "I understand. Holocaust survivors feel the same way." He brought the book and she signed it and then he signed it. She gave me a hug and Dr. Pearl and I shook hands. "We want to put you to work," she said, smiling. She meant that she wanted me to help them on the Daniel Pearl Foundation.

As I drove away I looked at the high school next door where their son had gone. BIRMINGHAM HIGH SCHOOL, HOME OF THE PATRIOTS, it said on a wall. I saw a group of boys running together, like on a track team. Daniel Pearl had started there before he went out into the world.

Back in New York, I called Dovid Efune and we had coffee near his office. I thanked him for coming up to me that night after I gave my talk, and told him about my meeting with the Pearls. I didn't tell him then, but he inspired me to begin my journey back out in the world to find the truth behind my kidnapping. That felt like my responsibility.

Chapter 11

Local and International

In 2012, I had to move to a smaller apartment. After the financial crisis of 2008, my apartment in New York, a co-op, like thousands of other apartments and houses in America, plummeted in value. The building did not own the land on which the building sat. While I was in Afghanistan, the co-op board began to negotiate with the owner to buy the land. It purchased the land for $50 million and my maintenance quadrupled. I also had a mortgage. I hung on for two years and then I could no longer afford to live there. After *Captive* appeared in 2010, I tried to get another book contract, to supplement my CBS contract, the only way I could afford to stay in my apartment. I wanted to write about the Kajaki Larah, the Black Way, a story, little known then, of the largest underground railroad in the world, the thousands of Afghan boys who, seeking a better life, crossed overland from Afghanistan to Europe and the UK. But publishers were afraid that something would happen to me. Sophie said that I could not travel east of Turkey. I eventually took the story to *60 Minutes*, and wrote an article in *Foreign*

Affairs, but no book. In 2012, I moved to a small rental apartment in Inwood, at the top of Manhattan, and started over, another ripple effect of my kidnapping.

I went to the Strategic Studies Institute (SSI) at the Army War College in Carlisle, Pennsylvania, for which in 2007 I had written a monograph titled *The History, Rise, and Present State of Islamic Fundamentalism in South Asia.* I wanted to write the same thing on the Middle East and combine the two monographs into a book. Since CBS would not allow me to return to South Asia I would go to the Middle East and expand my knowledge, be of more use to CBS, and have more opportunities. The United States was pulling out from Afghanistan. It, too, had lost, like the Soviets, the British, the Persians, and Alexander, but no one said that on television.

As I wrote my proposal, I thought why not include another one to study the links between Pakistani jihadist groups and the Middle East. So much of all that was going on there started in Pakistan. Al-Qaeda, the Chechens, the Uzbeks, the Uighurs of western China, all were linked to the Tribal Areas and to the Haqqanis.

In December, CBS asked me to go to Idaho to talk with Bowe Bergdahl's parents. There were rumors that the government was working on his release and CBS wanted to be first to interview him. The Bergdahls came to my hotel and they, open and Western, like people I grew up with, smiled warmly, happy just to see me. Jani Bergdahl said my being alive and well gave her hope that her son would come home again. That moment was worth the trip. We had dinner and started to get to know one another. Many people had come to see them, and they were nervous. Bob was upset by what some journalists had written after they had met with them. I had been in the army and knew how serious it was for a soldier to go AWOL, but I was not there to judge their son. I had to win them over for CBS, but more than that, I wanted to gain their trust and to be there for them. The Haqqanis had held their son now for four years.

On Sunday, Bob and Jani took me to their Presbyterian church and Jani sat on one side, holding her Bible, the same kind that my mother and sister had, and Bob, with a long beard, wearing a white Muslim prayer cap, sat on the other side. He wanted to be close to his son and to win his captors over. He posted messages on the internet. We had lunch at the church and that evening we sang Christmas carols with their congregation. They took me for a ride out into the country and we stopped, to my surprise, at a small monument to Hemingway, who had lived nearby with his family at the end of his life. They felt that I would have a kinship with him. I did like the romance of Paris, his vigorous life, and spare masculine sentences, when I was younger, but the thought of his last days were depressing. I felt sad and dark walking among the trees. I felt death hang over me, and realized that I was a different man now since I was kidnapped. I had looked death in the eye. I was grateful when we drove on that Bob and Jani and I had established a bond. We went to a café dedicated to Bowe. Men from all over the country came there to support him. Over the next two years we would call, text, and write to one another.

SSI awarded me the contracts but would not provide expense money. Richard Perle introduced my work to the president of a national security policy foundation. A grant officer sent an e-mail and pointed to seven words in my proposal: *"the Haqqani Network in the greater Middle East."* He wanted me to research this. I was excited, as I once was when *National Geographic* magazine asked me to travel the lengths and to find the sources of the Brahmaputra and the Amazon. It was a different form of exploration.

On February 26, 2012, I came home from work late to find a letter from the US Department of Justice, Federal Bureau of Investigation.

Dear Mr. Van Dyk:

This letter is to provide you with an update to the case by which you were previously referred to the FBI's Office of Victim Assistance. As this time, the Federal Bureau of Investigation has closed its investigation into your hostage taking. The FBI has jurisdiction to investigate terrorist attacks against US citizens. It is not possible at this time to proceed further toward filing of charges therefore the investigation has been closed. The FBI will re-open the case if any information is developed in the future.

I understand how this decision may be difficult to comprehend. It is not intended to diminish your experience. Please feel free to contact me at [here was a phone number and an e-mail address] if you have any questions.

Sincerely yours . . .

The FBI had run into a dead end. It didn't seem to know who kidnapped me or how to find them. Abdullah and Shahwali had got away with it. I was upset, but resolved: I would do this myself.

It took six months to write a proposal, to go through the vetting process, and to convince the board of directors, one of whom was a former director of the CIA, of the merits of my thesis: that the Haqqanis had a presence in the Middle East. Not everyone agreed with me. I received the grant that I applied for, but the foundation stated in my contract that I was never to acknowledge its name. I wondered, just as I did when I became the director of the Friends of Afghanistan, just whom I was working for.

I had to have an acceptable think tank and fiscal agent through which, for accountability, the foundation could send the money. The Council on Foreign Relations agreed to take me on as an adjunct senior fellow. "You must get insurance," said Sophie. "You can never say that you work for CBS." Again, as in 2007, she had to protect the corporation. I understood. Again, she was afraid that I would get in trouble. Ana Real, the deputy foreign editor, had said that if I got in trouble again, CBS would not bail me out. I couldn't find a company to insure me. I was a kidnap victim. This time I was on my own.

I contacted Rosanne Klass and we had dinner at a diner she liked near her apartment. She was in her eighties now, overweight, and she still ate too much, especially desserts, but at least she had stopped smoking. She used a walker, but her mind was sharp. "The State Department hates me," she said. I had heard this for thirty years. "Do you think they remember me?"

"No, I doubt it. They're all younger now," I responded, wishing I hadn't said this. She nodded. We still argued over politics, but we went to musicals together. She told me about the time that she wrote a ballet for George Balanchine. She loved the arts and show business, the reason that she came to New York, this hard-line, no-nonsense, anticommunist advocate for Afghanistan, who was my biggest supporter.

She was far from unknown. In 2010, she contacted the *Weekly Standard*, and they assigned her to write what was a long and positive review of *Captive*. We argued that night briefly over dinner, and it bothered me because we were so close. We were old Afghanistan. I walked her back slowly across Broadway to her apartment. It was like I was walking my grandmother home. We arrived and the doorman came out to help her up the steps. I put my arm around her and kissed her on the head, the first time I had ever shown such emotion. It was the last time I saw her. She died a month later. The *New York Times* wrote a wonderful obituary about her. The *Wall Street Journal* wrote an editorial praising her work on Afghanistan. They hadn't forgotten her.

One thing I couldn't bring myself to tell her that final night that we were together was the consequence of her recommendation, in 2003, that I should see Professor Rasul Amin. Through him I had met a young, pretty Afghan woman called Sameer, who in turn had introduced me to Amin's nephew Shahwali.

The Council on Foreign Relations wrote a letter announcing my title and obligations. I had a book contract and funding from a foundation. I felt, for the first time since I was kidnapped, that life was beginning again. I flew to London and Bryn Padrig, to whom I felt close because of all that he done for me when I was in captivity, gave me an office. I had dinner with a former CBS intern who had worked on the foreign desk in New York and who, when she heard me say that I wanted to go to Yemen, said her father, Taher Qassim, a Yemeni activist, could help me. I went to see him in Liverpool. He gave me some names of men in Yemen, making the introduction. I contacted freelance journalists and scholars who had worked there. In September 2013, I flew to Sana'a.

A Yemeni journalist I had contacted picked me up at the airport. "It is very dangerous here now," he said. "An American photographer was kidnapped off the street three days ago." I became nervous. The journalist took me to a hotel where he said that it was safe. The next night one of my new contacts came and we walked through the city, and I felt more relaxed. A week later I moved to a school in the Old City run by the Muslim Brotherhood and began my project on the Haqqani Network. I did radio interviews for and sent memos to CBS on the country. I kept thinking of the photographer, Luke Somers, who had just been kidnapped. He had probably been taken by tribal leaders. They often kidnapped people and treated them well, a way to demand in exchange electricity or, say, a new road from the government. Three months later, I went one night, dressed as a Yemeni with a Yemeni guide, to the grocery store where Luke Somers was taken, in part to be close to him, a form of solidarity. I met with a Yemeni journalist who had ties to al-Qaeda, hoping to learn more, but he had a vaguely sinister way about him and I kept quiet about Luke, afraid of what might happen to me.

On November 25, over sixteen months after Luke was taken, the US finally felt that it had intelligence on where he was and mounted a secret rescue attempt, but he wasn't there. On December 4, al-Qaeda in the Arabian Peninsula, which I had been told had a direct link to al-Qaeda's leader, Ayman al-Zawahiri, in Pakistan, posted a video of Luke online. He wore Western clothes and was outside, and the weather looked warm. He had been moved from the mountains down into the south—al-Qaeda territory. Al-Qaeda in the Arabian Peninsula had never killed a foreign hostage, and it did not demand a ransom, but Luke was nervous and I was afraid for him. On December 6, the US launched a second rescue attempt, but Luke and another Western hostage, Pierre Korkie from South Africa, were killed. I watched the story on the news and felt empty and weak.

I learned in reading the news after Luke was killed that Korkie was a schoolteacher and that a small South African charity, for which he worked, had paid a ransom of $320,000 to his kidnappers and that he was scheduled to be released on December 7. How could the US, with all its resources, not know this? Or did it know, and went ahead anyway? I would try to find out.

✣ ✣ ✣

IN FEBRUARY, 2014, I left Yemen and flew to Dubai to meet with two journalists from the Tribal Areas of Pakistan to learn about the routes that jihadists took from the Tribal Areas to the Middle East. I flew back to New York to do my taxes, go to the dentist, and see Sophie. She wanted me to return every three months. I walked into the newsroom and she welcomed me back. That was all that counted. After three days, with a snowstorm coming, I returned to London and flew to Cairo. I spent a month in Egypt, a hard, angry country now, with supporters of the Muslim Brotherhood on one side and those who backed the military on the other. I went one afternoon to al-Azhar University for a meeting in the office of the Grand Mufti, after which I walked down the road to Khan al-Khalili, the bazaar built in the fourteenth century. Two hustlers approached me and I let one guide me through the labyrinth. He took me to a mosque and we walked up the dusty steps onto the roof and he pointed out sites. Sundown approached and we listened to the call to prayer. I silently watched the city. "You remind me of another American journalist who came here some years ago," my guide said. I knew instinctively what he was going to say. "His name was Danny."

We walked down the steps and he took me to a shop where a friend sold paintings on papyrus. I knew that I was supposed to buy something, but I went with him to see where this would lead. The shop was closed but he found the owner and we went inside. I walked to the owner's desk and looked at the business cards beneath a glass desk top. There, on the right, was Daniel Pearl's card. The owner brought glasses of tea and I sat and told them the story of Daniel Pearl and me.

From Egypt I went to Saudi Arabia. After a month, it grew hot and when the wind came up at night I felt the sand in my face. On June 14, Bowe Bergdahl was released. Bob and Jani had told me about their dealings with the government, and I felt happy for them as I watched television, but I was afraid of the backlash that would come. They knew it would.

I saw Bowe sitting in the gray 4×4 blinking his eyes and rubbing his face. They had blindfolded him, I felt, and removed it when they reached the release point, just before they started the video. He wouldn't be able to tell anyone where he had been held. I remembered when they removed my blindfold and I couldn't open my eyes for a minute, the first time I had seen the sun since I had been taken. Bergdahl had been kept in a room, perhaps in the dark, for five years. I understood, even as an outsider, the anger that soldiers felt if he had gone AWOL, but no one could understand what it was like to be in a Taliban prison for five years.

I watched Bob and Jani standing with President Obama, and then the politicians voiced their anger. The anti-Bergdahl rhetoric grew fiercer the following day. Everyone hated him, it seemed, especially soldiers. I couldn't argue with them. America called itself a Christian country, but those who wanted to punish were louder than those who were willing to forgive Bergdahl. Bob told me that military officers told them that they didn't want to prosecute him. He had been through enough, but now the public was taking over, calling for blood.

I flew to Bahrain, to Qatar, and down to Sudan, where bin Laden had lived and from where he had returned to Afghanistan. From Khartoum, I returned to Cairo. I was trying, among other things, to find the Egyptian army major who had stayed with Haqqani when I was there. I was sure he was one of the original members of al-Qaeda. Drawing on my links to the past, I met, nervously, with members of al-Gamma al-Islamiyya (the Islamic Groups), who said they still considered Ayman al-Zawahiri to be their leader though he was far away, stuck in Pakistan. (Al-Zawahiri is also the leader of al-Qaeda.)

One evening in August 2014 I took a taxi across Cairo. A man standing on a corner was about forty; he wore an open-neck shirt and sport jacket. We walked into a small dusty store with electronic equipment and used televisions. An employee inserted a CD, a compilation made after 9/11 of interviews with Arab jihadists in Afghanistan, and Osama bin Laden came on the screen wearing an Afghan turban and an army fatigue jacket.

There was another clip of bin Laden, his beard long, and he wore a white kaffiyeh down to his shoulders, Salafi style, meaning that his headdress hung loosely down all sides with nothing to hold it in place. *Salafi* to an Islamist means "pious ancestors"—those earliest Muslims, the companions of the Prophet Mohammad and those who came immediately after, when Islam was young and pure and men were confident that God was on their side, they who followed the true Islam and carried it to the farthest reaches of the world. "This is a famous speech," said the man. "It is the first time that Osama said the real enemy was the West." How could a young man have the audacity to call for war against anyone? Where did he get the confidence? It was a wish for martyrdom. I later remembered that I had had dinner in Islamabad in 2005 with two Pakistani journalists who told me that in February 1998 the ISI drove them across the border to Afghanistan, where they attended the press conference that bin Laden held, with other jihadists, and where he announced the formation of the "International Islamic Front for Jihad against Jews and Crusaders." They were effectively telling me that in their view the ISI had backed, if not helped to create, al-Qaeda. Samad, my bodyguard who had betrayed me, told me that Pakistan used the Taliban for local purposes and al-Qaeda for international. In August 1998, al-Qaeda attacked the US embassies in Kenya and Tanzania.

Abdullah Anas was next in the video, a clip filmed in the 1980s of an engaging, smiling young man with a bushy beard, explaining that jihad was now required. I had seen him a few weeks ago, in London: heavier, distant, circumspect, his beard neatly trimmed. Gone for him too was his happy, youthful confidence. He lived a quiet life with his family. He was an executive now. But I learned later that he knew Hajji Din Mohammad. There was a network here that reached back, always, to Afghanistan, and to the Tribal Areas of Pakistan. I began to think, as I watched, of returning to Afghanistan.

There were short clips of other Afghan-Arabs. "We worked with the CIA to drive the Russians out of Afghanistan and then they decided we were terrorists. How did this happen?" said one. As I looked at the men, I thought of my time in Afghanistan during that war, of the passion and romance of that time. I had been traveling through the Middle East for months now and always Afghanistan was on my mind. Everything started there, including ISIS. I was having trouble with my project on the Haqqanis in the Middle East. It was hard to get to jihadists, and dangerous. People were afraid to talk to me. They didn't know who I was. I had wondered, ever since I looked down at the mountains with

Bob and John, the FBI agents beside me as we left Afghanistan after my release, if I would ever return to Afghanistan. I was still uncertain, still afraid of Taliban with shaved beards waiting for me in Kabul. But I would try.

I decided right then to leave Egypt immediately and to return to Afghanistan. The most important thing I had to do was to see Din Mohammad to apologize for betraying him. He had sent a driver to my guesthouse to take me to safety, but I chose instead to say no and I crossed the border with Abdullah's men, who were at war with his family, and they kidnapped me. Hajji Zahir, Din Mohammad's nephew, and Hazrat Ali, his ally, had killed Abdullah's cousin. In turn, Abdullah, backed, I felt now, by the ISI, had killed Din Mohammad's brother, and Zahir's father, Hajji Qadir, a vice president of Afghanistan. Samad had told me that the two clans were at war. I, seen as allied with Din Mohammad, was in the middle.

I needed help to get a visa and to find Haqqani contacts in the Middle East. I was still angry at Sami Yousafzai, my former fixer in Afghanistan, and ever since he suggested leaving me in Khost along the border in December 2006 when I was researching the death of Pat Tillman I was uncomfortable around him. But he had contacts no one else had.

He had reached out to me after I was released from captivity. He was apologetic, and appealed to our shared experience of being kidnapped. In 2002, he had sneaked Eliza Griswold, an American journalist, into the Tribal Areas, but quickly got caught. The authorities released Griswold but put Sami and his driver in prison for forty-three days. I wondered what happened to him. I had watched him get out of his car and berate a Pakistani policeman in Islamabad for stopping us one evening—a recklessly arrogant act for anyone, but especially for an Afghan living on a visa in Pakistan unless he had special support he could count on.

Sami said that he knew Taliban in exile in Ankara, Turkey, and in Dubai. He was coming to London and offered to meet me there. It was interesting that even after 9/11 he, an Afghan, could fly easily between Pakistan and the UK. We met on a bench by the CBS bureau. He hugged me gently. He was kinder and more respectful than before.

We walked to a café near the bureau in Chiswick and sat in the sun. It was Ramadan and he was fasting, but he urged me to have coffee. I just wanted to talk.

I asked how it was that he could travel back and forth so easily to Pakistan. He said that he had a house now in London and that his children were in school there. His mother was there with the family. His daughter was in university. He was maintaining two homes, one in London, maybe the most expensive city in the world, the other in Islamabad. I didn't ask where he got the money to live like this, but I assumed he did well, working for American, European, and Japanese news organizations, all of which needed fixers (especially those rare men with good Taliban contacts). I knew, for example, that in November 2008, he was driving his car in Peshawar with a Japanese correspondent he was working with when the Taliban shot him. I had read about this attack. Sami described it to me in detail. He recognized a man with henna in his beard coming toward him in the street with a pistol. He shouted at the Japanese correspondent to get down, raised his hand to protect his own head, thinking that he could survive a bullet to his arm or hand. The man shot Sami in the left arm and hand, while another man tried to open the other door and kidnap the correspondent. But Sami, though wounded, got the car away quickly and saved the correspondent and himself. The correspondent flew back to Tokyo. Sami's contact had turned on him. I didn't believe for a minute that Sami was involved in the kidnapping. The Taliban wanted to kidnap Japanese correspondents because Japan paid so much money, quickly, to secure their release. It was the Trade.

Sami still had some shrapnel in him and said that the Japanese had paid his way to London for medical treatment. It was his second trip there. I believed him.

We talked about my work in the Middle East, but I kept it vague. I said I understood that he worked on my case—that much Bryn Padrig, Nafay, and Michael Semple told me. He began to tell me, in a sporadic way, some of what he did to help me.

"We found out who the *chakador* was," he began, "and Bashir and I went to his house in Landi Khotal."

Chakador meant "guard" or "watchman" in Pashto. They wanted to leave a message with the chakador's family that they knew who he was and where he lived. They were squeezing the circle. The chakador had to be Gulob.

I didn't know who Bashir was but then I recalled that he came on the phone briefly just after Bryn Padrig and Michael Semple, when they called me after I was released.

"Bashir is the brother-in-law of Gohar Zaman," Sami Yousafzai continued. Bashir's father was governor in Jalalabad under the communists. To make any payment legal, Sami said, the money had to go to Gohar Zaman, who sent it to Kabul. "It was for Mohammad Feridoun."

If any money ended up with Gohar Zaman, he was not a simple old policeman, as I thought, maybe incorrectly, that Semple had led me to believe. If he sent it to Feridoun in Kabul, I had to find out what happened to it after that. I didn't know then that he sent it when I reached Feridoun, safe with him and his men.

Sami said that Abdullah was behind my kidnapping, that he was a criminal and did it for money. Sami, who said he was in Jalalabad at that time staying in a guesthouse, said he got involved when he got a call from Bryn Padrig. But Bryn and Nafay told me a different story. They both said that it was Sami who first told *them* that an American had been kidnapped.

Sami said that they, meaning the CBS team, got my phone records, and Shahwali's records, from Fazul. Then out of the blue Sami talked about Hajji Zaman.

Hajji Zaman was a Khoughani, of the same tribe as Yunus Khalis, born in the foothills of Tora Bora, but for some reason chose to go with a different mujahideen political party. After the Soviet war ended Zaman left Afghanistan and settled in Dijon, France. It was from there, wrote Peter Tomsen, chief US diplomat to the Afghan resistance under George H. W. Bush, that the CIA after 9/11 lured Zaman back to Afghanistan, where he and his men became one of the three militias hired by the CIA to find bin Laden at Tora Bora.

Hajji Zaman was considered an ISI asset, and was allegedly the man behind Abdullah when he and another, unknown, person assassinated Hajji Qadir in July 2002. Sami said that the Taliban had killed Zaman in 2010 because he had worked for the US at Tora Bora trying to kill bin Laden. This did not make sense since both the Taliban and Hajji Zaman were ISI assets. There was no reason for the Taliban to kill an ally. The truth was that Hajji Zaman was working for the ISI when he moved slowly against bin Laden, then established a truce with bin Laden and then let him and the Arabs with him escape down into Pakistan. Sami told me in 2006 that it was Yunus Khalis's two sons who led bin Laden down from Tora Bora into Pakistan.

It was the link between Abdullah and Hajji Zaman, and between Hajji Zaman and the ISI, and the CIA, that ultimately interested me more than anything else.

It would take more than two years, but in May 2017, after hearing many stories about Hajji Zaman from people who never knew him, Ehsanullah introduced me to Shahmamood Meikel, a clean-shaven man wearing a tie and jacket, about 5'9" and in his early sixties. He was polite, well-spoken, a Pashtun former journalist for the VOA during the Soviet war, later deputy minister of the Interior, and then country director for the US Institute for Peace. We talked about Peshawar in the 1980s—lunches at Green's and Jan's; mutual friends, all of us beginning journalists; his friend Steve McCurry, the photographer who took the famous picture of the Afghan girl with green eyes, and who later introduced me to *National Geographic* magazine. "I knew Hajji Zaman. I liked him, he was an intelligent man," said Meikel.

He said that after the Soviet war and the rise of the Taliban, Hajji Qadir and Hajji Zaman, opposed to the Taliban, fled to Pakistan but were expelled for anti-Taliban statements. Qadir went to Germany and Zaman took aslyum in France. Qadir, a Pashtun, returned to Afghanistan and joined the Northern Alliance with Hazrat Ali, his ally. They were both from different ethnic groups, both opposed to the Taliban, and to Pakistan, which backed the Taliban. Hajji Zaman returned to his home territory near Jalalabad and Tora Bora. He had built up power during the mujahideen time, and thus became an obstacle, Meikel said, to the Northern Alliance's attempts to take control along the Pashtun border region.

"There was a lot of money available then for anti-narcotics programs along the border," said Meikel, "and a power struggle developed among Qadir, Hazrat Ali, and Zaman, for this money. The US was allied with Qadir and Ali, less so with Zaman."

The US chose all three men, each with a militia, to go after bin Laden at Tora Bora. "Zaman told me that they divided up Tora Bora, each man taking his own territory," Meikel continued. Seven months later Hajji Qadir, now a vice president of Afghanistan, was assassinated. "Zaman said he was not involved. The rumor was that the Northern Alliance killed him [Qadir]."

This was new news. I said that I heard that Zaman worked for the ISI.

"I don't believe that Zaman was an ISI agent," Meikel replied. "He was a sincere person, and he had an independent quality about him. He was not ISI."

Then why did people say he was?

Meikel sighed. "You know what it was like during that time. All the mujahideen commanders and the leaders had ISI contacts." He was right. The ISI controlled the flow of arms and money to the mujahideen. "If you had contacts with the ISI [it did] not mean that you were, or are, an ISI agent."

Three weeks later, I met again with Moustache, the journalist, in Pakistan. He wore dark shalwar kameez and sat calmly across from me drinking hot milk tea. Five days before he had told me, "I knew Hajji Zaman well." He read from the notes I had asked him to prepare. "His name is Mohammad. He lived in France and after 9/11 returned to Afghanistan. He was one of three men hired by the US to find bin Laden at Tora Bora. He told me that he got money from the Americans and then he went to al-Qaeda and got money from them, and then went back to the US and convinced them to stop bombing, and then he led al-Qaeda down from Tora Bora into Kurram Agency, Pakistan."[12] He put down his notes and looked up, his eyes hard, dark, and clear: "He [Zaman] was working with the ISI and they paved the way for al-Qaeda into Kurram."

He drank more tea and said, "On June 7, 2002, Hajji Qadir, the governor of Nangarhar province, was killed in Kabul. My source, who is a very deep source, said that Hezb-i-Islami, meaning Gulbuddin Hekmatyar, killed him on orders of the ISI, because he was too close to the Northern Alliance and was fighting the Taliban. His brother, Din Mohammad, became governor of Nangarhar. Then President Karzai, under pressure from the US, made Gul Agha Sherzai, who is from Kandahar, governor of Nangarhar."

It is well known, and much has been written about, how close Sherzai, a rough, burly man,[13] became to the US military in Kandahar. Moustache continued, "Sherzai immediately told Karzai that he needed Zaman, who was known to have worked for the CIA at Tora Bora, and the ISI, the Afghan government, al-Qaeda, and the Taliban, as his deputy chief of police for Nangarhar."

Moustache paused and put his glasses down, "Nangarhar, because it is on the border with Pakistan, and because of the drug trafficking routes that pass through there, is maybe the easiest place in Afghanistan to make a lot of money. Sherzai could never have got that job if Abdul Haq and his brother Hajji Qadir were alive." He was quiet, thinking.

"Zaman might have killed Qadir not just on orders from the ISI because he was backing the Taliban, but because he and Sherzai had planned it this way," I said.

"Yes," he agreed, his eyes dark and piercing now. He was afraid to say this directly, afraid that the ISI would find out that he had said this to me. "Hajji Qadir tried to create a multi-ethnic Northern Alliance group to fight the Taliban. He was killed for this. In 2010, Hajji Mohammad Zaman was killed by a suicide bomber."

I told Moustache that Din Mohammad had told me, indirectly, that his family had killed Hajji Zaman. It was revenge because Zaman had killed his brother, Hajji Qadir, "There is peace between our families now," Din Mohammad had said. Moustache nodded, accepting this. He understood revenge. He, too, was a Pashtun.

But I didn't know all this information in late August 2014, when I sat with Sami in London. I was just beginning my search.

"Abdullah knew," Sami concluded, "that people were getting close to him." By "people" Sami meant the CBS team, of which he was a part.

I remembered Gulob saying to me one night, menacingly, "They have tried to capture Abdullah, but this time he has escaped. If they capture him, it will be very bad for you." It seemed now that he was telling me the truth.

He said that "everyone," meaning his contacts in the Taliban, knew about my case. He said that the CBS team gave $500 to an Afghan journalist to go to Abdullah's house, but he wasn't there. The noose was tightening, but they were afraid Abdullah would sell me. I was a commodity, well known now, and it was too dangerous to keep holding me. Abdullah had to protect himself and by selling me he could make quick money and be free of me. The word was out, Sami repeated: "An American has been kidnapped."

Sundown was approaching and Sami was hungry and said we would talk more later. He wanted to say hello to Bryn and then to go eat. I went with him to the CBS newsroom. We walked in and Sami saw friends and started talking to them. Bryn saw us and came over, happy to see Sami, and they shook hands warmly. "It is interesting," I said, "that Sami can travel so easily back and forth from Pakistan to London." Bryn smiled. "We all know that Sami has a special relationship," he replied. Exactly what that was, he didn't say.

Sami and I drove to a halal or "lawful" restaurant in West London, which was filled with people, it appeared, of Pakistani heritage. I thought I was in Pakistan. We had iftar and I told Sami that I was trying to get a visa for Afghanistan and Pakistan. Sami said that the Afghan ambassador in London was a friend of his. He would think how to get a visa for me for Pakistan. Again, he was being kind, in complete contrast to when we worked together in the mountains in December 2006. I said I had heard that Asif Durrani, the acting ambassador of the Pakistani embassy in Kabul in 2007, when I was there, had been transferred and was now the high commissioner for Pakistan in London. No, Sami said. Durrani was no longer the high commissioner in London, but was the Pakistani ambassador now in Dubai. He would find Durrani's phone number and e-mail for me. I was impressed that he knew the Afghan and Pakistani ambassadors personally. I kept wondering about what Bryn described as Sami's "special arrangement" with the Pakistani government. I wanted to return to Pakistan to see Gohar Zaman, but I was afraid to go back to where I had been kidnapped. "We will not let the bird out of the cage a second time," Gulob said to me. I didn't know what the links were between Abdullah and the government. I didn't know what they were, or even if they existed, between Sami and the government. I didn't know who might be waiting for me. But I had to go.

The next day I called Durrani in Dubai, used Sami's name, and left a message, but he didn't respond. I sent him an e-mail, but he didn't respond to that either. I was afraid that he would blackball me again. Professor Amin had said that Durrani had blackballed me after I went to see him in the fall 2007. Sami called to tell me that the Afghan ambassador in London would see me. I went to the ambassador's office, in his home. He promised to give me a visa. The embassy gave it to me the next day.

On August 19, still in London, I was walking through the CBS newsroom and looked at a television on the wall and stopped. Jim Foley, the American journalist kidnapped by ISIS on November 22, 2012, in an orange prison suit, was kneeling in the sun, and a man in black holding a knife stood next to him. I knew that he had been kidnapped and was being held in Syria. No, I said silently. No, no. I turned away and then I looked at another image of him taken from the side with his eyes shining. "That poor courageous man," I said to myself. He was holding his head high, his back straight, and he was waiting. He knew what was coming. He'd been preparing for this for weeks. I didn't think at that moment that maybe ISIS had demanded a ransom, that what had begun with Daniel Pearl had now reached Syria, that journalists were no longer observers, but a central part of political theater, and war, and that the Trade was a part of both.

I thought only of Jim Foley's bravery and courage, of how he must have been trembling inside, but would not let it show. I could see it in his eyes. What a great, courageous man. I walked away, my stomach in a knot, crying inside. He had not flinched in the face of death.

I walked to my office, put my head on my desk, and then I went outside for a walk.

The next day I met with Sami again. He knew a man in the Pakistani embassy in Kuwait and another in Amman. He would contact them for me. I said that I wanted to meet a member of the Taliban in the Middle East who would know about Haqqani. He had an idea.

I flew to Amman, arriving at midnight, and the man at passport control looked at me, this American with gray hair and a long beard with visas for Yemen, Saudi Arabia, Egypt, and Sudan, and hesitated, too long I thought, before he stamped my passport. A tall thin man came up to me and said my name, took my bag, and we walked outside. His name was Eamon, a Palestinian who worked for the main CBS fixer for the Middle East; they were both based in Amman. Eamon had short hair, wore jeans and a T-shirt, and had a hip, no-nonsense way about him that was comforting. Eamon was an Irish name. He nodded in agreement. His parents liked it. We drove through the hills with pine trees, and quiet streets, to my hotel. I had breakfast outside, and then the fixer came in an SUV and took me to a café. We sat in a corner and a man pitched his idea for a television production company. The fixer was a Christian Palestinian, a businessman, fixer, and wheeler-dealer.

I wanted to learn about ISIS, and the differences among ISIS, the Taliban, and al-Qaeda, if there were any, and about links to the Tribal Areas. The fixer introduced me to people and I went from there. It was always the same, whether in the Amazon or Afghanistan. I met one person and he, or she, led me to another. Everything was based upon instinct and trust.

Sami sent me the name of a man to see at the Pakistani embassy in Amman. A receptionist directed me to his office. A man in his thirties put down his newspaper and asked what I wanted. He took my passport and went into another room and ten minutes later returned. "You have to go back to your country of origin. We only issue visas for people who live in Jordan."

Always, it was the same with Pakistan. It hadn't given me a visa since March 2007.

❖ ❖ ❖

ON SEPTEMBER 2, I watched Steven Sotloff, the next American jour-nalist kidnapped by ISIS, on August 4, 2013, on his knees in an orange prison suit. He too held his head up, his back straight, while the same man who'd held a knife to Foley stood next to him, all in black, holding a knife to Steven and ranting against America. I shivered. For days now it had been coming: ISIS said that he was next. I had watched his par-ents plead to his captors to save their son. But ISIS wanted war. Men in Saudi Arabia told me that ISIS fighters were fighting their parents, for their weakness against dictatorships. Steven Sotloff, I would learn, loved his parents, and they loved him. All I knew then was that Steven had possibly become the next man caught in the web of this unbearably cruel and vicious trade, this selling of human beings, this act of war, this murder of innocents. Steven too was so courageous, kneeling with his head high, never flinching, facing the camera, not giving in. "Everyone has two lives," Steven wrote to his parents while waiting in his cell to die. "A second one begins when you realize you only have one."

I was living a second life. I had a responsibility to Daniel Pearl, but also now to Steven Sotloff, to Jim Foley, to Nicholas Berg, beheaded in Iraq in May 2004. I didn't know then that ISIS had demanded a ran-som of 100 million euros ($137 million) in exchange for the release of seven US and British captives, and that the US government said that it could prosecute the families, and others who tried to raise money for them, for trying to ransom their children. I didn't know either that Mr. and Mrs. Sotloff would learn about their son's death by seeing him on television, just as the Pearls had, just like the Foleys. Before them in Afghanistan and Pakistan it had been Sayed Agha, Daniele Mastrogi-acomo's driver in Afghanistan in 2007, slaughtered like an animal, and then Ajmal Naqshbandi, and then Piotr Stańczak, the Polish geologist, all killed because their governments didn't pay a ransom. They had all become pawns in war, shown on television.

The next day, I took a taxi to have lunch at a man's house. I asked the driver to stop at a grocery store where we were supposed to meet. I waited in the shade, moving from one spot to the next, not wanting to stand out, afraid, even in Amman, of being kidnapped. I called him and he picked me up in his car.

He was a prominent, independent analyst and was watched, he said, by the Americans. His teenage daughter won a scholarship to study in the United States, and was sitting on the plane waiting to leave and Jordanian officials came and took her off. The BBC had called to ask him to go on television that evening to talk about the death of Sotloff, whose murder resonated not just in America but across Europe and the Middle East. The BBC called him often, he said, a sign that it respected his analysis. His two sons were with us in his house. I expected them to be pious, quiet young boys, wary of a foreigner, but one boy, about ten, talked to me while on his computer. His older brother was studying to be an accountant. The analyst, at my request, had asked two men from ISIS if they would see me. I was afraid, but wanted to talk to them. I had been waiting for almost a week.

We sat in the living room drinking tea. "It's time for me to go back to Afghanistan," I said. It was the first time I had shared my growing conviction with anyone else. I thought about it all the time. He shook his head. He had done research on me. "I advise you not to go back there. It makes me nervous." I wished that I hadn't told him. "Maybe you're right," I said. It was better to keep quiet. He drove me back to my hotel on his way to the BBC. "Don't go," he said again. We shook hands and I thanked him.

That night we spoke again: he still hadn't been able to reach the ISIS men. I was glad that they weren't available. Fireworks went off outside my window. I thought it was gunfire, turned out the light, and went out to the balcony, but it stopped. A wedding. I went back to bed and the fireworks started again.

The next day I went to the fixer's office where I was working. He was in Baghdad with a *60 Minutes* crew. Eamon and I sat at the same long table. "The ISIS people won't see me," I said.

"What about your visa for Pakistan?" he asked.

"They said I had to apply from my home country." I was nervous. ISIS had just beheaded Jim Foley and Steven Sotloff. The only difference between them and me and Daniel Pearl and me—and it was all the difference in the world, and I didn't deserve to even talk about it—was that the man standing behind me, when he went to pull the knife out, left it there. I was traded, I thought, my life for money. I didn't know then that there was more to it than money. Eamon looked up from his computer. He too had done research. He looked at me hard. "It's very dangerous for you. Don't go."

"Maybe I won't," I said, but I knew that I would end up going. It was Friday, and the office closed early. I walked that afternoon through Amman and returned to the hotel. I called the travel agency I used in London and booked a flight that night to Kabul. I had to fly to Dubai and catch a morning flight from there. I wouldn't sleep. I sent a note to Bryn Padrig. I asked the front desk to check me out. I called Eamon. "I am leaving tonight. Can you take me to the airport?"

He understood. "It's Friday and I have to be with my family, but I'll call someone and he'll come and take you. All the best to you, my friend." I felt the warmth in his voice.

I checked my e-mail and there was a note from Bryn Padrig. The new CBS manager would meet me at the airport. "No chances. Take great care." He too was nervous. The new CBS manager had replaced Fazul, who had left, worn out after thirteen years of late-night phone calls from London and New York. The taxi came and we drove through the warm, clear night. I looked at the stars and talked with the driver about the Jordanian royal family, once the ruling clan of Mecca, placed in power by the British.

"They are thieves," Eamon had said in the office. "Everyone hates the government. We trust the army and the border patrol to protect us from ISIS, but the royal family just steals money to enrich itself because it knows the end is near for them." Other men said the same thing. I never read this at home.

I stared out the window as we flew to Dubai. For six years, I wondered if my name was on a secret list at the airport in Kabul. The Taliban underground would alert their people when I passed through customs and they would come after me.

I tried to sleep in the Dubai airport, but I couldn't. Just before dawn they called the flight and we boarded a bus and rode out onto the tarmac and stopped, and I stood with Afghan passengers, feeling distant from them. I couldn't turn back now. Finally, the doors opened and we walked onto the plane. I didn't sleep a minute. We flew over water, and then the sun rose and rolling gray mountains appeared with wisps of thin gray clouds hanging over them. I had looked down at these mountains when I left Afghanistan in 2008. I kept staring at them. I saw a village in a valley and other villages appeared, and then a military base with rows of tan trucks, and the settlement widened. It was Kabul.

I had my visa from London, but I walked slowly into the terminal, wondering what would happen when the visa officer saw my name. The Taliban were everywhere. They were not just bearded men in the mountains, but were men with clean-shaven faces, teaching in schools and working in government offices, and, I assumed, stamping passports in the airport. I stood in front of a dark wood booth and an agent looked at my passport, and then he looked at me and back at my picture. I waited. He stamped my passport and I walked into the baggage room. The first time I had come here with Kody we drove to two adobe huts in a wasteland on the Iranian border and I had to get stamps from men in both before they would let us in the country. Back and forth we went, laughing at the absurdity of it all. Dusk came and we had to sleep in the car, but it didn't matter. We got our visas the next morning and drove to Herat. It was an adventure.

It was simpler now, and scary. A man held up a sign with my name on it. He picked up my bag and we walked out into the sun. I smelled the air of Afghanistan, a distant mixture now, once strong, of burning wood, sewage, and mountain air.

The CBS manager, a short man in his twenties, smiled and introduced himself. "We have to walk. The road is blocked. A soldier said they found a car with a suicide bomber and diffused the bomb." We walked through stalled traffic and I could feel tension in the air, but there was more energy here than in Amman. People were not as beaten-down as they were in Arabia. Dur Mohammad, the CBS driver, gave me a big smile as I climbed into the SUV. I felt warm seeing him again after six years. I asked about his family.

Cars started to move and we slowly made our way down streets I knew well. A van stopped in front of us and tried to turn around. Traffic stopped and a lanky man holding a rifle in one hand and a walkie-talkie in the other casually directed it. No one honked. "Who is that with the rifle?" I asked.

"NDS," said the manager. We drove down a narrow, curved road lined with gray cement barricades or high gray cement walls and it was like driving through an ugly urban canyon, but then we passed a modern white building near the foreign ministry and for a moment Kabul looked prosperous. We reached the Serena Hotel, where a German shepherd sniffed our bags. I was back in Afghanistan, and my life, and everything I knew about my kidnapping, was about to change.

Chapter 12

Meetings with
Four Important Men

A STEEL DOOR OPENED AND AS I ENTERED A SMALL ROOM, A GUARD told me to empty my pockets onto a tray. He frisked me gently, and another steel door opened, and another man frisked me and then I walked across the courtyard and entered the lobby of the Serena Hotel, once the Kabul Hotel. Here, on the morning of February 14, 1979, US ambassador Adolph Dubs was brought, after being kidnapped from his armored car by four unknown men, one of whom may have worn a police uniform. The US advised caution, but Afghan communist security forces, overseen by Soviet KGB agents, rushed the room, and during a firefight Dubs was murdered, shot in the head from six inches away. Ten months later, the Soviet Union invaded Afghanistan. To this day no one appears to know who killed Dubs, or why.

There were guards in the lobby now with hard eyes and unshaven faces, in bullet-proof vests, holding rifles. I promised Bryn Padrig that

I wouldn't leave the hotel grounds. CBS considered the hotel safe, but I wasn't sure. On January 14, 2008, the city was quiet and we heard the bomb go off, a suicide attacker detonating his vest. There was gunfire and then sirens wailing. The Haqqani Network killed six that day.[14] On March 21, 2014, the first day of spring—and the Afghan new year's day, a secular holiday in Afghanistan that Gulob, my jailer, told me that the Taliban do not celebrate—four teenage Taliban, hiding small pistols in their oversized shoes, passed through security and attacked hotel employees and guests, killing nine, among them Ahmad Sardar, an Afghan journalist with Agence France-Presse, his wife, and two of this three children. The next day the hotel manager, from Pakistan, did not come to work, but went back to Pakistan.

I checked into the hotel. The desk clerk, a woman, gave me a room on the second floor across from the CBS office. I unpacked and went down to the restaurant to have lunch with the CBS manager. While I waited, I went through my mind whom I needed to see in Kabul, the most important of whom was Din Mohammad, to apologize for betraying him and his family. I also wanted to talk to Fazul Rahim, my friend, the former CBS manager, who risked his life to lead the search for me inside Afghanistan. We didn't have a chance to talk before I left in 2008. I hoped he could help me get to Feridoun, who had brought me to the US Army base in Jalalabad, and maybe I would see Shahwali. I was afraid of him and would only meet him with Fazul in an outdoor public place, like Shar-e-Naw Park, with bodyguards. I wanted to see Enayat, the tribal chief who had taken me to the border in 2007 into Kurram Agency, and who would know people who could tell me about the Haqqani Network. Finally, I wanted to see Ehsanullah, my old journalist friend and, I hoped, a neutral observer.

The CBS manager and I had lunch, and he talked about his family. "We are going to see a friend of yours tonight," he teased. I tried to guess who he meant.

"No," he replied, "Hajji Din Mohammad."

I couldn't believe that he had arranged it. I had sent him *Captive* and asked him to take it to Din Mohammad, whom I had known for so long, I felt, and considered my most trustworthy friend in Afghanistan, although, in truth, I didn't know him well. I had met him with Yunus Khalis in 1981 and liked him, but we were together not more than two hours, and then I saw him again in New York in 1984 when he came to the door at the suite we rented at the UN Plaza Hotel to introduce the Afghan mujahideen government in exile to UN representatives. Still, twenty-four years later, in my ambition to cross the border, I ignored Din Mohammad's driver, who had come at the last minute to take me to safety, and had entrusted my safety instead to a criminal, Abdullah, who was maybe a member of the Taliban, maybe tied to the Pakistani government, maybe not, but who had murdered Din Mohammad's brother, and who was at war with Din Mohammad and his family. I couldn't believe that I had done it.

"Yes," said the CBS manager, "he is coming at five p.m." He was pleased that I was pleased.

I changed my clothes and put on a suit. The manager called to say that Din Mohammad would be late. The afternoon passed. I tried to concentrate, but couldn't read or write. I made tea and went across the hall to the CBS office and sat with the manager and discussed Afghan politics. Finally Din Mohammad phoned to say he would be there in five minutes. We went downstairs to meet him as he walked across the lobby, solidly built, six feet, slightly stooped now, with a white beard, a black turban with white stripes, and in white Afghan clothes and black sandals. An assistant walked behind him. We shook hands warmly. I wanted to hug him, but I couldn't, not in front of others. He was powerful, the lead negotiator with the Taliban.

The Pashtun doorkeeper, with his rugged face, different from the urban Tajik and Hazara staff, said hello. They shook hands and we walked together to the elevator. It wasn't working. Did he mind taking the stairs? He smiled, of course not, and he climbed them easily. I was glad that he was still strong. The CBS manager brought coffee to my room, but I didn't want any. I didn't want the manager there, but I let him stay. Din Mohammad sat silently. The power in the hotel went off. The room was suddenly dark. Was this a prelude to an attack? The lights came back on and I relaxed a bit. He waited and I began:

"In 2007, I was here for CBS and I also had a contract to write on what the West calls Islamic fundamentalism in South Asia—Afghanistan, Pakistan, India, Kashmir, and Bangladesh." He nodded, understanding. "Just as I was finishing, I got a call from a publisher and I returned to New York and the editor asked if I could go into the Tribal Areas and write about what he called 'a blank space' on the map, unknown to the West. The CIA didn't seem to know where bin Laden was. I had wanted to do that for the past five years and to see Haqqani. I had already seen Yunus Khalis. I thought if I could get to Haqqani I could learn about bin Laden.

"I didn't know where to begin. The CBS manager in Afghanistan took me to see Mirwais Yasini to talk to him about a story on drug trafficking. He was head of an anti-drug commission. He said he had been with Yunus Khalis in the 1980s and took Dan Rather into Afghanistan."

Din Mohammad smiled. "Dan Rather, I remember." He had arranged his trip, as he had arranged mine.

"That September, I went back to see Yasini on my own, to begin my project, separate from CBS."

"If you had come to me, I could have arranged for you easily to go," said Din Mohammad, "and to stay there for a week or two, and nothing would have happened to you."

I put my head in my hands. If only I had known how to find him, everything would have been different. I could have gone many times. Maybe I could have seen Haqqani and learned about bin Laden. I would never have been kidnapped. I would never have made all those crossings into the mountains, going with the Taliban, living on the edge.

After the Soviets left Afghanistan in February 1989, I continued to think of Din Mohammad and other Afghans I knew, but as the years passed I forgot his name, and those of many Afghans from the 1980s. It was Ehsanullah who reminded me of Din Mohammad's name and gave me his phone number, and then Shahwali brought his book to me.

"Yasini invited me back and the next night I went to his house again, and again I asked him," I continued. "He knew a man who might be able to help me, but it would take a few days. Three days later he introduced me to Mullah Malang. He said that he fought in Kandahar during jihad, with seven hundred men under him, and was part of the Yunus Khalis's network."

"Was Yasini there when you talked with Malang?" Din Mohammad interrupted.

"No, he made the introduction and then left. It was just the two of us. He said that he knew a man who could help me. His name was Abdullah. He was from Jalalabad. He killed a man and had to leave Afghanistan. He moved to the Tribal Areas and joined the Taliban.

"Malang said the only way that Abdullah could come back was under a reconciliation program and that he needed him, as a member of parliament, to help him. I assumed he would protect me because of this and that I would be his guest and under Pashtunwali he had to protect me, on his honor, as a Pashtun. I thought I would be safe."

Now came the part I dreaded. I had to tell Din Mohammad that I betrayed him.

"I was told and then my guides confirmed that Abdullah killed or was part of the group that killed your brother Hajji Qadir. By going with Abdullah I was aligning myself with your enemy. I betrayed you." There, I had said it. I felt a mixture of relief and shame. "One of Abdullah's men, either a member of his family, or part of the Taliban, or both, who was imprisoned with me, said that they were in a feud with your family. After my book came out I got a letter from a man with al-Qaeda, in prison—"

"Here?"

"No, in America. He lived in the Tribal Areas in the 1980s and '90s, was part of bin Laden's group and said I was kidnapped because I got caught in the middle of a feud between your family and Abdullah's family. I was tied to you, and that kidnapping me was a way of getting back at you."

The room was silent. Din Mohammad sat looking at me, thinking, impassive.

Finally Din Mohammad spoke. "When my driver came back he told me where you were staying, and I became afraid for you."

"I trusted Mullah Malang," I said, "but not completely. I later heard that he worked for the CIA."

"He worked for everyone."

"Do you know Michael Semple?"

"Mullah Malang is close to Michael Semple."

I sat in silence. I didn't know this. I remembered again what Bryn Padrig, who had been in Pakistan for CBS directing the search for me, said on the phone from London, after I was released: "Michael Semple saved your life." I remembered that Semple told me that when I was in captivity Malang called Abdullah to his house in Islamabad and told him to release me and not harm me.

"Mullah Malang and Michael Semple are very close." I was concerned that Semple and Mullah Malang never told me this. Maybe it wasn't important.

I thought back to August 2007, when I had been looking for help along the border and Roshan Khadivi urged me to call Semple. He spoke Dari and Pashto, she said. He was the best man to help along the border.

Semple had been warm and friendly when we met in Washington in 2008, but again I felt that he had been holding back. Maybe it was just the way he worked. I assumed that he didn't want to reveal his sources, which was normal. I would be the same way. Semple was an accomplished man, number two in the EU mission in Afghanistan, and, if it was true what people said and articles implied, perhaps close to British intelligence. He knew the Taliban probably better than any Westerner. He was unique, a Westerner working for powerful Western institutions, a Muslim, married to a Pakistani, living in Pakistan.

How did Semple find me, and get me out, I wondered? I could not explain why the Maulvi had kept saying, "Congratulations on escaping death." Something told me that it wasn't just because I was ransomed. A small part of me wondered if Haqqani wasn't involved in getting me released. I had mentioned his name enough, hoping that the Maulvi would find a way to get to Haqqani to ask him about me. After all, this was one reason why I had come to the Tribal Areas: hopefully, to find Haqqani. "You were kidnapped by a criminal gang, not the Taliban," Semple had said, with conviction. I still wasn't convinced, six years later. If they were criminals, why did they spend hours trying to convert me, talking about Islam every day, giving me four books on Islam to read, preaching to me, patiently showing me how to pray, like a Wahhabi? Gulob told me where to hold my hands, when to bow and how many times, standing behind me or beside me, reciting the full Kalima, making sure I said each word correctly, like the best teacher one could have. I went along, feeling nothing. Gulob knew that I wasn't Muslim, but said, toward the end, that I was drawing close to Islam. I felt like a charlatan, but I was afraid, trying to stay alive. Gulob seemed fervent in his beliefs. We listened for hours to Taliban suicide tapes. Gulob sat on his knees, clenching his fists, looking upward, his eyes glistening, as he listened to the young men chanting, like a haunting Vienna Boys Choir. "I have been trained to be a suicide bomber," he said, "and so have my children." He came in one night, took a box of ammunition that was on a barred window sill, put it on his shoulder, and left. He was going on jihad. "We are Wahhabis," he said. "You must learn to pray as a Wahhabi." Bin Laden was a Wahhabi. Their preachers were Wahhabis. Was this all a ruse? If so, they should be on Broadway. They were remarkable actors.

I had asked Semple in Washington how he learned Dari and he told me enthusiastically that some UN people had been kidnapped and he had been asked to help. He was sitting in a car, a book in his lap, learning Dari while going to meet with the kidnappers to negotiate. He was laughing infectiously as he told me the story. I repeated the story to Din Mohammad.

"In 2003 or 2004, some UN people were kidnapped in Kabul," he responded. "The ransom demand was 15,000,000 euros. Mullah Malang was involved in this case. The hostages were released, but just then the police and the NDS came in and the money disappeared. I asked Mullah Malang where the money was and he said he didn't know."

The *New York Times* and other papers reported that on October 28, 2004, three UN employees, two women and a man, were riding in a white SUV with the pale blue UN letters on the side, in Wazir Akbar Khan, the diplomatic enclave in Kabul. A black SUV, with tinted windows, cut the UN vehicle off, and five men in police uniforms jumped out, grabbed the three UN employees, beat their driver, and drove away.

At six thirty in the morning, on November 23, the three employees drove a car to a meeting point where a UN vehicle was waiting, got out, climbed in the UN vehicle, and left. The interior minister said that no ransom was paid.

It was the first kidnapping of UN employees there since before 9/11, the first kidnapping of foreigners, I believed, since US ambassador Dubs. If the ransom demand was 15 million euros, that was 5 million euros, or nearly $5.5 million, per person. If the kidnappers spoke Dari, as Michael said, that meant that they were probably Tajiks and it was a criminal operation. The Taliban were Pashtuns. Din Mohammad was changing my view of Semple. But this was before I would learn the other sides to this case.

I changed the subject. I said that Sami Yousafzai, an Afghan journalist living in Pakistan, told me that Abdullah worked for Hajji Zaman, one of the three men hired by the CIA to find bin Laden at Tora Bora.

"Hajji Zaman worked for the ISI," said Din Mohammad.

Again, I was silenced. If this was true, and Abdullah worked for Hajji Zaman, that meant that Abdullah very possibly worked, in some capacity, for the ISI, which meant the ISI knew about my kidnapping. I based this thought, at first, only upon my sense that there were unknown people behind the Maulvi directing my kidnapping and that just before I was released, I was at some type of military base with Abdullah. I kept wondering about the links between the CIA and the ISI. They once worked together and still did. I thought all the time about the man at the US Army base who said they knew all about me. From whom?

Din Mohammad said that Malang worked for everyone, and Semple said that Malang had a house in Pakistan. It was illegal for a foreigner to own property in Pakistan, but Afghans with connections—either with businessmen, if they were doing business, or with the government—could avoid the law. I wondered why Malang, an MP with no known business ties, had a house in Pakistan unless he had ties to the government.

Further, if Hajji Zaman worked for the ISI, this would explain why he had not tried to kill or capture bin Laden. He took the CIA money and let bin Laden, it seemed, get away. Was he behind my kidnapping?

I told Din Mohammad that one of the men in the cell with me, meaning Samad, said that his family, but not he himself, had killed and wounded nineteen members of Din Mohammad's family in a feud. Din Mohammad didn't flinch.

"Abdullah thinks that my nephew, Hajji Zahir, was involved in the death of his brother," said Din Mohammad. "That is why Abdullah went to Hajji Zaman. It's not true. He wasn't involved."

I asked if Abdullah had assassinated his brother, Hajji Qadir. He said no. So what Malang, Razi Gul, and Samad told me was a lie. Either they didn't know the truth, which I didn't believe, or they lied to confuse me, or to keep me away from Din Mohammad. Or, was Din Mohammad lying? I didn't want to believe that. I was entering a dark world.

I asked about Mullah Malang. Din Mohammad said that he had a place in the National Security Office. He worked for everyone, meaning Afghanistan, Pakistan, and the US. "He is from Badghis," he said, "and fought jihad, with our party, in Kandahar. He lives in Kabul now."

By "jihad," he meant the Soviet war. *Badghis* means "home of the winds," which come off the Asian steppe. It is in the northwest on the Turkmenistan border. It was interesting, although not unheard of, that a man would travel hundreds of miles from his tribal area and become a guerrilla commander, and now work for different countries. He had gone, as a young man, from Badghis to Kandahar, seeking his fortune. This is where he would have become close to Pakistan, which was close and which controlled the arms supply to the mujahideen. He was an outsider, maybe a soldier of fortune. I wanted to find out more about him.

I asked Din Mohammad if Malang was fighting his family, meaning the Arsala family. He waved his hand. He couldn't harm them. "He was either trying to trap me by kidnapping you," he said, "because he knows we are friends, or he is a dealer between the kidnappers and those who are kidnapped."

Maybe he was a professional go-between, an Afghan part of the Trade. I remembered when he showed me the picture of the Gandharan statue and asked if I knew someone who wanted to buy it in New York. He seemed like a man who would do anything for money. Sharif said that Malang, while a prominent commander during jihad, had lost his luster toward the end of the war by getting involved in unsavory business deals. But then Sharif, I was certain, had betrayed Sean Langan, and probably got a portion of the money that Channel 4 paid. The business of the Trade had gone on for decades along the Afghan frontier, but now it involved the betrayal of guests, of outsiders, and deceit, but also beheadings. The Trade was now a $1.5 billion international criminal enterprise.[15] Al-Qaeda franchises across Africa and the Middle East had developed a protocol for kidnappings. In January 2014, in Sana'a, Yemen, former prime minister Abdul Karim al-Eryani told me that British prime minister William Hague[16] told him that al-Qaeda there had made $35 million from kidnapping. Mullah Malang may have seen an opportunity in a growing business and wanted to make money. It was better than trying to sell ancient Afghan artifacts. But I didn't know the truth.

Din Mohammad continued: "Mullah Malang got money in the UN kidnapping case. He took it and told the kidnappers to release the victims. The police came and Mullah Malang wouldn't give them the money and now there is a problem between them. There was a deal between NDS and Malang, a competition for the money. I think you were probably kidnapped for money. There is a rule in Afghanistan. 'He who is involved gets his share.'"

I sat there quietly. I was in shock.

This meant, if I was ransomed, and it appeared I was, that not just Malang, but possibly Abdullah, Gulob, Shahwali, Razi Gul, Samad, Hajji Zaman, and who knows who else may have received a "share." They were all contractors brought in on this business deal. That would explain why Shahwali was happy at the US base in Jalalabad and for the first time didn't ask me for money. The Pearl Project listed twenty-seven men involved in Daniel Pearl's kidnapping. I wondered now how many were involved in mine. The Trade was a business with a payroll. In Yemen, it involved criminal gangs, al-Qaeda, its government backers, and the tribes that let al-Qaeda live on their land. In Pakistan, especially along the Afghan border, and in Iraq, it involved murder, now of foreigners.

One year after I sat with Din Mohammad that night, I learned that Peter Jouvenal, the former BBC cameraman in Afghanistan and the former owner of the Gandamack, who had gone to Afghanistan, as I had, in 1981 but who stayed on, was involved in trying to resolve the UN kidnapping in Kabul.

"The US was worried, after the kidnapping in Iraq in 2004, that Iraq was spinning out of control and that kidnapping of foreigners, and demands for ransoms, would spill over into Afghanistan and it wanted to send a message immediately that this would not be tolerated," Jouvenal said. "The Karzai government, which was a transition government, which had been appointed in December 2001, was preparing for Afghanistan's first ever presidential elections, on October 9, and the US didn't want a prominent kidnapping to affect it." The kidnappers, calling themselves the Army of Muslims,[17] took the three UN employees, who had worked on the elections, on October 28. They were released on November 24. "Before, there was the perception among Afghans that you could go after an Afghan businessman and that government wouldn't do anything. There had been hundreds of kidnappings of Afghans over the years, but never of foreigners." Jouvenal had forgotten about Adolph Dubs, the US ambassador, but the US probably had not. "I had been involved in helping resolve many kidnappings during the Soviet time, and in Pakistan, but they never involved ransoms," he said.

Jouvenal was right about US fears. After the kidnapping was resolved Zalmay Khalilzad said, "It is a major defeat to terrorists who wanted to export an Iraq-style of hostage-taking in Afghanistan."[18]

The BBC reported that Jouvenal was suspected of being involved in the kidnapping,[19] and the Afghan government took him into custody.

"I was asked to get involved in the UN kidnapping. I made contacts with a Yunus Khalis commander," Jouvenal responded. He didn't remember the commander's name. "I met Behgjet Pacolli,[20] a Kosovo businessman—one of the UN kidnap victims was from Kosovo—whose hobby was resolving kidnappings. He decided to try to negotiate the release of the three hostages. He came with a suitcase filled with dollars. Pacolli gave it some tribal leaders, and I don't think he saw it again."

Since 9/11, it appears that more than one hundred foreigners, approximately, have been kidnapped in Afghanistan,[21] twelve of whom were journalists, and approximately a dozen foreigners, three of whom were journalists, in Pakistan. The Taliban demanded a ransom[22] for Piotr Stańczak, the Polish geologist, and that Poland withdraw its twenty-six soldiers in Afghanistan, just as they demanded of Italy that it withdraw its soldiers in exchange for Mastrogiacomo. The Poles refused to pay the ransom. The Taliban asked Stańczak, who was Catholic, to convert, but he held on to his faith,[23] and they executed him, the next Westerner after Daniel Pearl to be kidnapped and murdered in Pakistan. One report said that Stańczak got caught in a feud between two rival Taliban groups and one, in anger, beheaded him.[24] When I read this, I understood better why my kidnappers wanted to keep me hidden. Italy paid a ransom and Mastrogiacomo is alive.

Again, I felt that my case was different, but I didn't know why. Somewhere behind Abdullah lay Hajji Zaman and the ISI. Again, I asked Din Mohammad who killed Hajji Qadir.

"There was a huge conspiracy behind this," he answered softly. "It was Hajji Zaman." There was no problem today between Hajji Zaman's people and the Arsala family. They had a tribal *jirga*. A jirga is like ancient Athenian democracy, when elders come together to discuss a problem, choose a leader, or settle a dispute; they vote openly, never secretly, for a man can say one thing publicly and vote another way. "A deal was made between Pashtuns and the deal is safe," said Din Mohammad. Hajji Zaman was killed in 2010. After this there was a shura, meaning a tribal council. I called it a peace conference. He was admitting that they had got their revenge. There was now peace between the families.

Din Mohammad was saying, without spelling it out again, it seemed, that the ISI ordered the killing of his brother and that Hajji Zaman, who worked for the ISI, pulled the trigger. It would be dangerous, but I had to find out if the ISI ordered Hajji Zaman to kidnap me, and if so, why.

Hajji Zaman, like Yunus Khalis, grew up at the base of Tora Bora, near Jalalabad, of the same tribe, and I assumed joined Khalis's mujahideen party,[25] to which Malang and Yasini belonged, and which, like the other six mujahideen parties, was controlled by the ISI. I wondered if I had met Zaman when I lived with Haqqani. We were allies then.

I reread the passage in the memoirs of one of America's premier diplomats of that era in which he wrote that the CIA had lured Zaman back from France to Afghanistan after 9/11.[26] On December 3, 2001, his private militia, one of the three hired by the CIA—the other two were led by Hazrat Ali and Hajji Zahir, Hajji Qadir's ambitious son—began to move slowly up toward Tora Bora after al-Qaeda. On December 12, Zaman and al-Qaeda called a cease-fire. The next day al-Qaeda was to surrender. US forces at Tora Bora, under the control of military commanders elsewhere, were angry, and in the confusion, the remaining al-Qaeda forces escaped down the mountains to Pakistan. Hajji Zaman fled to Pakistan.

I needed to find a credible, neutral party to tell me who killed Hajji Zaman. I couldn't prove that it was the Arsala family, and I was afraid now that his death might have had something to do with my kidnapping, especially if Zaman (which I couldn't prove yet) worked for the ISI, whose tentacles seemed to be everywhere.

On July 6, 2002, two men fired over thirty bullets at Hajji Qadir—then both governor of Nangarhar Province and a vice president of Afghanistan—and at his son-in-law and driver, killing them in their vehicle outside Qadir's office in the center of Kabul, and then fled. Din Mohammad never said that the ISI killed Hajji Qadir, or his other brothers Abdul Haq and Mohammad Qasim Arsala, or his own son Izatullah in 2001, only that the Taliban killed them. I had to learn more about Hajji Zaman.

There was a link here among Zaman, the death of Abdul Haq, and me, and I had to figure it out because somewhere in there was, maybe, one reason why I was kidnapped. Robert McFarlane, President Reagan's national security adviser from 1983 to 1985, when he met Abdul Haq at the White House, wrote an article in the *Wall Street Journal* all but blaming the CIA, which he considered incompetent, for Haq's death.[27] He didn't mention the ISI.

It was getting late, but neither Din Mohammad nor I moved from our chairs.

I asked Din Mohammad if, after 9/11, the US wanted Abdul Haq to be president. I thought that this was one reason why he went into Afghanistan to rally tribal leaders, to convince America that he still had power. After Haq was killed, the US chose Hamid Karzai, in December at the Bonn Conference, to be president of the interim government of Afghanistan. Din Mohammad was very careful in his reply. He was afraid. I had to be careful, too. He wouldn't answer directly. He said that some people in the US wanted to solve the problem of Afghanistan politically, without violence, and wanted Abdul Haq to make a political deal with the Taliban. He confirmed that after his brother was killed, the US went with Karzai.

I asked who wanted to solve this politically. He didn't know if it was the CIA or the Pentagon, or which was opposed. He looked at me. "Maybe people will come after you if they find out that you are trying to find out the truth about what happened to you. As a friend, I warn you be careful."

Would they come after me here? Would the ISI come themselves? Would they send someone? I was afraid. I imagined them sending someone who could ghost into the hotel, pass unnoticed through the security checks, take out a pistol, and shoot me. Din Mohammad said that Kabul was full of ISI operatives, "It would be easy for them, if they felt you were going to expose them, to send someone, or to come after you directly."

Din Mohammad had to go, but before he left I asked him about Haqqani.

"We will meet and talk again," was his reply. He said that the man who came with me to see him in 2007 was called Shahwali, correct? It was a question, but he knew the answer. "He was from Kunar." I said yes. I wondered if he was going to do anything to Shahwali. I reminded him that Rasul Amin, head of the Afghanistan Study Centre, introduced me to Shahwali. He nodded. "Rasul Amin died," said Din Mohammad. "Yes," I acknowledged, "in 2009. Shahwali wrote to tell me."

Din Mohammed was silent for a moment. "Think about everything," he said. "Be careful. Look at all sides. My advice is to leave it. It's too murky."

We walked down to the lobby and the CBS manager walked him outside to his SUV. He returned ten minutes later and brought with him three books that Din Mohammad had written. "As we were standing outside," the manager said, "Hajji Din Mohammad said, 'Tell Jere to be careful. It is very dangerous for him. It was a conspiracy and by exposing it he will put himself in danger.'

"Money can do anything," said the manager. "They could send someone after you. I think you should leave immediately."

I wondered who "they" were, and what the conspiracy was. The manager was ready to go home to see his wife and daughters. He had shown me his children's picture. They were darling, smiling little girls. He asked if I trusted Hajji Din Mohammad. I didn't like this question, or him, for casting doubt on him. But I was worried that Din Mohammad couldn't tell me the whole truth, not just because he was afraid that I would write something that would harm him, but if he did tell me everything that I would lose respect for him and his family. We were friends and friendship, like trust, was everything. I needed him.

⁜ ⁜ ⁜

AMRULLAH SALEH, FORTY-THREE, a Tajik, former director of the NDS, clean-shaven, in khakis and blue sport coat, was in his sitting room. I had come to ask for his help. First, I needed to give him some background. I told him about my time in Afghanistan in the 1980s, and about my kidnapping in 2008. He listened. He would make this simple. Did I know the movie *Twelve Years a Slave*? I said no. I had been traveling for a year in the Middle East. "Go see it," he said. "It is about a good man, a violinist, captured by his friends and sold into slavery." According to Saleh, I was that man.

He began by telling me that Feridoun Mohmand, who picked me up after my release, was from the Mohmand tribe, as was Yasini, the MP who had introduced me to Mullah Malang. Then he added: "Feridoun Mohmand is an agent of the ISI."

My stomach tightened. The man who took me to the US Army base in Jalalabad after I was released worked for Pakistani military intelligence? "He was in touch with the US Army the whole time," said Fazul years later. So that was why he knew where to go.

"Feridoun Mohmand and Mullah Malang are best friends with Michael Semple," said Saleh. "Semple, the former deputy chief of mission of the EU in Afghanistan, is a subcontractor to MI6 and works with the ISI. What is an EU diplomat doing in Helmand Province trying to promote a reconciliation program with the Taliban? This was why Karzai kicked him out of the country. Michael Semple's wife is the daughter of a Pakistani army general."

I knew some of this, but not that Semple may work in some capacity for the ISI, or that Malang and Feridoun were friends, or that Feridoun was an ISI agent.

"Didn't you ask yourself: Why would he help me? What does he get out of this?" Saleh was exasperated at my naïveté.

I was embarrassed, but Semple had explained to me on the phone the night I was released why he got involved. I had believed him, and still did. He helped me "as one old Afghan hand to another." I loved that. It was the warmth of Afghanistan, surely?

David McCraw, the assistant legal counsel at the *New York Times*, had asked me the same question about Semple as Saleh did. I was told that Bryn Padrig had brought Semple in and I just assumed that CBS paid him a fee.

"In 2004, about October, this time of year, four UN employees were kidnapped," Saleh continued. "We could not get to them. It became a huge issue. Then comes Michael Semple and tells us, 'I know Mullah Malang, who knows how to get to the kidnappers.'" Saleh then said the NDS delivered five million dollars to Michael Semple and to Mullah Malang. The UN employees were released. Semple had not told me any of this; I would have to talk to Michael about this but first I had to hear Saleh out. He was, after all, a former head of Afghan intelligence.

"There was another case of a foreign national being kidnapped, an Italian." Saleh rubbed his forehead, closed his eyes, thinking. "His fixer was killed." I reminded him: "Yes, Naqshbandi was his fixer. It was an Italian journalist. Mastrogiacomo."

The Karzai government released five Taliban prisoners in exchange for Mastrogiacomo but refused to release any for Naqshbandi, which was why the Taliban beheaded him. Saleh asked where they took me. I described the route that we took toward Torkham, the border crossing. Saleh asked if I was kidnapped by Haqqani or by a kidnapping cell. I didn't know.

He said that his experience was that Haqqani would not have released me for so little money—my kidnappers had wanted $1.5 million, initially, and three prisoners from Guantanamo. I was taken into Khyber Agency, then Mohmand, maybe up to Bajaur. He took my notebook and drew a map.

"There is a lot of kidnapping in the area where you were. We get word of kidnappings every day. You were probably in the Gandow area, in Khyber Agency. That is Afridi territory or Mohmand. They are gangsters, mafia, and gun sellers.

"My advice is that you leave immediately," Saleh continued. "There is no government in Afghanistan today. If they cannot control Kabul, what about the rest of the country? Wait three months, send me an e-mail, and come back. Then we can interview people. Right now it is too dangerous. I am protecting myself. Those are my bodyguards outside. Kandahar is not reporting to Kabul. Mazar-i-Sharif does not report to Kabul. Even the city is not Karzai territory."

We walked outside. Men with rifles stood around us. There were barricades at each end of the bumpy dirt street. This all cost money. We had talked in a new, modern room in his house. He must have earned a high salary as head of the NDS. Again, he told me to leave immediately. He said he was talking to me like a brother.

We drove back over other bumpy streets. "I think you should leave tomorrow," said the CBS manager. I couldn't. I was still, without knowing it, in shock at what I was learning. I wanted to learn more, and I wanted to learn more about Haqqani, my original reason for embarking upon this whole trip. I was becoming Ahab and Haqqani was Moby Dick. Nobody associated with my kidnapping knew I was here, only Fazul, the new manager, Din Mohammad, Saleh, and Ehsanullah, my journalist friend. There were other men I wanted to see, but now I was worried. I was relatively safe in the hotel, although anyone could just walk in.

The manager called Bryn Padrig, who also said that I needed to leave immediately. I asked the manager for a CBS phone. Fazul always gave me one the day I arrived. It would take the new manager a week, and many requests before he would give me one. He was too busy with his new power running the CBS bureau. Besides, his father had worked for the NDS.

❖ ❖ ❖

I CALLED EHSANULLAH. On Friday, September 12, he came to the hotel and we sat in the courtyard. He looked around as men walked by looking at us. I had been in Kabul six days. Bryn called every day to ask when I was leaving.

Ehsanullah said Mullah Malang was a friend of Abdul Haq and Peter Tomsen,[28] the US diplomat. I told Ehsanullah—who like many Afghans only had one name—of my meeting in September 2007 with Asif Durrani, the acting ambassador at the Pakistani embassy, who Rasul Amin later said had blackballed me, and that Durrani had asked me to find information about Khalilzad. "Why would he do that?" I asked. I felt that Durrani was ISI and wanted to find out if the ISI put me on its radar in early 2007.

"Pakistan is after Zalmay Khalilzad," he said quietly, "because he is very anti-Pakistan. They killed his brother-in-law and two nephews. Zalmay means young. Khalilzad means son of Khalili. His family is from the east, but he grew up in the north. He had an office in the palace during the Karzai era. He was a virtual king here. Pakistan would want to target him, so maybe the ISI is behind Durrani."

Khalilzad had told me in the 1980s that the US could get his family out of Afghanistan anytime.

I asked why the Taliban had become so cruel and violent, beheading people. "If you push me up against the wall, the only thing I think about is revenge," Ehsanullah explained. He agreed to do research for me, but I had to pay him in dollars. That evening, I convinced the CBS manager to take me to a grocery store where there was an ATM. We drove past high gray concrete barricades, the ruination of Kabul, this once open city. I felt vulnerable away from the hotel, wondering if the Taliban knew I was there.

⁂ ⁂ ⁂

BRYN WAS DAILY putting more pressure on me to leave. I had called Fazul as soon as I got a phone, but he didn't want to talk in the hotel. He worked for NBC now and it was awkward with the CBS people, all of whom he had brought into the company, including the new manager. He invited me to dinner.

I put on Afghan clothes, the first time since I was kidnapped. I was returning to the past. I was nervous. Night came and Fazul called; he was waiting outside. I walked down the hallway, down the steps to the ground floor, and through the lobby, ignoring the hotel staff watching me, and walked outside, hesitated and then put on my *pakhool*, my felt hat. I felt so comfortable, but I was afraid. I didn't think that I would wear Afghan clothes again, especially this pakhool. I had slept on it in the cell.

I opened and walked through the steel doors to the outside wall. A guard stood by the last steel door, on the outside wall, looked through a peep-hole, waved at me, opened the door, and I walked onto the street. I felt vulnerable and quickly got in a blue SUV waiting by the door. It was dusk and the street was empty. Fazul smiled broadly. His infant son, Yusuf, was with him. He had his arm around him.

We drove thirty yards and sat at a red light. It was the first traffic light I had ever seen in Kabul. The city was becoming part of the modern world. I looked to see if the Taliban were coming for me. We drove past a checkpoint. The city was still busy and dusty with guards and concrete barriers. We pulled into a courtyard. There was a new house on one side and a new apartment building on the other. Fazul, his father, and two nephews (his son was too young to eat with us) and I ate dinner, watched the news, and the boys asked who my favorite football player was. They loved Messi, from Argentina. I smiled. Once there was no television here. Now they were part of the world.

Everyone left and Fazul and I drank saffron tea and he began the story that I had come to hear.

"I was in Peshawar. I had taken my mother there for a checkup. I remember clearly, it was late February. I last heard from you on the fifteenth, when you sent an e-mail saying you were leaving soon to cross the border. The next day you texted to say you were going. We had an agreement that you would text me every other day or every seventy-two hours." When, he had asked, should he start panicking—after three days?

I remembered. I thought he was being overly protective, but I did what he asked. I had been going for months up into the mountains, but each time I was with the Taliban for only an hour or two, and although I twice slept in the village afterward, and had been in a house just across the border, I always returned to relative safety.

"I was in the Peshawar Rahim hospital. My Afghan phone was on, in case I got a call from an Afghan number. I hadn't heard from you in over a week and was waiting."

I remembered sitting on the floor in the cell, wondering when Fazul would know that I had been taken.

"Bryn knew this. We had started panicking a bit. Nafay, Bryn, and I had a spontaneous call, each one of us calling the other because we hadn't heard anything." I felt badly that they had been so worried. "I got a call, in Pashtu. 'Is this Fazul? Do you know Jere?' I said yes. I knew immediately. He asked if I had a fax number. I gave him the one in Islamabad. 'We will fax you the message,' said your kidnappers. I called Nafay and told her to be prepared for bad news. I called Bryn."

I felt emotion welling up in me. All that I had pushed deep inside for six years was coming back. I knew pretty much what happened in the cell, but almost nothing about what happened on the outside.

"In less than half an hour, Nafay called and said the fax had arrived."

It was the ransom letter that I had written as the gunmen stood over me.

"'We'll call you back,' they said, and they hung up. I called Bryn and he said to call Michael Semple and gave me his number. I told Michael everything I knew. Bryn said to move to Islamabad. 'We'll set up a team with Michael.'"

The *Wall Street Journal* had set up an office for Daniel Pearl in Karachi.

"I moved to Islamabad. Nafay and I went to Michael [Semple]'s house outside of Islamabad and it was beautiful. I loved it there. It was a typical South Asian home, surrounded by fields where he grew vegetables and had people working for him. He is married to a Pakistani. He offered us the best coffee and delicious pastries. He lived very well with many servants. His wife's sister is a famous classical dancer, a big star. A day or two later we got another call, but no news. Almost every evening we went to Michael's house. Bryn wanted Sami Yousafzai there, because of his contacts with the Taliban, and so we brought him in.

"Another man came, Gohar Zaman, a former head of IB in the 1970s." The Intelligence Bureau was the oldest of Pakistan's intelligence agencies. "He was in his late seventies, and we didn't want him there because of his ties to the ISI, but Kroll, the CBS insurance company, had connections with a Pakistani insurance firm. He was with the insurance company and it said we must have him there. The first thing he asked was what kind of alcohol did we have. He wanted Russian vodka. He wasn't too helpful, but he was a character and Michael's house was a good retreat."

Kroll is a multinational corporate investigative agency and risk consulting firm, a growth industry since 9/11, and a part of the Trade. Zaman, it appeared, was Kroll's man in Pakistan, or one of them. It was he who sent the money, Sami said, to Feridoun, who, Saleh said, was an ISI agent. And there was more. Gohar Zaman was far from a simple man.

"After three or four calls from your kidnappers, we got new phones that recorded calls. We had a few long conversations and then they started talking. 'I am the person who can make this happen,' I said. They said, 'Give us one million dollars and we will release your guy.' I was very forceful with them. I said, 'That's not how this is going to work. We just can't give you the money and hope that you will free him.' They got angry and were very threatening. 'Give us this money or we will kill him.'"

I cringed. I wondered who said this and how close I had come.

"In time they calmed down. We knew we had to keep the line open. Most of our conversations ended properly. Immediately after their calls, they turned their phones off and when they called again it was always from a different number. It was always two or three people who called, and they never gave any names. It was always in Pashto.

"After a few more calls and a few discussions with Michael, I wrote down everything I knew about you: I knew you were going to see Abdullah. I knew about Shahwali and that he was a teacher in a private school. I knew that you had gone to see Rasul Amin and there had met Shahwali. I knew you had met Mullah Malang at Yasini's house. I sent this information to Michael, to Bryn, and to Sophie."

It was how it worked: one person led to another.

"Michael said we should focus on two tracks: Who is Shahwali and his family? And, who is Abdullah and his family? Our focus was not on the men who had you, or the phone calls, but on Shahwali and Abdullah."

"Ahmed Jan and Ahmed Shah went to work on Shahwali." Ahmed Jan, a Tajik, was Fazul's friend and a cameraman for CBS. Ahmed Shah was his cousin and also with CBS. Ahmed Jan had driven me in 2002 down to Khost, deep in Pashtun country. He was with Fazul when Feridoun brought me to safety. "They found Shahwali's school, and from there his address, and from there his family and their address in Peshawar. His house was small and looked right. His father was there. They didn't know where Shahwali was and were worried. They said he was working with an American journalist." That was me.

All Fazul could tell Shahwali's family was that I was alive and well and with some bad people: either criminals, or Taliban. "We want your support to help bring your son back," he told them.

Fazul said that Michael Semple's contacts were working on trying to find out all about Abdullah. Semple asked Fazul to go to Jalalabad to meet the former governor of Paktika Province. Fazul learned from him that Abdullah was a Mohmand and that Abdullah's relative, Khorsheed, a former mujahideen commander, was killed or ordered killed by Hajji Qadir in the late 1990s. Abdullah, in revenge, was suspected of assassinating or being behind the assassination of Qadir. That was why he was an outlaw living in the Tribal Areas. He could not go to Afghanistan. He was not Taliban, but a contract killer, a drug smuggler, and kidnapper. Abdullah also had a problem with Hazrat Ali, the former mujahideen commander and ally of Din Mohammad's family, over a drug deal.

Din Mohammad had said that Khorsheed had set up an illegal checkpoint, was a thief, and that "the mujahideen council" had decided to pick him up. Din Mohammad's brother, Hajji Qadir, the provincial governor, gave the order. Hajji Qadir and Hazrat Ali were all accused of being drug dealers and warlords.

"The provincial governor brought in a dodgy fellow," continued Fazul. "I gave him some money and asked him to tell me where Abdullah was and what he was doing." The man told Fazul that Abdullah was in the Tribal Areas. The governor knew why Fazul was there, and knew not to say anything. Fazul called and asked Ahmed Jan and Ahmed Shah, his cousins, to come down from Kabul with his computer and satellite phone. "On our way from Paktika Province to Peshawar, as we passed through Jalalabad, I called Shahwali's father, in Peshawar. Someone else answered the phone and said that Shahwali's father was in Jalalabad and gave me his number. I called him. His father said, 'I have good news. Come. I have Jere's phone and his passport.'"

Fazul continued the story of his conversation with Shahwali's father. "'Why are you here?' I asked. He said he was buying a plot of land. 'How can you be doing this while your son is in prison?' I asked. He didn't answer. Back in Peshawar, I told the others: we can't work with this family."

A few weeks after I was taken the Maulvi came into our cell and said that they were negotiating with Fazul and with my family for the money. A week or two later, the Maulvi came into the cell, gave me a sheet of white paper, and told me to write a letter to Fazul telling him to transfer the money—I had no idea what that meant: whose money?—to Shahwali's father quickly and secretly. He told Shahwali to write a letter to his father. If his father talked to anyone, we would be at risk. Shahwali and I read the letters into my digital recorder and the Maulvi left the cell. Maybe an hour later the Maulvi returned and handed me another sheet of paper and told me to write a letter to Fazul to tell him to work with Abdullah, Mullah Malang, and Shahwal's father.

I understood none of this. I wondered if it was a smokescreen to confuse me. Why Abdullah? Gulob said that my people, whoever they were, were trying to arrest him, but I thought he was on my side. And why Mullah Malang? I thought he would be in Kabul trying to help me.

The Maulvi later told me that that the money was in Pakistan. He seemed pleased with himself. He added that they would send a suicide bomber to the exchange. I understood none of this at the time, and less so now as I listened to Fazul.

"Michael [Semple], meanwhile, was working his back channels. I have no idea who he was talking to. Michael has so many contacts. He was working a back channel to Abdullah, and brought the money down to five hundred thousand dollars. The front channel was at one million."

Everyone in Afghanistan was desperate for money, it now seemed, even baggage handlers at the airport and children in the streets. I would learn in 2017 that after the *New York Times* had wired money to a bank in Kabul, that bank then took a large fee. Sayyid Qutb had called money the "American god," and it flowed like a wide, rushing river into Afghanistan, one of the poorest countries on earth, fostering corruption and greed. No one seemed to trust anyone any longer; thirty years of war, the country's transformation to a gun and drug culture, and the kidnapping epidemic had tended to destroy trust.

Even after David Rohde and his fixer Tahir Luddin escaped, David's brother Lee and wife Kristen were afraid, after dealing with David's case for seven months, that the Pakistani helicopter due to carry David from the army base in Miran Shah—to which he and Tahir Luddin had escaped—to Islamabad might mysteriously disappear. McCraw, on behalf of David's family, called US ambassador Anne Patterson, who assured him that the Pakistanis were nervous about the whole episode and said not to worry. I did not know what amount the Haqqani Network had demanded to release Rohde, Luddin, and their driver, who chose to stay behind, but maybe it was similiar to what Abdullah and his gang had demanded for me. Maybe that was the price of a hostage then.

"Bryn prepared to go to Heathrow to fly to Pakistan. Nafay worked her magic to get him to the VIP section of the airport and we put him in the Marriott."

Again, I felt emotional. All this work that they were doing, all the chances they were taking, had been for me. I had stayed in the Marriott many times. The CBS bureau was there for years. In September, five months after I was released, the Taliban blew it up, killing fifty-four people and injuring hundreds.

"Every two or three days when we went up to Peshawar, in case anything happened, we took money in a big bag and walked into the Pearl Continental." Fazul shook his head, smiling. I had stayed in the Pearl Continental more than once; two of my uncles had introduced me to this part of the world. In June 2009, the Taliban blew it up, killing at least eighteen people. "We sat in the restaurant drinking coffee and tea, waiting, wanting to be in place," Fazul explained. "We knew the money would be changed in the *chow-ka-gha*, the money exchange place in the old bazaar."

It was a labyrinth of small open shops selling brass pots, sandals, old artifacts, prayer caps, clothes, food, and spices. There was a mosque where men prayed and slept on the carpets in the summer heat, a romantic part of old Peshawar. I first visited there in 1973 when Peshawar was safe, and walked everywhere unafraid. It was a stopover on the Hippie Trail that began at the Pudding Shop in Istanbul and ended in Kathmandu, or the beaches of Goa. When I returned in 1981 Peshawar was darker, crowded, and freelance journalists and photographers started to appear, at what had become a base camp for Afghanistan. We ate at Jan's, or Green's, crowding around the tables of these restaurants in the old British hotels, or even in Dean's with its dark furniture, white linen tablecloths, heavy cutlery, and waiters in frayed, starched white jackets. Peshawar became like Casablanca during World War II, a city of intrigue, foreigners, arms deals, and Afghan refugees, where you could make a phone call or send a telex. It was the headquarters of the mujahideen political parties, and later al-Qaeda.

It is a modern, much larger city today, and Dean's is now a boring glass and steel shopping center, and it is hard for a foreigner to get permission to go there. On January 14, 2016, the police arrested forty-five money-changers in the chow-ka-gha for terrorist financing. Peshawar has gone from being a romantic, sleepy town in the 1970s, filled with flowers, to an unruly urban center of global terrorism today.

Fazul continued. "Sophie called and asked if we should tell the US government, and we decided it would be best to let them know. She did this and immediately the FBI mobilized. I got a call from Bob in Kabul. He said, 'We hear you are trying to rescue some innocents and so please keep us informed.'

"The next day the FBI broke the lock to the door of your room at the Gandamack, went in with gloves, photographed everything, put items in special bags, and then, as Nafay called it, we were water-boarded in Islamabad." He meant that the FBI interrogated them intensely. "Trudy Campbell, I think her name was, of the FBI, came and took us from the Marriott to the US embassy. We told them all we knew.

"By then, Ahmed Jan and Ahmed Shah had your phone records and we went through all your calls for the last six months. We narrowed it down to four numbers. We found two in Pakistan that were still operational. We asked the FBI for the records of these numbers. 'We have these numbers,' they said, 'but they are classified and we can't share them with you.'"

This was the first indication, to me, that the FBI wanted to take over my case. The numbers on my phone were important for my work, but the only reason to call them classified would be to keep them from the CBS people. The FBI had shown, in their 2013 letter to me closing my case, that they didn't seem to have done anything with the numbers, some of which were for Mullah Malang, Abdullah, Shahwali, Sameer, and Sharif. I had nothing to hide, but I felt naked that other people had the numbers of all my contacts.

Fazul: "Michael [Semple] now started talking to Feridoun Mohmand. We wanted to keep it simple and not have so many people involved.

"Every three, four, or five days, Feridoun would give us an update. On March 28, he called Michael and then Bryn and said to come to Peshawar tomorrow. That was it. Feridoun had done the negotiating. He is the son of Ferdaz Khan, the grand khan of the Mohmand tribe."

Fazul raised his hands to emphasize the breadth of his power. He was the chief, like Sitting Bull.

"Abdullah was still negotiating or being difficult and threatening, Feridoun said, but he couldn't stand up to the head of the tribe. He was told: 'You will get your money but I want this man in one piece.'"

I cringed again. Abdullah was threatening to kill me right up until the end. This was why the Maulvi had said to me in the cell, too many times, that final day, "Congratulations on escaping death."

"We rented a meeting room at the Pearl Continental. Feridoun came. We met in the room. He would get up and go make a call and come back. In two hours, the deal was done. Once Feridoun became involved it was out of the FBI's hands." It was in the hands, possibly, of the ISI.

Fazul said that they agreed on an amount. Feridoun and Fazul went to Torkham, the border crossing, and with Feridoun's bodyguards to his guesthouse. That evening Fazul moved to Jalalabad. Bob, the FBI agent, called, asking where they were.

I didn't ask how much the payment was. I didn't want to know. Whatever it was, the CBS team, plus Michael, Feridoun, and Zaman, had saved my life.

The FBI chartered a plane and flew to Jalalabad on March 29, the same day that Fazul, Ahmed Jan, and Ahmed Shah met there. I was to be released that same day but there was a battle between the Taliban and the Afghan army in the area and so they postponed it to April 1. In the meantime, Fazul and his cousins had moved to Feridoun's house. The FBI kept calling him. Fazul was nervous but Feridoun was calm and confident. "It will happen," he said. "You have my word."

On the night of March 31, Fazul and Ahmed Jan left Jalalabad to get me, but they didn't know where I was going to be released. Fazul made Ahmed Shah stay behind at Feridoun's house. Ahmed Shah would tell me later that it made him angry and that he began to mistrust Fazul.

On the way, Fazul told the FBI that he would call them. Bob, the lead FBI agent on the ground, said that they would have a doctor ready at the PRT—Provisional Reconstruction Team, a civilian-military unit, of which there were many in Afghanistan—at the US Army base in Jalalabad. Fazul then told Feridoun that they would take me to Jalalabad.

"We drove through bazaars and villages and everyone stood and waved as the great khan passed," Fazul said. He, a Tajik, now deep in Pashtun country, was relaxed. He was with Feridoun, chief of the Mohmand. They picked up more gunmen as they drove east. They had fifteen riflemen by the time they reached the last village before the border. They stopped at the house of the khan of that area and had dinner. All the elders of the region came to pay their respects to Feridoun. They knew something important was happening for their leader to be there but they didn't know what. Fazul went for a walk with two gunmen and saw riflemen on the roofs of houses. He was in Feridoun's kingdom and safe.

Chapter 13

Your Input Is Very Welcome . . .

I walked into my apartment in Manhattan and I was home, and felt the warmth of my carpets, the piano, photographs and paintings from different countries, bow and arrows from the Amazon, nomad knives from Tibet, and maps, my talisman, my security, books and stacks of paper, the memories of my nomadic life. It was October 2014. I went to CBS. Sophie welcomed me warmly and gave me a new desk in the newsroom.

In mid-December, I came home one night and there was a letter from the Department of Justice, Federal Bureau of Investigation. Nervously, I opened it.

Dear Mr. Van Dyk,

We are forwarding the attached letter from Lisa Monaco, Assistant to the President for Homeland Security and Counterterrorism.

The letter invites families of US citizens who were held hostage by terrorists or pirates since 2002 to provide feedback on their experiences interacting with the US Government officials during the period of their loved one's captivity. This effort is part of the review directed by the President that is intended to inform the actions of the US Government in future overseas kidnap and hostage-taking situations.

We respectfully encourage you to have a discussion with your family members to determine if they would be willing to participate in this process.

As always, please do not hesitate to get in touch with us if you have additional questions or if there is anything we can do to assist you.

Sincerely,

Lisa Skolnick

Victim Services Manager

Office for Victim Assistance

I was frankly surprised that the government remembered and knew how to find me. The letter from the White House was dated December 17.

Dear Families,

President Obama has heard the concerns expressed by some of you about your interaction and communication with US government officials regarding efforts to secure the safe return of your loved ones. To that end, the President has established a team of senior officials to conduct a review of how the United States government responds to these cases.

Specifically, we are examining how we can communicate most effectively with you to achieve our shared goal of bringing Americans home safely. Your recommendations and reflection on your experience will be a critical element of this process and invaluable in informing our efforts.

As part of this review, we will be guided by the principles that we should share as much information as possible with the families of hostages, while protecting the safety of your loved ones, the integrity of investigations, and the sensitive sources and methods through which we develop information. The President also remains firmly committed to denying hostage takers any benefits of ransom or other concessions. Therefore, the scope of this review will not include a reconsideration of our no-concessions policy.

The Administration's goal has always been to do whatever we can within our capabilities and within the bounds of the law to assist families to bring your loved ones home. On behalf of the interagency review team, I would like you to invite you and members of your family to provide input to this effort.

Sincerely,

Lisa Monaco

Assistant to the President for

Homeland Security and Counterterrorism

The letter gave the name of the review team leader, Bennet Sacolick, his phone number and e-mail address and said if we wished to accept the invitation to contact him. My case was closed, but not, apparently, forgotten. I sent an e-mail to the team leader. I would participate but I was leaving to go overseas, and would have to talk from there.

January came. Suddenly, Nafay, in Islamabad, called. Her father had called the consul general in New York and asked him to give me a visitor's visa. It would only be for two weeks, but after eight years of rejections a door had just opened. I called the consul general's office and he told me come over. It was snowing. He welcomed me into his office. There was another man with him. He had a refined air about him and wore a dark, expensive suit. We drank tea and the three of us talked. The consul general asked what kind of work I did. I said that I was a freelance writer—for *National Geographic* and *Smithsonian*—and a consultant to CBS.

The consul general was taken aback. "If you say you are from CBS then I have to send your application to Islamabad." He had to protect himself. Since Sophie had said a year and a half ago that I could never say on this project that I worked for CBS I would not be doing anything for CBS in Pakistan. I removed the reference to it on the application.

The next day I returned and a man in a brown suit with a thick head of hair gave me my visa. It seemed too easy.

I walked back to CBS. I had to tell Sophie that I was going to leave soon. I still did radio commentary, went on late night television, wrote for the website, helped correspondents and producers with contacts in the Middle East and South Asia, but it was not like before. I no longer felt fully a part of CBS. Afghanistan rarely made the news. By 2014, the US was focused on getting out. In May, there were 32,000 US troops in Afghanistan, but President Obama said he would bring that number down to 9,800 by the end of the year, and cut that number in half again by the end of 2015. But the Taliban were gaining strength and in July 2016 he announced that the US would leave 9,800 troops in Afghanistan. Back home few seemed to care: America was tired of Afghanistan.

CBS had hired a former deputy director of the CIA, and he and other men talked about Afghanistan, Pakistan, and the Middle East on air now. I felt like a remnant from the past, so it wasn't a complete surprise when I got an e-mail from Sophie's secretary saying she would like to see me in her private office.

She asked when I was leaving again to my project. I said in three days.

"I am ending your contract," she said, looking at me coldly. "You have to leave by the end of the week."

My stomach knotted, in shock. I told her I'd be out in two days.

"Fine," she said. She didn't smile.

I said good-bye and she nodded. I went back to my desk. In a moment, Sophie appeared next to me. I stood up out of politeness. The producer who sat next to me was away and she sat in his chair and brought it close. I sat down. "You can stay until the end of June"—a reprieve of six months.

"Thank you." June represented the last day of my contract. If she broke it maybe she was afraid that I would sue her. I would never have done it, not to her, not to CBS, not after all that they did for me.

"Good." She smiled, and touched my arm. "Have a good trip." The personal bond was still close between us.

Three days later, I flew to London and went to the CBS bureau, but I no longer felt at home there. The next day, February 2, I got an e-mail from Lieutenant General Bennet Sacolick.

Dear Mr. Van Dyk,

Thank you for your email. My name is Lieutenant General Bennet Sacolick. Although an Army general, I am currently assigned as the Director of Strategic Operational Planning at the National Counterterrorism Center. In my current position, I write counter-terrorism strategies and make policy recommendations in support of White House priorities. As referenced in the letter you received, I am leading a White House-directed comprehensive interagency re-view that examines our government's coordination and interactions during a hostage situation. As part of my review, I am very inter-ested in your viewpoint on the US Government's efforts to support your family during these situations. We greatly value any reflections and/or recommendations you have based on your own experience and would like to have the chance to discuss them with you.

Regarding the time constraint you reference I wanted to invite you to participate via phone or in writing as this review will be com-plete by the time you return in April. The discussion would entail a brief call with a small team (2–3 people), which can be entirely anonymous if that is your preference. We would be happy to receive your thoughts in writing as well. We want to ensure that we choose a venue that is convenient for you.

I am grateful for your willingness to participate in this important effort. I look forward to sharing our findings with you and other fam-ilies once this review is complete. Please do not hesitate to contact me or my staff if you have any questions or concerns during this process.

Warmest Regards,

Bennet

I would participate, but I was about to leave for Paris to meet a pro-fessor at the Sorbonne and a Saudi expert at Sciences Po. I met a Yemeni in a café whom I knew from Sana'a who introduced me to men in the government, part of an underground that I could never meet on my own. She gave me the phone number to General Yahya Saleh, the former chief of staff of Yemen's Central Security Forces, its counterterrorism unit, who was living in Beirut.

I flew to Beirut, arriving at night. I didn't tell anyone why I was there. I was going up into the mountains to find a man who had killed many men, to sit and talk with him, all because I had been kidnapped. That was what led to this project, an attempt to come back, to stop being a victim, to put my kidnapping behind me, and go forward. I thought of Daniel Pearl, Jim Foley, and Steven Sotloff, and now Peter Kassig, the former Army Ranger who had created an aid organization in Syria and who had been kidnapped on October 31, 2013, by ISIS. Even though he had converted to Islam in prison, ISIS called him a crusader and killed him, a strong, silent American, before the world on November 16, 2014. I thought of Kayla Mueller, killed in a bomb attack, and Luke Somers, killed in a rescue attempt, and later of Alan Henning and David Haines of the UK, which also didn't pay a ransom, killed by ISIS. I felt guilty that I was alive. The ripple effects, Michael Semple had said, would go on and on. He was right. This is what kidnapping does: it poses questions that run for a very long time to some very remote corners, and it forever separates you from others. I was out here alone, but I was grateful. I was alive, and others were not.

I didn't feel comfortable talking to the government yet. I wanted to find General Saleh, a nephew of Ali Abdullah Saleh, who had ruled Yemen for over thirty years, to see what he knew about Haqqani's Yemeni family, Haqqani's unique access into the Middle East. I called and left messages. I wondered if anyone was monitoring calls to his number. I would see him and then return to Kabul and talk from there, of all places, to the US government. If it wanted to learn about kidnapping, they needed to hear from someone in Kabul. So much began and ended there.

I wrote back to the government.

To: *Brenda J. Cottonwood*
Subject: *Re: Discussion with the Policy Review Team*

Dear Ms. Cottonwood,
I will talk with your people. I assume that they want to focus strictly on the government's dealings with family members while someone is in captivity. I will do this, although my kidnapping involved others also. In addition, please note that the government also plays an important role, as I am sure you know, in the life of each hostage if he or she is fortunate enough to be released, or escapes. The government can, in both cases, help or cause damage.

I am in Beirut. I am not sure when I will be free tomorrow and will let you know as soon as I can in the morning, my time. I am staying at the Movenpick. The number XXX-X-XXX-XXX, Room 628. I am also on a UK cell phone: XX.XXXXX-XXXXXX. If tomorrow doesn't work, I will be here through Sunday, leaving that night for Kabul. I will be available there from, say, 4 p.m. Kabul time on Monday.

Sincerely,
Jere (pronounced Jerry) Van Dyk

I realized that I was still angry. I didn't feel like a criminal or that I had done anything wrong on my assignment into the mountains, interviewing the Taliban, crossing over secretly into Pakistan, until I arrived at the US base in Jalalabad, and the man with a pistol on his belt said, angrily, "We know all about you." Some welcome. Then the FBI agent said that I had broken the law by going into Pakistan without a visa. Then the FBI agent in New York asked why I had gone to Morocco in 2006. I was afraid that the government was wary of me, that it saw me as a traitor who was too at ease with the Taliban, and yet I wanted to be accepted by it.

I hired a car and went up into the mountains, went into a ski lodge, and sat at the bar and waited for General Saleh. I felt like I was in the West and didn't like it. A man who had drunk too much came over and wanted to talk. I said a few words and tried to ignore him. The general arrived, about five foot nine, well built, smiling, ordered a drink, sent messages on his smartphone, and told me about himself. I ordered mineral water. He invited me to his home, and he drove fast in a new BMW through the mountains and we went to his basement, sat next to a swimming pool, and he brought out a bottle of vodka and at that moment I knew that he wanted to forget what he knew.

He talked about working with the Americans and how he admired their patriotism. He didn't know about Haqqani's family and I knew I had to look elsewhere. We had dinner and I enjoyed being with his family. It grew late and he ordered a car for me. As I rode down the mountains, I realized that I should return to Yemen. I wanted to find Haqqani's family there: he was the only Afghan of influence to have married outside his tribal and ethnic family. And he married an Arab.

The next day I ran on the quay along the Mediterranean. Although I was the only Westerner out here, no one seemed to be following me. I thought of Terry Anderson, the AP reporter who had been running the same path in 1985 before he was kidnapped by Hezbollah (Army of God), a violent Shiite group backed by Iran, in the middle of the day. He was held hostage for nearly seven years.

Anderson was kidnapped along with over one hundred other Westerners, all pawns caught in a war among Israel, Iran, and Arab nations in the 1975–1990 Lebanese civil war, during which the US sent a Marine expeditionary force, France sent paratroopers, and Italy two thousand soldiers as peacekeepers to Beirut. On October 23, 1983, Shiite suicide bombers attacked the US Marine Corps barracks in Beirut, killing 241 US Marines and other servicemen; other suicide attackers reached the French barracks in another part of the city, killing fifty-eight paratroopers. Hezbollah, afraid of revenge from the US and France, began to kidnap Westerners as protection. In 1985, the US, under President Reagan, and under pressure from hostage families and the media, began secret negotiations whereby Israel would sell US arms to Iran, which was at war with Iraq and needed weapons desperately, in exchange for the American hostages, and the US would reimburse Israel; the US would use the profits from the sale to secretly fund anticommunist guerrillas in Central America: Iran-Contra.

In 1987 President Reagan, who said that he would never negotiate with terrorists, was forced to go on television as the scandal deepened to tell America, and the world, that what started out as a strategic opening to Iran became, in the end, an arms-for-hostages exchange. I wondered if it wasn't a hostage-exchange from the beginning. Some hostages were killed, some released, new ones taken.

In 1987, Terry Waite, an assistant to the archbishop of Canterbury, came to Beirut as a special envoy to negotiate the release of Anderson, and other hostages held by Hezbollah and Islamic Jihad, and was himself kidnapped and held for nearly five years, four of which were in solitary confinement. When he was released and returned to England, pictures show him, a tall thin man, laughing at the airport, shaking hands with the archbishop. He was home and the world knew of his extraordinary efforts and suffering, but not that he felt that he had been used by nations.

Waite came to New York and we had coffee in his hotel. He asked if I had gone through mock executions. I said yes. He, too, worried in captivity—not about dying, but how bad the pain would be when they killed him. I thought again of the fear in the eyes of Jim Foley, Steven Sotloff, and Peter Kassig. The Trade had almost nothing to do with religion. It was only sometimes about money, but always about murder, and publicity, and revenge. I remembered the scream of Nick Berg.

I flew late at night to Dubai and just before dawn boarded a flight to Kabul. I stood at passport control, wondering again if they, whoever they were, were waiting for me. The agent looked at me, looked down at my passport, again a long time, and finally stamped it, and I walked into the baggage claim room where a man was indeed waiting for me. We passed quickly through customs and went outside. I glanced around. I watched men watching all the passengers. I wondered who they worked for in their hearts. I went back to the Serena Hotel. Three months had passed since I was last there. Afghanistan had at last formed a government.

This time I called an Afghan female friend. The line was silent at first. "You've come back here? You're insane," she said. She would come see me for coffee. That evening I sent a note to General Sacolick's team in Washington.

> *Dear Brenda,*
> *I just arrived here in Kabul. I am staying at the Serena. The number is XXX-X-XXX-XXX, room 395. I will be here all week. Alternatively, my UK mobile phone: XX.XXXXX-XXXXXX.*
> *Sincerely, Jere*

I received an e-mail from a woman I will call Rhonda.

> *Sir,*
> *We're just waiting for our boss to return from a morning meeting with the Director. We will ring you shortly!*
> *Rhonda*

Finally, they called. Rhonda mispronounced my first and last name. I realized that they were just a group of people who had to call a list of former hostages, ask a series of questions, and check them off. She said that they were in a rush and had people to talk to. Her tone suggested that I was talking to a group of bored telemarketers.

We talked for an hour and a half. I told them, politely, about my experiences, which I felt were insignificant against those who had been killed. I once trusted the government, but now, since I was kidnapped, I was wary of it. It didn't seem to trust me.

I sent Rhonda a letter in which I talked about my family, the CBS involvement in my case, the trouble that those working on it had with the FBI, and I reminded Rhonda about Gracia and Martin Burnham, the missionaries kidnapped by Abu Sayyaf, the guerrilla group in the Philippines, named after a member of the Afghan mujahideen, and the quiet decision the George W. Bush administration had made to pay a ransom.

"Mr. Van Dyk," she responded,

Thank you so much for taking the time to write this and share it with us. Your input is very welcome and helpful. We will add these to the notes from the team's conversation with you last week. Thanks again for taking the time to participate and provide input to the policy review.

Best,

Rhonda

I let it go, feeling like a fool.

PART THREE

"This is the work of ghosts.

You are part of a gigantic picture here."

Chapter 14

The Work of Ghosts

Once my work with the government was over I could begin my own projects again. There was a light snow on the ground. I had a cold, but it was good to be back in Kabul.

Ehsanullah, my journalist friend, and I sat drinking green tea by the window away from others in the Serena Hotel. A man sat in a corner, smoking. A waiter took his time setting the table next to us. Ehsanullah wouldn't talk until the waiter left, and then he spoke in his low, gravelly voice.

The previous September, when I despaired of ever getting a visa to Pakistan, I had sent him, at his urging, to the Tribal Areas to do research on Haqqani, but the explanation of my kidnapping now consumed me. The two topics were separate, but I felt that they merged somewhere. I wanted to go to the heart or get as close as I could to both. No one, outside of the Afghans I met with in Kabul, and possibly Bryn Padrig, and Sophie, if he told her, knew where I was.

"The Pakistanis are making it hard on us again," Ehsanullah whispered. He got a visa, but the embassy stamped it in such a way that it was a signal to others to watch him. They insisted at the border that he give them the address where he would be staying. His cell phone didn't work in Pakistan and he had to borrow one from a man cleaning the floor to call his office in Islamabad. He was paranoid, but then maybe he was right. If he was lying, and only using this trip to make money, I wouldn't work with him again. I read his reports, picking out as best I could, like a miner looking for gems, what I felt was true.

"Is Yasini tied to Pakistan?" I asked. "He lives very well."

"Karzai never gave him a good portfolio in the government because he always considered him to be a Pakistani man. So many people are. Your friend, Hajji Din Mohammad, has a home in Peshawar and property there. The ISI works with all the ex-mujahideen leaders."

The ISI had killed Din Mohammad's three brothers, and his son, yet he kept a home in Pakistan. He was trapped, I felt, trying to stay alive, keeping on good terms with Pakistan, working with the Afghan government, and the West.

"Yasini has money," Ehsanullah continued, "because he was deputy minister for counternarcotics in 2002, when the US gave money to farmers along the border region to stop growing poppies. He also borrowed one million dollars from the Bank of Kabul and he hasn't paid it back."

I liked Yasini. He was a gracious host, was part of the Yunus Khalis group, and had warned me about crossing the border. But he had also introduced me to Mullah Malang. He was from the border region and a prominent politician. I wondered if he knew General Babar, the man who founded, with government approval, the mujahideen.

George Washington University, under the Freedom of Information Act, acquired documents related to Afghanistan from the National Security Archive and posted them online. One, from 1994, read: "This memo to the State Department's Afghanistan Desk shows concern over Pakistan's now-notorious Inter-Services Intelligence Directorate's (ISI) involvement in the Taliban's takeover of Kandahar. A hand-written note states: 'This AM I've heard that General Babar is running this

Taliban op.'" Babar was interior minister then under Prime Minister Benazir Bhutto.

General Babar had explained to me, taking credit, how he created the mujahideen, but he never talked about his involvement with the Taliban.

Ehsanullah continued: "Your friend Hekmatyar, who became prime minister in the mujahideen government, wanted to fight the Taliban, but all his leaders along the southern border up to Kabul, except a few, refused to fight because all the Taliban leaders were in Pakistan. Hajji Qadir, head of the Jalalabad Shura [council], told him, 'If you fight the Taliban they will go to Pakistan where Babar will protect them.'"

"Hekmatyar hates the Taliban," I said, "and they hate him. He wants to rule Afghanistan."

Ehsanullah said that he was like Islamic militants in the Middle East. He paid allegiance to his backers, in his case Pakistan and Iran, but had his own agenda.

Ehsanullah was sure that the ISI nonetheless controlled Hekmatyar. I knew that and felt that Hekmatyar might know who was behind my kidnapping. I had two ways to get to him, but I was still afraid of him after his death threat against me. I changed the subject and asked about Feridoun. I would focus on him. I wanted to know about his ties to the ISI and his link to Michael Semple.

Some years ago, Ehsanullah said, a Pakistani kidnapped a French female aid worker, but she was released thanks to Feridoun. Ehsanullah said, "I heard the French paid $1 million, but only one lakh ($100,000) went to the kidnapper."

I had never heard the story about the French woman before.

"Maybe it was you he kidnapped, but I heard it was a French woman," Ehsanullah responded. "Mullah Malang probably got money from your kidnapping." He said both these things casually. Malang called the night before I left, trying to save me. Michael Semple said that Malang called Abdullah to his house in Islamabad and told him not to harm me. He and Michael, it seemed to me, saved my life. How could he possibly be part of my kidnapping? I asked who else might have been involved. "One of Haqqani's main sources of income is kidnapping," he said, "but my sources say he is finished. Pakistan has officially banned the Haqqani Network."

I didn't believe him. Pakistan would not ban the Haqqani Network; officially, under pressure, maybe, from the US, but never in fact. Pakistan had a history of banning Islamist parties that came back under different names. Again, I wondered if Haqqani was involved or knew of my kidnapping.

"Even if the network breaks up the cells will operate on their own," said Ehsanullah. "Few people remain in the family." So many had been killed. He said that Ibrahim, Jalaluddin Haqqani's younger brother, was the leader now, that there were criminal gangs in Kabul and along the border who kidnap people and then negotiate with the Haqqanis, the Taliban, or other groups who have a political agenda, and sell the victim to them. A hostage was a form of hard currency. The Trade, like money, knew no boundaries and was growing worldwide. It is estimated that in 2003 the al-Qaeda franchises in the Arabian Peninsula and Africa got an average of $200,000 per hostage. By 2015 the figure was $10 million. The kidnap and ransom industry has grown to the point that today 75 percent of all US Fortune 500 companies carry K&R insurance.[1] Even Ehsanullah said he was afraid of being kidnapped. There was a price for everyone. "They love to kidnap Japanese," he said, "because they pay so much money. The US pays, but does it through NDS, so I am told."

A woman I knew who worked at an intelligence agency, which she would never name, said after I was released, "There is money out there for discretionary spending." She believed that the US government had ransomed me. I gave a talk one night at a dinner for executives in the K&R industry at a restaurant on Wall Street. There was an ex-FBI agent at the dinner, and a former Marine Corps officer who worked as an advisor in the R&R industry, both of whom said afterward, separately, that they were certain the US government ransomed me and said it was wrong that no one told me what went on to release me.

"There is a new way to send money, called *Handi*," said Ehsanullah. "Say I went to send money to Peshawar. I will call my friend there and tell him to provide the money, which he does. It's all private. *Hawala* still exists, but there are taps on the phones now and it is under constant surveillance."

I asked about Hajji Zaman, wondering if the ISI had brought Feridoun into my kidnapping case, in some way involving both of its assets. "Zaman was pulled back from Tora Bora by the Karzai government," said Ehsanullah. I had never heard this before. Everyone had a different story and it made me distrust them all. "After the Taliban fell, Hajji Zaman went from Peshawar to Jalalabad. Hajji Qadir and Hazrat Ali came from Nuristan[2] where they were fighting the Taliban. The US paid all three to fight in Tora Bora. They became part of the government. Hajji Qadir [he said Qadir but it was Qadir's son] was close to Karzai. Hazrat Ali killed Abdullah's nephew, Khorsheed."

Ehsanullah's version of the story was like Din Mohammad's, except he had said that Khorsheed was Abdullah's brother, not nephew. But Ehsanullah had just explained why Hazrat Ali was afraid of Abdullah. He was tied to the ISI.

Ehsanullah, made anxious by too many men around us, left. We would meet again. I called Mirwais Yasini. He didn't know who I was until I reminded him of my kidnapping. "Can you come to my house for lunch today, and we can talk over a nice meal?" he asked. I hesitated. Yasini sensed my uncertainty and said quickly, "I will send my black Suburban and some bodyguards over to pick you up." Two minutes later he called back. "Can you come over now?"

I put on a warm coat and my *pakhool*. I took it off, held it in my hand, still uncertain, and walked outside into the courtyard of the Serena, put it back on and went through the locked steel doors to the outside wall and told the guards that a black vehicle would come for me. The car arrived and a guard opened the door and I walked out into the street, feeling exposed.

Two girls, fully covered, rushed out from behind a tree and came up holding ballpoint pens for sale. They pulled on my arms. They were cute, but they grabbed me in desperation. I climbed in the car and they banged on the window. We drove to the corner and waited at the light. I waited for the girls to run up. A policeman with a white mask to protect him from the fumes and the dust waved us forward.

We passed buildings with sandbags in front, rows of concertina wire on top, and small gray cameras watching. Once school girls here wore short dark skirts and long white socks, and white scarves, and laughed in the streets. There were few cars and no one had ever heard of magnetic bombs or suicide bombers, and you could see white stars in a jet-black sky. I loved Afghanistan then, the only country I visited (I remember again) where I never saw a child begging. They were poor, yes, but there was once dignity here that I never saw anywhere else. Now children begged and little girls banged on car windows and soldiers in bullet-proof vests stood beside high concrete barriers.

But still, the streets were crowded. Men still wore turbans and traditional clothes, and the shops were still small, made of wood, and the streets dusty. The stone barrier in front of the Interior Ministry was identical to the barriers outside the White House, the State Department, the US Capitol, and on Wall Street, all in place because of what started here.

Inside Yasini's compound, there were two coffee tables with trays filled with nuts, fruit, cookies, and soft drinks. Pictures of Yasini giving speeches, and with his children, dotted the room. Another man came in and checked on me. I heard a man walking down stone steps and Mirwais Yasini, in traditional clothes and sport coat, the man who had introduced me in his back yard to Mullah Malang, welcomed me and sat on my right, in a smaller chair. I was his guest, in the seat of honor.

We looked at one another, remembering how we looked in the late summer of 2007, when Kabul was filled with journalists, aid workers, soldiers, businessmen, and hustlers. Peter Jouvenal put on dinners at long tables on the grass at the Gandamack. I enjoyed that time. One night I looked out from my room at the tables with wine bottles and beer cans, and meat grilling over open fires, and men and women laughing, and I thought of my Aunt Elva and Uncle Woody in Shanghai in the 1930s, an expat world of high heels, mink stoles, and martinis. Aunt Elva was my mother's older sister, who got in an argument with my grandmother, dropped out of the University of Washington, took a slow boat to Shanghai, and got a job in the US consulate. She met her future husband, a pilot, who would become the first man shot down by the Japanese in the invasion of China—a tale portrayed, along with other war stories, in a comic book for children during that time. He survived and later in the war became the first man to fly over the Himalayas. I had eleven books from that time in which they were mentioned, and the comic book showing Uncle Woody in the water. They told me stories of Chiang Kai-shek, Hemingway, Clare Booth Luce, and Theodore White. It sounded wild and improbable. The scene of Kabul in 2007 already seemed just as fantastic.

Fazul had taken me in August 2007 to see Yasini, deputy minister of counternarcotics, to talk about a story on drugs, making the introduction. He was reading the Qur'an and he preached to me gently about what he had been reading and offered me tea. He said that he had taken Dan Rather into Afghanistan in the 1980s and was part then of the Yunus Khalis network. He was from the border area and according to Fazul was by 2007 a powerful member of parliament.

I remembered his big backyard with a thick green lawn, the delicious food we had for *iftar*, the men standing around and Yasini talking to each one, his hand on a man's shoulder, a political wheeler-dealer. He couldn't have been more gracious. Two months later, I was walking in Kabul and he saw me, and his SUV pulled over, and he invited me to lunch. I was traveling in the mountains then and I politely declined. Six years later, we were together again.

He told me to tell him my whole story and I did.

"There was a breakthrough with the American soldier who was kept by the Taliban," he responded. He was referring to Bowe Bergdahl. "It was the first time that the Taliban had direct contact with the US government."

I told him about Shahwali, Professor Amin, and Abdullah, who, I was told, killed Hajji Qadir. I skipped many parts, but said toward the end that Feridoun Mohmand, a tribal chief, picked me up after I crossed the river and took me to the US base in Jalalabad. His eyes narrowed and his face darkened.

"Why did Feridoun get involved? Was it at the beginning?"

I didn't know. "I'm looking for information," I responded.

"You can't quote me," he said, before he relented. "You can call me an Afghan intellectual and politician from the border region. Number one, after you left"—meaning, I felt, after I stopped coming to his house every night for iftar; I didn't think until later that he might have known, somehow, and thus meant after I left to go up into the mountains—"Mullah Malang disappeared. He didn't say anything and this angered me. I am angrier now." He slumped in his chair. He was a powerful man. I wondered if he would extract revenge from Malang for taking advantage of his hospitality, and for shaming him. "Number two, you were not kidnapped by the Taliban, but by a group of criminals. It was all arranged. Three, I know what kind of man Mullah Malang is."

Why then did he introduce him to me? How did he know that I was kidnapped by criminals, and not by the Taliban? I didn't trust this version of the story.

"Number four, Malang and Michael Semple are close. Malang went to Semple and brought him into this.

"Number five, MI6 was involved. They released you. The British have more experience here than you Americans do. This is the work of ghosts. You are part of a gigantic picture here."

He was saying that MI6 was involved in my kidnapping, maybe with the ISI, and perhaps also in my release. I was worried about the CIA, which loomed above them. Yasini rose and walked slowly around the room, his hands behind his back.

"The world is at a crossroads of destruction. Unfortunately, the 1979–1989 Afghan-Russo war plays a role. The United States brought Arab mercenaries here, giving them full-fledged support, and a free hand militarily and financially. This was made a war between communism and Islam, where the West played an integral part and supported, controlled, and ruled over the mujahideen. The pity is that Afghanistan was abandoned and there was no plan for the postwar world. All the mercenaries scattered over the world were pieces of the bonfire and all that has happened in the Middle East, Indonesia, Kenya, Tanzania, Madrid, London, and 9/11."

By mercenaries he meant what the US called Afghan-Arabs, those who had come from around the world to fight communism. I had met some of these men in the Middle East on my trip who told me that they had gone to an office, in Riyadh, and Sana'a, where men registered them and gave them a plane ticket and expense money, to Pakistan, and from there they went into Afghanistan. The "bonfire" was the victory that these men felt that they won, with God on their side, and they brought their glory and their passion back home and this fire burned in al-Qaeda, ISIS, Abu Sayyaf, and many others.

"If this bonfire is not extinguished it will enflame us and because it is so strong if it is not extinguished in a proper way, Afghanistan, geographically, geopolitically, and geostrategically, will become a brain tumor for the world."

He was like a professor, walking back and forth. I didn't like that he blamed the West for creating the mujahideen and al-Qaeda and exonerated Pakistan. Both sides were involved. Ehsanullah said that Karzai didn't trust Yasini because of his ties to Pakistan. Neither did I, now.

"I have two options," he said. "To abandon Afghanistan and run away and lecture in some university, and do business, or, form a political party based upon democracy, upon noble causes of equal rights and human rights, good governance, and a good society. The West, after thirteen years of war, did not invest in our society, only in the government. I need your help to enlarge democracy. If we don't do something, Afghanistan will become like Yemen, Iraq, and Syria. The clock is ticking. The situation will change."

He was not the first Afghan politician to ask for my help. They thought I had power.

"My father was killed. I don't care if it was by a sword or a knife, either by Daesh[3] [ISIS] or the Taliban. I am positive they will return. I know the blood of our people." Yasini lit a cigarette. "We need to bring civilizations closer together."

I asked him if he knew what kind of man Mullah Malang was, why did he introduce me to him? Again, he gave me a hard, dark look. I was questioning his honor, but I had no choice.

"I didn't think you would go so far with him and do such things," he said darkly.

He knew exactly what I was trying to do. I didn't blame him. I was the one who, against his advice, decided to cross the border, repeatedly, to go up into the mountains, and to go into the Tribal Areas. He and Malang warned me. I had come to him as a journalist. Now, by saying that he needed my support, Yasini was assuming I was in some way part of the government and could help him to achieve his ambitions.

The next day Ehsanullah came to my hotel again and we sat in the corner, ordered green tea, and waited until the waiters moved away. I told him that I had seen Yasini.

Ehsanullah leaned forward and whispered, "When Hajji Qadir was killed, they took his body to the army hospital in Kabul. His brother, your friend, Hajji Din Mohammad, went to see the body, pulled back the shroud and said, 'Congratulations, you died a martyr. You did not accept to become a slave.' The health minister was there and told me what he said. Later, his family accused Hajji Zaman of killing him. Zaman was later killed under the pretext of a suicide bombing. The families have now reconciled."

Din Mohammad was proud of his brother, who had refused to bow down to the ISI, who had used Hajji Zaman to kill him. Qadir had fought, to the end, for Afghanistan. Din Mohammad had also said that the families had reconciled. I didn't like to hear that Din Mohammad considered himself a slave, caught in the ISI web. This link, this slavery, this web, went back thirty years, to when the US and Pakistan were backing the mujahideen, when the US and Pakistan brought the mujahideen to New York, pawns in the great fight against communism—and I escorted them.

"There was no stigma then for an Afghan commander to work with the ISI," Ehsanullah reminded me. "You know. You were here then. Everyone was working together in a great cause to fight the Soviet invader." He was right. I rarely even heard ISI mentioned. "All the commanders had ties to Pakistan then. That is where the arms and ammunition came from."

I had admired most of the mujahideen, the poor men living in the mountains, walking for hours, living on little, sharing what they had with me. Others were men I didn't like, men like Hekmatyar and Rabbani, and hard men who talked of stoning adulterers or threatened me if I took a photograph of their women. But educated, urban Afghans and tribal chiefs like Enayat hated every one of these rough religious men who fought, as he said, for the CIA, the British, Pakistan, and Saudi Arabia, destroying Afghanistan. I had lived with these men, and understood them, I felt, in part, because I saw a similarity in their toughness, and in their strong faith, to my own religious upbringing. My father told me that he wanted to come with me here. He loved the idea of the adventure. I was kidnapped because of the lure of that adventure.

The next morning, he returned to the hotel. We met in the lobby and walked to the restaurant, where again, because of his paranoia—he didn't want to have a spy overhear him—he handed me a sheet of paper on which he had written the following:

"Commander Abdullah, in his 40s, is a small commander in the Kunar Salafi network."

Kunar was the province north of Nangarhar along the border. Rasul Amin and Shahwali came from there. *Salaf*, again, means ancestor in Arabic. Specifically, it refers to the earliest companions of the Prophet Mohammad and their righteous followers in the early, exciting days of Islam. Salafis revere these men, as Christians revere the disciples of Jesus, as secular Americans revere the founding fathers. Salafis want to re-create this glorious past when men were pious and strong. Salafis, in the Middle East, in my experience, are nonviolent. In Afghanistan, Salafis and Wahhabis are identical, a violent brotherhood, at least part of which is linked to al-Qaeda. Ehsanullah was saying that Abdullah was linked to al-Qaeda.

"Abdullah stutters when talking," wrote Ehsanullah. "His uncle was Malik Nabi, former commander of Harakat-e-Islami Afghanistan,[4] led by the late Maulvi Mohammad Nabi Mohammadi."

Nabi Mohammadi's party was one of the seven official mujahideen parties, backed by Pakistan and the US, in the Afghan-Soviet war. Mullah Omar, I would learn soon in Pakistan, was one of his bodyguards. Mohammadi later supported the Taliban. He died in Pakistan in 2002.

Ehsanullah said that Abdullah was from Bela, a village half in Nangarhar Province and half across the border in Mohmand Agency, in Pakistan. The Kunar River, like the Rio Grande, was the border dividing the Mohmand tribe. Ehsanullah was describing, in his note, where I had traveled across the river, up into the mountains, and back. I had been, it seemed, in Abdullah's traditional territory.

"Abdullah's family is considered of the criminal type," Ehsanullah wrote. Abdullah's uncle was dead. His son, Abdullah's cousin, Khorsheed, was killed by Hazrat Ali and Hajji Qadir. After his death, Abdullah, as a family elder, began to take his revenge. But because Abdullah had a bad name, meaning he was a known criminal, the Taliban would not accept him. He therefore joined the Salafis in Kunar, where he still lived.

Maybe Abdullah was using Kunar as a hideout. Shahwali was from Kunar. If Abdullah was a commander in a Salafi network, he was also Wahhabi. Gulob had said that he and his men were Wahhabis. Bin Laden was Wahhabi. Gulob said that they fought under Abdul Wali, who was Taliban. Which meant that there was no difference among Salafi, Wahhabi, and Taliban. They were all fighting the infidel invaders, they all wanted money, and to me were using religion as a cover and a shield.

"Abdullah and his family respect Feridoun Mohmand greatly," Ehsanullah wrote. "In tribal life, you need to have good relations with the tribal elders who protect you, and your future, in society."

Abdullah, above all, it appeared, was dependent on Feridoun, who was ISI, and leader of his tribe—a more important influence than al-Qaeda.

If Abdullah was in Kunar, he might have been able to put pressure on Shahwali after they met to coerce him to work with them by suggesting that Abdullah maybe would harm Shahwali's family.

Ehsanullah, still afraid of being overheard by waiters or men at other tables, took the paper and wrote: "On the day when the ex-mujahideen Commander's Council, called the 'Nangarhar Jihadi Council,' led by Hajji Qadir, lost to the Taliban, Abdullah and his cousin, Commander Khorsheed, took this opportunity to disarm ex-commanders, including

Maulvi Yasini, the uncle of Mirwais Yasini, and took their arms and vehicles, in the name of the Taliban, to Mohmand Agency."

If true, this meant that Abdullah, using the Taliban as his cover, had humiliated Yasini's family, which would explain why Yasini was angry. Yasini knew that Malang was linked to Abdullah, who had shamed Yasini's family, which would explain why Malang disappeared. He was in some way a marked man. A man could not shame another man's family, disparage his honor, and his dignity, without paying a high price, unless he apologized and asked forgiveness. Yet Yasini brought Malang to me.

I asked Ehsanullah if he remembered Professor Rasul Amin, the minister of education in the first Karzai government. Ehsanullah twisted his face. "He went with prostitutes."

A light went on. Sameer was a prostitute. That would explain why she acted like she did with him, sitting so close to him, tickling him, turning his face red: he paid her. She was the sole breadwinner for her family. She needed money. She was probably involved, maybe from the beginning. It was she who introduced me to Shahwali.

Chapter 15

The Story of Fazul Rahim

IN FAZUL RAHIM'S NEW OFFICE SPACE, THERE WERE HALF A DOZEN desks with computers. We walked into a smaller room with two small desks and no computers. When Fazul worked for CBS he had a big office, a giant executive desk, a television, computer, bathroom, and a galley kitchen in a new hotel. He was now with NBC, starting over, like me.

There was a *bokhari*, like a Ben Franklin stove, in the center. A small fire crackled inside and the room was warm; outside it began to snow gently. A Turkman bow and arrow and a sheaf of arrows hung on the wall. When Alexander marched crossed Afghanistan in 330 BC, Turkmen attacked him, leaning under their horses, like American Indians, shooting their arrows. A guard entered and brought us glasses of green tea and a bowl of nuts.

Fazul wore jeans, a blue shirt, and dark sweater, his laptop on the desk in front of him. There were three clocks on the wall giving the time in Kabul, London, and New York.

I told him about my meeting with Din Mohammad and Amrullah Saleh, and their feeling that I had been betrayed. I told him about my lunch with Mirwais Yasini. I said that I wanted to go see Feridoun Mohmand, to thank him for his help, and to learn about Abdullah.

"I called Feridoun," said Fazul. "He said it was one hundred percent safe, two hundred percent."

I thanked him for calling. What would I do without him? Fazul told me to tell him the whole story. He became agitated when I started to talk about the role of Michael Semple.

Semple, he said, was much more than a simple UN person, as he had showed by bringing the warring sides to the table in his improvised truce in Musa Qala in 2007 in Helmand Province. Musa Qala, or Fortress of Moses, had about twenty thousand people, with about the same number in the surrounding area. In 2006 a small British and Danish force based themselves in or near government buildings and patrolled from there. But the Taliban and local people resisted. The British garrison was under siege, attacked, soldiers said, as many as thirteen times a day. Semple—trying to stop the fighting, to reduce civilian deaths and Taliban influence—orchestrated an agreement among tribal leaders, British troops, and the Taliban, who ceded control of the town to tribal elders. According to Fazul, Mullah Abdul Salaam Alizai, governor of Urzgun Province under the Taliban and a member of the powerful Alizai tribe, agreed to fight other Taliban in exchange for a position of power. The British and the Taliban agreed that neither would go within five kilometers of the town.

On February 1, 2007, US Army general Dan McNeill took over command of the International Security Assistance Force (ISAF), that is, all NATO and allied forces in Afghanistan, from British general David Richards; fundamentally opposed to the truce, McNeill immediately began a bombing campaign that provoked the Taliban to retake Musa Qala, who kept their hold on it for ten months. On December 5, Afghan and ISAF forces launched an attack on the Taliban and after a week retook Musa Qala, in part thanks to successful Afghan negotiations with Mullah Salaam. On December 26, 2007, the *Daily Telegraph*[5] reported that a secret meeting over Musa Qala had taken place between

MI6 agents and the Taliban in 2007. A day later, Michael Semple and Mervyn Patterson, a British expert on northern Afghanistan, were, it was reported, arrested with $150,000 on them, and information on their laptops about previous payments to the Taliban in 2006, implying that Semple had negotiated the 2006 truce also. Amrullah Saleh, then head of the NDS, was angry at this outside interference and went to Karzai, who declared Semple and Patterson persona non grata and kicked them out of the country.

Fazul was right. Semple was no ordinary man.

Fazul recalled the story of the three UN workers kidnapped in broad daylight in Kabul in 2004. "We," he went on, "journalists, later found out that they never left the city." Fazul asked Semple about money in exchange for their release. Semple said that he was not supposed to talk about money. Fazul said that there were rumors that MI6 paid off the Taliban in Musa Qala. Karzai later did the same thing, Fazul said, buying off the Taliban. Saleh, I saw, had a reason for being angry with Semple.

It grew dark and a man brought in a tray with two bowls of beans and potatoes, round, warm Uzbeki bread, and more green tea. We sat by his desk and had dinner. It felt good eating with Fazul, unlike eating with Yasini. I looked at him, his hair receding, heavier now. I had known him for twelve years. We started at CBS at the same time and I could never repay him for all that he did for me. We ate quietly. "We need to see Shahwali," said Fazul, changing the subject. It had been seven years. To me, it was like yesterday since we had last seen one another. I didn't want to see Shahwali again. A part of me wanted to beat him and then throw him in Guantanamo, another part of me was grateful to him for helping me when no one else would. He still called, still harassed me. "I know he betrayed you," Fazul said, "but we could learn a lot from him."

Eventually I agreed to see him, but only in a public place, with bodyguards around. Shahwali would have people there, hiding. He could hide a gun in his vest. Fazul's men would have to frisk him before I got close to him. I got angry even thinking of seeing him and his betrayal. I couldn't forgive him. I asked Fazul how he could find him. He had his brother's phone number. He told me not to worry. We would have men there.

I remembered the first time Shahwali had come to the Gandamack and we sat under a tree, his big smile, hustling me. I didn't trust him then, but I went along, desperate to cross the border.

Before I saw Shahwali I wanted to see Feridoun.

Fazul said that Feridoun had to stay in Jalalabad. There was a fight between two villages, and he, as head of the Mohmand tribe, had to negotiate peace between them. Last September I wouldn't leave the hotel; now, I was thinking of going to Jalalabad. I asked if the road was safe. If we left early, spent two hours with Feridoun, had lunch, and returned before nightfall, I wouldn't have to tell anyone.

Fazul said that he could call Feridoun again and ask him to send a car and bodyguards to take me down to see him and bring me back. Fazul got on the phone with a district police chief in Logar Province, south of Kabul, where suicide bombers had killed a dozen policemen that afternoon while they were having lunch. He finished his call, typed up some information, and called NBC in London. He was finished for the evening. He called Feridoun again. He gave me the phone. Feridoun's voice was warm, confident, welcoming. I must come to see him. It was completely safe. Fazul took the phone and talked for a minute. We would work something out.

We relaxed. I looked at the snow falling gently. A guard came in, took our bowls, and gave us more tea. The fire burned low in the bokhari and the room was still warm. This was old Afghanistan, quiet, warm, peaceful. It reminded me of sitting in a *chi-khana*, or teahouse, in the mountains. I asked Fazul about his life. He had told me parts of it over the years, but I wanted to hear the whole story.

"I was born in 1977 in Khinj, a village today of about one thousand people, in the lower Panjshir Valley."

Panjshir meant "five lions," referring to five brothers who lived in the valley in the eleventh century. It was one hundred miles northeast of Kabul, by the Hindu Kush. It was Tajik country, home of Ahmed Shah Massoud, the now mythical guerrilla leader, a valley which neither the Soviets nor Taliban could conquer.

"As a boy, I went to a *maktab* in the morning and a madrassa in the afternoon.[6] There was not enough land to work for food. Each extended family shared about one acre. My own share as a boy, which was part of our family plot, was no bigger than this room." It was eight feet by twelve feet. "I later bought land for sixty to seventy thousand dollars but that was much later in life."

It would have been after the Soviet Union invaded Afghanistan in December 1979, sending tanks and armored personnel carriers over the Hindu Kush, down the narrow paved road past the Panjshir Valley to Kabul, and east to Jalalabad and south to Kandahar. Fazul continued, "In 1980, when I was two or three"—no Afghan knows his exact age—"the Soviets invaded the Panjshir, and the whole valley evacuated up to almost the very end.[7]"

By June 1982, the Soviet Union had invaded numerous times, sending hundreds of helicopters, fighter jets, bombers, tanks, and thousands of troops into the Panjshir trying to quell the resistance,[8] led by Massoud, who had fled Afghanistan in 1973 to Pakistan where he helped form, with Hekmatyar, the mujahideen, and who became a symbol, like Haqqani for the Pashtuns, of the resistance. Fazul and his family had to walk or take horses through banks of snow over mountain passes time and time again.

"My father was with the mujahideen, one of thirty men who once went to meet Massoud—we called him Amir Saheb—when he returned from a trip," Fazul said.

"The commander of my father's unit was killed and my father was chosen to take over, but he was hit by a grenade and had twenty-three pieces of shrapnel in him which shredded his back. There were no doctors or hospitals and we lay him on a bed on his stomach. He couldn't move or talk. The next month the Soviets attacked and we made a straw bed and put him on a horse and walked up to the end of the valley. We stayed two months. Six months later the Soviets attacked again. Massoud had the best intelligence.

"Eventually my father started to walk with a crutch, and we walked twelve hours through the Hindu Kush to another village for six months."

When the Soviets left, pushed back by the mujahideen, Fazul and his family, like other families, returned. Fazul continued, "The lapis and emerald mines were still open in the Panjshir and my father would go to Pakistan for weeks at a time to sell stones." Panjshir has been famous for centuries for its silver and precious stones. "One night some men learned that we had some money from a sale and came with guns. 'Don't make any noise or we will kill you,'" they said. "My father took off his gold watch and sneaked it to me and I put it in my pocket under my vest. They broke all the boxes in our house and took my mother's jewelry, all our clothes, and beat my father. I was nervous and a man saw that and came to me, found the watch and slapped me hard across the face. I was nine and I never forgot it."

They had to leave Afghanistan. They became refugees walking through mountain passes up through Badakhshan[9] and down into Chitral, Pakistan. Fazul said, "It was the first time I saw the outside world, paved roads and electricity. It was too dangerous to try to go to Kabul. There were few roads in Badakhshan. KhAD[10] was everywhere and people were afraid of them. We had enough money to rent a house in Peshawar and I went to a Jamiat-i-Islami (Islamic Society) school with a boy named Jaal, who was Rabbani's son, but I didn't know that." Fazul was in the fifth grade.

Burhanuddin Rabbani was the professor who brought back the works of Sayyid Qutb, bin Laden's favorite author, and translated them into Dari.[11] Rabbani became president of the Islamic State of Afghanistan when the mujahideen came to power in 1992. He was killed by a suicide bomber in 2011.

Fazul said, "In 1989, we got word that the Soviet Union was leaving and we returned from Peshawar to Kabul, where my grandfather owned a home, and then in the spring we returned to Panjshir." But there was civil war now between the the mujahideen and the Afghanistan communist government left behind by the Soviet Union. Schools were closed and Fazul convinced his parents to let him study in Pakistan. He went alone, following a mujahideen arms supply route for seven days through the mountains back to Pakistan so he could go to school. "The bottom line was there were paved roads and there was electricity." He had an aunt and uncle living in Peshawar and went to a mujahideen school.

"I was twelve in 1992 when the mujahideen came to power. We were so excited. The war was over and I could go to school in Afghanistan." He lived in his grandfather's house in Kabul. But then civil war erupted again; their house was hit repeatedly with bullets and the Kabul River became the front line. "I didn't like Najibullah," Fazul noted, "but I was sad when he was killed, because of why and how. I went to see him at Ariana Square in Kabul, and wish I hadn't. He shouldn't have seen justice that way."

Najibullah, the former head of KhAD, which tortured and killed many of its prisoners, became the last president of the communist Democratic Republic of Afghanistan left behind by the Soviet Union, from 1989 to 1992, when he had a chance to escape Afghanistan but chose to stay. The war among the Northern Alliance, led by Massoud, Hekmatyar, and the Taliban, lasted from 1992 to 1996. In 1993, Hekmatyar fired hundreds of rockets a day into Kabul. Schools were closed. When the Taliban took Kabul in 1996, the Taliban castrated Najibullah and hanged him in the square.

"I went to Jamiat Lycee mujahid and then to the first modern high school in Kabul, Estiqkal, which means freedom, the French high school. Classes were in Dari. Today all schools require Arabic and English."

"I was graduated finally in 1996. During our second day of exams, the Taliban took Kabul." Ten days later, the NDS, now under the Taliban, picked up Fazul and three cousins because they were from the Panjshir, home of their enemy Massoud, threw them in prison, and beat them for four days with electric cables, demanding to know where they were hiding weapons. His parents paid $2,000 and bought his release. He went back to the Panjshir for a year and then returned to Kabul. Fazul continued his story:

In 1997, I took the Kabul University exam. If you got the highest marks you went to the medical school, then the engineering school, political science, and so forth. I was thirty-seventh out of eight thousand students and got accepted to medical school. I was there for two years. One day we had a chemistry exam. Armed guards lined the walls. A mullah, who had a stick, was in charge and said we could not use any books. There were two hundred students taking the exam and I was a little late and didn't hear the instructions. I sat down with my books. The mullah came over and hit me twenty times. I went home and decided I wouldn't go back. In 1998, I went to Peshawar and worked for a year in a shop that my uncle owned. You could retake an exam if you passed it. I came back in 1999, took the exam and passed again.

I had a classmate whose father, from Kandahar, was deputy chief of police. I was nervous sitting next to a Kandahari[12] with a black turban, but we became friends and went to each other's homes. I had a motorbike and one day he came to me nervously. "Give me the keys," he said, "go to the back of school, jump over the wall, and disappear. The Istakhaborat [Internal Security] is here. [This was the Ministry of Defense Intelligence, run by a friend of Mullah Omar. Fazul's classmate would move the motorbike and give it back to him later.] There are two trucks outside and they have a list of fifteen names and yours is second on the list. Get out of here." I jumped over the back wall, took a taxi to my uncle's house, and went back to the Panjshir.

At the time, a human smuggler would fly you to London and sneak you through customs for eight thousand dollars. Some friends of mine were going, one who is our senator today, and I was going to go with them, but I didn't have the money, and didn't want to borrow it. Five months later, I came back to Kabul from Panjshir and got married. It was 1999. I returned to Panjshir and worked for six months in the mines.

In the spring of 2000, elders came to me and said, "You are the best educated person here and we would like you to be a teacher." [There was only one university educated teacher, the rest were mullahs. It paid less than fifty dollars a month.]

At the time half the Shomali plains [north of Kabul] were under the control of the Taliban and the northern half was under the control of the Northern Alliance. I found two teachers, and fixed the school. Most of the teachers were mullahs. I taught English, geography, math, and science. The mullahs taught religion. People heard about my classes and came from faraway villages to attend. I used the IRC [International Red Cross] system, which I had learned in Peshawar.

I am most proud of those two years. There was energy and enthusiasm and it was wonderful. We had poetry classes and mullahs gave speeches. We had a conference to celebrate the birth of the Prophet and three thousand people attended. We did everything by hand. Massoud heard about what we were doing, focusing on the natural sciences and English, but we needed money. We applied to the district governor and a week later we got a letter to go see him. They had two hundred million Afghanis and gave us half.[13] Massoud approved the money. The students learned more in four months than they had learned in the last four years. We had proper books and paper. We were making up for all the time that they had lost. People came from six villages. We had five hundred students.

When school started in 2001, they made me the principal. I still taught English. It was a middle school and we made a high school so our students wouldn't have to walk six miles each way to a high school. I was twenty-three. A French NGO, which was working in the valley, asked if I would teach English to their staff. I started at five a.m. and worked until evening. I was making two hundred dollars a month, one of the highest salaries in the village.

At that time, Iran and Turkey each were giving one hundred scholarships to our region. Massoud said to divide them between north of the Hindu Kush and south. We were living in a tiny valley surrounded on three sides by the Taliban. The only exit was through Badakhshan. Over three thousand students took the exam. I got the second highest mark in the valley and while I was waiting to see about the scholarship, 9/9 happened [he was referring to the assassination of Massoud on that day, international calendar]. You cannot imagine how devastating it was.

Two men on Belgian passports, who said they were journalists, came to the Panjshir to interview Massoud. A bomb in their camera killed him and the cameraman. The other man tried to escape but was caught.

It has never been proven, but it is assumed that al-Qaeda killed Massoud. The news went around the world.

"Massoud was everything to us. He was king. Even if he couldn't solve the problem, just to see him made you feel better. It was not imaginable that something could happen to him. A week after the attack, they announced that he was dead. Thousands upon thousands came to his funeral."

Fazul's eyes were watery. He had been talking for two hours, and now became emotional.

"You have to put yourself in that hopelessness. No matter if you were a mullah or a liberal, educated or illiterate, I had never seen such sorrow. Then 9/11 happened. Our only source of news was the radio and we listened to the BBC and VOA [Voice of America]. I have never seen such emotion. We were surrounded by the Taliban."

The watchman came to put more wood in the bokhari. Outside the muezzin called the faithful to prayer. Fazul got up to wash and pray. It was the final prayer of the evening. He returned twenty minutes later.

"There was tremendous fear and complete hopelessness. Massoud was our only hope. He had top lieutenants but no second in command." He mentioned other guerrilla leaders, strongmen still in power. He drank some tea.

Afghanistan, where women in Kabul once dressed like women in Europe and America, where Kody one night went to a discothèque with a strobe light, where Kabulis went to the movies and sat in outdoor cafés, fell into chaos.

"Before the Taliban, Massoud was amir of Kabul and the northeast. Ismail Khan ruled in the west. In the east was Hajji Qadir. The south was chaos."

The Taliban, backed by Pakistan and Saudi Arabia, couldn't take eastern Afghanistan, under the control of Hajji Qadir, who had become therefore the enemy of Pakistan. Someone had to kill him.

"The Taliban went after Hekmatyar. He went to Massoud, his enemy, who saved him. In 1996, the Taliban turned on Hajji Qadir and in three months overran him all the way up to Kunar. Massoud was trapped and knew that he would be overrun. Within twenty-four hours he marshaled ninety percent of his forces and returned them to

Panjshir. He had no choice but to let the Taliban take Kabul. On September 26, 1996, they entered the city. Massoud blew up the bridges entering Panjshir. He brought Hekmatyar to Tehran, where, as soon as he arrived, he turned on Massoud."

Fazul described in detail the war that engulfed Afghanistan and the leaders, once American allies against the Soviets, who turned on or allied with one another. "Rabbani was still president, a figurehead for the world, living in a hotel in Mazar-i-Sharif. In 1999, the Taliban launched a major attack and took the north. The only part beyond their control was Panjshir.

"Arabs were the fiercest fighters in the front lines. Massoud would listen to their radios, so the Taliban would make fake recordings, of Arab voices, to frighten him. The Arabs would fight to the last bullet whereas the Taliban preferred to take prisoners. There were Punjabis [Pakistanis][14] fighting with them. We found a Punjabi wandering in the streets. He had a knife and we took it and put him in a room for two days, fed him and told him not to try to escape, saved his life really and took him to NDS.

"We never thought the fighting would end. My life was moving from one place to the next. It was difficult, but we could live through it. I was only hoping to live somewhere in peace. I was still hoping for my scholarship, but the director said to just live. 'How can you even think of this now?' he asked. We had to survive without Massoud, who had negotiated our scholarships. If it hadn't been for 9/11, we would not have been able to hold out longer than six months. It was my last year teaching.

"I was going back to Panjshir and stopped at a guesthouse and saw one of my students. It was too late to travel that night and so I stayed with him. His brother worked for MSF and he had another job offer at ICRC and said I should take the job with MSF. Our exit plan was to be involved with foreigners. The UNHCR and the WFP were here.[15] My friends working for them were immune from the Taliban wrath.

"An Australian doctor interviewed me for the job at MSF, but said what we really need is another doctor, but if we change, because of your language skills, you will be our first option. I felt hopeless. The future was dark. I stayed that night in the guesthouse.

"There were more foreign journalists and photographers all around. A man said, 'Your friend is with CNN, which has the biggest operation.' My friend said CNN didn't need any more people. More foreign teams were coming in and I saw that my students were getting jobs. I was sitting there despondent and saw a friend from Peshawar. He was running the office. He said, 'I've been looking for you. Where have you been? Just stay here, I will let you meet the big networks. Stay away from photographers and writers. They won't be here long. Go with the big companies.' The requirement was that you either had to have a car or to know English.

"I was standing there and two men came up to me, Randall Joyce and Jim Axelrod.[16] Randall asked me a few questions. They wanted to know if I could speak English well enough, and they asked my friend if they could trust me. That was it. We set up an office and Jim, who had never been anywhere, was happily surprised. I asked how much I would earn and Jim said one hundred fifty dollars. The next night we went down to the front lines and filmed there and we went down there again. Randall said, 'We have to pay you more for this.' It was dangerous. He gave me another hundred dollars, so I was making two hundred fifty dollars per day.

"I remember the joy that first week taking $1,700 home to Panjshir and giving it to my family. I never had that joy before. I loved teaching, but with this job, when it gets in your blood you can't get it out."

Fazul has a brother and nine sisters. One sister is married, the rest live at home. He, even though we had been through so much, looked at me coldly when I asked about them. Here, a man must never ask how many daughters or sisters a man has. You must always protect your women.

"My family is getting too large and my wife and I want to move to an apartment in our compound. My father doesn't want us to move, but my wife is desperate for some privacy. I always bring my money home and give it to him. He doesn't have a stable income now. We won't be eating together, and with Yousef [Fazul's son] now three, our cost of living will rise. Mom is on my side."

He was thirty-seven, but his father was head of the household.

"The only time I've ever had any stability was in the past fourteen years. My story is one story. There are hundreds of thousands of people with stories more interesting than mine."

It was late. He had been talking for three hours.

"It was so exciting in 2001, 2002. After 2010 I got tired. It was like being on a bicycle and never getting off to rest, round and round we went. I wanted to meet new people and deal with new ideas."

He was buying houses and land. He had become a wealthy man.

"I lost touch with the real world." Fazul still wanted to return to CBS, just as I never wanted to leave. We had once been part of a family, when it was exciting; we didn't think about the end.

❖ ❖ ❖

ON THE MORNING of February 22, Ehsanullah came to the hotel again and brought more information on Haqqani drawn from his trip into the Tribal Areas and to Peshawar. I didn't tell him that I had a visa for Pakistan. The next day there was an avalanche in the Hindu Kush and people were killed and missing. The CBS crew left for the mountains. I called Fazul, but there was no answer. Two days later, he called back and apologized for not calling me back sooner. He had been in the Panjshir to cover the avalanche. Two of his cousins had been killed and seventeen others from his village. "You get used to this here. You just go on," he replied. He stayed for the funeral. There would be another service in Kabul the next day.

I went again over the names of the people I wanted him to contact. I knew Din Mohammad was busy and had asked me not to call him again, but I was running out of time. I asked about Feridoun.

"I called him, but he didn't answer," said Fazul softly. He was tired. There was a landslide on the Jalalabad Road and it was closed for two days. That was probably why Feridoun had not come up. He would call him again. Fazul had families to console, including his own.

After lunch, I checked my e-mail in my room. There were two notes from Sami Yousafzai, who was back from London, now in Islamabad. The subject line on one read: "Jery's Fridun."

"I am sure you remember faridon Momand," he wrote.

Good news he survived but numbers killed.
    @pajhwok: #AFG An #Afghan MP FaridonMomandunhert in a suicide attack in eastern #Nangehar province. Two killed and 10 wounded in attack.
    Best rgds

I stared at the screen. Feridoun had been attacked by a suicide bomber. "It is completely safe here, no problem whatsoever," he had said. He guaranteed it. There were so many questions I wanted to ask. I thought of Yasini, with whom I had just had lunch and who was angry that Feridoun was involved in my case. Could he be involved in this? Was it coincidental? Feridoun had finally agreed to come up to see me but his convoy had been hit by a suicide bomber. Someone had been paid to assassinate him.

I wrote back to Sami and said that I had talked to Feridoun on the phone a week ago. I hoped he wasn't hurt too much. I didn't tell him that I had wanted to go see him partly because he would be able to tell me more about Sami. Newspaper reports appeared over the next two days:

Three persons were killed and 13 others wounded when the convoy of Wolsei Jirga (Parliament) member Faridoon Momand came under suicide attack in Jalalabad City, the capital of eastern Nangarhar province on Friday, officials said.

Ahmad Zia Abdulzai, the governor's spokesman, told Pajhwork Afghan News the attack on Momand took place late Friday. Momand was on his way to Jalalabad City from Kama district when a suicide bomber riding an explosive-laden car attacked the MP's convoy near Kama Bridge. Humayun Zahir, director of Nangarhar Civil Hospital, said receiving three dead bodies and 14 others wounded with most of them in critical condition.

Asadullah, an eye witness, said that the suicide bomber exploded his car when Momand's car crossed the bridge. No group so far has claimed responsibility for the attack.

Chapter 16

A Rising Star

EHSANULLAH SAID I SHOULD TALK TO A MAN CALLED ARIFULLAH Pashtoon. His father was an elderly, distinguished tribal leader near Khost. I didn't know him, but agreed to see him. Again, one man was leading me to another, and this time it would lead me to where I never expected to go.

A man who looked to be about forty came into the hotel. He had short hair, wore white shalwar kameez, a black vest, no hat, and black polished loafers. I was sitting in the lobby and watched him walk past, looking at his phone. Ten minutes later he returned and we shook hands. "I had to perform my ablutions," he said. Muslims had to wash before praying to be clean before God. Islam is as much a social ritual as a religion. We went to the café and sat in the corner.

He was a member of parliament, and chairman of the Senate Foreign Relations Committee. He came from an old, prominent political family. "The communists asked my father to join them, but he said, 'I only have one party, the Party of God,'" he said proudly. A waiter came over and Pashtoon ordered tea and cookies. "I was only three when the Russians invaded." He was a new generation of political leaders, not yet forty. I listened.

"I am young and want to shine in the politics. Sitting here is an opportunity for me. The other, older men, why won't they talk? They are afraid. They are not independent." They were controlled by their past, when they aligned themselves with Pakistan or Saudi Arabia, seeking money and power, like most men, in the wars that have engulfed Afghanistan since August 1975.

He talked for the next hour about himself and his family. He talked about working in the Gulf. "In 1995 I was working in Doha and studying English and computers at night. I was living with twenty-two Afghans and one night I brought a computer back and they asked if it was a piano.

"I am a rising star," said the ambitious young senator. He told me about his experiences as a politician visiting India and Pakistan. I drank tea and waited. I knew I had to be patient. "There is no standard sandwich here—no McDonald's. We don't even have decent medicine or a decent standard internet. There are US, Spanish, German, and British Muslims in the Tribal Areas who have joined al-Qaeda and the Taliban." Finally, we were getting somewhere. I had no sense if I could trust him, but I listened. The Taliban were working with Daesh, he continued, using the Arabic pejorative acronym for ISIS.

He talked about the links between Saudi Arabia and Pakistan and negotiations with the Taliban. He wanted someday to be president. He had to go to a meeting. I walked him to the door. I had spent almost two hours with him; it was time wasted, I thought. I was wrong.

I returned to my room and late that afternoon Enayat, the tribal leader who had taken me into Kurram Agency, called. I had been trying to reach him for five days. "I have been gone," he said. "How can I help you?"

I wanted to see him and to tell him what had happened since we last saw one another, when we had walked through savannah grass into Kurram Agency, and I had gone ahead, like a pilgrim seeking nirvana.

I told him I was working now on another project, like the last one. He knew that I was talking about the Haqqanis. I asked if he knew someone who would talk with me. I was looking for an introduction, which he would provide, and which would become the missing link.

The line was silent. "People are scared. You are writing about a sensitive subject. Where are you staying?" I told him. "I have a meeting there and will come at five p.m."

I waited in the lobby. He came at seven p.m. and we recognized one another immediately. He wore Afghan clothes and a pakhool, looked older and heavier, and walked with the confident air now of authority and success. We went to my room, which was maybe bugged, but we felt safer there than downstairs, where men were watching. We talked like old friends about our trip to his village and into Kurram Agency. "It was very dangerous what we did, going on those roads. There had been so many bombs there." He shook his head. I told him about my kidnapping. He looked at me differently and asked me questions. "You are lucky to be alive," he said.

I explained that I had been traveling in the Middle East and what I wanted to pursue.

He was quiet for a second. "It is very dangerous what you are doing, but you know this. You must be careful." He was referring to himself also. If he helped me he would expose himself to danger. There was, as we both knew and as he would never say directly, especially in my hotel room, an ongoing assassination program against tribal leaders. He was in danger, possibly all the time, of being targeted by the ISI. He would help me, but I had to give him time. That was all I needed. This was the opposite of the Trade. It was, in all its beauty, and simplicity, one man helping another. He asked me to come with him and we went downstairs and sat with an Afghan businessman and three other Afghans, all in suits and ties. The meeting was in Pashto. It was too hard for me to follow, but I was fulfilling my role by sitting there. I had met the businessman the day before. He lived in Washington and had government contracts. He mentioned Khalilzad. I said I had worked with him. We moved in the same circles, he said. I had helped Enayat, I hoped, by my presence in the meeting.

After an hour, I excused myself and left. I had dinner and late that night I was reading a report on Haqqani by Thomas Ruttig, a linguist, Afghanistan scholar, and cofounder of the Afghanistan Analysts Network. We had never met, but I sent him an e-mail hoping to find him in Berlin where he lived.

Instead, Ruttig was in Kabul and sent me a note back inviting me over the following night. I wore Western clothes and took a special taxi for foreigners across Kabul, turned down a dark, bumpy dirt street, and stopped where an Afghan stood by a light outside a compound. Ruttig, his wife, and I sat in the living room. Kate Clark, a former BBC correspondent who worked with Ruttig, joined us briefly before she left to go to a yoga class. Even now Kabul was a mixture of Afghanistan, terrorism, and the expatriate West.

We sat in the living room and I felt at home. We talked about the Haqqanis, and then we shared stories about our experiences in Afghanistan over the years, moved to the dining room for dinner, and it was a delightful evening. Later, over green tea, I brought up that I was also researching my kidnapping.

"Michael and Malang are buddies and have been since 2004, I think," said Ruttig. He was head of the UN in Gardez before 9/11. Semple was with the UN then and with Ruttig helped implement the Bonn Agreement of 2001. "Michael and I organized the first *jirga*," he said.

He was being modest. He and Michael had organized the first Loya Jirga, which means "grand meeting," after 9/11. A Loya Jirga includes all the important leaders of Afghanistan, who are called together to discuss and vote upon the most important national or international problems facing the country. It would take remarkable diplomatic skill, fluency in Pashto and Dari, the respect of elders, and knowledge of Afghan culture to do this. Few if any foreigners could possibly accomplish it. We talked about Malang and Semple and then I said that I had met Malang, through Mirwais Yasini, and asked how he had the money to buy such a big house in the center of Kabul.

"Yasini was the head of one of the nonregulated counternarcotics programs that, maybe, the British set up. He was a midlevel mediocre commander at the time." The British were creating alternative livelihood programs for Afghans and Ruttig thought, maybe (although he didn't want to say, and I understood his fear), that Yasini may have been the director of one of the counter-narcotics programs. I recalled that in 2006, Fazul had taken me to meet Yasini for a story that CBS wanted to do on narcotics. He was the director of a counter-narcotics commission at the time. "A lot of this money disappeared," said Ruttig, "and the British didn't care." He spoke of forged documents and forged farmers' signatures, part of the the corruption that was the ruination of Afghanistan.

Ruttig spoke clearly, accepting, as he had to, the corruption that now pervaded since 9/11 when the US and other countries poured billions of dollars into one of the poorest countries in the world. I asked about the kidnapping of the UN employees in Kabul in 2004.

Ruttig had been involved in the attempts to free the UN workers. "We figured the kidnappers would try to take their hostages to Pakistan and so I went to Logar Province and other areas where they would come through on their way and talked with tribal elders and asked them to watch out for them coming through their territory."

I asked how much the ransom was. "I never heard anything about a ransom," he replied. "I missed the exchange. I overslept the morning that it took place."

Everyone working on my case knew all about the money, but here it was a mystery. It was central to most, but not to all, kidnappings, depending on the kidnappers' priorities. Hezbollah in the 1980s in Lebanon used the hostages as a shield against a US and French attack in revenge for killing their servicemen.

In Yemen, in 2014, Luke Somers's family said that the FBI never said anything about a ransom. On March 28, 2012, a year and a half before I arrived in Yemen, al-Qaeda in Yemen, officially called al-Qaeda in the Arabian Peninsula (AQAP), kidnapped the deputy Saudi Arabian consul in Aden, the port city near where AQAP operates, and called the Saudi embassy, threatening to kill him.[17] When I visited Aden in January 2014 everyone I met talked about this kidnapping. AQAP demanded $10-, then $20 million ransom, plus the release of all AQAP prisoners in Saudi Arabia in exchange for his life. AQAP posted numerous videos of the diplomat. The word in Aden, however, was that

Saudi Arabia was holding five female members of al-Qaeda who had gone there to fund-raise and AQAP wanted to exchange them for the diplomat. On March 2, 2015, he was released.[18] There was no official information. In 2012, an Iranian diplomat was kidnapped in Yemen. He, too, was quietly released, in 2015. Iran said he was rescued in an intelligence operation, yet another report said that he was exchanged for an ISIS prisoner held in Iraq.[19] In March 2017, over two years after Luke Somers was killed, his younger brother Jordan sent me a Reuters article[20] that the FBI had just sent him, which said that AQAP had posted a message online claiming that its sole demand for Luke's release was that the US release, in exchange, two prisoners: Sheikh Omar Abdel-Rahman, the famous blind sheikh, in federal prison on charges related to the 1993 World Trade Center bombing; and Aafia Siddiqui, an MIT-trained Pakistani neuroscientist in federal prison on attempted murder charges. AQAP said that the US refused to negotiate. The FBI wouldn't comment. It was the Trade in all its darkness.

In the West, in the kidnap and ransom industry, the captors are considered the "producers" and the hostages are the "product," and the forced "transaction" is "the trade."[21] There was no "transaction," apparently, in the case of Luke Somers. In the 2004 UN kidnapping case in Afghanistan it did not seem, at least according to Amrullah Saleh and Hajji Din Mohammad, that the UN had a risk management plan in place, or if it did, it was chaotic.

Michael Semple had told me he was involved, but only as a negotiator, so I pressed Ruttig gently about Semple's role. Kate Clark came back after her yoga class, listened, and assured me that Semple was a good man. I felt guilty questioning him, but I had to ask because I was still uncertain. I was driven to understand my case, not aware that it would take yet another turn. I asked why Saleh would go after Semple as he did. I wondered if it wasn't because Semple and Mervyn Patterson had established on their own a truce between the Taliban at Musa Qala and the British Army, angering Saleh and the Americans.

"I studied the truce at Musa Qala, and while a lot of people supported it, the Americans were opposed and sabtoged it." They didn't want any compromise with the enemy. Saleh, close to the Americans, went to President Karzai, and Semple and Patterson were thrown out of the country. "What was political may have become personal," said Ruttig. And I had just been caught in the middle.

"There were hints also," Ruttig continued, "that the kidnappers were from the north."

"Were they from the Panjshir?" I asked.

Ruttig didn't know, or if he did, wouldn't say. Saleh was part of the Northern Alliance and from the Panjshir. Again, my kidnapping had just taken another turn.

Soon it was nearly eleven o'clock. It had been an enjoyable evening and I felt a kinship with Ruttig. We had both fallen, in our own way, for our own reasons, in love with the wild romance of Afghanistan. There was plenty more to talk about. He kindly invited me to come over the next night. I accepted. Just as I was leaving my cell phone rang. It was Enayat. I said I was having dinner with friends and could I call him later. I didn't want to talk in front of anyone else. "I'd like you to talk to someone," he said.

I agreed to, wondering who it was. I said that I would call him when I got back to the hotel. Two minutes later, my phone rang again. "Mr. Jere, this is Pashtoon"—Arifullah Pashtoon, whom I had met with in the hotel the day before. Something was up. I knew that Enayat was behind this. I agreed, but with reservations, to a rendezvous at two p.m. at my hotel.

I called Enayat from the taxi. He confirmed that he wanted me to meet with Arifullah Pashtoon. It would be good for me, he assured me. I said okay and thanked him. Two people now, Ehsanullah and Enayat, neither of whom I felt knew one another, had told me within the last day to meet with Pashtoon, both making the introduction. I didn't know what was going on, but I would see him again. Kabul was dark, the streets empty. I was afraid of the Taliban appearing in the road and forcing us to stop.

The next day, Arifullah Pashtoon was waiting in the lobby, wearing a tan sweater, dark scarf, and an elegant camel-hair jacket with dark shalwar kameez. We walked to the café. He said that after 9/11, he returned from the Gulf and became one of his father's bodyguards. It was total lawlessness then. There were no police, no army, nothing. Men with long hair and rifles, rocket launchers, everything, were walking around. His father, still a prominent tribal leader, gave an interview to the BBC and said, "Please do not bomb us. The Taliban are gone." America wouldn't listen. All the tribal elders prepared for a meeting. Haqqani sent a note to his father saying, "We are coming."

Pashtoon talked for an hour about what he had seen in recent years along the border and in the Tribal Areas, the links among the Arabs, the ISI, and the Haqqanis. There were Arabs, Americans, British, French, Germans, Canadians, and they trained Chechens, Uzbeks, and Tajiks.

Then Pashtoon got to the point: Anas Haqqani, one of Jalaluddin Haqqani's sons, and a man called Hafiz Rashid, also part of the Haqqani Network, had been arrested in Doha. Pashtoon said. "Ibrahim called me. 'Please help us,' he said. I went to the jail to see them. 'We feel like we are guests here,' said Anas. 'We are being treated very well.'"

"Wait a minute," I exclaimed. "Ibrahim Haqqani called you?" I asked.

"Yes, why not?" he replied casually.

This was why Enayat had called. I was being vetted the first time to see if Pashtoon trusted me. Here was my link to the Haqqanis. Ibrahim was Jalaluddin's younger brother. No Western journalist, to my knowledge, had seen them in at least two decades. I had been trying to get to them since 2002. I had been kidnapped trying to do this.

On October 16, 2014, the *New York Times* had reported that Anas Haqqani and Hafiz Rashid, a senior commander of the Haqqani Network, were arrested in a "transit hub in the Middle East" and were now in Afghan custody. The US said that Haqqani had been fund-raising in the Middle East and the paper reported that Rashid was related to Mohammad Nabi Omari, who had been transferred from Guantanamo, in conjunction with the release of Bowe Bergdahl, to Qatar.[22] This meant, to me, that Rashid was visiting his brother in Doha, the capital of Qatar, where the US probably kidnapped him and Haqqani. I would meet with NDS officials soon and learn more, and I would learn a different side to this story in Pakistan. It was the Trade raised to a whole other level.

"Can I see Ibrahim?" I asked.

He hesitated. "I will talk to him," he answered.

I went to my room and brought back *In Afghanistan*, and showed him a picture of Jalaluddin Haqqani sitting with his men on a tank, and pictures of me in the Haqqani compound. I wanted him to see these pictures so he could tell Ibrahim Haqqani. I forgot that Enayat had looked at my book in 2007. He would have told Pashtoon about me. I couldn't believe that I might have a chance to talk to the Haqqanis, the oldest, and arguably the most lethal anti-Western terrorist organization, including ISIS, in the world.

Pashtoon gave me his phone number. "This is a special number," he said. "I will call your friends, but you must do something for me also. I want to work for the CIA."

Chapter 17

Closer

THE ROOM WAS BLACK. I SAT ON A SOFA AND SAW THE LOW ORANGE glow of an electric heater in the center. I took off my pakhool and put my notebook on the glass table in front of me. Gradually my eyes adjusted, but I could only see a few feet ahead. There were two stacks of Din Mohammad's books on a table next to a chair and a table in front with a button to summon an assistant.

After about forty minutes he came in, a bit hunched over, a white cap on his bald head, wearing a beautiful, long, thick, multicolored coat. We shook hands, leaning forward, greeting one another, bringing our heads close together. I told him how much I liked his coat.

Din Mohammad apologized for keeping me waiting, but he had been busy with meetings. They were there until eleven o'clock last night, he said. I assumed that "they" were his team of officials preparing for the upcoming peace talks with the Taliban. "The Pakistanis are saying that the Taliban are not quite ready to talk. You know how they are," he said. "They can't do anything without Pakistan." He would be the lead negotiator for Afghanistan in the first peace talks with the Taliban that would take place in July 2015 in Murree, Pakistan.

I told Din Mohammad that I had talked with Yasini. He listened as I told him about our meeting. I said that Yasini said that Malang was not a good man. "Then why did he introduce him to you?" Din Mohammad asked.

I had asked him the same question. Yasini didn't think that I was going to get deeply involved with Malang. Din Mohammad gave me a look. Again, he warned me to stop looking. It would not be good for me. Three times now he had warned me. He was trying to protect me, and himself. I told him why I had left quickly, without saying good-bye, last time. He listened, but didn't let on what he was thinking. Again, I told him that I wanted to talk about Haqqani. He picked up his phone and called a man who would talk to me. He will come over now. Din Mohammad didn't want to talk about Haqqani directly with me, afraid, I felt, of what I might write and that the ISI would come after him.

I asked one last time about Haqqani.

Din Mohammad hadn't seen Jalaluddin Haqqani since 1996, nearly twenty years. The Pakistanis and the Taliban used his name but he didn't have ties to them. Din Mohammad seemed to be protecting Haqqani. The US made Haqqani more important than he is, he said. Maybe there were other reasons to make him seem dangerous.

He was being too cryptic, but I felt that he was saying that the US focused on, talked about, and reported on the Haqqani Network too much, making the Haqqanis more important than they were, as if the US was creating an enemy to justify the war it had fought for fifteen years. The US might have greater geopolitical reasons, he was saying, for promoting the power of the Haqqanis. I would find out more in Pakistan.

He said that Jalaluddin wanted to fight the Taliban when they came and went to Yunus Khalis who counseled him not to, and said not to join them. Khalis was opposed to internecine warfare, but he didn't know how to stop the Taliban, sponsored as they were by the ISI.

The man Din Mohammad had summoned to talk about Haqqani didn't come. Din Mohammad had to go. We agreed to meet the following day. I called him the next day, but he didn't return my call. He didn't want to talk anymore.

I had been in Kabul a month. I decided it was time to go to Pakistan. I called Pashtoon. He hadn't talked to "my friend" yet, meaning Ibrahim Haqqani. He would call me when I got to Pakistan. He too was afraid to mention Ibrahim Haqqani, now the head of the Haqqani Network. I had been told that Jalaluddin had a stroke and was partially paralyzed, or that he had hepatitis. President Karzai said he was dead. Din Mohammad said that Jalaluddin spent his days quietly reading the Qur'an.

I still wanted to see Feridoun, and Shahwali, but I was afraid that if I told Shahwali that the FBI had wanted my help to find him he might harm me, that he would come to our rendezvous with a gun. He had betrayed me once already. I was afraid, too, that if I probed too deeply with Feridoun that he would alert the ISI, and that they would come after me. Din Mohammad had warned me three times. I was paranoid, still trapped, still a victim of the Trade. But I was at the same time excited. Haqqani was close.

Chapter 18

The Pakhtun Festival

I left Kabul on a cold Sunday morning in March. At the airport, I checked in and looked out the window to the north. The jagged Hindu Kush were stark white with snow, shining in the sun. There was the Afghanistan that I loved. I had waved good-bye from this airport, when I was here in my twenties, climbing the stairs to the Aeroflot plane, my hair long but wearing a tie and the full-length wolf coat that I bought in the bazaar for $12, on my way to Moscow and back to Paris.

The Pakistan International Airlines plane, a twin prop, was small and cramped and the seats were narrow and frayed. I sat toward the back. Two men in rumpled leather jackets walked up and down the aisle. One carried a metal ruler, like a swagger stick.

We touched down briefly in Peshawar and two men in blue uniforms, with stewards and hostesses, commuting to catch a flight, got on and we bounced and swerved through a storm to Islamabad. Officials waved us through customs. I saw Nafay, the CBS manager, with a streak of gray in her hair now, come through the crowd and we hugged one another. "You made it," she said, smiling. Yes, finally, I felt comfortable and safe. "Mugaddir is here. He was our driver during the whole time when we were trying to get you released. We have a tank here now to protect us," she whispered. There was indeed a small tank with camouflage netting across the street, and around a corner a Humvee with a machine gun on top.

Mugaddir, six foot three, slim, smiling, his beard dyed red with henna like the Prophet Mohammad's, came forward and we hugged one another. For eight years, Pakistan had refused me a visa but now, through Nafay's father, the door had opened.

Islamabad's Serena Hotel, on a hill behind a black high wrought iron fence, was the only major hotel that the Taliban hadn't bombed. I checked in and Nafay went outside to have a cigarette. "I smoke because of you, you know," she had said when she came to New York. We had lunch and talked for three hours. I asked her to thank her father for my visa. I wondered if he knew why I had come.

I explained the Haqqani project. She knew people I should see. She announced that she and two other women were putting on the first-ever Pakhtun[23] festival, celebrating Pakhtun culture with films, music, dancing, and panel discussions. They were bringing a delegation from Afghanistan, the foreign minister of Pakistan, and speakers from all over Pakistan. They had raised over $80,000.

Her father was Pakhtun, a minority in Pakistan, and her mother Punjabi, the main ethnic group in the army. Her parents had met in Peshawar, the largest Pakhtun city in the world. Her father became a diplomat and she went to high school in Pakistan and Mexico before she went to Pepperdine.

I didn't tell her what I had learned in Kabul: that my kidnapping was different, it appeared, from what I thought. I now wanted to learn from her, and I wanted to talk with Gohar Zaman, whom Michael Semple said I must see before my investigation would be complete.

"I will send Mugaddir over tonight with a phone for you," she said. That evening we sat in the lobby and he gave me the phone. "Everyone was so worried," he said, looking kindly at me. "Mr. Jere has been with us from the beginning. He is our friend." I felt myself becoming emotional. No one in America talked to me about my kidnapping or showed any affection. There, I was a problem. Mugaddir and I had spent hours together over the years, my Pashto instructor and guide.

Sami Yousafzai called and I invited him over. He wouldn't come inside the hotel. The security forces were everywhere, he said: the waiters, the hostesses, the cleaning people. He insisted that I go to a guesthouse but I had to stay in the hotel. It was the safest place for a foreigner, and I had to be especially careful. If I was going to try and reach the Haqqanis I had to do it from the Serena. My phone would be tapped. I would be watched constantly. I was afraid to stay at Sami's place. I couldn't be seen to be tied to him, and I would be too vulnerable there. They, whoever they were, the ISI or the Taliban, could see me there and come for me.

At the hotel, there were guards and barriers below to stop a suicide bomber in a car. Sami wanted to meet outside but I didn't want men to see me getting into his car.

I called Mahmud Mohmand, whom had I gone to see, thanks to Michael Semple, in New York. He lived in Peshawar, two hours away from the quiet streets of Islamabad. The man with him in New York knew Ibrahim Haqqani. "Where is Michael?" Mahmud asked. "I do not have a current e-mail address for him."

I gave it to him. If Mahmud couldn't come to Islamabad, I would see him in Peshawar. I called Moustache, the journalist from the Tribal Areas, whom I had brought to Dubai in February 2014. "The Serena is not a good place, but I will call you and come to see you there," he said quietly.

I called Pashtoon in Kabul on my CBS UK phone and left a message. I went down to the lobby, past a man standing at a podium by the elevators, monitoring everyone. I went for a walk on the hotel grounds under the gaze of a guard with a rifle on a balcony.

The next morning Pashtoon called to say that he had talked with Ibrahim Haqqani and told him that I wanted to talk with him. Haqqani did not say no. Was it possible, after all these years? "I am talking to you on a mobile that US Special Forces gave me. They said no one can hear us. I want to work with the CIA. Can you introduce me?" He was asking me again. I didn't believe that his phone was secure. Mugaddir, the CBS driver, had told me of an army friend who listened to foreigners' phone calls.

I told Pashtoon to remind Haqqani that I lived with him and his brother when they were fighting the Russians. I said to tell him that I was writing a book and wanted to give him a chance to tell his story. It was an opportunity for the Haqqanis to talk. He promised to do this.

That afternoon, Nafay and I met in the upstairs lounge. I told her about the call from Kabul. I had to trust her and couldn't do this alone. It was too dangerous. She had contacts with the ISI, but most importantly she had done all she could to save me. Her eyes were wide. I reminded her that the US had kidnapped Anas Haqqani, Jalaluddin's son, last October, and a man named Hafiz Rashid, part of the Haqqani Network, and given them to the Afghans, and that Ibrahim had called my friend and asked for his help. Both men were now in prison in Kabul. My contact went to the jail to see Anas. I didn't tell Nafay that he was playing both sides, but like all Pashtun tribal leaders along the border, he was trying to survive the ISI's assassination program, and he was ambitious. If he got a job with the CIA, he would be playing three sides, unless US and Pakistani intelligence still worked together, which I believed they did, in which case it was four.

Nafay smiled. The stars were aligning. I said I was afraid. I couldn't afford to get kidnapped again. She said we would meet Ibrahim in Islamabad, or in a safe house in Peshawar. I would be watched, but we would be okay. She asked where Jalaluddin was living.

How could she be so confident that I would be fine? She was admitting that the ISI would be watching us. They kept files on journalists. I had gone once to the Office of External Publicity, which oversaw visas for journalists, to register, as I was supposed to every time I visited. A woman took a legal-sized red manila folder, my file, from a cabinet next to her and looked through it.

I told Nafay that Behroz Khan, whom she knew, had once told me that Jalaluddin lived in a safe house in Rawalpindi, right near the Pakistani army's General Headquarters. Rawalpindi is an ancient city,[24] and the headquarters since the founding of Pakistan of the Pakistani army.

Behroz Khan (whose brother would soon be killed) was the Pakistani journalist who took me to dinner at the home of Asif Durrani, the acting ambassador, in Kabul in 2007, now the ambassador in Dubai. In 2006 Behroz introduced me to Sami Yousafzai in Peshawar.

I didn't want to get excited because the chances of meeting Ibrahim Haqqani were still remote. Nafay started talking about all that had gone on while I was in captivity. It had become, it seemed, an important part of her life.

We went outside the hotel so she could have another cigarette. The air was cool and the sun was bright. I asked if people knew who Ibrahim Haqqani was. If he walked down the street would people recognize him? Nafay said no, that only security people would recognize him. I said that the Pakistani defense minister said that there would be no peace talks on Afghanistan without the Haqqani Network. She walked over to a table, pushed her cigarette into an ashtray. "That's right. That's how important he is. Nothing will happen without him."

Din Mohammad had said the exact opposite.

That night Pashtoon wrote and asked if I had the messaging app Viber. I tried unsuccessfully to install it. Pashtoon didn't have any information yet, but would call me, he wrote again. I told him to remind Haqqani that I had seen Yunus Khalis before he died. I wanted to see Jalaluddin again.

Pashtoon called that evening. He had talked with Ibrahim. He would meet with me, but I had to wait until he called Pashtoon again.

Could it be possible? I had been kidnapped partly because I wanted to see Jalaluddin, now men were opening the door for me. I thanked him and said that I would do my part. I would have to talk to the CIA on Pashtoon's behalf to introduce him. At eleven thirty, Pashtoon wrote again: "Hi dear how are you doing there tomorrow I want to call that guy have a nice night."

Two days later, Pashtoon called. They would talk with me. He would give them my number and he would send me theirs. The next day a man called and left a message in English. I felt a knot in my stomach telling me to be careful. I didn't know who it was: only a couple of people had the phone number—Moustache or Mahmud,

Semple's Pakistani friend whom I met in New York, in an apartment. I called back. A man answered and I introduced myself. Was it Ibrahim? Could it be?

"It is Mahmud," he responded, somewhat annoyed. He was coming up tonight and would see me for dinner. He called that night and said he was downstairs. In the lobby, I walked past a man with dark hair and a dark beard and hard eyes, but he had a book next to him. I kept going. I walked to the front door where other men were loitering and I slowly turned back. There were many men standing around, watching perhaps. I saw a young woman, about twenty-one, with curly hair, in a bright-colored skirt, and black tights, carrying a backpack like an art student or hipster in the West, standing out in this expensive, proper hotel where women mostly wore saris and shalwar kameez.

I walked back across the lobby, looking at every man standing or sitting until I reached the one man sitting alone, with the book: Mahmud. "You look completely different," he said. Yes, I was heavily bearded now, older and darker inside, and he too was lighter in his manner in New York. I gave him a choice of hotel restaurants and he chose Pakistani and picked a table with no one around. I liked this man, instinctively, as I had in New York. A waiter came over and he ordered fresh grape juice. I did the same.

He asked where I had been traveling. I listed the countries and told him a bit about my project. "In Kabul, people were afraid to talk to me," I said. "They told me the opposite of what I thought I knew about my kidnapping." I mentioned Din Mohammad and Mirwais Yasini, whom I felt hated or was competing with Feridoun Mohmand. I assumed that Mahmud, from the Tribal Areas, would know all these people.

"Feridoun has many people who have enmity with him. But he is very powerful. No one is more powerful than he is in Mohmand. He is fine." Mahmud drank some water. He was a Mohmand.

Feridoun wasn't fine. He had barely survived a suicide attack.

"It is not that people are afraid of what you are doing," said Mahmud, responding to my comment that men in Kabul were afraid to talk to me. "They are afraid that by talking with you, they will be seen by others as working with you, who is CIA, and that the person talking to you is therefore working for the CIA, and has millions of dollars and they can kill him. People are afraid for their lives."

I understood. Mahmud too seemed to think that I might be a spy of some sort.

"More than one thousand tribal elders have been killed in the Tribal Areas since 2004," he said in his formal way. "The tribal chief, and I am one, is approved by the political agent and the governor. Each receives five hundred to ten thousand rupees,[25] as a token of respect; he is responsible for playing a key role in the affairs of the tribe." He was saying that Pakistani officials had to approve his selection as chief of his tribe, and paid him a small bribe to follow orders. He was a lawyer and believed in the law, yet also in the tribe: a man torn between two worlds. He said that since 2004 in the 880 square miles of Mohmand Agency alone over two hundred tribal chiefs had been assassinated, and their positions filled by "corrupt men appointed by outsiders."

Pakistan was using the Taliban to destroy the Pashtun tribal system. The British, with air power, were never able to bring the Pashtun tribes to heel, but Pakistan was determined to protect itself from being surrounded by India, therefore to assert its writ over the Tribal Areas and Afghanistan, and to re-create the Muslim Mughal Empire, stretching from Lahore to Tashkent, including all the Sunni Muslim nations of Central Asia. President Karzai told me that he lamented the loss of that part of Afghanistan, now called the Tribal Areas, taken by the British when Afghanistan was weak against the British Empire—as Afghanistan is weak today, with Russia to the north, and Iran to the west, and to the east an ambitious, nuclear-armed Pakistan.

"We don't want corrupt bureaucrats to exploit our resources," Mahmud continued. He said the government takeover of the Tribal Areas started during the Soviet invasion, even earlier. Where once Pakistan used the mujahideen for this purpose, now they used the Taliban. He cited Article One of the Constitution of Pakistan, which declared that the Tribal Areas will be supervised by a governor; beneath him, by a chief secretary and other officials. Under them was the political agent, one for each Tribal Agency.

The political agent for Mohmand was clearly a key figure in my kidnapping. He had to know who was behind it. Mahmud could in theory introduce me, but it was too dangerous, especially if I was trying to see Haqqani. "People know about the links among militant groups but they don't want to take the risk of talking to you because they want to live," Mahmud said. To them I was a CIA agent. I had seen this paranoia in the Middle East, this fear that came from living under authoritarian governments, and corruption, and secret police.

"The government reads our e-mails, plants chips in our phones. It even sends 'smart girls' to me who ask if I want to work for the Americans, to test my loyalty." As he talked, the young woman with the backpack, who stood out so glaringly, came in and sat at a table across from us. A few minutes later she got up and left. Mahmud glanced over meaningfully. "Like her."

Mahmud said he had met with the US ambassador Richard Olson, and that after this an intelligence agency picked up his younger brother and tortured him severely. "'It is because your brother is a friend of the Americans and is working for them,' they said. They said my brother supported militants." He had petitioned the court on behalf of his brother, who was under a death sentence and being tortured in prison.

A waiter kept coming over and pouring our water. "I don't like these people, always watching and listening." He too wanted to go to my room. We finished dinner and walked to the elevator. It would be obvious to anyone that I wasn't a simple visitor, as my visa said. He showed me a brief he was carrying. Mahmud was representing Shakil Afridi, the doctor whom the CIA hired to help find out if bin Laden was staying in the compound in Abbottabad and who then Pakistan imprisoned. It was dangerous to represent Afridi, all but considered an enemy of the state. It was as if Mahmud was working in some capacity for the US. He was playing a very dangerous game. I wondered now, again, why Michael Semple had sent me to see him. At first, I thought it was to help me, but now I didn't know why.

"We want to stop the government from using our land for its terrorist activities," Mahmud went on.

I wondered if there was a camera watching or if someone was recording us. "We are trying to bring the Tribal Areas into the mainstream. We are treated like slaves. I told the US ambassador, 'You have murdered our women and children and continue to, because you have given money to our government which targets us, and it is always the innocents who are killed. The government doesn't target militants.' The ambassador smiled, while a man with him took notes. 'You have devastated our region,' I said."

Mahmud was angry at the US, but how did he get an audience with the US ambassador and was so important that an aide was there taking notes? I had to find out more about Mahmud.

He continued, lamenting that his friend and colleague, whom I had met with him, was killed, and Mahmud was attacked, after they returned from studying the US court system. By whom, he didn't know. His uncle, a peace activist, was wounded in an attack. "I meet with generals in the army, and I tell them our problems, but they have no control over our secret agencies. There are twenty-six of them now." He started naming them and gave up. The US, to my knowledge, had seventeen.

Mahmud left to stay somewhere else. The next morning, I was having breakfast when he appeared at my table. His phone rang and he told me it was an official from the US embassy. He would be back in thirty minutes. I waited an hour and went to my room.

He never explained, but he did report that two security men stopped him after he had met with the political agent and asked what they had talked about. He didn't seem worried, but I was. He had just met with a US government official, in public, who knew to find him here at this hotel.

"Some people say that the Pashtuns are related to the Kurds. They are strong fighters and they hold their land, but they are divided up into four countries. There is an international conspiracy against the Kurds and the Pashtuns. The Punjabis are afraid that the Pashtuns will unite."

The last sentence was true. That was one reason why the ISI, led by General Babar, created the mujahideen, to divide and conquer the Pashtuns, of which he was one, in Afghanistan. "All our invasions come from the West," an aide to President Musharraf told me in 2006. He meant Mahmud of Ghazni, Babur, Tamerlane, Alexander, and most recently, in the eighteenth century, Ahmed Shah Durrani, the Pashtun leader, of Kandahar.

I asked Mahmud to call Ibrahim Haqqani for me. It was dangerous for me to call. I was taking a chance with Mahmud, but there was no one else. Pashtoon was in Kabul. He switched on the television and turned the sound up and called. He talked for a minute and closed the phone. "He said 'we will call you.' Everyone's life is in danger. Each one of us must be careful. If anyone is seen talking with an American it will be dangerous for you and for him."

I made green tea for us with the kettle in the room. Mahmud was implying that any meeting would be behind the backs of the ISI. How was such a thing possible? Mahmud talked about journalists in the Tribal Areas killed by the security agencies, specifically in Mohmand Agency. He had taken one to the hospital and peeled off his shirt, soaked in blood. They were courageous, but why was he telling me this—to scare me, or to warn me? "There are many courageous people in the Tribal Areas," he said. "I know a man who killed ten militants, including a cousin of Abdul Wali. The militants came and said, 'Come with us,' and he and his wife, his sister, his brother, and his father all fired their weapons, killing the militants. He has moved with his family to an unknown destination."

I froze. He had just said "Abdul Wali." It was the first time I heard this name since I was taken. Gulob, my jailer, said that Abdul Wali was their leader. "He knows you're here," Gulob said once. Another time Gulob said to be silent because Abdul Wali's men were next door. I had watched the shadows of men walking by the barred, blackened window. I wondered if Abdul Wali could find me now, in the Serena. Why, of all people, did Mahmud bring up his name? I decided to keep quiet and listen as Mahmud continued.

"If I don't criticize the militants, they won't bother me. They respect me. It is the same with the security forces. They will give me things. Everywhere there are militants and terrorists who want a free hand to do what they want. If anyone tries to expose them, or their weaknesses, they will kill them. I know many things but I cannot tell you because I don't want to be slaughtered. There are many who know far more than me, but if they talk to you their lives will be in danger."

Why was he talking this way, other than to scare me or show his influence and power? Mahmud was playing at least two sides. He didn't criticize the Taliban, nor did he criticize the security agencies. He was a tribal chief, and yet the Taliban, with their assassination program, backed by the ISI, left him alone. He talked with army generals and had met, at least once, with the political agent at the US embassy, and he lectured the ambassador. He had power, yet his brother was in prison. I didn't understand.

I needed to find out about Haqqani and Abdul Wali. I had been traveling for a long time but I felt that I was close now to the source.

Mahmud quoted Khushal Khan Khattak, a seventeenth-century Pashtun poet-warrior: "'There are thousands of people who can wear turbans but there are few who deserve to wear one.' You should not be deceived by a man's appearance, but look in his heart to see if he is sincere with you or not."

Mahmud took off his socks and rolled up his sleeves. He wanted to go to the mosque. I didn't know that he was religious. The muezzin's call, once haunting and luring me in, came through the open window. He went to the bathroom, washed, and returned. "If you keep throwing rocks at a man he will soon have a pile of rocks next to him. What does this mean?"

"That he can hurt you more?"

"Yes, that is why a man must be careful."

"Aren't you going to the mosque?" I asked.

"It is too late now. Shah Sab was a spokesman for militants and later he joined ISIS."

Out of the blue, another name had just popped up. I hadn't heard the name Shah Sab in seven years. When we were hiking into the Tribal Areas, Samad, my bodyguard, said the area we were in was controlled by Shah Sab, and Pakistan supported his training center. Razi Gul, Samad, and Shahwali told the Maulvi, and Gulob, the night we were captured that Shah Sab invited us. "We will investigate," the Maulvi said. "If Shah Sab invited you here then you will be free to go. If not, we will deal with you under Sharia." I shuddered then and did now when I heard Shah Sab's name again.

Maybe the mention of Abdul Wali and Shah Sab was a coincidence because Mahmud was from Mohmand Agency, but I didn't think so. He was telling me that he knew more about my case than he was letting on. He had done research, maybe, after we had met in New York and he had read my book. Shah Sab was now ISIS, an implacable foe to any American.

"Empirically, the Taliban are the most dangerous terrorist group in the world," a scholar told me in Kabul. Maybe. But I still felt that the Haqqani Network—led militarily by Sirajuddin Haqqani, who was also the military commander of the Taliban, and which was linked, and had been for decades, to the highest levels of the Pakistani army, the sixth most powerful in the world—was more powerful, and thus more important even than ISIS. If the men who captured me were criminals, why would they talk, almost reverently, about Abdul Wali and Shah Sab? I was afraid to discuss this with Mahmud and I didn't want the US embassy to know that I might meet with the Haqqanis.

Mahmud went on. "Ask one hundred percent of the people about the TTP and they will know about it, but not five percent will know anything about the Haqqanis; even I don't know." The TTP is the Tehrik-i-Taliban, aka the Taliban Movement or the Pakistani Taliban, a coalition of militant groups. "Abdul Wali is the leader in Mohmand. Shah Sab came in and competed with him but lost and Abdul Wali remains in charge."

He was helping me understand my kidnapping better, but confusing me about the Haqqanis. It seems that I had been kept in Mohmand Agency, where Abdul Wali and Shah Sab lived. Maybe I was driven in circles for two hours instead of going north, if my kidnappers were telling me the truth about their ties to Abdul Wali and Shah Sab. It also meant that Mahmud, who said that he was on good terms with the militants, knew these men. He was able tell them where I was. He gathered his papers and said he had to leave.

I had tried for weeks to get kidnap insurance, following Sophie's advice, but no one would insure me, a kidnap victim. If I hadn't been kidnapped, there was only one place to go for K&R insurance and that is Lloyd's of London, within which there are twenty insurers, part of a sophisticated syndicate that has grown up, with its own protocols, for underwriting and controlling the growing kidnapping insurance business.

Few if any companies, families, or NGOs can afford to operate in weakly or corruptly governed territories, like Mali, Somalia, the Sahel, Nigeria, the Tribal Areas, where the role of the kidnappers is to maximize ransom money and to exert pressure on the victim and his or her employer, family, or government. Today, international firms pay roughly $250,000 annually in kidnap and ransom insurance to operate in high-risk areas, what I call the wild. The Pashtuns, like Yemeni tribesmen, have kidnapped people for probably centuries, but now kidnapping has become, for the militarily weak, a part of modern warfare, like suicide bombers. I literally couldn't afford to get kidnapped again.

Early in the afternoon, I went outside to have lunch in the sun when my phone rang. The caller identified himself as Ibrahim Haqqani's son and that his name was John. It was his nom de guerre. He spoke English in a calm, confident manner. He was returning my call. I told him that I had lived with his uncle at Shah-i-Kot during jihad and had written a book about this. I was now writing a book about his family and wanted to give him a chance to explain the Haqqanis from his point of view.

"Okay," he said, "where should we meet?"

It was too quick and too easy. I asked if he was in Peshawar.

"No, we are near the Serena, but we cannot come there." This phone was being tapped, if not by the Pakistanis then by the Americans. It had to be. Yet he was talking so freely.

"I don't know. Let me think. Are you sure you can't come to the Serena?"

He said they could not. It was better if we met at a guesthouse. Did I know F-7 area? It was a wealthy area, one of the best addresses in Islamabad. He told me to find a guesthouse there and let him know.

Could they kidnap me from a guesthouse? The Haqqani Network could do whatever it wanted. But they were letting me choose the place. If I were a spy I could fill it with people and capture them. The government had to be watching us. Would they take me in or throw me out of the country?

That night I went to Nafay's Pakhtun festival. Sami Yousafzai, my former fixer, was there. He introduced me to a female politician, a member of the Kabul Pashtun elite. He told her that I had been kidnapped. She asked if I was treated well. That was all she was concerned about, that they had been good hosts.

"We have respected our traditions for centuries," Mahmud had said earlier. "Don't kill women or children or innocents in combat. The militants are not tribal people. They have been created to show a different picture to the world." They were poor, deracinated men from Afghanistan, brainwashed in religious schools financed by businessmen and princes in Saudi Arabia and throughout the Gulf. The *New York Times* said Anas Haqqani had been fund-raising in the Middle East when the US took him.

A famous singer from Kandahar performed, and he sang louder, with the drums, the tabla, and the flute, and the crowd stood, clapped, and sang, and the Pakistani Rangers, in berets and carrying rifles, stood in the back, and the Pakhtuns, in their minds, were ready to march, as their ancestors had, on India. "My border and my river are the Attock," they sang. The Attock to the outside world is the Indus River, the life blood of Pakistan.

"This song was banned under Zia-ul-Haq," said Sami. "The Punjabis are afraid." Zia-ul-Haq was the American ally and dictator during the Afghan-Soviet war.

"The US has given billions of dollars to the Pakistani government, which uses this development money to make the Pashtun belt a slaughterhouse," Mahmud said. "The suicide attacks, whether they are done by men trained by the security forces or others, target the innocent. It is the women, children, journalists, lawyers, and tribal elders who suffer."

"Tribal customs and systems have been destroyed by the courts, which do not give speedy justice to tribal people," Mahmud wrote in my notebook. He, like Ehsanullah, preferred to write some things rather than talk. "We have our centuries-old customs and traditions, which we have deemed sufficient. But the government destroyed them and the Taliban established their courts."

Why would Pashtuns go against their own people and with a Punjabi-led government?

Mahmud implied that Gulob, Razi Gul, Samad, Abdullah, the Haqqanis, Shah Sab, and Abdul Wali, all Pashtuns devoted to Islam in what Mahmud called the Pashtun belt, from Western Pakistan into Afghanistan, cared more about power and wealth. They needed Pakistan to gain power, and to establish Sharia, their vehicle, and were therefore prisoners of Pakistan, which had its own geopolitical agenda.

Abdul Wali rose in this cauldron. Gulob and Mahmud said Wali was the Taliban leader in Mohmand Agency. I wondered if it was a bomber working for Abdul Wali who had tried to kill Feridoun in the suicide attack, so that he, Abdul Wali, a rising star, also under the control of the ISI, could rule Mohmand Agency. This war of ghosts was at heart a struggle for power, of one man against the other, of tribe against tribe, of one ethnic group against the other, of nations against nations, and faith was a weapon.

"What do you think of Michael Semple?" I asked. "I hear stories about him and Mullah Malang, and my kidnapping, and money, and I am confused."

"Michael came to me some years ago," replied Mahmud, "and got much information from me. Since then I have not heard from him. He has become ever more mysterious."

Like Mahmud himself.

⁜ ⁜ ⁜

MUGADDIR AND I sat in the big tent at the festival. Another group of musicians was playing Pakhtun music, a mixture of Central Asia and India. Mugaddir was born in the mountains near Miran Shah. The Haqqanis still had their headquarters in Miran Shah according to Din Mohammad. Haqqani was at home there. It was his tribal territory. "The Hotaks are fierce fighters, Mr. Jere. Oh, yes. They would come down from the mountains and fight the British," said Mugaddir, proud of his tribe. Mugaddir was born in the exact area that I had hiked up through years ago, into Afghanistan. Haqqani, like Mugaddir, like Nafay's father, all came from the Tribal Areas.

We watched young men dance the *atan*. The music grew louder and faster and the men swirled their long hair and the audience stood and clapped. I went up to say good night to Nafay. She took me to her father, who was sitting in the front, clapping, his face red with emotion. We shook hands and he smiled warmly, welcoming me.

As I rode with Mugaddir back to the hotel I thought again that I was here because Nafay's father had called the consul general in New York, who had worked for him. I once told Sophie at CBS that Nafay's family had contacts in the government.

⁕ ⁕ ⁕

THE FOLLOWING NIGHT, Mugaddir drove slowly down the driveway to a guesthouse. Inside two journalists, one with a mustache, another with a beard, both from the Tribal Areas, were watching television, which showed rioting Christians burning two men alive out of revenge for the suicide bombing of their church. The religious wars were here as much as in the West.

I had come here to learn about Haqqani in the Tribal Areas. We drank black tea, with milk, and then we drank green tea, and they explained how ISIS came to Pakistan and then to Afghanistan. They talked about the Haqqanis' links to Pakistan, al-Qaeda, the safe houses, and the land and sea routes that jihadists took to East Africa, the Arabian Peninsula, and to Iraq and Syria. "I am afraid of you," said the man with a mustache. He didn't believe that I was a journalist. We were wary of one another.

"Pakistan has created many Taliban groups," said Moustache, "to divide and rule them better but they have found that they cannot control what they have created. Mullah Fazlullah created the TTP, and then Pakistan created a TTP splinter group called Pakistan Jamaat-ul-Ahrar,

the Pakistani freedom fighters group. It was led by Mullah Qasim Khorasan, also known as Abdul Wali, in Mohmand Agency."

I was quiet. So, Abdul Wali's nom de guerre was Mullah Qasim
Khorasan. Khorasan referred to ancient Afghanistan, the name used by
ISIS. The ISI protects the TTP.

"Pakistan is using the tribal people to get money from the US to buy
weapons and for its own use," Moustache continued. "The Americans
are killing us by the Pakistani government. The war since 9/11 has been
a tsunami against the common people."

We drank more tea and the night grew late. Mahmud and Din Mohammad had insisted that the Haqqani Network was not important,
but the two journalists here, based in the Tribal Areas, spoke of its vast
reach and growing power. Mahmud and Moustache agreed on the ori-
gins of Abdul Wali.

"First came the mujahideen," Mahmud said at the hotel, then came
"the Black Turbans," who were led by Sufi Mohammad and Fakir Mohammad. They merged the Black Turbans into the TTP. Fazlullah established a madrassa and an FM radio station in Swat." "Mullah Radio,"
men called it. "Fazlullah beheaded people and hanged them," Mahmud
said bitterly.

"Fazlullah was not strong enough among the Mehsud,"[26] Moustache
continued.

The Mehsud were the largest and strongest tribe in the Tribal Areas. They looked down upon the Waziris, the second most powerful
tribe. The Mehsud and the Waziris live in Waziristan, the place of
the Haqqanis and al-Qaeda headquarters. Sir Olaf Caroe, last British
governor of the Northwest Frontier Province of India—today, Khyber
Pakhtunkhwa Province of Pakistan—wrote, romantically, that there
was something "to their air and carriage. The nearest I can get to it is to
liken the Mehsud to a wolf, the Wazir to a panther. Both are splendid
creatures; the panther is slier, sleeker and has more grace, the wolf pack
is more purposeful, more united and more dangerous."[27]

"Pakistan created the Mehsud Group led by Khan Syed Sajna," said
Moustache. "They all became too powerful." He opened his laptop. "Abdul Wali started out in Mohmand as a journalist and then joined Haro-

kut-ul-mujahideen,[28] in Kashmir, fighting India. He is a poet and has written a book on Pashtun poetry. He started his group in 2007–2008 just after the Red Mosque massacre in Islamabad. He wanted to create his own Red Mosque in Mohmand. You are extremely lucky. He was just starting when you were kidnapped, trying to prove himself killing so many people, creating terror everywhere. He could have easily killed you. You are so lucky."

If Abdul Wali fought in Kashmir, he was under the control there of the ISI. It would cost money to build a mosque and madrassas like that of the Red Mosque, money which would have to come from kidnappings, or from the Persian Gulf and the Middle East.

If Abdul Wali wanted to create a new Red Mosque, it was also to accrue further power with the government, and to create more jihadists. Gulob, the jailer, had told me that they were afraid that other militant groups, other producers, would learn about me and muscle in on their territory, like the mafia, and steal me, a valuable product, and sell me to another group. Maybe they did have to hide me from Abdul Wali. Maybe they were just criminals, but to me now, there was no difference between being a criminal and being a member of the Taliban. Abdul Wali was a poet, a thief, and a thug, and killing was his way to power.

In the kidnapping and ransom industry, it is only considered legal to pay ransom in criminal kidnapping, seen as different from terrorism. It seems, from the outside, that all kidnappings are criminal, but in the industry, and in the Trade, it's not so.

It is illegal in the UK under law, and thus at Lloyd's, to pay, facilitate, or reimburse terrorist ransoms. In 2015, 80 percent of all kidnappings worldwide were considered criminal. The average ransom, on land, was $250,000, but the amount was higher at sea among Somali pirates. As far as the insurers are concerned, only crime pays. Terrorism doesn't. So terrorist kidnappers had a motive to appear to be "simple" criminals.

Moustache turned his laptop toward me. "This is Abdul Wali." I stared at the photograph. He was in his forties and had hard, dark, penetrating eyes, a wispy beard, and long, black, lanky hair. He wore a brown pakhool, dark shalwar kameez, and a vest, this poet, this writer, this killer with dreams of glory.

It was midnight when Mugaddir drove me back to the hotel. I spent the next day typing up my notes and preparing questions for the Haqqanis. Pashtoon, in Kabul, sent me a text. Did I have the meeting yet? I said no. The Haqqanis were waiting. But I needed an interpreter, and only trusted Nafay.

She called that evening. She had booked a place for the meeting on a quiet street, but was looking at one more house and as soon as she was certain she would call me. She asked if I would call "John," the man who said he was Ibrahim's son. I placed the call, but he wasn't there. Five minutes, ten minutes passed. Normally he called right back. Maybe he was out or the phone wasn't his. An hour passed, then two.

"Don't put your hand in every hole, or a snake may bite you," went the Pashtun proverb. "I can't keep pressing my luck," I thought. I remembered Gulob had said that if I came back he would "not let the bird out of the cage a second time." Nafay sent the address where we were to meet. "No word yet," I wrote. "They'll call," she wrote back. "You know how things work around here. Just takes a little longer, usually."

❖ ❖ ❖

NAFAY CAME THE next day and we sat outside at the Serena. She said that we would be safer there talking than inside. I had to trust her. Again, she wanted to talk about my kidnapping.

"We decided to call the US embassy," Nafay said. "The FBI called us back. Fazul and I met them at the Marriott and they put us in their car and drove us to the embassy. They took us to the Homeland Security office downstairs and they made us put our phones outside the door. There was a third man there who said, 'I'm with the IRS. Everyone's afraid of the IRS.' They asked us everything: what were our phone numbers, where we were born, what we did for a living, and where we worked before. They asked all about our lives and then they started asking us about you.

"We insisted that it was important that both Shahwali and you got out. The Afghan had to come also. The kidnappers called multiple times a day. 'Where is the money?' they asked, 'When will we get the money?' We told them that we were working on it and not to hurt you. The evening before, there had been a bombing at the Italian restaurant, the Luna Caprese, here in Islamabad, and four FBI agents were wounded."

The bomb attack was on March 15, which suggested that Nafay didn't learn of my kidnapping until a month after I was taken. I was quite certain, however, that she and the others knew earlier and that she was compressing time. Ahmed Shah, Fazul's cousin, knew within a few days. Roshan Khadivi called CBS within a week. I wrote my ransom letter nine days after I was taken. The Taliban Military Committee, as they called themselves, demanded that I do it quickly.

"We all got new phones, SIM cards, and Skype addresses and began skyping with Bryn in London. We started tracing Shahwali and Abdullah. Bryn flew out and he, Fazul, and I went to Michael Semple's farm. Bryn had his name only, they had never met. The first call that Michael made was to Mullah Malang. He identified Abdullah, and Fazul called Rasul Amin to get Shahwali's phone number. Fazul, who didn't speak Pashto very well, got in touch with Shahwali's father, who didn't seem worried at all that his son was kidnapped. Sami and Bashir Khan went to Abdullah's house in Landi Khotal." Bashir Khan was Gohar Zaman's brother-in-law. "Once the FBI got involved and Kroll came in the decision was made to pay the ransom."

Michael told me that he learned that I had been at Yasini's house. That's where he started. He would have received that information from Malang, who was close to Semple and Yasini. It was strange that Malang had not told Semple already. I let it go.

Everyone (including Gulob) seemed to be from Landi Khotal. Fazul had called Kroll "the insurance company," yet Bryn Padrig supposedly had brought money out as well. I didn't want to ask Nafay about this yet. I wanted her to talk freely, to get out what was on her mind.

"Gohar Zaman said it would not be that much money." Later, Nafay said that Zaman had said that $20,000 would be enough, that these people had never seen such money, which made me wonder where the rest might go. "Bryn came out with money. . . . I told Bryn to go into the VIP lounge at the airport. Fazul, in a shiny suit, met him there." She was confirming that Bryn came out with the money, but Gohar Zaman seemed to be the one who knew how much to bring.

"Bryn was going stir crazy and so we would go to Michael's farmhouse. He loved Michael and was also I think jealous. Michael got to live this exotic life, going where he wanted. Michael had to find out who could influence Abdullah. Gohar Zaman sat there doing nothing, keeping his eyes on us. Fazul and I got a call from someone asking, 'Shahwali, Shahwali, is that you?,' then realizing it was us, hung up immediately. We knew therefore that he was involved. Gohar Zaman, it seemed, was key here, this character, this simple old man.

They had drawn CBS into the Trade, using Shahwali's brother as collateral, just as Gulob had wanted to use Shahwali's father as collateral before sending Shahwali to Kabul to negotiate with Fazul for my release; just as the malik of Ducalam had used his brother, he said, as collateral with the family of the military intelligence agent who supposedly came across the border to see me.

"We asked for proof of life, and they played your voice recording to us over the phone," said Nafay. "'If you ever want to see him again,' they said, 'get us the money.'"

I still didn't feel I knew what ultimately drove my case. It may have been simply about money, but like the hostages in Syria, I didn't think that it was just about money, certainly not if $20,000 would be enough. Not for those making the ultimate decisions. I kept thinking now about Abdullah's modern camp, and wondered about Feridoun's driver, who knew exactly where to go on the US Army base, and the American with the pistol on his belt who said when I arrived, "We know all about you," and the navy woman flirting with Shahwali.

I told Nafay that a woman in the navy claimed that she had been in touch with CBS and Fazul said that she had been lying. "Everyone knew about you, Nafay countered. "We got a call from people who said, 'We are military intelligence and the CIA and we want your man handed over to us.' We said, 'We don't want to talk until Jere Van Dyk is handed over to us.' Everyone wanted a part of this."

Everyone had a different story.

Nafay said that Semple had found that Abdullah was part, as she put it, of "Feridoun's court"; he was a member of Feridoun's tribe and had to pay allegiance to him, the great khan of the Mohmand. "Michael called Feridoun and Feridoun told us that to get you out quickly and quietly we would have to give him money and treat Abdullah in such a way so that he feels that he is important. We were to appeal to his pride, and not humiliate him."

So, I thought, the money would go to Feridoun and he, as the tribal chief, would distribute it. This would not be, it seemed to me, what Abdullah and Shahwali planned. Din Mohammad said that "everyone got his share."

Nafay continued: "Fazul and Bashir were going to meet Shahwali's father a second time at a kabob place on Charsadda Road in Peshawar. Bryn was getting frustrated and wanted to go in with guns blazing. 'What kind of gun do you want?' Fazul asked." So, Abdullah would be watching from somewhere, maybe sitting in the restaurant. Nafay smiled, nodding her head yes. I trusted Nafay. The others, all men, implied that she just handled logistics, but she was the only Pakistani among them in Islamabad. She had ISI contacts as part of her job. No journalist in Pakistan went against the ISI. She had to be careful, but she was not doing anything except trying to help me. I wondered if she was holding any information back, as a friend, to protect me.

"The FBI was interested in us, took our addresses, e-mail addresses, and phone numbers," Nafay continued. "They were convinced we were involved." The kidnappers kept calling. "I called Trish Williams to ask if she could trace the calls. She said, 'Oh, I'll see.' They did nothing. I told Fazul to get back to Kabul as quickly as possible to get to your personal things before the FBI did. When he got there an FBI agent was caressing your laptop in his arms."

I thought Fazul stayed along the border the whole time and hadn't seen his family in seven weeks. He would have seen his family if he went back to Kabul, I assumed. Everybody wanted to take some credit, I understood that. It gave them stature, their lives meaning and purpose to be a part of something greater than themselves, something dangerous and exciting, something honorable, like the rescue of a friend.

"Every time the kidnappers called they asked for Michael directly. We knew that it would be safer for you to be released in Pakistan. The fax to us at the beginning came from Bara, which is near Peshawar. All the phone calls came from Pakistan." It would be safer for me in Pakistan only if they knew that they could control my release and guarantee my safety. Only the government or a tribal leader, or both, could guarantee that.

Chapter 19

The Mystery of Gohar Zaman

I PUT ON MY GRAY SHALWAR KAMEEZ, TOOK THE ELEVATOR DOWN-stairs, and walked past the podium where a man stood with his clipboard, through the lobby and outside into the sun, down the stairs, and to the parking lot. I had just worked out in the gym and felt light and free, for the first time in years, no longer beaten down and defeated. I felt young, like a boy. Men looked at me but I didn't care. I was approaching the end, I thought, finally. We were going to Peshawar to see Gohar Zaman. A foreigner needed government permission to go, but Nafay wasn't worried about this. Mugaddir stood by his car, smiling. "You look like a real Pashtun now," he said. I sat in the backseat. Nafay sat up front in shalwar kameez, the first time I had ever seen her in Pakistani clothes.

The four-lane highway was like one in America. We drove past villages, grassland, rocks, trees, and buildings here and there toward Peshawar. We reached Attock, and then the stone arch, still in the Punjab, paid a toll, crossed the Indus River, and drove on into what the British called the North-West Frontier Province, or NWFP, now Khyber Pakhtunkhwa, the land of the Pashtuns. It felt rougher now and there was energy in the air.

Piotr Stańczak was kidnapped in Attock in September 2008. His driver, assistant, and paramilitary guard provided by the government were killed, and the Taliban took him by boat,[29] across the Indus River into NWFP on a fourteen-hour trip into the Tribal Areas, sneaking him through checkpoints, down into South Waziristan. The Taliban kept him there for five months. He was beheaded in a town in a semi-tribal region, near Peshawar. I had never heard of a ransom demand, only a strange demand that Poland not send troops to Afghanistan, that the government release five Taliban from prison including Ahmed Omar Saeed Sheikh, imprisoned since 2002 for the kidnapping and murder of Daniel Pearl. These demands suggested to me, in a convoluted, murky way, that the ISI was involved in Stańczak's murder or that some were trying to pin the blame on the ISI. A similar thing happened in 2008, just before I was kidnapped, when the Pakistani ambassador to Afghanistan chose, inexplicably, to drive through the Tribal Areas to return to Afghanistan instead of flying, as he always did, and was kidnapped—all part of what an Afghan commentator on television called of the "strange game of the ISI."

Poland, unlike the United States in the death of Daniel Pearl or in my case, chose to pursue justice for Stańczak. The Polish government was negotiating with the Taliban, but then supposedly talks broke down. Elements of the Pakistani government, and certainly the political agent in South Waziristan, had to know about these talks. I felt that Stańczak was a pawn, caught maybe in the hands of the "bad Taliban," as Samad, my bodyguard, had called them.

In 2009, the *Guardian*[30] reported that a Pakistani politician linked to the Taliban was behind Stańczak's kidnapping. In 2012 Poland, again unlike the US, pursued the case and attempted to put Stańczak's kidnappers on trial, in absentia, in Warsaw. Poland sent a top law official to Pakistan to get records of the investigation and evidence, but the government refused, citing lack of a legal framework to exchange documents, to provide information. Poland demanded that Pakistan sign a treaty allowing this exchange, and Pakistan complied, but since then nothing has happened and it appears now that Pakistan wants to use bureaucratic red tape to bury this case, as it has, with help from the US, buried the case of Daniel Pearl. The Trade has become since 9/11 an instrument of, at the least, elements of the state.

We approached Peshawar, and on the right, I saw the white Mogul architecture of the Darul Uloom Haqqania, the Haqqani House of Learning, also now called the International Islamic University, the seminary where Jalaluddin studied and from which he took his name. There was now a cacophony of sounds, of horns from buses, cars, trucks, the buzz of rickshaws, and people shouting. Once this city was quiet and filled with flowers. We drove through a residential area, stopped in front of a gate, and guards opened the door and we entered a compound with green grass and drove up a narrow driveway and parked.

Gohar Zaman, a man of medium height and a lean, solid build, came out, walking quickly, and we shook hands and his grip was hard. He told us to come inside. He had a brusque, vigorous military way about him. He was balding with thick white eyelashes. He wore a yellow shirt with cufflinks, tan trousers, and light tan shoes.

We entered his home and there was a dark wood dining table set for six filled with food. He took me into a bedroom and introduced me to his wife, an attractive younger woman with long brown hair and wearing shalwar kameez, and we shook hands. She welcomed me warmly. Another man, in shalwar kameez and a green Shetland sweater, came into the room. It was Bashir, Gohar Zaman's brother-in-law. His eyes and voice were softer than Zaman's. Zaman said it was time to eat and I sat down across from him and Bashir sat next to me. Nafay sat next to Zaman. His wife did not join us. A servant brought out more dishes of kebabs, rice, and vegetables, a feast. We chatted, but ate too quickly. I took out my notebook but Zaman said we would talk later. Too soon, we finished and Zaman brusquely told us to get up and come outside. We sat on the porch, with birds singing, the lawn enclosed by a stone wall, the muffled sound of traffic on the other side, and old rifles on the wall behind us. Zaman finally started to relax.

"I commanded the Frontier Constabulary and I was head of intelligence for Pakistan," he began. He was clearly not a simple old man, as Fazul and Michael Semple had seemed to describe him, if he was once head of intelligence. Abu Hamza, the Taliban leader in Kunar, and Abu Omar, the Taliban leader I interviewed in Chitral, both told me that they worked for older men, "graybeards," they called them: former military, and I assumed ISI men, the most famous of whom was retired lieutenant general Hamid Gul, former head of the ISI, Milt Bearden's counterpart when he was with the CIA in Pakistan in the late 1980s.

Gohar Zaman was a policeman for thirty-five years, including being police chief for Baluchistan, the large Pakistani province south of Afghanistan that takes up half of Pakistan (the province is roughly two-thirds the size of California). The capital of Baluchistan is Quetta. The Quetta Shura, or the Taliban leadership council, was in 2008 in Quetta. Maybe he still had authority there. When I listened to Taliban suicide recruitment tapes, of young men singing in haunting voices good-bye to their mothers, and, romantically, of death, I saw that the tapes were made in Quetta.

Gohar Zaman talked about a time he was in a cabinet meeting with Nawaz Sharif, during Sharif's first time as prime minister,[31] who told him to take his personal plane to Baluchistan to oversee a kidnapping case. There was little about the mujahideen or the Taliban, these Pakistani proxies, that Gohar Zaman, a former head of intelligence, wouldn't know about. Semple was right. The story of my kidnapping needed Gohar Zaman's side to be complete.

We had tea. "The Taliban are in disarray," Zaman began. "The Haqqanis have been moved across the border to Afghanistan." As soon as he said this I realized I couldn't trust him. He was lying, or this was what he had been told. I knew the Haqqanis were in Pakistan—I was talking to them and would, possibly, see them soon, in Islamabad. He also said that the Haqqanis "had been moved," implying what Pakistan never said publicly, that the Haqqanis were under Pakistani control.

"A debriefing is so important," he said. He asked how I got out. I told him the whole story. "You crossed at Lapura. My village is near there. There is a bridge there now."

I remembered crossing on the ferry and felt nostalgic that a bridge had replaced it.

"The American effort in Kabul was zero," Zaman said, meaning that in his eyes, the FBI did not do anything. This would include, if Nafay was right about who else had called them, the CIA and the Army's Military Intelligence Corps. "All the US wanted was to know how successful we were." I didn't know how he would know what the US government did, or did not do, in Kabul, unless he had his own contacts there. But it mirrored what Bryn, Fazul, and Nafay had said, that if it hadn't been for Feridoun they would still be groping in the dark.

"Abdullah was lying to us all the time," Gohar Zaman said, "and he was very smart. The man at Kroll, Mr. Hildred, was very good to me." He met Hildred, the Kroll man, in Washington in the summer of 2013. Kroll then was working almost exclusively in South America. We learned so much from you, they told Zaman. "It is all very different here," Zaman said. "You need an intermediary who must be powerful. You need a way to get to the top man."

Kroll may well be—like companies hired by the *New York Times*, like famous former CIA agents, like the US government, like powerful politicians—aware in the post 9/11 world of everything related to international security matters. But it appeared to me that when it came to Pakistan and the Tribal Areas, no one knew very much. Or maybe I was blind, and the government had its own reasons for not pursuing a kidnapping.

"When Feridoun came and he talked about his family, and I talked about mine and we saw that we had a link, then I knew for the first time we were going to be okay," said Bashir. From then on there would be no danger. He looked at me with wide, staring, soft, penetrating eyes. "Feridoun was close to Najibullah, who was then a member of parliament."

Fazul had said that Feridoun had come to Peshawar and negotiated my release, but it sounded as if Bashir and Gohar Zaman were in charge, perhaps together with Michael Semple. Most importantly was the news that Feridoun, who Saleh said was ISI, came to Zaman. Bashir had said that Feridoun as a very young man was close to Najibullah, but that

Bashir's family, including Zaman through the marriage of his sister, was as well. The US and its allies had spent billions of dollars, beginning in the 1970s, backing the mujahideen with Pakistan in the grand war against communism, when in fact, through family ties, at least here, Pakistan and Afghanistan were allies.

Zaman, Bashir, and Feridoun were Mohmand, all the same tribe. But above them was the ISI.

No wonder the FBI, whose agents rotated in and out Afghanistan every ninety days, didn't seem to know what to do and were relying upon the CBS team to find me. When the British ruled here, their agents stayed for sixteen years before they could take home leave. They knew the culture and the languages. US State Department officials rotated every three years. In April 2007 I had lunch at the US embassy in Islamabad and Elizabeth Colton, the press attaché, said that Ambassador Ryan Crocker, leaving to become ambassador in Iraq, called Pakistan the "murkiest country" in which he had ever worked. We were like children here, it seemed, lost in a maze.

Mahmud, like Fazul, said that Feridoun was khan of the Mohmand, meaning the most powerful man there, but the ISI would be above him. Feridoun was playing all sides, concerned, like any man, with keeping his power. I wondered where Abdul Wali fit into this. I still didn't know whether Abdullah and the Maulvi and his men were criminals, or Taliban, or both. Were they tied, through Abdul Wali, to the ISI? I didn't know who they were. The Maulvi had said during an interrogation that they would like a donation to the TTP—the Tehrik-i-Taliban, which would be the main Pakistani Taliban organization created by the ISI and run by the murderous Fazlullah. Or, they could all be lying, creating a smokescreen, like driving me in a circle when I was blindfolded.

Fazul said that Semple got Feridoun involved. I had assumed that Semple therefore brought Feridoun to Zaman. But Zaman was waiting all along for Feridoun to come to him. I wondered who was stronger: Feridoun, the tribal chief, or Abdul Wali, the Taliban leader.

A year later, in 2017, I went with Mugaddir back to Peshawar to see Rahimullah Yusufzai, doyen of Pakistan journalists, along the border. He lived in a large house with a high wall and a lawn in the back in Hayatabad, the wealthy area of Peshawar, where bin Laden and his fellow Arabs lived in the 1980s. There are police cars on corners to protect the residents. "Security is better now here, but the Chinese are worried. They bring me over to talk at think tanks. For them the number one concern is security." A week ago, China announced to the world its vaunted $54 billion China-Pakistan Economic Corridor (CPEC), part of its much larger Silk Road project to establish links to the West. At the same time, unknown people kidnapped two Chinese Mandaran teachers in Quetta, along the border. The Chinese came to Yusufzai asking for his assistance. "I've had a lot of dealings with kidnapping here."

He was surprised to learn about my own. "I never heard anything," he said his eyes wide with surprise.

"Abdul Wali is the most extreme, the most radical, the worst of the worst. Feridoun does not have good relations with him. He is under the control of the Afghans now."

What? I thought.

Nafay, in elegant dark pantaloons and a long black and white shalwar kameez, listened, smoking. "I quit smoking in 1999 and started in 2008, because of you," she reminded me again.

"Bryn was willing to do anything to get you back," said Bashir. They had a saying in Pashto: "If the time was not right, two stones, one your head was resting on, and the north stone, on top, would not move, but if the time was right you could remove the stones easily."

Gohar Zaman confirmed that another Kroll person arrived to see how the CBS team was proceeding. He stayed in the Marriott and didn't do much of anything but watch, Zaman said.

"He had big ears, I remember," Nafay said. "He was quiet."

"I had to find a path to follow," said Gohar Zaman. "In a kidnapping, you reach a dead-end street and you go back and start over." He was called in on the Daniel Pearl case, but was told that the prime minister was involved. When the state took over, you had to just step aside. If the Pakistani government took over, that meant that it was above the Karachi police. It would mean intelligence agencies. It was interesting that the government would ask him, a Pashtun from Peshawar, to go to Karachi, eight hundred miles away, the same distance from Chicago to

New York, where the main language was Urdu, not Pashto. But there was a large Pashtun population in Karachi, and he was, after all, a former head of intelligence. There were stories that Pakistan had moved Mullah Omar and the Taliban leadership from Quetta to Karachi, over four hundred miles away, to hide them from US surveillance.

"I have never seen so much money," said Gohar Zaman. Like the others, he would never say how much.

Gohar Zaman was clearly in charge, and he had money from Kroll. In April 2003,[32] not two years after 9/11, Kroll added kidnap and ransom insurance to its portfolio of security services, to be brokered by Asset Security Managers, a subsidiary of Aon Limited. Aon was a member of the K&R syndicate that governs the worldwide criminal kidnapping market, at Lloyd's. My captors were the producers, and I was the product. Kroll was the broker. Zaman was Kroll's man on the ground.

"Feridoun also knew that we had connections at a high level." Again, Gohar Zaman meant the government—above the level of the political agent for Mohmand Agency—and the Pakistani military, which controlled Pakistani foreign policy, and its joint military intelligence agency, the ISI. "The British were here for centuries and they really knew the country, the people, and the language." He paused, selecting his words, so as not to offend me. "The Americans are a different species."

He didn't respect the Americans, who didn't seem, to him, to care about and thus to understand his culture, or to learn Pashto, or Urdu, the official language, while he spoke perfect English.

"Bryn cried when he learned that you had been released. Abdullah was a minor Taliban commander. My concern was that you would be passed on to or sold to a bigger commander or another Taliban group and that would have been difficult."

My captors had worried about the same thing. They, the producers, didn't want to lose their product, their golden goose. I was part of what Semple had called on the CBS Evening News a cottage industry. He was referring to the Afghan-Pakistan theater, but it was now, since 9/11, a growing, worldwide criminal, government, and terrorist enterprise.

Gohar Zaman said that Abdullah and his men were Taliban. Maybe Michael Semple had said that I was captured by criminals to protect whoever paid the ransom money. It would be easier, politically, to give money to criminals than to the Taliban. Or, as he said, it was an unauthorized operation, meaning not cleared by Abdul Wali. I thought back, again, as I did on occasion, of what the malik said in Mohmand Agency when I sat in his compound during Ramadan: *"You Americans are playing a double role."* I was beginning to feel that the ISI didn't want me sneaking across the border, traveling in the mountains, and after watching me for months talking with the Taliban, their proxy army, and afraid of what I would write or show on television, decided to teach me a lesson.

The alternative explanation was that my kidnapping was opportunistic, random. Sameer met me, listened as I talked with Professor Amin, called, got to know me better, talked with Shahwali, brought him in, and introduced him to me. I hired him and he tried to lure me in with the malik of Ducalam, but that didn't work, and then the Wahhabi joined us, and through him I met with Abu Hamza, but they couldn't lure me in either. Then I introduced him to Abdullah, and he joined with Malang, who was already planning something, as Saleh implied, maybe part of his fight against Din Mohammad's family, the paladin against the aristocracy, which was why he didn't want me to talk with Din Mohammad. And I was taken simply to make money, like selling artifacts. But there was something more there. Din Mohammad had said that if I talked to Malang that he wanted to be there with me. There was something between the Arsala family and Malang and I had walked into the middle of it. It had to do with the death of Hajji Qadir and Hajji Zaman.

In the end, CBS got involved and Bryn came in, got Michael Semple's name from someone, and called Semple and Sami Yousafzai. The first call Semple made was to Malang. Din Mohammad and Saleh said that Malang and Semple were friends. Then there was a link, according to Saleh, between Semple and Feridoun. Hovering above all of this was the spector of the ISI, and over it, or with it, in my mind now was its ally, the CIA. And maybe MI6. Maybe it was a conspiracy and maybe I should leave it alone, as Din Mohammad said.

I felt now that Malang might have called me the night before we left because, whatever complicated feelings he may have had about me at that moment, he wanted to save me. Maybe he sensed that I was in serious danger, and he tried to stop me. I, too headstrong, went ahead, and after I was taken he called Abdullah, as Michael told me in Washington, to his house in Islamabad, and told him not to harm me, which I felt was Semple's polite way of saying not to kill me. There was a balance of power, Michael and Razi Gul said, between Malang and Abdullah. The only one who could resolve this, it appeared, was Feridoun, the tribal chief, and his ally, through family and maybe the ISI, Gohar Zaman. But I was guessing. Everything was still a guess. It was very dangerous for me to even try to resolve it.

Maybe the Taliban had acted on their own. They attacked their masters, after all. Abdul Wali had sent suicide bombers all the way across Pakistan to a park in Lahore, the capital of the Punjab, on March 27, 2016—Easter—where they killed over seventy Christian women and children. He had sent suicide bombers to Karachi, killing women and children. He later attacked Quetta also, this man whose men let me go.

Still I was bothered by my reception by the US government when I was released. Two years later, David Martin, the CBS Pentagon correspondent, read *Captive* and said, after he interviewed me, that he couldn't understand what my reception at the US base was all about. At first I thought that when the US got word that I was taken, a couple government agencies did some research, learned of my time with the mujahideen and with the US government, were upset that I had gone with the Taliban, and were either involved, or gave permission to the ISI to take me.

On January 27, 2011, Raymond Davis, a CIA contractor, shot and killed two Pakistanis in Lahore, setting off demonstrations and causing a public rift in US-Pakistani relations. On May 2, 2011, Navy SEALs flew, secretly, we were told, into Pakistan and killed Osama bin Laden. On August 13, gunmen scaled the wall surrounding Warren Weinstein's house in Lahore, overpowered his guards, kidnapped him, and took him across Pakistan to the Tribal Areas. On December 1, Ayman al-Zawahiri, the head of al-Qaeda after the death of bin Laden, announced in a video that "the Jewish American Warren Weinstein" was being held captive. I called the company where Weinstein worked, in northern

Virginia, and told a woman who answered that I had been kidnapped and held in the Tribal Areas and offered my help. I called twice. No one called me back. I understood. I was one person, not the US government, and it maybe appeared quixotic, even strange, certainly naïve, but I felt that I might be able to find out about him. Then, on April 23, 2015, President Obama announced that the US had just learned that Weinstein, and Giovanni Lo Porto, an Italian aid worker, had been killed, accidentally, in a counterterrorism operation, a drone strike, on January 14, 2015, that had targeted militants in the Tribal Areas. Then it came out that one of the terrorists killed, a man with a bounty on his head, was Adam Gadahn, the head of al-Qaeda's media operation, and Weinstein's death became clearer, at least to me.

Gadahn—who had listed me, among others, as an American commentator on al-Qaeda in a memo to bin Laden that the SEALs found at bin Laden's compound in Abbottabad in 2011—was a Jewish Muslim convert. Many jihadists had never accepted him because of this. Gadahn had for years issued videos, with his American accent, on behalf of al-Qaeda against America and his allies.

Weinstein and Lo Porto were, inexplicably, living in the same compound, maybe in the same house or even the same room as Gadahn, just as I had shared a room with three men. Maybe it was a coincidence, but it was interesting that Weinstein and Gadahn were together. Maybe al-Qaeda brought them together, in kindness, so that Weinstein would have a fellow American to talk to, or his captors felt that Gadahn would be able to possibly help convert Weinstein to Islam.

After Weinstein's death was announced, one of his captors said that he was studying to become Muslim. Where, I asked myself, had the US got its targeting information? Did it have its own assets on the ground? Maybe, but I doubted it. The US had placed a drone over the area where I was being held, but never said that it knew where I was. Jack Cloonan, the former FBI agent, told me that the US did not know where David Rohde was being held. It did not know where Bowe Bergdahl was being held. It did not know where Weinstein was being held. The political agent in North Waziristan would have known. If Gadahn was with Weinstein, as the US said, the ISI certainly knew where he was. To me, it appeared that the ISI decided to give up Gadahn and told the US where he was. The US, through its drones, watched the compound, and in time fired the missile that killed Gadahn and, collaterally, Weinstein. Daniel Pearl, Adam Gadahn, and Warren Weinstein, all Jewish, were dead, and I was alive. Maybe Dovid Efune was right. Maybe I survived because I wasn't Jewish.

"Siraj would have been easier," said Gohar Zaman, breaking my thoughts. "I have a way of getting to him." Sirajuddin, Jalaluddin's son, was now the Taliban military commander. Gohar Zaman was saying that he, as a former head of intelligence, could still get to the most powerful Taliban military commander. I told my stories of living with Haqqani and of my experience with Hekmatyar. Gohar Zaman called Hekmatyar a bloodthirsty animal who killed people for nothing and who was now negotiating a job with Ashraf Ghani, the Afghan president. I had heard this, too. Months later Hekmatyar, after thirty years of fighting in the mountains, where President Karzai told me that Hekmatyar was happiest, would indeed come in from the cold. In May 2017, the Kabul political elite, led by President Ghani, welcomed him back to the presidential palace. Hekmatyar called the Taliban his brothers and asked them to lay down their arms. Only Amrullah Saleh had the courage to publicly criticize him for not even remembering the victims, the thousands of innocents he had killed.

I told Gohar Zaman what Hajji Din Mohammad and Amrullah Saleh told me in Kabul about Michael Semple. I kept wondering if Saleh still held a grudge against Michael for his work toward bringing peace in Musa Qala, when Saleh and the US Army had preferred to fight.

"I found Michael Semple to be a mysterious fellow," he responded quietly. "I have had experience in police work and in the border regions for thirty-five years. I found that there were gaps here and there in his background or what he was saying."

Two years later Nafay told me that during this time when the Islamabad Shura was together, Zaman went to Dubai to have open-heart surgery, and that he called from the hospital and told Bashir, in a weak voice, to send the money to Feridoun, and that Bashir then disappeared and Nafay didn't see him until we met seven years later. And, I kept thinking, Zaman said that $20,000 was enough. He was not just an old policeman, but, it seemed, in charge. Finally, it appeared that Feridoun, great khan of the Mohmand and according to Saleh, the former head of NDS, was an ISI asset, just like his father. He took possession of the money and no one seemed to know if he gave any of it to anyone else.

"I have a BS degree and an MA from Sweden," Zaman continued. "I have contacts in MI5 and MI6. I know a chap who is the head of counterintelligence at MI6. The next time I'm in London I am going to ask him about Michael Semple."

Yet Gohar Zaman had been at Semple's farm and was linked to the highest levels of the Pakistani government. He knew Nawaz Sharif, the prime minster, after all. He had to know if Semple had ties to MI6 and the ISI as Saleh said. And so what if he did? As Bryn said, he saved my life.

Gohar Zaman said that he tried five hundred times to talk with Abdullah but never succeeded. Semple gave Abdullah's number to Bashir.

Bashir looked at me. "Feridoun then contacted me," he said.

Abdullah, it appeared, contacted Feridoun, deferring to him, chief of the Mohmand. Feridoun then took over and became the negotiator between Abdullah and Gohar Zaman. At least this was Zaman's story. Nafay sat quietly and did not contradict him.

I told Gohar Zaman that the FBI wanted me to go back to Kabul, find Shahwali, and send him to Guantanamo.

Zaman looked at me painfully. "Abdullah is such a small man, like Shahwali. Why would they go to all that trouble?" Then he added casually, "I thought I would kidnap Abdullah."

The old man who had asked if they had Russian vodka, as Fazul said, had casually suggested that he could mount an operation to kidnap Abdullah, who had thirty men around him.

Gohar Zaman kept talking, apparently aimlessly, telling me his thoughts, it seemed, as they came to him.

"We put Shahwali's brother in a guesthouse with Bashir as his chaperone in case Shahwali called his brother."

Nafay chimed in. "We were having a group meeting at Michael's farm and Fazul's phone rang. I remember it vividly. I was sitting next to him. One of the kidnappers called and said, 'Shahwali?' He probably hit the wrong number and accidently called Fazul. Not the brightest bulbs, your kidnappers. That's why we thought Shahwali might be playing for the wrong team. And so, we focused on his next of kin for a while in our quest to locate you."

Shahwali, it appeared, was clearly involved, and yet Fazul gave him $200 in Jalalabad and let him go. The FBI—Bob and John—let him go. They took him to the shower and brought him breakfast. Maybe the FBI didn't know anything then—yet.

"I talk to local people and then I get the tribes involved," said Gohar Zaman. "I was the secretary general of the police of all of Baluchistan. If something happens to a foreigner and their diplomats come they think we tell them lies all the time."

I wondered if he didn't know that the Haqqani leadership was in Pakistan.

"Journalists were skeptical. 'Who is this Jere Van Dyk?' they would ask," Nafay went on. "'What does he really do? Who is he really? He has an air about him.' You know you have that." She looked at me. I had heard this before. I did keep my distance from people. I had felt separate since I was a boy. I liked working on my own, like my father.

I didn't know who the journalists were that Nafay was talking about except possibly people at CBS, one of whom did say, out loud, that he thought I was with the CIA; others said behind my back that I was different, and they couldn't understand me. I didn't go out drinking with them, and wasn't part of the pack. I had friends from grade school, high school, college, the army, the Senate, friends overseas, track friends, people from my Assembly, but ultimately, I kept myself separate. Maybe everyone is like that. We are all different. We all have our own struggles. It is part of the human condition, but I always came back to the Bible verse pounded into me when I was a boy: "Wherefore come out from among them and be ye separate, saith the Lord"—and my father—"and touch not the unclean thing; and I will receive you."[33] I was never the Christian that my father wanted me to be. "No one knows me," he once said to me. I felt that I understood him.

"You must always think," Gohar Zaman continued, "what is the escape route they could have taken? You study this in an intelligent, systematic way. How do I find this? I was pretty sure you were here in Pakistan. We were all very tense. Every day we were nervous and waiting, but we had to be logical. There are no shortcuts. It takes time.

"As a principle, I never handle money. Or, I get a hold of a powerful chap and say find this man and bring him to me. How much money do you want? I know someone like that and he owes me. If I need something I always go to the political agent. He knows everything in his agency."

Again, here was confirmation that I had to find the political agent for Mohmand Agency. But Gohar Zaman did not go to him. He worked this out with Feridoun. Or so it seemed. He had just said that he never handled money, but Ahmed Shah had told me he wired it to Feridoun in Kabul. No, he went to Dubai, Nafay said, because a special doctor, who he had been waiting for, came in from Europe and he went for open-heart surgery. He had his brother-in-law touch the money. Everyone had seen the money, but no one would admit to having touched it.

Chapter 20

Ibrahim

THE GUESTHOUSE IN ISLAMABAD WAS BEHIND A HIGH WHITE WALL and had a number on the dark wood gate, the only way Nafay knew that it was the right place. She wasn't familiar with it; maybe someone else arranged it for her. A man opened the gate and Mugaddir drove into the compound. There were no guards, no police, just a brown stucco house and a small lawn, surrounded by a high stone wall. Nafay told Mugaddir that she would text him when we were ready to leave.

"I didn't tell him who we're meeting," she said. She was confident and at ease. The men on the Islamabad Shura said that Nafay's role was limited to listening and some logistical work, but she was evidently more capable than they implied. She said that she knew a few ISI people as part of her job, but I knew from working with her over the years that she knew some of the men whose names I read in the paper who were highly placed in the military, and the women, too, in government and in the media, and she knew how to find them. We walked into the reception area and a man stood behind the empty counter, quietly smiling.

Three other men, who looked to be in their thirties, sat on couches; one, a thin, smaller man almost lying down, relaxed against the far wall. He smiled warmly and openly, as if to reassure us. Another man, unsmiling, a little older, sat alone in a chair against the back wall. I felt that we would be fine, and I relaxed a bit. Nafay didn't pay any attention to the men. I knew not to ask who they were. She exchanged a few words with the man behind the counter and we walked down a narrow hallway to a room. No one asked me to register or identify myself. The room had two chairs, twin beds, a small bathroom, a telephone, and cost 20,000 rupees a night, over $190.

I sat in a chair and waited with Nafay. It was 12:30 p.m. We were thirty minutes early. "Who were those men lounging on the couch?" I asked. I knew, without asking and with no proof, that she had called her contacts to tell them that we were going to meet the Haqqanis, and to ask them where we should meet. No journalist in Pakistan, I had heard many times, could work in the national security area and stay alive without staying in touch or following the orders of the authorities. No one dared to go against them. I had heard about and read stories about men who been killed.

"Don't pay attention to them," Nafay answered blithely. "They're nothing."

She didn't answer my question, but I let it go. I felt at that moment that this was all being arranged and that she had become part of it. I called "John" at 12:55: "We are in room 101."

"I see that," he said softly. "We're on our way." I was all but certain now the men outside were ISI. I didn't think, until later, that they could very well have been Haqqani men, that John had told Nafay, in their conversation, the address where we should go, or, she could have told him where to come, and that they would have sent some of their people there. They wouldn't dare come alone. Which meant that the meeting was sanctioned, if not approved, by the ISI. I had never heard of any US government official, Western journalist, or scholar meeting with the Haqqanis since 9/11. I didn't know if any Western official had met with them. I thought again of the man on the couch smiling in a way as if to say, "Relax, we're not going to do anything do you." We kept waiting.

"We are sitting ducks here," said Nafay. She had seemed relaxed when we came in, but now, after an hour had passed, she had started to worry. Perhaps it was a setup? Did we do all this for nothing? At 2:00 p.m. I called again. "We got stuck in traffic. We will be there shortly," said John. Part of the leadership of the Haqqani Network, one of the most powerful terrorist organizations in the world, was stuck in traffic. They belonged in the mountains, not here.

At 2:25 p.m. John called. "We are out front."

I felt energy and excitement rushing through me. It was only polite to go outside and greet them. We walked down the hallway out into the sun as an SUV with tinted windows pulled into the driveway. The driver wore a brown pakhool. He was Afghan. A sturdy man about six-feet-one, in white shalwar kameez with a black beard and a black-and-white striped scarf over his head, Salafi style, got out smiling broadly, and I felt warmth flow through me. We were going to be fine. We hugged one another gently, a form of greeting. A man in his twenties, in black shalwar kameez and a black jacket, came around the other side, smiling, and we shook hands. It was John.

We entered the front room, and the clerk still stood, smiling enigmatically now. I didn't look over but I knew—without any proof, beyond the genuine warmth with which he greeted me and the power he exuded—that the tall man was Ibrahim Haqqani. We walked straight down the hallway and into our room. He sat in a chair. Nafay sat in front of him, John on his right side, his back against the wall. I sat between Nafay and Ibrahim on John's left. I wondered if he was armed. They were so calm. There had to be people watching us, and protecting them. No one knew what to expect or do. I thanked them for coming. Ibrahim smiled, looking at me. I looked back trying to recognize him and remember him. Had he recognized me, or was it a show?

I picked up the book I had written on my time with them in the mountains when they were a small group of men fighting the Soviet Red Army. When helicopters flew slowly over our compound, like giant grasshoppers in the sky, or hovered there; when we went at dusk to attack an Afghan army base; when we massed in a much larger group in a field, and they carried rifles from different countries. We raced horses across a grassy plain, and I laughed in the wind. I watched them line up and put their rifles in front of them and bow their heads in the dirt.

I gave Ibrahim a picture I had taken of Jalaluddin. I showed him a black-and-white photograph of Din Mohammad and me at the UN Plaza Hotel in New York. He pushed it away in disgust. "I can't look at him," he said. I had made a mistake. He was now the enemy. Now I understood. This was why Din Mohammad didn't want to talk to me about the Haqqanis. They had parted ways.

In July, four months later, Ibrahim Haqqani and Din Mohammad would sit across the table from one another in the first Afghan-Taliban peace talks, in Murree, north of Islamabad, where Mike Kaufman, the *New York Times* correspondent and my mentor, and I had once stood in the trees looking west into what Mike called "darkest Afghanistan." The talks didn't lead anywhere. To date, there haven't been any more since then.

I told them why I had come to see them. I was writing a book on them and I wanted them to have a chance to tell their story, in their words, from their beginning all the way up to today. I talked about our time living together in the mountains. I said that I wanted to start when they were born, and to learn about their father and what they did growing up and how they had become what they are today. I didn't know how much time I had. We seemed safe enough. I didn't know why they had agreed to do this, and wanted to find out, but that would take time. I knew that I had to progress slowly, and carefully. I couldn't alienate them. From experience, I knew that everyone wanted to talk about his or her life. It was the most important thing in the world to a person. I wanted Ibrahim to feel comfortable with me and then I would get to the hard questions, if I had the courage, to ask about their ties to Pakistan and to Saudi Arabia, and why they sent suicide bombers into Afghanistan, killing innocent people—hundreds, even thousands of them by now. They had been fighting for over forty years and they were, it seemed, stronger than ever. What were their goals? How big did they want to become?

I didn't know why, but for some reason this door had opened to me. I would go one step at a time. I talked briefly about our time at Shah-i-Kot and then I asked where they were born and what their father did for a living.

Nafay's cell phone pinged. It was her older sister, checking to see that she was okay. She had told only her what we were doing. I didn't tell anyone. An hour later, during a pause, as she started to translate a question I asked, she stopped, looked right at me, her eyes wide, staring at me. "I don't believe this is happening. Who are you really? I mean, who are you?" We had known one another for twelve years, she worked to save my life, and she suddenly felt that she didn't know me at all. She was afraid that I was a spy, but she didn't move. She translated from English to Urdu and to Pashto and back. Who was I that I got to meet with the head—it was clear now, based on our conversation—of the Haqqani Network? And why would they meet with me? It had to be something more than the past. I wasn't sure why this was happening either, but I was led here. I had no thoughts of where it would lead.

Hours passed and Ibrahim got up to pray. When he finished, John got his shoes for him, gave him his scarf back, and stood carefully beside him, the dutiful son, and then he prayed. While we waited for him to finish Ibrahim sat back down next to me, picked up *In Afghanistan*, and leafed through it. He stopped and looked at the pictures. I pointed to Mallem Jan, my interpreter, whom I had wanted to find again. Ibrahim said that he was in another country, dismissing him. He had given up and run away. John returned to his seat and I told them briefly about my kidnapping.

"I was trying to get to you," I said, "and was led to believe that I could." I meant, but didn't say, that Mullah Malang said that Abdullah could maybe take me to Jalaluddin. I remembered the letter I had to write that Abdullah would take to him, and that I didn't like writing it. The Haqqanis were now terrorists, but now here I was talking with Ibrahim, Jalaluddin's younger brother, the head now of the infamous Haqqani Network. "I used Jalaluddin's name often to stay alive." Ibrahim smiled and laughed warmly.

I felt awkward and strange saying how close I felt to them, meaning him and his brother and Mallem Jan. I was living in the past. I remembered the moment when I had arrived in their compound, and Jalaluddin gave me a plate of honey to go with my tea and asked kindly where I was from, welcoming me, and where I ran through the forest, watched every day as the Soviet helicopters flew over us, and huddled with them one day when a helicopter gunship came in low and stopped and hovered above us, waiting to drop its bombs, and when we shared gritty rice, bread, and green tea in the snow, and they heated water for me to take a bath.

"I didn't know that you were kidnapped," said Ibrahim. "We were not involved. Kidnappings can have a very good outcome, or they can end in disaster."

I believed him. I knew that they had power in eastern Afghanistan, in Kabul and beyond—even, I was told, across to the Iranian border, going against everything I read that US officials and experts believed, and I knew now of their influence in the Middle East, but I still wasn't sure of the extent of their power in the Tribal Areas. Mahmud said it was very limited. Amrullah Saleh, the former NDS head, said if I was kidnapped in Mohmand the Haqqanis were not involved. Their power came from their closeness to the ISI and to the leadership of the Pakistani army. Behroz Khan, my Pakistani journalist friend, said that he had watched retired general Hamid Gul, former head of the ISI, say on television that "Jalaluddin is more Pakistani than [Pakistani nationals]." He was living in Waziristan, where his tribe, the Zadran, had lived for centuries, long before Pakistan even existed. Haqqani was an Afghan. He was Pashtun. The Pakistani army was primarily Punjabi. The Pashtuns had once ruled the Punjabis and wanted, in their dreams, to rule them again. Further, Jalaluddin was deeply religious. I had watched him call his men to prayer before dawn in the snow. He once wanted to drive out the godless communists and to live in a world that he had grown up in, where God ruled, not man. I understood the power of the brotherhood of the mujahideen and the Taliban, of their belief in God and in the righteousness of their cause, ridding their country of the evil, foreign, Christian invaders. I had listened to their suicide tapes, of young men chanting of Afghan geography and history.

I felt the American policy of killing young men who were fighting to get rid of us, foreigners in their land, was wrong and that our real enemy was that part of Pakistan that indoctrinated and trained these men, and those in Saudi Arabia and Qatar and Kuwait and every other Muslim dictatorship that sent money to Pakistan to train them. Perhaps the Haqqanis would fight against their country for their faith, but I didn't believe that they truly believed that Pakistan was more Muslim than Afghanistan. They were Hanafi, he said. They were not Wahhabis; they were not ISIS. These were Arab imports. I felt that they were trapped, seduced by their power and the money, and trying to stay alive.

Nafay's phone pinged again. It was another message from her sister. She was afraid. Were we safe? I didn't know. Nafay sent a message.

"We want to establish an Islamic state. We have been deprived of our freedom and of our right to establish Sharia," Ibrahim continued. "If I fight against the Russians I am a good person. If I fight against the Americans I am a terrorist. We haven't changed, only America has changed."

Evening turned to night. They seemed in no hurry to leave. Nafay called on the room's phone for something to eat. A man brought a tray of soft drinks and chicken sandwiches. It was strange to sit next to this famous mujahid whom I had last seen in the mountains, and to watch him eat French fries, a chicken sandwich, and an American soft drink. It wasn't right. It was too modern, too common. He needed to be up in the mountains, with a rifle, walking on a hard dirt path, going into battle, protecting his people from the infidel invaders, and sitting on the ground eating around a fire.

"We will do research and find out all about your kidnapping," Ibrahim said.

"Thank you," I responded gratefully. Was it possible? My old friends, but not really, one of the most powerful terrorist groups in the world, would find out who kidnapped me? This was what I needed.

But it would take time and I would have to come back. I only had a few days left in the country.

It grew late. Ibrahim talked about his nephew, Anas, in prison in Kabul and how the US broke its promise, as part of the Bowe Bergdahl agreement, to let the Haqqani family travel to the Middle East. Instead the US had kidnapped Anas. Ibrahim was angry. The US, he said, had lied, and he didn't trust it. He was admitting that the Haqqanis had held Bergdahl. I asked him about this. "We didn't hold him directly," he responded, waving his hand dismissively. He told me how Bergdahl was captured, a different story from what I heard in the West. Someone under them held Bergdahl, but he didn't tell me who. We would talk about this more another time. It sounded like they had many groups under them. I would learn that they were like a holding company, with an array of groups under their control, far beyond their tribal reach. It was the power of Jalaluddin and Ibrahim, warriors during the great jihad against the Russians. Din Mohammad told me that when Jalaluddin went to the Middle East when he was younger to raise money, the Arabs interviewed him on television and that many women contacted him. He was a famous mujahid, the great, fearless, masculine Afghan warrior fighting for Islam. "They all wanted to marry him," he said, smiling.

I had met with men at NDS headquarters in Kabul and they said that the Afghans had captured Anas in Afghanistan, but it wasn't true. It was a smokescreen to take credit for what others did. The *New York Times* reported[34] that a US official said that Anas and Hafiz Rashid were captured in a Persian Gulf country, but the name was being withheld to protect the country. The paper did not say who kidnapped them. Pashtoon, who called the Haqqanis for me, was the intermediary between them and Anas and Rashid.

Midnight came and passed. We had been talking for over eight hours. Nafay's sister sent five messages checking on her little sister. Twice, Ibrahim stopped the conversation and he put his hand on my wrist. "We only trust you," he said, smiling. We had crossed a line. Somewhere along the way as we talked he had made, I felt, a decision. He saw, I felt, that I was there not to talk as a US government official but as one truly interested in them. I was the same man who had been with them before and hadn't changed or shown that I was different. "Finally," he said, smiling happily, "the truth will come out." Twice he said this. They would have the opportunity to tell their side of their story.

He had decided that I was not like the other journalists who were in Afghanistan now writing on behalf of the West. I was with them when their backs were against the wall against the Russians. He talked proudly about the time that he had started the Russian tank that they had captured and hidden in the mountains. I remembered that time, and the smoke and the noise and Ibrahim, in his twenties, laughing.

How proud he was that he had started the engine. During that month, I had been part of their small band, their brotherhood.

Then, he became serious in a way that I didn't expect. He said that they had twice met with CIA agents, but they didn't like either one. He said he wanted to meet again, in Dubai even, if I could guarantee their safety. I told him that I didn't have the power to guarantee their safety anywhere. I sensed that this had something to do with his nephew, Anas. I told him that my visa was almost up, but I would return. It was past midnight. I wanted to keep talking, but felt that I should end the meeting. I knew that he would have talked all night. They wanted my help and I had to be careful.

Nafay asked if we could take a picture of her and Ibrahim. He said no, but finally relented when I said I needed proof that we had met, and Nafay took a photograph of us together. "No one in Pakistan must see this," he said. "There are many Afghan spies in Islamabad," said John. "It is very dangerous for us."

I said I would like to see Jalaluddin. Ibrahim smiled and was quiet. We hugged one another, shook hands, and said good-bye. I shook hands with John. He told me his real name. "Please stay here," he said.

Nafay and I waited in the room. She called her sister. "Who are you?" she asked again, staring at me. She couldn't get over what we had just done. She had helped to arrange this meeting, and she didn't really feel she knew who she was arranging it for: whether it was just for me, or others. We went to the front office and the staff stood up and we walked outside. The men on the couches were gone. It was cool now and dark. Mugaddir drove into the courtyard. I had just spent eight and a half hours talking with the leader of the Haqqani Network. We had agreed to meet again. The Haqqanis, America's archenemy, would find out the truth for me about my kidnapping. I was almost there.

We drove back through the night, cool and refreshing after sitting all day in that room. I couldn't get over the fact that Ibrahim Haqqani had offered to tell me how I was kidnapped and why, and who, ultimately, was behind it. America's enemy would help when no one else would.

I would learn soon what they wanted in return.

Chapter 21

A Promise Kept

I CALLED JOHN AGAIN, BUT HE TOOK A DAY TO GET BACK TO ME. THEY were far away and he apologized for taking so long to call back. I wanted to see him again, but we both realized I would have to come back to Pakistan to learn the truth about my kidnapping. I had overstayed my visa, and with all that I'd heard I wondered if I would ever get a visa again. I had to leave without delay and at the airport I hugged Mugaddir good-bye and gave him a tip. It changed our relationship but only for a minute. I was a day late and officials asked why I had overstayed my visa. Nafay said that it wouldn't matter, but it did. I couldn't tell them what I was doing. I told the officer that I had no excuse. I thought I could stay an extra day and apologized. He stamped my passport.

I slept on the flight to Dubai. There, despite a heavy cold, I asked for a good barber who cut my hair and trimmed my beard down to an acceptable length. My time with jihadists was over for now. Ibrahim's beard was dark and shorter than mine.

I went back to the hotel, put on a suit, and took a taxi to the US embassy. The driver stopped by the road, and I walked across the grass to a single-story building that said CONSULATE OF THE UNITED STATES OF AMERICA. There was power in those words in their big, confident, gray metal letters. Two men in blue shirts and pants with black pistols on their belts came out and stood between me and the building. "Are you here for a visa?" a guard asked. The other man stood back ten feet and to his side. I said no. I showed my passport, but he didn't move. I was American, wore a suit and tie, and it didn't matter. "I'd like to talk to a political officer, if I could."

"Are you working here?" They still didn't trust me.

"No, I have some information and I'd like to talk to someone." I smiled, being friendly. "That's all, nothing more." I looked at the stone building, the thick glass darkened windows. Once, a US embassy was a welcoming place. They weren't going to let me close to the building. It didn't matter. All I had to do was to give Pashtoon's name and phone number to someone who would take it to the right person.

He went inside and I stood in the shade. The other guard, with a gentler voice, came over and stood next to me. "What do you want?"

"I was working with someone and he asked me to pass along some information. That's all."

"Is it sensitive?"

"Yes." He nodded. I was no longer, at least to him, a threat. He left and I walked back out into the sun. I assumed that people were watching me. Ten minutes later I heard a man's voice, turned, and saw a man with a short haircut and a polo shirt standing at the window open at the bottom, like at a bank.

"How can I help you?"

I gave him my passport and letter of introduction. "I'm working in the Middle East. I'm an Afghan-Pakistani specialist and I was working with a politician in Afghanistan and he helped me a great deal, and said, in exchange," and I lowered my voice, "that he wanted to work for the CIA." I took out a piece of paper from my shirt pocket with Pashtoon's name, phone, and e-mail, and slid it under the glass. "That's all, nothing more. I didn't want to go in the embassy in Pakistan. I didn't want the wrong people to see me, so I came here."

He looked at me. "Can I make a copy of this letter?"

"Yes, you can keep it." The letterhead was from the most establishment think tank in America, yet still he was wary.

He took my passport. "Do you mind waiting just a few minutes?"

"No, that's fine." He walked away. I went back and stood in the sun. Ten, fifteen minutes passed.

He returned to the window. "Do you mind coming in for five minutes?"

"Sure," I said. I wasn't sure that I wanted to, but another part of me did. I heard a thick click and the door opened and I stepped inside. Two guards approached and I had to empty my pockets. I walked through a metal detector and a man ran a wand over me. I had to take off my belt. Again, he ran the wand over me. I felt like a foreigner.

"Just leave everything there," said my escort.

"I better put my belt on. I'll look kind of funny." We walked to the back and he waved at a young man in fatigues and a door opened and we walked outside down a walkway. He was a step or two ahead. "Do you like living here?" I asked.

He turned, smiled. "Hey, it's Dubai."

"I feel so much more relaxed here than in Pakistan."

"I've worked there. I know what you mean."

We entered another building, and again I went through a metal detector, stretched out my hands, and took off my belt. We stopped in front of a door that said INTERVIEW ROOM, and it opened and we stepped inside. There was a small wood desk, with two chairs on both sides and two phones. He pointed to a black princess phone, at least twenty years old. "This phone's going to ring in about five minutes. You just pick it up and talk to the person on the line."

He closed the door and I felt like I was a suspect in an interrogation room. There was a small refrigerator on the other side with an open box of tea bags on top and a file cabinet. I casually looked around for a camera. If it was there, I didn't see it. I waited. Fifteen, twenty minutes passed. No call, nothing. Were they watching me, to see if I was nervous or moving round too much? This was impolite. When I was twenty-seven I put on a tie and walked in the embassy in Kabul and sat at a desk and a man politely talked to me. That was another era. A back door opened and a woman in her late thirties or early forties, with blond hair, brown slacks, and a blouse, came in carrying a notebook. She smiled and sat down.

"Thank you for coming by." She had an open, Midwestern manner, but she didn't introduce herself or shake hands. I told her why I had come and how I met Pashtoon, and through him the Haqqanis. I told her the whole story. I said that Pashtoon wanted to be president and wanted to work for the CIA. I assumed he thought that if he did this that the CIA would put him in power.

I described my meeting with the Haqqanis, not everything we talked about, but I told her that I was afraid of the ISI. She asked for Haqqani's number, but I wouldn't give it to her. I talked with her for two hours and she only asked questions.

I said that the Haqqanis used different numbers. I couldn't betray Ibrahim. I felt that he wanted to use me to help get his nephew out of prison, but I was using him too. We had once been young together living at Shah-i-Kot. He said that he trusted only me. He had let me take his picture.

I gave her some information about Haqqani and was angry at myself. She raised her eyebrows, took notes, and I felt uneasy. I was talking too much, and just handed over information I had worked hard to obtain.

John told me in our last conversation on the phone that he was reading *In Afghanistan* and how much he liked it. "I like how you got the letter from the *New York Times* and all you went through to get here. I want to get your other book from Nafay." It was strange to be in the middle between the Haqqanis and the US government.

The woman at the consulate asked where the meeting with Haqqani had taken place. I didn't tell her. I told her that they had let me choose the place, and the time, and that they would be there. I couldn't tell her where we met in case we met there again. For that, perhaps they would put me on a watch list and they would know what plane I took and when I arrived they could have a local person follow me.

"How long are you going to be staying in Dubai?" she asked. She was interested in my Yemeni visas. She asked if I knew people in Yemen. I said yes and that I was going from Dubai to Yemen. There was a former al-Qaeda person there who had been in Guantanamo and who knew Haqqani and I wanted to talk to him. I would be in Dubai for five or six days. There were people I had to see also.

She raised her eyebrows. "Did you mind if we get together again?"

"No, that's fine."

"Would you like to come here, or meet in a café?"

"Either place is fine. No, a café would be good." I preferred some-place more neutral, where maybe I wouldn't give her so much power. I gave her my phone number. "You have my hotel. It is there on the sta-tionary, Room 407." She looked at the hotel stationary on which I had written Pashtoon's e-mail addresses and phone number.

"I will call you next week."

"Okay. What should I do about Pashtoon? Should I tell him that someone will be in touch with him?"

"No, don't do anything. I have all the information."

"Do you have a name at all?"

She rose and smiled without flirting. "Shannon." We shook hands. "Someone will open the door for you. If you can just wait a few minutes, it's how we have to do it." I understood. They had their rules. "Again, thank you." She smiled pleasantly and opened the door behind her and left. I sat there for ten minutes and then I heard a solid click and the door swung open and a woman with long dark hair and wearing a black pants suit and black heels stood there, her arms out. "Come." She didn't smile. We walked to the first building.

"Do you like living here?" I asked.

"I do. I like the weather. It's the Middle East."

"I got a note from a friend in New York. It's still snowing there."

"I don't care if I don't ever see snow again in my life."

We reached the other building and stood by the door. I picked up my watch and nervously put it on. Why was I nervous around these people? I was giving them too much power. I was afraid of them. I didn't know how close the CIA was with the ISI. "Do you have your passport?"

I took one out of my pocket, and then the other. I picked up my phone. "Was I supposed to give you, no, Shannon, no—that's right, forget it."

She raised her hands up. "I know nothing."

She opened the door and I walked out into the sun. The door closed. I walked down the street and waited for a taxi. I had fulfilled my part of the deal with Pashtoon.

PART FOUR

" Friendship is forever, but money is only for a few days. "
—Ahmed Shah Amin

Chapter 22

Taliban Military Council

I WENT BACK TO THE HOTEL. IT WAS A THURSDAY. FRIDAY WAS A DAY of rest. Shannon from the consulate wouldn't call me until Monday. In fact, she didn't call then, nor did she call Tuesday or Wednesday. I could only guess why not.

Sami told me that he knew a member of the Taliban military council living in Dubai who knew Haqqani and would arrange for me to meet him. I met Sami at breakfast at his hotel and we planned the meeting. "I think it's safer if we meet in my room," he said. I returned that evening, and we sat on his balcony overlooking Dubai. It was getting hot and muggy and I felt my cold returning.

At around nine thirty Sami's friend called and we went down and stood on a street corner. A very thin man with a long dark beard, a black Kandahari cap, in white shalwar kameez and a dark vest walked slowly toward us. We shook hands. He had a soft voice and manner. We went to an Iranian restaurant nearby. He knew people who ate there, and worried about being seen with me, but we could eat there anyway. The food came and I prayed in Arabic: "*bismillah ir rahman ir rahim*"—"In the name of God, the gracious and merciful," the words we had used when we ate in captivity—and his eyes brightened. Was I Muslim? No, I was trying to make him comfortable and to protect myself. "We can't talk here," whispered Sami. I paid for dinner, over his objections. He was Pashtun and had to be a good host.

They walked to Sami's hotel. I walked behind them and sat in the lobby. A man in a suit with a white cord reaching to his ear stood at the elevator, suggesting an important official was nearby. I waited ten minutes and I walked to the elevator. "Good evening, sir," he said. I went up to Sami's room.

The three of us sat in chairs facing one another. "What is it like, as a Pashtun, and as a devout Muslim, to live in Dubai?" I asked. There were massage parlors, prostitutes in the streets, and night clubs.

"It is not an ideal place to be a Muslim," he admitted. "There are temptations and you have to suppress your evil desires. It is very hard to see people kissing in the street, or to see a woman walking in an un-Islamic dress, or to see men and women talking. It is hard to keep your children from seeing men and women holding hands."

It seemed especially incongruous that members of the Haqqani family, so austere in Jalaluddin's generation, might spend time in Dubai. The Taliban explained why the Haqqanis felt appreciated in the Gulf.

"There were more Arabs around Jalaluddin than anyone else," he said. "The Arabs respect us here because we gave up everything to protect bin Laden and to fight for our country. We have never given in and we are an inspiration to them. The Taliban have inspired Daesh." He, too, used the Arabic slang for ISIS.

"There is strong support here for Afghans because they sheltered bin Laden. We have meetings with Arabs and they give us thumbs up for waging jihad, standing up to the Americans, and not giving in. We see the Afghan turbans and clothes that ISIS wear. They are all mujahideen groups and they are the same. The source is the same and the definition is the same."

The source was Afghanistan. They were all one, the Taliban and ISIS. An hour passed before he, this Taliban official, asked me, "Why are you doing this, coming here, talking to me and taking this risk?"

The question made me wonder if he could harm me. I didn't tell Sami or him that I met with Haqqani.

"The best message is that a man gets good treatment by the Taliban and tells the world. That is a success," he continued. Sami must have told him that I had been kidnapped. I was a victim, trying to become free of that, and even here I was still a victim to them. I was too negative, too paranoid. Maybe he was saying that he, the Taliban, would treat me well. He would not harm me.

"What was it like in prison for you?" I asked, knowing that he had been imprisoned by the new Afghan government after the US invasion.

"They came to our house and told me to come with them. I only had a pistol and said, 'I don't care if I die, but I will kill some of them before they kill me.' My family said 'no, they have surrounded the house and you must surrender.' They made me give up my pistol. I was in a KhAD prison from 2002 to 2006.[1] The guards saluted me because I was once the director. They tortured me. There is no dignity in torture. They tied my hands and feet and left me like that for thirteen months. I didn't see the sun. Once, it was so cold that there was ice on my handcuffs. They beat me forty-five days straight. My clothes stuck to my body, the blood and parts of my skin. I prayed and recited verses from the Qur'an. I was not afraid. We believe that if someone is going to be martyred that there will be no pain and there was none for me."

He said that he was fine, mentally, but that he still had physical problems from that time. That was why he walked so slowly.

"They came for me on the fourth day of my second marriage and I didn't have a chance to be with my wife. They charged me with twenty-five murders, including the death of Nazir Mohammad, the defense minister. They also said I killed Karzai's father. I came here and the NDS told the Dubai government and the government talked to me. The head of the NDS is from my village." He was betrayed here by someone from his own tribe. It meant, very possibly, that he was being watched. "It may be rude for me to say, but the Americans only met the people in power and they never truly reached the real Afghans."

I asked him about Pakistan. "It is using us like a gun and we have no choice. America threw us in front of the dog that is Pakistan."

"Is Pakistan using you today?"

"They use us but they cannot finish us. We are using them too. The Pakistani contribution has been very important to help us in winning this war. I have a house in Pakistan worth five thousand rupees. If I pound a nail into the side and force it to split it will crumble and I will have no home." He was saying that Pakistan was their home and if the Taliban fought in Pakistan that they would destroy their home. "I need my home to survive."

By now it was 1:30 a.m. We would meet the following night. I went downstairs and the man with the cord in his ear smiled and said good night.

The next morning I felt weak from my cold, which was getting worse, but went to a restaurant on the corner, sat outside, and had breakfast. I went for a walk and went to a travel agency. Shannon, at the embassy, had said that the Saudis would begin bombing soon in Sana'a and advised me not to return. Still, I asked about flights to Sana'a. There was one flight on Yemenia that day, but after that nothing. I decided that it was too dangerous to return to Yemen and called the travel agent I used in London and made a reservation to fly back there.

I slept most of the day. I felt sick, but called Pashtoon and told him I had done what he asked and now he must wait. He was excited and asked me what he should do. "Nothing," I said. "Live your life. I've done all I can."

Sami called and told me he was back in Islamabad. I felt too sick to travel and canceled my flight reservation. I went back to sleep and then late that afternoon I went for a walk by the water for twenty minutes. When I returned I couldn't find my phone. Where was it? It was with me all the time. I had it that morning because I talked to Sami. I hadn't left the room except to go for a brief walk. I looked everywhere, twice, three times, pulled the bed out, looked under every cushion. I used the hotel phone to call my number. It rang but there was no answer and I heard no ring tone in the room. I couldn't have lost it. There were phone numbers on there I needed and messages. I went through my room again and again. I went down to the front desk and asked if the cleaning people had come to my room and found a phone. No one had turned one in. I went to the Pakistani restaurant on the corner and a café I had been in the day before. Nothing.

The next day I felt somewhat better, but I was upset about the phone. It belonged to CBS. I used the hotel phone and rebooked my flight to London. I wondered if the man with the earpiece at the hotel wasn't watching the man from the Taliban military council. I wondered if Shannon, or her superiors, had the Emiratis sneak into my room and pick up my phone, or did an agent rub up next to me and steal it? I was paranoid. I had been with the Haqqanis and now with a high Taliban official. They would get Haqqani's number, which I had refused to give them. No, they wouldn't. I had only used a local Pakistani phone to call the Haqqanis.

I flew back to London. There, Bryn Padrig welcomed me back and said he wanted to talk when I had a few minutes. Six months before I had seen a notebook on his desk with my name and YEMEN on the cover. It was a list of everyone he should call if I got kidnapped again. He had always had my safety in mind. Three years earlier in a pub for the Christmas party I asked him about my kidnapping but he wouldn't talk about it. Almost everything had to be kept secret. I understood, but I felt under his thumb.

I followed Bryn into his large office, with glass walls, off the newsroom. He sat up straight behind his desk and came right to the point.

"You have made my life with Sophie very difficult," he said, his voice loud. She was his boss, the foreign editor and senior vice president. "You went over my head and wrote her an e-mail and made a comment about Mukhtar in Kabul." He was the new CBS manager whom Bryn had hired. "What's going on?" Bryn asked. I had never seen him like this. "I welcomed you here, gave you an office to use and you abused that. I did a lot for you."

I sat there, shocked. I had expected a pleasant conversation, one in which he would ask questions, as he had other times. The last time I sat in here with him, he asked if I would talk to the staff about Yemen.

"You implied that Mukhtar was not up to the job. What was that all about? Why did you go over my head to Sophie? She asked me to find out what this was about."

I didn't remember writing anything, and it is not something I would do, I thought, but I must have said something. Bryn thought it was because I was close to Fazul and wanted him back at CBS. I did. I liked the camaraderie, the friendship, the trust.

He looked at me. "You have made my life very hard."

"I am sorry," I said. "I apologize."

He wouldn't accept it. He kept lecturing me. Finally, he stopped. "Should we fire him? Sophie wants to know." His voice was not so angry now. It was hard for him to holler at me and then ask my advice. I didn't want to cause Mukhtar to lose his job. "Why didn't you talk to him directly if you had a problem instead of doing this?"

"No, don't fire him. I am sorry that I caused you all this trouble."

"How soon are you going to leave?" he asked.

"In a day or two."

"Good. Clean out the office and go. I don't want to see you here again."

I said good-bye and walked out of his office. I couldn't be angry at Bryn after all that he had done for me, but it hurt that we were parting ways like this. I owed him more than I could ever repay.

I went for a walk, came back, and cleaned out my office, feeling humbled and ashamed. I wanted to leave as soon as possible. I felt freer also.

I returned to New York. It was late April 2015.

I wrote a hundred-plus-page, single-spaced, heavily footnoted monograph on the Haqqani Network in the greater Middle East and turned it in to my funder.

In May I received a packet from the National Counterterrorism Center in Washington, DC, inviting me to attend a series of meetings on the new US hostage policy, the result, in part, of the conversations, written reports, and e-mails that we, former hostages and their families, had with government officials.

Chapter 23

The Families

I walked into the lobby of the hotel in Crystal City, Virginia, the concrete, sterile enclave near the Pentagon. There were small groups of people talking with one another. I saw John Solecki standing alone. We greeted one another happily. We hadn't seen each other in three years.

"I heard you went back to Damascus," I said. "Did you go back to see your first wife?" She was Syrian. I knew why he had gone back, looking for comfort and to test himself. He was drawn there, as I was to Afghanistan. David Rohde said that someday he would take his daughters to Afghanistan and tell them what happened. John smiled again. "No, I didn't see her. She lives in Cairo."

Returning to Syria was a way to overcome his fears and to go back to his youth. His parents had been archeologists there. They would be horrified at what was going on. "Fortunately, they're no longer here," he said. "All the destruction would be too much for them."

ISIS destroyed Christian churches, like the Taliban destroyed the Buddhist statues at Bamiyan, like the Spanish built churches over Aztec and Inca temples, like the communist Chinese destroyed Tibetan Buddhist monasteries. Each man thought his faith was the only true one.

Two women in their thirties, one with short blond hair in a green dress, the other with dark hair in a black pants suit, appeared at the door carrying folders and wearing government ID chains. "The buses are here to take us to the National Counterterrorism Center," said the blond-haired woman.

We filed outside to the buses. I saw a woman behind me and stopped to let her get on the bus first. She was attractive, had dark hair, and an energetic, lively way about her. I introduced myself. "Diane Foley," she said, smiling brightly. It was Jim Foley's mother. "It's so good to meet you, Jere. David [Rohde] has told me so much about you. I want to spend time talking with you."

She had suffered so much yet she was so friendly. "Your son was the most courageous man in the world," I said and immediately wished that I had kept quiet. "I do hope we can talk," she said. She got on the bus. I admired her son so much. Jim was strong kneeling there, his back straight, and waiting. He kept his head high.

John Foley was a ruddy-cheeked, white-haired man in a tie and jacket. We shook hands and he smiled warmly. They knew that they had no choice but to go on or die inside. I thought of the devastation that had been wrought upon them. A man in a dark blue shirt and jeans, in his sixties, approached. His wife, attractive, with gray-blond hair, in a light-colored dress with a shawl, was behind the Foleys. "Art Sotloff," he said quietly. We shook hands and I introduced myself. "Shirley Sotloff," said the woman. I felt humbled before them also. I said that Steven was the most courageous man in the world. He was. He, too, had kept his back straight and he kept his head up waiting for the knife to come. He didn't flinch. He too had died with dignity. The Sotloffs climbed on the bus. Daniel Pearl went through the same thing that Jim Foley and Steven Sotloff did; so did Nicholas Berg, Peter Kassig, David Haines, Alan Henning, and Piotr Stańczak.

I climbed on the bus, saw a seat toward the front next to a woman, sat down, and said hello. We rode quietly for a few minutes. "Are you a family member?" she asked.

"No," I said, "a former hostage. Afghanistan. 2008."

We introduced ourselves. Her name was Reverend Kathleen Day. "I'm with the Muellers," she said and looked at the couple across the aisle. I looked at Carl Mueller, in his fifties, blond-brown hair, slightly tanned, with a solid build. He wore a dark shirt and a gray sport coat. Marsha Mueller was a pretty, all-American-looking woman, with blond-brown hair. She looked out the window. They lost their only daughter, Kayla, just four months before. I was ransomed. I could never discuss it, especially not here, but everyone presumably suspected it. The people here would have given anything to have been able to ransom their children.

"The government did nothing to help us," said Reverend Day. "The FBI didn't do anything. We, I mean the Muellers and I, tried to do all we could to free Kayla and bring her home. We had word that the kidnappers wanted to negotiate. We were trying to raise money. We were in contact with people in Syria and Turkey. The government did everything it could to prevent us, it seemed, from freeing her."

The Muellers had to act on their own. They didn't have a big company behind them. "Kayla was such a sweet girl growing up, always wanting to help others, and to think that the government would do nothing to help her."

We drove past the Pentagon, along the Potomac, past grass and trees, bicyclists and joggers. It was quiet and sunny in the early summer morning. The bus turned up a winding lane, past manicured green lawns and government buildings nestled among the trees, all part of the new, unseen world of the US war on terrorism. The buses pulled into a circle and stopped in front of a building.

The blond-haired woman stood up front. "There are people outside waiting for you. Just follow their directions. Remember to turn in your cell phones." She got off the bus and joined about eight others, who stood in a row, smiling, welcoming us. We walked slowly past them.

One of the men in line was a tall three-star general in dress blue uniform with his pants tucked into his high black spit-shined boots.

"That's quite a get-up," said Shirley Sotloff to the general.

I smiled to myself. The general spread his arms out, like a scarecrow, and turned, twisting his body, getting ready to twirl around. "Ma'am, this is a uniform," he replied, a three-star general twirling in the morning sun.

"Whatever," said Mrs. Sotloff. She kept walking, unimpressed.

We entered a lobby where stern-faced men and women wearing government chains and badges watched us. Two women stood behind a table, holding blue folders, anxious to help. There were name tags on the table. People put their cell phones in a locker. It was hard to believe that I was a part of this. I walked to the other side of the lobby. Carl Mueller came over and we introduced ourselves. "Are you a family member?" he asked.

"No, former hostage, Afghanistan, 2008." It would become my mantra.

Carl Mueller nodded when I said that I was kidnapped and seemed to draw closer. Marsha Mueller joined us. She too asked if I was with a family. I told her. I said that Kayla was such a strong, remarkable young woman. She said thank you. "I wish we had known you before, we could have really used your help." I sighed. I should have gone to them.

We walked down a hallway with floor to ceiling windows, paintings, photographs, potted plants, and rolling lawn and trees outside. All this and so much more built to fight al-Qaeda, the Taliban, ISIS, and other groups in the Middle East, Africa, and the Philippines. The seventeen US intelligence agencies had somehow failed to help these people.

Young employees stood against the walls, directing us. We entered a room with ten round tables and five or six chairs at each one, with a writing pad and pencil at each place. There was a lectern with a seal of the US government on the front, and a white screen lowered from the ceiling. Breakfast was laid out on a table in an adjoining room. I took some food and returned to my seat.

The Muellers were sitting on my left, Kathleen Day across the table. John Solecki was sitting at the next table. A woman in a dark blue dress came over to the Muellers, spoke warmly with them, and put her hands on Marsha's shoulders. She nodded curtly to me and sat down next to me, consulted her notes, and got up to talk to a man in a dark suit. "I guess if you've been out a while, they don't treat you so well," said Marsha.

The woman walked to the lectern. "My name is Lisa Monaco," she said. "I am the president's Homeland Security adviser and chief counterterrorism adviser."

She was the name on the letter I had received last December, announcing the establishment of the Hostage Policy Review Team and inviting me to respond.

She said she appreciated how difficult it was for some people to be here, and thanked us for coming. She and her team wanted to explain the new Presidential Policy Directive and to answer all our questions. The president had heard our concerns about our interaction with government officials. "We know where we have come up short and where we have failed you. No one is asking you to move on. We own this," she said.

I admired her for saying this, but there were people around me whose children were dead.

"The government's mission was to firstly and most importantly, talk to you—family members and former hostages—as well as members of Congress, think tanks, other governments, NGOs, and individuals." She thanked us for our courageous and generous contributions. Then she said, "The US will maintain a no-concessions policy. We as a government believe that we cannot pay a ransom. That will remain unchanged."

Lisa Monaco continued. "We want to change the way we work with you, to trust you more and to work closer with you and provide as much information as we can. The administration's goal has been and will continue to be to do whatever we can within our capabilities and within the bounds of the law to assist families to bring their loved one home. But to pay a ransom only encourages more kidnappings."

There was a government representative at each table. She introduced people from the Department of Defense, the Department of Justice, the FBI, the State Department, and the White House. Other men and women were sitting at tables and standing in the back. We all had received a letter from General Bennet Sacolick inviting us, she said, to take part in their planning. He was the head of the task force. The general stood up, taking command of the room. "I want to welcome you all here today. Thank you for all your help. We look forward to engaging with all of you."

I didn't know how he could help. In 2010 Navy SEALs flew into Kunar Province, Afghanistan, and one threw a grenade where Linda Norgrove, a twenty-six-year-old Scottish aid worker they had come to rescue, was hiding. Didn't they know that they could have negotiated her release instead of heroically trying to rescue her and killing her?

In December, the SEALs flew into southern Yemen, hiked to a village where Luke Somers and, unbeknown to the SEALs, Pierre Korkie, a South African schoolteacher, were being held by al-Qaeda. A South African charity had paid a ransom to free Korkie the next day, but the US apparently didn't know. The US embassy had been working on this for a year yet no one knew that the South Africans had paid a ransom? Korkie died in the SEALs raid, alongside Luke Somers. Al-Qaeda said that they would kill a Saudi Arabian diplomat also, but they freed him in 2015. Al-Qaeda in Yemen still had never, to my knowledge, killed a foreign hostage. The Trade, for AQAP, was too profitable.

The SEALs said that a guard dog alerted the al-Qaeda fighters and a battle broke out. A man ran inside a building and shot the hostages. There are dogs in Yemeni villages, but dogs, as a rule, are unclean in Islam and I had never heard of dogs being around al-Qaeda. But it was possible. I wanted to learn more. The SEALs were happy to take credit for killing bin Laden but kept quiet about their failures. Maybe it was because I was in the army, but I preferred the Delta Force who did their work and didn't brag. Maybe, in truth, I was protective of hostages, like Linda Norgrove and Luke Somers, with whom I felt a kinship. And I felt guilty that I was alive.

Elaine Weinstein and her family were not at the meeting. They were in mourning. "We believed the president when he told us that rescuing American hostages was his highest priority," Mrs. Weinstein wrote in the *Washington Post*. "They told us for three years that 'everything possible' was being done to find and rescue Warren. We now feel deceived. How do I explain to my grandkids that the government could have saved their grandpa, but decided not to?" Weinstein, killed in a US drone strike, had been a captive for four years.

Again, why, I asked myself, did al-Qaeda kill Daniel Pearl in 2002, but not Warren Weinstein when it captured him in 2011? Again, why did Ayman al-Zawahiri, the head of al-Qaeda, post a video with Weinstein's picture, shortly after he was taken, and not kill him? Why would Pakistan, to which the US gave billions of dollars, not make any apparent attempt to find Weinstein? One reason, I felt, was that the terms of the Trade had changed. Al-Qaeda, and its backers, felt that it no longer had to proclaim its presence. Everyone knew al-Qaeda. Without being able to prove it, I knew, after traveling now for almost two years in the Middle East looking for the links among jihadist groups linked to the Haqqanis, that al-Qaeda did not exist alone, whether in the Tribal Areas or Yemen. It had powerful forces behind it. I agreed with Samad, my bodyguard, who told me that the Pakistani army used al-Qaeda as it did the Taliban.

Lisa Monaco introduced Mike McGarrity, of the FBI, in charge of the new Hostage Recovery Fusion Cell. McGarrity, in a dark suit, smiling, walked quickly to the white screen filled with bullet points.

"The Hostage Recovery Fusion Cell will serve as the full-time, operational focal point for coordination of all US response activities related to the hostage taking of US nationals abroad. I will be the federal government's primary operational coordinator . . . We will bring together people from across the federal government to coordinate activities . . . We will focus on developing and executing individualized recovery strategies. We will . . ."

I lost interest. Maybe the government would do all these things, but the people in the room simply wanted to know why the government hadn't helped them, and that their children did not die in vain. I kept thinking as I sat there how fortunate I was, and I felt guilty being alive among these people. A journalist said to me that the ancient Greeks would say that I was twice-fated, meaning that my fate was to be kidnapped yet to survive. I was extremely lucky, he said. Now I had a second fate. I didn't know, as no man can know his fate, what that would be. But I knew that I had still a responsibility, and within that I felt I might find some redemption.

Gracia Burnham, who spent a year in the Philippine jungle as a hostage of the Abu Sayyaf with her husband, Martin, forgave her kidnappers. The Abu Sayyaf are Moros, from the Spanish "moor," meaning Muslim, the word the Spanish used for the Muslims who ruled Spain from 711 to 1492. The Moros were a small minority in the Philippines, which was a Spanish colony from 1521 to 1898. Then came the Spanish-American War, and the Philippines became a US territory. Muslims in the Philippines are the poor underclass; many are from Mindanao Island, in the south. My father, a marine, waded ashore there in World War II to fight the Japanese.

The Abu Sayyaf, which means "father of the sword-bearer" in Arabic, was founded by Abdurajik Abubakar Janjalani, a Filipino man who played soccer against the Arabs at a camp overseen by Ghulman Rasul Sayyaf, an Afghan member of the mujahideen, who changed his name to the more Arabic "Abd al-Rabb al-Rasul Sayyaf." The bond created among these young men by playing soccer would extend around the globe. Sayyaf, today a proud, vocal member of the Afghan Parliament who has successfully pushed through legislation to protect mujahideen for past crimes, was close to bin Laden. In 2017, I watched him welcome Hekmatyar, called the "butcher of Kabul," back to Kabul on television. In 2002, President George W. Bush, a Christian, nonetheless quietly went against longstanding US policy to try to ransom the Burnhams, because, I believe, they were Christian missionaries and he wanted to save them, part of his Christian constituency.

A statement at the time said: "It is US government policy to deny hostage takers the benefit of ransom, prisoner releases, policy changes or other acts of concession. In the event a hostage-taking incident is resolved through concessions US policy remains steadfastly to pursue investigation leading to the apprehension and prosecution of hostage-takers who victimize US citizens. US Foreign Service posts can be actively involved in efforts to bring the incident to a safe conclusion."

The ransom payment of $300,000 disappeared. Abu Sayyaf, which has focused on kidnapping Christians since the 1990s, continues to take hostages, demand ransom payments, and sometimes kills the hostages.

For Abu Sayyaf, the Trade is not just about money, but is an instrument in a defensive holy war, a jihad, against Christianity.

In Pakistan, the Trade is not just about money, but part of the quiet war, I believe, that Pakistan feels compelled to lead. More than once, I heard in Pakistan that it was afraid that the Israelis would attack Pakistan's nuclear arsenal, from their secret base[2] in Azerbaijan. That is why, I realized later, the Taliban I met with high in the mountains south of Tora Bora, said, for the first time, that the Taliban would go anywhere, "even Azerbaijan." I wondered then how they even knew where that secret Israeli base was.

I believed one reason why I survived, and Daniel Pearl, Adam Gadahn, and Warren Weinstein did not, was because I wasn't Jewish. Because of the visceral fear of Israel among some members of the Pakistani security apparatus, a Jewish journalist or a Jewish kidnap victim is always more vulnerable than a non-Jew.

Mike McGarrity was still talking: "We want to engage other actors to help us. We are going to think outside the box to do all that we can to bring future hostages home. We will talk with journalists. They often know more than others. They are on the ground and have a lot of contacts. We want to work with the families as well as with entities throughout the government." He meant well, but he was preaching to people they had failed.

"The US government will work closely with all of you to proactively share as much information as possible. We have heard your complaints and are committed to change. Our job will be to coordinate diplomatic intelligence, law enforcement, and military components of hostage recovery efforts."

Diane Foley stood up.

"My name is Diane Foley. We lost our son Jim in Syria. We hope that you will change. We will watch and see. I don't want to feel that my son died in vain. That I cannot accept. Frankly, you must convince us that you are going to change. I really feel that our country let Jim down. As an American I am embarrassed and appalled at the supposed efforts to rescue him. The American bombing caused Jim's death. He was sacrificed because of a lack of communication, of coordination, of prioritization, in the most horrific way. We, as a family, had to find our own way. On our own."

The room was silent. I admired her courage. She wasn't holding back.

"We knew everything before the FBI, or anyone else in the government. Everyone was kind and supportive, but the FBI used us for information. For the first year, it knew nothing. Can you imagine? For a whole year you had no information, nothing at all. It is appalling. And you expect us to believe that you will change now. You have to convince us. Because we did everything we could, we annoyed people. We bothered them. The problem was our desperation to bring Jim home did not seem to be in the strategic interest, if you will, of the United States."

She sat down. John Foley, a doctor in New Hampshire, had said in an interview that he was prepared to go and exchange himself for his son, that he "would have gladly traded places so that he could be free."

Bob Bergdahl said that he would trade places with his son Bowe so that he could be free. Admiral John McCain went to the North Vietnamese border to be close to his son, John McCain, now Senator McCain, when he was a POW in Hanoi.

Mrs. Foley continued: "The government acted like they didn't have time for us. I was so surprised that there was so little compassion. We were doing everything we could to bring our son home and we were told that what we were doing was illegal and that we could be prosecuted. We were told that we could not do anything. The government was so patronizing, and our son was being tortured every day."

The room was completely still.

Paula Kassig, a tall, slim woman with short black-gray hair, stood up in the back behind me. She spoke quietly. "I am Peter Kassig's mother," she said. She was a nurse in the public health department in Indianapolis. Ed Kassig, a high school science teacher with a mustache and a big chest, sat next to her.

I couldn't hear her very well, standing in the back of the room. They had adopted Peter as a baby. He ran track in high school and joined the army, but he, too, always wanted to help others. This came from his grandfather, a Methodist minister, who wanted to help Muslims whom he felt were kept down by their own governments. Peter converted to Islam and changed his name to Abdul Rahman. His parents were heartbroken, but Paula said that he died because of his love for the Syrian people. There was a strong Midwestern dignity to her as she stood stoically, a kind, devastated mother. They were incredibly proud of their son for listening to his own voice and following his humanitarian calling. They too would work every day of their lives to keep his legacy alive.

The room was coming closer together. People knew that they could talk here. We were part of a small community, but those who talked were part of even a smaller one. We had all been hostages, some in captivity and some at home. The kidnappers controlled our lives.

"We will be watching closely to see what the government does," Paula Kassig ended. She sat down.

Ed Kassig spoke up, his voice strong and deep. "We will be watching. Talk is easy. You must walk the walk." Lisa Monaco walked over to our table, made a note, and returned to the podium.

A woman in the far back on the other side of the room, with gray-brown hair and in a dress with a light cardigan sweater, stood up. She was smaller and her voice was soft. There were no microphones and it was hard to hear her also.

"I am Luke Somers' mother. Luke was a freelance photojournalist kidnapped September 2013 by al-Qaeda in Yemen and killed in December 2014." It was just six months now and here she was. "I feel that my son would be alive today if the US had not tried to rescue him. Luke is dead. What am I to do? Why are we here? How do we know that you are going to change, and what does it matter? For the future, yes, and if other families will be spared what we have had to endure and to live with every minute of every day, that will be good. But you didn't listen to us before, why would you listen now?"

Paula Somers, too, was a mother, now alone, her voice cracking, spilling her broken heart.

"We got no help from the government. In fact, it told us to be silent. I asked why and they told us not to tell other family members or close friends that Luke had been taken hostage. I didn't say anything at my work. I had to keep quiet."

Again, I saw Luke standing beneath a leafy tree, pleading for help. He wasn't skinny and he wore Western clothes. They were feeding him and he wasn't tied up, at least not then, but he was scared.

"Luke loved the Yemeni people and only wanted to help them. He was my son. He was all that we had." She sat down.

Lisa Monaco stood in front, her hands clasped together, her face flushed. It was she, I heard, who felt so badly about all that had happened that she and Jennifer Easterly—director of counterterrorism on the National Security Council, and a mother, sitting at a far table—went to the president. Lisa Monaco knew that she had to stand and take it.

Behind me, a sandy-haired, bearded man in a dark jacket stood up. It was Michael Semple. What in the world was he doing here? I had been asking that question for years now, and I didn't have an answer. How did he get here? He must be working for the US government. He was articulate and spoke vigorously, but I was so shocked by his presence that I didn't remember a word he said.

"There are thirty-five Americans being held hostage right now," Lisa Monaco said. "Most of them are in Mexico." They are all linked to drug trafficking. "There are five Americans being held in Pakistan."

Suddenly, perhaps triggered by the shock of seeing Semple, I realized why Ibrahim Haqqani made his remark that he only trusted me, why he talked about his nephew, Anas, and wanted to meet in Dubai: the Haqqanis were holding the American hostages and wanted to negotiate. They were suggesting me as the middle-man. Maybe Semple was involved in this.

"Let's take a five-minute break and then we will continue," said Lisa Monaco. I went up to her.

"My name is—"

"I know you are," she said. I wondered what she thought. I had, after all, gone off with the Taliban.

"I would like your advice. I have been working on a project for the past two years on the Haqqani Network in the Middle East. Three months ago—"

Michael Semple came over and stood beside me, interrupting my conversation with Lisa Monaco. "What are you doing all dressed up like this? You look like a government official. What has happened to you?" He was smiling. Lisa Monaco stood there.

I shook his hand but I wanted to talk to Lisa Monaco alone. I waited until Semple finally moved away.

I continued quietly. "I met with Ibrahim Haqqani, the first non-governmental Westerner, I believe, to meet with the Haqqani leadership in two decades. Maybe I can help. What do you suggest I do?"

"Talk to Mike McGarrity," she said.

He was walking through the crowd. I introduced myself and told him what I had told her. He was taken aback. "Did you meet with Siraj?" He meant Sirajuddin Haqqani.

"No, with his uncle, Ibrahim, and another family member." I didn't name "John."

He gave me his card. "We'll come up to see you in New York or you can come down here. We'll set up a meeting with the Fusion Cell." I didn't know if it was a good idea, but I wanted to help. I would also be helping Haqqani.

He left and I saw Art Sotloff standing near us. "How are you doing?" I asked gently.

He shrugged sadly. "There is no closure for us. There won't be until we get our son's body back."

I hadn't thought of that. How would they ever be able to do that? Maybe someday they could go to where he is buried and bring him back. He took a rubber bracelet off his wrist and gave it to me. It said, "*Remember Steven J. Sotloff. 2LivesFoundation.Org.*" I thanked him and put it on my wrist.

"Everyone has two lives. The second one begins when you realize you only have one," Steven had written to his parents from prison. How was I going to live that life?

"He's been there," said Michael Semple effusively, joining us. "He knows."

Over a lunch break I wrote down some of my observations and then got up to wash my hands and saw Ed Kassig in the hallway. "I just confronted the assistant director of the FBI," he said. "I asked him if he would have been so certain in his statements opposing paying a ransom if it was his child. I challenged his moral authority. They didn't do anything, nothing to help Peter. They made it worse."

I wished that I had been there to see him challenge the number two man in the FBI, and to stand his ground. I admired his willingness to confront them: I was too polite and it was killing me in a way that I didn't know. I didn't confront Sophie Roland-Gutterman, or Sean McManus, the CBS president, after I was told that he asked whether CBS was obliged to help me. I was angry then sad that Zalmay Khalilzad, ambassador to the UN, and Elliot Abrams, number two on the NSC—powerful men—who wouldn't even talk to Sophie on the phone when she asked for their help to get me released. An Afghan female friend who had heard about my kidnapping told me she had been to see Khalilzad at the UN in 2008. They were friends. "I am going to see Jere tonight," she told Khalilzad. "Jerry who?" was Khalilzad's response. She told him. "Jere Van Dyk." "Did you hear what happened?," Khalilzad responded, "he was kidnapped in Afghanistan. I did all I could to help him." I didn't say anything when she told me. I wanted to believe him, but I believed Sophie more.

I walked into the lunch room where Paula Kassig, standing in the back looking over the sandwiches, was next to another woman, with gray-brown hair. I walked over toward them and the other woman looked up. "I am looking for something vegetarian," she said. "My name is Paula Somers."

I didn't recognize her at first for a second. I felt a combination of warmth and sadness. "Oh, you are Luke's mother. I heard so much about him. I lived in Yemen last year briefly. He was such a fine young man."

She sighed. I stood there. She and I said hello to Paula Kassig and they commented that they had the same first name, two mothers who had just lost their sons in the most brutal ways.

I kept thinking of Luke. A week after I arrived in Sana'a, an Irish journalist, in an abaya, took me on a tour of the Old City. "Don't tell anyone you are American," she advised. "They hate America here because of the drones. It is not Afghanistan. The Yemenis are gentler. We call it al-Qaeda light here, but you must be careful." I had thought Luke would be released.

I took a sandwich and a bottle of water. Michael Semple came over and we stood by the door. I knew I had to ask him: "I've been gone for two years in the Middle East. I went back to Afghanistan. I don't understand. Why do people say—"

"That I kidnapped you?" He laughed. He didn't even let me finish the sentence.

"Yes, why would they say that?" I was concerned that Amrullah Saleh, a former head of NDS, a man profiled on *60 Minutes* who was close to the US, would blame him for kidnapping me.

He laughed. "You know Afghanistan, you know the Afghans. They're paranoid about everything. They believe all kinds of things, create stories, and wild ideas." He talked fast and I couldn't keep up. I couldn't get over that he interrupted me, as if he was expecting my question. I wanted to take notes, but I had a sandwich in my hand. A woman told us to return to our seats.

Lisa Monaco asked another man to come to the front. A slim, intense, dark-haired man in a blue suit, a bit hunched over, put one hand in his pocket and paced back and forth. "I'm with the Department of Justice. We intend to do everything we can to bring the people to justice who . . . have killed Americans. We are committed to that." He rubbed his chin, looked down, thinking. "At no time were we ever going to prosecute any of you for trying to deal directly with the terrorists. I know you've read that and I know you think that, but I'm here to tell you that it's not true. It never entered our minds. The person who told you that is no longer here."

Army colonel Mark Mitchell, tasked to the NSC, had told the Foleys, the Sotloffs, and other families that they could be prosecuted for trying to save their children. "Saving American hostages is a priority, but not a top priority," he stated in a television interview. "He threatened us three times," Diane Foley said. He had no compassion, she said. He later denied ever saying this, insisting that he did not have the power, but the families insisted that he had threatened them.[3] What had become of the United States that it would prosecute a family for trying to save a son or a daughter?

I was happy when I heard that $1.5 million and three men from Guantanamo had been demanded for me: it meant that there was a chance I might survive. There was a financial incentive to keep me alive—I was a commodity. At that moment I had no idea that any payment for me might be illegal. I was preoccupied with the thought that I might have to raise the money.

The prosecutor kept pacing back and forth. "I want to repeat this. We never intended to prosecute anyone for trying to negotiate with terrorists or trying to free their loved one. We never even thought of it." He stopped walking. "If you fund the terrorists, then you are encouraging them."

Carl Mueller leaned over and said in a low voice, "There is no accountability."

His daughter was killed and he wanted justice. What man wouldn't? Marsha Mueller looked up at the prosecutor. "We were trying to do everything we could to bring our daughter home. You say that you weren't going to prosecute anyone, but we were told that we couldn't even talk to the people who had Kayla. What were we supposed to do?"

"We knew that you were doing that."

"What?" Marsha Mueller asked. "How did you know? Were you reading my e-mails when I was in contact with these people?"

"Yes, we were reading your e-mails."

Marsha's voice rose in anguish. "You never told us. While we were trying to save our daughter's life you were reading my e-mails and you did nothing to help us. You were spying on us. One of your people was telling us that we were breaking the law." Her voice broke and she wiped tears from her eyes. "How could you be this callous? It was my daughter. I was trying to save my child."

I saw that she and Carl were holding hands under the table.

The prosecutor turned and was pacing again. "We weren't going to prosecute anyone. The person who said that is no longer here. We are changing now. We have listened to all of you. That is why we are here to announce our new policy. The United States will not pay ransoms, but our no-concessions policy does not mean that we will not allow any communication with terrorists."

Hostage families could now talk to the kidnappers. Marsha wiped tears away. It was all too late.

Art Sotloff stood up and introduced himself. "We lost our son Steven nine months ago. We are angry. I am grateful to the FBI. They contacted us, but this is all too late for us. Our son is gone. We tried all we could, but . . . it didn't work. Our government couldn't do anything."

He sat down and again it was quiet. What else could he say? Everyone knew about his son.

Debra Tice sat at a table in the center. She had long gray-brown hair and wore bright red earrings. Her husband, Marc, gray-haired in a gray pin-striped suit and tie, sat next to her. He rose, holding some papers, and spoke in a calm level voice, as if addressing a board meeting.

"Our son, Austin, is thirty-four and has been in captivity in Syria for three years and still no one knows where he is, or even for certain if he is alive. Our government has been helpful. We have met with a great number of people in government and out."

In 2017, there was still no news of their son. Five weeks after Austin Tice disappeared a grainy video of him, blindfolded, appeared, confirming that he was alive, but no one knew who had kidnapped him. In November 2016, the Newseum in Washington, DC, displayed a banner outside its building, on the route that presidents take after their inaugurations, to remind the world that Austin Tice was still missing. US officials believe that he is being held by the Syrian government. Marc and Debra and I talked one night in New York. They were trying to get Secretary of State John Kerry to ask Russian president Vladimir Putin to talk to Syrian president Bashar al-Assad. The Trade had now reached the highest levels of international diplomacy, this soft, insidious weapon of the weak against the strong.

"Fundamentally, it seems, in reading through all the material here that little has changed," said Marc. "There is still a no-concessions policy. There will be no ransoms paid. But at least we are told that we can talk to our son's captors, if we knew who they are or where they are.

We are still not allowed to do anything and everything we can to try to bring home our son."

He sat down and Debra Tice stood up. "I will have nothing to do with this," she said loudly, her voice resonating across the room. "I have been and will continue to do whatever it takes, go anywhere and everywhere, talk to anyone, to bring my son home. I live in fear every day that the government will kill my son, either in a drone strike or a military raid. I demand assurance that the government consult with us before it tries any rescue attempt. I am terrified at what my government might do if it sent drones over near where my son is being kept, do you understand, terrified?"

Again, there was silence as her voice and passion lingered in the air.

In the back, on the other side of the room, Jim Coleman, a stocky man in a dark shirt, rose. "Our daughter Caitlan was kidnapped in Afghanistan, with her husband, in October 2012. She was pregnant at the time. Our grandchild was born there. We got a video in 2014, but there was no picture of our grandchild. We are afraid of the drones, and of the terrorists."

Erin Boyle, in her thirties, a Canadian schoolteacher, sat at another table, closer to the front, behind me. Her brother Joshua was married to Caitlan. I heard the Coleman family was angry that Joshua, her brother, took their pregnant daughter to Afghanistan.

In December 2016, a video appeared online of Caitlan Coleman and Joshua Boyle, kidnapped in 2012, and their two children now, both born in captivity. Joshua Boyle and his two boys wore Western clothes and looked to be well-fed. I knew now that the Haqqanis had them and that they would keep them and wanted to exchange them for Anas Haqqani, Jalaluddin Haqqani's son, and for Hafiz Rashid, and probably other hostages. The Haqqanis posted a proof-of-life video online of Coleman and Boyle in August 2016, which was then shown on US television.[4] In December 2016, a second video appeared online showing the two boys.[5] This Trade was now using television advertising to get the attention of governments to cause them to act.

Paula Somers stood up again. She mentioned Rachel Briggs, the director of HostageUK,[6] who was in the room. Briggs worked with Terry

Waite. "I felt alone, with no help coming from anyone in the US, and under orders 'not to tell a soul' about Luke and so I reached out to Rachel, who offered to put me in touch with Diane Foley. I am sorry now that I didn't do that. We could have helped one another."

President Obama called Paula Somers the night of the raid to tell her that Luke had been killed. When she and Jordan, Luke's younger brother, met with the president she asked him for all the information that the government had gathered about Luke, and a record of all that took place, including when and how he was killed. The president promised it but she had yet to receive anything. "It seems only fair that I and other parents whose children didn't come back have this history."

It would take another year before the government gave her even a part of the information that she requested.

Jordan, about twenty-five with long, curly dark hair, sitting next to Paula, stood up. "The government did nothing to help us. For fourteen months Luke was in captivity and the government only lied to us. It's clear now that the government didn't know what it was doing." His voice was strong and intense and carried across the room. He started to become emotional. "I don't even know why we are here. Is this a conciliation prize, a trip to Washington? Is the government trying to appease us? It gets my brother killed and then invites us here to say that it will be different in the future. What will be different? My brother is dead. Nothing will help us.

"Luke was my older brother. I looked up to him. He was everything to me. The US military and the CIA, with its drones and its torture program, did not help us; in fact, I think they are responsible for my brother's death. Pierre Korkie, the South African schoolteacher who was with my brother, was going to be released the next day. His people paid a ransom. We didn't have that opportunity. We were trying to do all we could, but we didn't get any help. Why are we here? To hear more lies? My brother is dead.

"I don't even like the name 'Fusion Cell.' To me, this new collection of people doesn't inspire any more trust than before. It's comprised of the same entities that got my brother killed. I suggest having an outside representative or organization involved. We were treated horribly by the FBI's so-called victims specialist. HostageUK was a saving grace. For the US government, its interests overshadow those of the common man—the corruption in education, in health care, and our situation is no different. Higher interests are always served. They were served far more than mine, my mom's, and especially Luke's. If my mother and I had the means, I'd take us and get the hell out of this country."

He sat down and the room was quiet. People didn't know that General Sacolick had called Jordan after Luke was killed. They spoke for more than an hour. It didn't diminish Jordan's fury.

Shirley Sotloff, sitting at the table behind me next to her husband, leaned over and whispered, "He better be careful. They'll throw him in jail."

"No," I whispered back, "he'll be fine." He could say what he wanted.

There were other victims present: Brenda Wright-Rockamann, whose brother, a ship captain, was taken hostage by Somalia pirates; the German mother of Michael Scott Moore, a German-American held by al-shabab[7] in Somalia; Jonathan Alpeyrie, a French-American photographer, taken in Syria, who said he was all for keeping everything quiet. But he was alive, ransomed for $450,000. Randal Rhoade with CARE, who was kidnapped in Somalia and who came all the way from Laos, where he now worked, didn't talk; neither did a family of Syrian-Americans. Nancy Curtis rose to say that her son Theo[8] was not there because he was suffering from the aftereffects of his torture.

Midafternoon came. We had been together for much longer than planned, but even though we were tired, no one wanted to leave. There was sadness, sorrow, and anger, but there was warmth here too, and a feeling of camaraderie. The meeting broke up finally and the government people smiled, trying to be friendly, as we left the room. Some people went out to the buses and back to the hotel.

I went with the Foleys and the Kassigs on a tour of the National Counterterrorism Center. We stood on a balcony looking down at a large cavernous room with an array of computers, with only a few people there. A man explained their mission, but he spoke in bureaucratese and military jargon and I was bored, and then he explained how they monitored drones from there. I had been under them and asked how they knew when to fire. He explained in jargon how they had to be certain of their target, but I felt terrible asking in front of the Foleys and Kassigs, thanked him, and walked away.

Back in the hotel everyone was in the lobby. No one wanted to be alone. We felt separate from others in our own cities and towns, but here we were part of a family. I went over to John Foley. "I'm glad we met," he said. So was I, even more that he accepted me. "Come, sit down," he said. He raised his hand toward a bartender. I admired him for trying to enjoy life. "I have five children," he said. "It's easier than if you only have one." He was being strong. I had watched him cry on television.

We went to a table and others joined us. Soon there was not enough room and we had to get more chairs. I sat there, but a part of me felt like an interloper. Diane Foley and I sat across from one another. "I do want to talk," she said, but not in such a large group. She put her head down slightly. John Foley sat next to her, subdued but smiling.

Jane Larson, whose husband, Paul Overby, a writer who was assumed to be held by the Haqqanis, and Erin Boyle, Joshua Boyle's sister, came across. I didn't recognize Overby's name at first although Jane asked if I had met him in the 1980s, but nineteen months later, on January 4, 2016, the *New York Times*[9] published an article about his captivity in what was the first public acknowledgement, a joint family–Fusion Cell initiative. I looked at his picture and read about him. He was older than I was, but I vaguely recalled him being around then. There was only a small group of journalists, photographers, writers, and activists then interested in Afghanistan. Overby looked in the newspaper photograph like an Afghan, maybe a convert to Islam. Perhaps he too had been lured back by the romance and excitement of the past.

Jane Larson and Erin Boyle asked me to join them with Jason Amerine. David Rohde had urged me to meet with him. He was in his forties, slim with short hair and wearing civilian clothes, open-neck shirt and khakis. He was a lieutenant colonel in the army. He talked softly, holding a pen.

"I was tasked by General John Campbell, head of US and NATO forces in Afghanistan, to think outside the box and do anything I could to secure the release of Sergeant Bowe Bergdahl and the other hostages. I had an office, still do, a staff, funds, and complete freedom to do whatever it took. We have contacts throughout the tribal regions of Pakistan."

"How did you get them?" I asked.

He put up his hands. "We just have them. I know a lot of people."

In late October 2001 Amerine was the Special Forces officer in Uzbekistan preparing to go into Afghanistan to rescue Abdul Haq, Din Mohammad's brother and former mujahideen leader who had gone into Afghanistan to rally tribal leaders against the Taliban before being surrounded by them. Amerine and his team were later dropped by helicopter into southern Afghanistan, where they met up with Hamid Karzai and brought him through the mountains, through US bombing raids, firefights, more bombings, in which some of Amerine's men were killed, others wounded, to safety. He was a West Point graduate, a highly decorated soldier, an Arabic speaker, on his way up, now trying to save hostages. But ten days before he met with us he had appeared before a congressional committee to explain what he called the "dysfunctional" hostage policy of the United States. Amerine was the subject of a nine-month criminal investigation, behind which was the FBI.[10] He had revealed publicly that the Pentagon had, in effect against US policy, paid a group under the control of the Haqqanis for a proof of life video of Bergdahl, in effect a ransom for proof that he was alive. The money disappeared. The CBS team had asked for proof that I was alive, and I sent a voice message; the Haqqanis posted a video of David Rohde as proof that he was alive.

Now the Haqqanis had raised the ante and demanded and received money in exchange for proof that Bergdahl was alive. The Trade had taken another turn. Mirwais Yasini was right. The US government had negotiated for the first time officially, although secretly, acknowledging the Haqqani Network. I wondered if Pakistan was behind this, or if the Haqqanis were doing this alone because of Anas. I felt that Pakistan had to know. The Trade had possibly become, although I couldn't prove it, a government instrument, a weapon, of a weaker government—Pakistan, which was ostensibly an ally—against the stronger United States.

"I am very impressed with the Haqqanis' counterintelligence operation," Amerine said. "My main problem was with the FBI, which feels that this is their domain, specifically with one man, who is a wretched human being. He did all he could to stop us." I would later meet this bearded, edgy man, friendly to me but who bragged of his work in Afghanistan—yet another official pounding his chest about his toughness there, and I saw why Amerine felt as he did.

The FBI threatened to sue Amerine, who had criticized the Bureau for its incompetence. The FBI, in charge of kidnappings of American citizens anywhere in the world, was as interested, it seemed, in maintaining control as in freeing hostages. This was turf warfare. When I was in the army, I would hear, half-jokingly, that the enemy was not North Vietnam or the Soviet Union, but the navy. It was the battle for funds, for influence, for power. It was more important to defeat your enemies in Washington and to protect your tribe. Little, it seemed, had changed.

"We think that another child was born in captivity," said Amerine. "I used every resource available but I failed the hostages. The White House led the release of Bowe Bergdahl. It all depends on the investigation against me. I am being punished for announcing that we paid a ransom. I think I'll retire and go sit on the beach in Hawaii."

He was a good man and he seemed defeated. Why Hawaii? I asked.

"I grew up there," he said. He would go home. I kept secret that I had been ransomed. I wanted to protect the company that saved me, and to possibly prevent anyone there from becoming a target in the future because of what was done for me. In a week, my time at CBS would be over. Amerine paid a ransom to get proof of life, and it cost him his career. I later watched a video of Rear Admiral John Kirby, a Pentagon spokesman, responding to the news about Amerine. "I'm not aware that any money changed hands," Admiral Kirby said. "There are such exchanges." He was contradicting himself—acknowledging that the government paid for information.

"We can't do anything now," said Amerine. "The Haqqanis control everything. We have to wait."

"They won't even give us proof of life," said Erin Boyle. "We don't know if anyone is even alive."

"They're tough," said Amerine, referring to the Haqqanis. That they were. I watched Jalaluddin climb on a roof in the snow and call his men to prayer, and I watched them put their rifles down and pray in the dirt. They had God on their side and would never give in. I couldn't tell the families that I had so recently met with the Haqqanis.

The Foleys, the Sotloffs, and the Muellers came in and sat at a table next to us. They were a family within a family drawing strength from one another. The Tices sat alone. It would be too awkward to sit with the others. Their son was still alive.

David Rohde and Kristen Mulvihill, his wife, came into the dining room and joined us. I got up to get another chair. At the same time, Shirley Sotloff got up from the table beside us and walked by me.

"Did he suffer much?" she asked softly, referring to her son. "No," I said, "two seconds, no more."

"Thank you," she said softly, and walked on.

That moment made my trip worthwhile. I didn't know for sure how many seconds. But I had seen a video in Pakistan, and other videos. When I was a captive, after my mock executions, I had felt my jugular vein and tried to calculate how long it would take. I wanted to alleviate Shirley Sotloff's suffering, to help her, the missionary in me. A year and a half later, I would bring her and Art to *60 Minutes* so they could tell their story, as I would work with Paula and Jordan Somers, and the Foleys, join the boards of the James W. Foley Legacy Foundation and HostageUS, and try to help the hostages in Pakistan. It was a mission born of guilt, of a desire to do something worthwhile, something for which I could quietly be proud and not be merely a victim, a form of redemption.

⁖ ⁖ ⁖

THE NEXT DAY we met in the lobby, most of us dressed differently now. We were going to the White House. No one was sure what was going to happen.

My first visit to the White House was on March 21, Afghan New Year, 1982. I stood in the East Room along with Afghans in exile and men and women from what the US called "Captive Nations," from Eastern Europe, under the control of the Soviet Union. President Reagan walked up to the front of the room, smaller in person than on television. He put his arm around an Afghan teenage girl wearing a colorful nomad dress and said, as the cameras rolled, "We are with you. You are like our founding fathers. You are freedom fighters."

I came a second time in 1984 with Zalmay Khalilzad and we had lunch with Walt Raymond, on loan from the CIA to the National Security Council, in the White House mess, after which we went to Raymond's office and he gave me booklets with CIA stamped on them and I wondered what I was getting into. It was now June 2014. The men we once called freedom fighters were our enemies. Ibrahim said that they hadn't changed, only we had changed. Not so: they now used suicide bombers and kidnappings to make money, which they no longer received from us, and as a form of war. We now tortured prisoners. This all came from Afghanistan.

Carl Mueller and I stood just outside a large room with a beautiful inlaid wood floor. "Now is the chance to say what you want to say," I said.

"I don't know," he replied. "I'm thinking. Diane Foley was talking to some reporters outside."

There was tension among some family members. She spoke out more than others and the media gravitated toward her. "Don't hold back," I said. "This is the place to talk. You can't go any higher."

"Thanks. I don't know," he shook his head. "We can't let these people get away with this. We just can't."

But how would he find those men who hurt his daughter? He and Marsha would learn new information from the government while we were in Washington. Kayla Mueller was blamed online for being a sympathizer and pro-Palestinian. She had a Syrian boyfriend. People were blaming the victim. "I hope you talk if you want to," I said again. I wanted him to say whatever he needed to say.

I found my seat next to General Sacolick. We stood as the president of the United States came around the room and we shook hands. The vice president sat next to him.

John Foley, famous in a way that he never wanted to be, spoke first. His voice was scratchy and he cleared his throat. He asked if the new hostage policy that we had all worked on would stay in place with a new administration, and if it could be formalized through Congress. The president responded that to get Congress involved would only make it more vulnerable. "It will be a fixture. If someone harms an American, we want them to face the judgment of the law. There is no statute of limitations for these crimes committed against Americans." He added, "I have to take into consideration foreign policy when I make a decision."

Debra Tice held her hand high and the president called on her. She stood up. "I want a commitment from you, Mr. President, that you will not launch a rescue attempt or send a drone missile down on where my son is being held. I want you to tell us beforehand. I am afraid that what happened to others will happen to him. I don't want the United States to kill my son. His life is the most important thing in the world to me. We want him to return home alive."

Obama responded quietly. "I can't do that. Foreign policy must play a role in my calculations. I know that sounds harsh, but I can't avoid it . . . We know that there will be other Americans kidnapped. These things take place in failed states, where US power is limited, in areas controlled by ISIL, in the Federally Administered Tribal Zones of Pakistan, in parts of Libya, Somalia, and Lebanon. Concessions are one of the toughest things I grapple with in this office."

It was the interests of America against the life of one American. But what if it is your child? He said that he would do anything to save his daughters. Vice President Biden talked about his son, who served in Iraq and who died of cancer. "Nations have interests, not hearts," said Talleyrand, foreign minister to King Louis XIV.

The room was silent as the president talked. He took questions, and he listened. "Every three months I go, without the press knowing, to Walter Reed hospital and visit with men and women who are wounded and maimed for life as a result of decisions that I have made. I don't make those decisions lightly. I wrestle with them. I see the consequences in front of me. But I must think of the interests and the foreign policy of the United States.

"No one can know what each and every one of you in this room has had to wrestle with, the courage, the fear, and for some the devastation knowing that your loved ones have been killed. I am deeply aware of that. But we cannot, as a nation, give in to terrorism."

We had been there at least ninety minutes, longer than planned. "I am now going out to announce our new policy," said the president. "This is the result of your work. Thank you, all of you."

He stood up and walked slowly around the room again. He hugged Paula Somers. What else could he do? He couldn't just shake her hand. Six months earlier he had ordered a rescue attempt that killed her son. He was saying that he was sorry. He couldn't comprehend the depth of her sorrow. He continued around the room. He had walked around the room when he entered an hour and a half ago; he didn't have to do this a second time—the first time, yes, but not the second.

He hugged Marsha Mueller and she reached up and hugged him back. No one seemed to know who killed Kayla. Maybe it was a US bomb, yet still Marsha Muller hugged the president.

Obama came to me and we shook hands again. He looked me in the eye gently and firmly, and walked out of the room, the Secret Service behind him.

The new hostage policy, if such it was, was an opportunity for the White House to say to the parents of those killed that it was sorry that the US couldn't save their children, and it was a gift to us, which meant a great deal to me, to meet the president of the United States. We got up from our chairs and I approached Jen Easterly, the deputy assistant to the president for counterterrorism. I told her what I had told Lisa Monaco. "Get proof of life," she said. She meant proof in some form from the Haqqanis that their hostages were alive. I stood there. I was about to enter a world that I had never been in before. I knew at that moment that I would return to see the Haqqanis, not just for myself, but for others, and with the tacit support of the United States. As I walked down the hallway after it was all over, I saw Lisa Monaco— tired, or relieved—and other officials walking toward me. She stopped, said hello to me, and we shook hands. I felt, for the first time since I was released seven years before, accepted.

I walked outside into the sun. I felt relaxed. I realized much later how important it was for me to meet the president, for him to say my name, to shake my hand and to say that it was good to see me, and later for Lisa to shake my hand. It felt like being welcomed home. I was accepted. I was part of America. Much later, when I realized fully what had happened, I broke down and cried.

The buses were waiting and we climbed on. David Bradley, owner of the *Atlantic*, was walking by outside and the families whose children were killed got off and went to him. He brought them together to his home while their children were in captivity and tried hard to help them privately. They were so grateful.

We returned to the hotel and I sat in the restaurant with Paula and Jordan Somers. "I don't know why we came here," said Jordan. "Nothing has changed. My brother is still dead. What was the point of this whole thing, to make us feel better? The US is responsible for the death of my brother. I feel used. This was all about making the government look better."

Paula drank her tea. "I don't know why we came either. I still feel that if the government hadn't acted that Luke would be alive. But now, I guess I'm glad that we did come."

The Somers seemed separate from the other families. Luke was born in England. He was killed at night by al-Qaeda and no one saw it. The Somers were like the Weinsteins. Both families felt that their loved one could have been saved. Few people remembered their deaths. There was little publicity and no one had seen them die. Luke had been in Yemen for a year and felt that he understood the culture.

I sat with Jordan the next morning in the hotel. He and his mother had a flight to Detroit and from there to Seattle. "I'm glad to leave," he said. "I hated it here. The only reason I am content at all about this trip is meeting you and Tik. Everything else sucked." Tik Root was a freelance journalist from Vermont whom I met in Yemen. He and Luke had been friends. Paula and Jordan wanted to get away and we went to a café in Washington and Tik joined us. We sat outside and Paula seemed to relax.

"It was strange being here," said Jordan. "It was so often unfulfilling meeting with other hostages and families from everywhere. It was weird. I hated having to shake hands with all these stone-faced lying government officials, and listening to Obama yesterday spew his generalized rhetoric, watching as so many of the friends and families nodded in awe at his very presence."

The next day, Paula and Jordan sat with Rachel Briggs, head of HostageUK. She would now, with the proper visa and with the help of funds from the James W. Foley Legacy Foundation, start HostageUS. Paula got a migraine on the flight home. She hadn't had one in twenty years, since her father died. She wanted to go to the hospital in Detroit but she kept going to Seattle. The White House meeting had been the opposite for her that it had been for me. There was nothing cathartic about it. It brought right back again all the pain she felt that night, six months before, when President Obama called to say that Luke had been killed. The only moment she said later that she liked, was sitting outside in the sun at the restaurant for lunch with Tik and me, talking about Luke.

I flew back to New York. I wanted to return to Yemen, to explore why Luke Somers really died, and to find more about Jalaluddin Haqqani's Yemeni family, and then to return Pakistan, to see the Haqqanis again and talk about the hostages. But it was now late June 2015 and I couldn't return to Yemen, not yet. Saudi Arabia was bombing Sana'a. My contacts in Yemen said it was too dangerous. They couldn't protect me.

On June 30, Sophie Roland-Gutterman asked me to send a company-wide e-mail to let people know that I was leaving CBS. I said good-bye to the president. "You know how these things are, Jere," he said. I did indeed. The US was pulling out of Afghanistan. The *Evening News* ended and Sophie came over and hugged me good-bye. A week later she and Ana Real, the deputy foreign editor, met me in a restaurant. We sat outside and as the evening passed I saw tears in Sophie's eyes. She asked about my trip to Washington and I told her the story. "You've come full circle," she said.

I wasn't finished. I knew what I had to do, but I couldn't tell her. We ordered dessert. "It was a budget matter," she said. "I had to do it." I felt lonely at CBS but I knew my life was changing, and I kept my distance from her now, but being with her at dinner made it hard to leave. We hugged one another and she smiled as the taxi drove away.

A week later, I met with the Fusion Cell at FBI headquarters in Washington. I talked to the Cell about my meeting with Haqqani. "Don't get ahead of yourself. We have many lines into Haqqani," said Mike McGarrity, then the director. I was put in my place: they didn't need me. He assigned a young female agent who was taking notes. She asked for my notes of my meeting with Ibrahim and for the photograph of the two of us. When I rode back that evening to New York, I decided not to give them anything. I didn't work for the government. I just couldn't give away the result of years of experience and work. I didn't trust them. The government hadn't changed. I would do this on my own.

Chapter 24

Ripple Effects

A MONTH LATER, JANE LARSON, WHOSE HUSBAND, PAUL OVERBY, had flown to Kabul in 2012 before taking a bus down to Khost along the border, hoping to interview the Haqqanis, sent me an e-mail. Jane had become close to Michael Semple, who was helping her. Semple was coming to Washington and wanted to meet David Rohde and me at Penn Station. I wrote him and said that I would meet him under the departure sign. He wrote from the plane to point out that there were two such signs. He knew Penn Station well. He picked a spot.

We greeted one another warmly and went into a restaurant and took a table near the wall. I watched two men walk in and sit at a table near us. They were from the Pakistani consulate. One was with me when I met with the consul general and the other gave me my visa.

"What are they doing here?" I asked.

He waved his hand. "They're just friends," he responded blithely.

"Where did you just come from, Pakistan?"

"No, Ireland," he said enthusiastically. "I went for a good run along the water this morning, caught my flight, and took the subway here. You can go through customs at Shannon and you don't have to here." It was strange—why didn't he fly directly to Washington? "I like to do it this way. I take the subway in from JFK and take the train down to Washington. I always fly coach class even if someone else is paying and take the subway instead of taxis. It's better to save money."

I again asked why people felt he was involved in my kidnapping. He repeated that Afghans were paranoid and made up stories. "I went back to Pakistan," I said. "I called your friend Mohmand. Thank you for introducing me. He was helpful. I saw Gohar Zaman."

Semple, sitting on my right, leaned closer, almost over me. "No, what are you doing?" His eyes were hard now. I had not seen him like this before.

"I met with Ibrahim Haqqani in March. I didn't expect this. I met him through tribal leaders in Afghanistan. He told me about his nephew Anas in prison. This is your world, not mine. I am not trying to move into your territory. You're the expert, not me. But I feel an obligation to do something. They said they trusted only me."

"They trust only you," he said softly.

"You're the expert. This is not my world," I said to Michael again. This was, I sensed, why he had come here to see me. He had sensed something, or he had learned, possibly through his many contacts, that I met with the Haqqanis. He seemed to relax when I acknowledged that it was his world, meaning the kidnapping world. I was saying that I was not trying to intrude on his territory.

"In any case," he said, "governments will take over. They will decide everything. Let's go."

We joined the two Pakistanis, and Michael switched to Urdu. I talked with the man I had tea with in January at the consulate. Semple and the other man kept talking in Urdu. "How is his Urdu?" I asked, to try to change the conversation back to English.

"Perfect," said the man with the mustache, "with no accent."

I asked Michael about his Dari. "Good," he replied. "I was on Afghan television the other day and talked for fifteen minutes in Dari."

Again, I was impressed. It was all very convivial, but I still didn't know why we were there. They went back to talking in Urdu and I talked to the other man in English. It came time to go and we walked out into the waiting area and Semple gave me a warm hug. He had a train to catch. "I have to meet people this evening and tomorrow," he said energetically. He was friendly again, the Michael I knew from before.

I wondered why he was going to Washington. He had wanted to see David Rohde and me. I felt that it had to do, probably, with the hostages. He had met with David and the families in Washington, but I had been unable to join them. I wondered how he, a foreigner, could be at the US National Counterterrorism Center. What was he doing there, and who was paying for his trips back and forth? I had been in Afghanistan and Pakistan too long, in the dark world of paranoia, and was still upset by my time in Dubai.

Nafay was visiting London. A friend loaned me his house in the country and I went there for a long weekend to work and called her from there at her hotel to tell her about my meeting with Michael. No one should trace the call from this house to a hotel. Still I wondered if someone would.

"He was introducing you to the ISI," she explained.

"I will never get another visa to Pakistan," I lamented. But I was wrong.

⁜ ⁜ ⁜

THAT FALL SHAHWALI called again. "My son has been taken prisoner by the ISI. You said that your neck is my neck and that you would take care of my children." He kept talking.

"Leave me alone," I said. "How can this be? What did you do wrong? I don't believe you. I have kept the FBI from coming back to find you. They will put you in Guantanamo, do you understand?" I paced the room in anger. He called again about his son. He wanted my help to get himself refugee status again, as he had asked me in Kabul. He tried to "friend" me on Facebook and I didn't accept it. He sent me messages and asked me to send my books to him. I found myself getting angrier at him. He tried to get me to get Fazul and Nafay involved to help his son. He started calling Fazul and Fazul sent me a note and asked me to have him stop. I told him to leave Fazul alone, and he did. He sent me a note asking for Nafay to meet him in Dubai to help him with his son. I worried that he would harass her.

⁂ ⁂ ⁂

THAT FALL I joined the board of the James W. Foley Legacy Foundation and attended a board meeting in Rochester, New Hampshire, where the Foleys lived. The foundation organized a road race and thousands came. A reporter for the Boston affiliate of ABC interviewed me. I felt relaxed and like I belonged as part of this foundation. I wanted to keep Jim's name alive as I did Daniel Pearl's, and Steven Sotloff's, and Peter Kassig's, and Kayla Mueller's.

The next morning, John Foley came to the hotel and he drove to the bus station from which I would take a bus back to New York. "We have to do something about those hostages in Pakistan," he said. "We just can't leave them there to be tortured every day." He, like Diane, knew that by helping others they were helping themselves. It was time for me to act.

I stayed in touch with the Haqqanis. I had three lines into them, but I wanted to keep them secret. I created my own simple set of code words, different for each line. I wasn't doing anything illegal and I let a contact at the NSC know what I was doing, but I didn't fully trust the government. I had assumed for years that my e-mails back and forth to Pakistan were not secure.

In November, I called Jim Coleman, Caitlan's father, and told him that I had met with the Haqqanis and that I was in contact with them and that I wanted to go back to finish my work and maybe I could find out something about his daughter. She had been a prisoner now for more than three years. There were no guarantees. I didn't know if I could get a visa for Pakistan. I called Erin Boyle, Joshua Boyle's sister, in Canada. Diane Foley, who liked advocating on behalf of hostages and monitoring in her own way the Fusion Cell and its work, was going to Washington to meet with the Fusion Cell, and to the White House, to continue this work. We talked about my plan to return to Pakistan to see the Haqqanis.

Two days later Jim Coleman called me back to tell me that someone from the State Department would be in touch with me. A few days later, a former journalist, then with the State Department and now with a think tank in Washington, contacted a producer friend of hers at *60 Minutes*, who contacted Ana Real, who said a man from the State Department wanted to talk to me. Mike McGarrity called as well, left his name, but no message. The former journalist came to New York and took me to breakfast.

"If you return to Pakistan, beware of being drawn in and double-crossed by the Pakistanis. It is impossible for a US official to meet with the Haqqanis because we have declared it a terrorist organization."

"What about the first peace talks held in July?" I asked. "Ibrahim Haqqani sat on one side of the table and Hajji Din Mohammad sat on the other. I read the *New York Times* article. I assumed that the US was part of this."

"No," she replied. "We did not have anyone in the room. There is no institutional understanding of Afghanistan or Pakistan because people change jobs every three years."

Ibrahim told me, in our interview, that no one had tried to contact them in months. The State Department official, whom I will call Harold, called. I said that I preferred to talk in person. I took the train to Washington and Harold and a female colleague of his, Anita, came to my hotel. We sat in the corner of the hotel coffee shop.

"It's been really busy," said Harold. "We had General Raheel Sharif here this week. He just left." He was the chief of staff of the Pakistani army. Harold and Anita, desperate for information, wanted to know all I knew about Haqqani. I told them some of what I knew—I was learning not to talk so much.

I told them about my meeting with Michael Semple at Penn Station. "I don't know what's going on," I said, "but I don't think I'll ever get a visa to Pakistan now."

"No," said Harold softly. "I don't see it that way. We have a hard time getting our people visas to go to Pakistan. I think the Pakistanis would like to hear from you."

I didn't understand at first, and then a light went on. He was saying that Pakistan might want me to come back. I would be used. That's how the world worked. I wasn't ready to go immediately, but I was intrigued.

Later that afternoon, an FBI agent, part of the Fusion Cell, as well as a man I didn't know, came to the hotel. We had coffee in a different part of the same café. I told them about Michael Semple, about what I felt was his effort to ruin my chances to return to Pakistan by introducing me to the ISI. He, too, thought that Pakistan would like me to apply for a visa.

I returned to New York. Laurie Caruso, I will call her, an FBI agent that McGarrity assigned to work with me, called. "Do you want to be involved or are you uncertain, or do you not want any part of this?" she asked.

I didn't trust the FBI after our meeting, and how the FBI treated the CBS team in my case didn't endear them to me, but I wanted to return to Pakistan, to see the Haqqanis, and to help the hostages. I read that Ibrahim had direct access to the head of the ISI and to the army chief of staff. If true, the Haqqanis had become not just a proxy militia, but a sophisticated part of Pakistani foreign policy. Ibrahim had told me how they began to work with the Pakistani army and how this relationship grew. This implied, maybe, that the Pakistani army had worked with the Haqqanis on the Bowe Bergdahl case. The proof of life ransom was a small fee that the Haqqanis took. It cost money to feed and guard, and protect, a hostage for five years. The Bergdahl Trade had become an instrument of a nation's foreign policy.

I would return to Pakistan and see the Haqqanis again. I told them briefly about my time at the White House and how I learned that they were holding hostages, and that it was only then that I realized why they had talked to me about Anas Haqqani and Hafiz Rashid.

"American and Taliban both care about their hostages. Both sides talked with one another," said Ibrahim. Yasini had said it was the first time that the Americans recognized the Taliban. The Haqqanis, by kidnapping, or simply taking into custody, one American soldier, had raised their own status to the point where they had negotiated equally, even if indirectly through Qatar, with the US, once their close ally, now their enemy. "We agreed on an exchange of five men from Guantanamo for the American soldier." I asked again how they captured him and if he ever tried to escape. "Mullah Sangeen captured him and gave him to Sirajuddin, who informed the Emirates of Islamic Afghanistan." It was the name of the Taliban government in exile. His nephew, Sirajuddin, was the emir.

"We wanted to exchange him for the prisoners. He was detained for four years. The leaders told Sangeen to treat him better than his own family, and he kept him in his own house. There were no guards. There were only women and children there. He escaped once, at lunchtime, and hid in a tree for three days. The Emirate of Islamic Afghanistan informed the US that he was in our custody. The people who had him took money three times for three videos."

Three times, he was saying, ransom money was paid for proof of life videos. I asked again how they captured the American soldier. "The soldiers were walking 20 meters apart in single file. They were in Paktika Province. The Taliban were waiting. He was walking in the front and they grabbed him and put a blanket over him and took him up into the mountains."

This went against everything I had read and heard. I had never discussed the moment of the kidnapping with Bob and Jani Bergdahl. Ibrahim said he wasn't there and admitted that they had used the American soldier as a political tool. It was impossible, as I sat there, for me to know the truth, but it appeared that the Haqqanis had used a kidnapping to force, for the first time, the US to negotiate directly with the Islamic Emirates of Afghanistan. Ibrahim had told me in our first meeeting about Skyping directly into the Oval Office. He described what he saw to me.

Back in New York I went for a run, as I did every day, in the park by my apartment. It was near the Hudson, which reminded me of the Columbia River. But my chest hurt, more and more now, as I ran. I rested, waited for the pain to pass, kept going, and gradually the pain went away. I was determined to tough it out. Every week I called a Dutch doctor friend I knew from Afghanistan, who lived in Brussels. He told me to stay away from American doctors. They gave too many pills and always wanted to operate. If the pain went away, I was fine. Besides, I had my cell phone with me, which I kept by a tree when I ran intervals, an older man pretending he was young. It made me happy to run.

Laurie Caruso called and was friendly and I was relaxed until her voice changed and became aggressive. "You did not want to show us the photograph or to allow us to look at your monograph," she reminded me. "Don't forget you are still a kidnap victim, and we treat this as an unfinished case."

I stopped and took a deep breath. She had just threatened me. The FBI had written me in 2013 saying that my case was closed, but it had the right to reopen it in the future. She was telling me that my case was still open or had been reopened, and that the FBI therefore had power over me. I was too afraid at that moment to question what she said.

"I will give you a copy of the photograph," I said, "but if you give this to your assets on the ground and they find Ibrahim and kill him I won't be able to live with myself."

"We are getting information from a lot of places, but you are getting a great deal," she replied.

I took the train to Washington and she and another agent were waiting in a car outside Union Station. We drove to my hotel and I checked in and met them downstairs in the restaurant, with menus in front of them. I put the photograph of Haqqani and me, in a large envelope, on the table. She opened it.

She looked at the photo. "You do blend in well."

I was upset that she had threatened me and I was nervous about giving them the photograph. I had promised Ibrahim that I wouldn't show it to anyone in Pakistan. Diane Foley called earlier and asked me to meet for lunch after which we would meet with David Bradley,[11] Gary Noesner, who was a former chief negotiator of the FBI, and others, at a meeting Diane had arranged to talk about the hostages. I no longer wanted to be around the FBI now once I had given up the photograph. I was afraid that they would take over.

That evening, "John," of all people, sent me an e-mail. He had talked with Nafay in Pakistan. I was glad to hear that she was in touch with him, but then Laurie Caruso, the FBI agent, mentioned that I was working with Nafay. Did I tell her that, or was she reading my e-mails? "Don't worry," said Laurie, "nothing will happen to Ibrahim if you are on the phone with him." She meant that the US would not use my phone call to target him with a missile. I didn't fully believe her. I was worried. I had given Ibrahim my word, the only thing I had.

That Christmas I caught a cold and it wouldn't go away. I kept running and the pain grew worse. It was hard to carry groceries home, my chest hurt so much. In February, I collapsed one night on the street near my apartment and the next day went to the hospital. I had atrial fibrillation, which I had inherited from my father. I needed heart surgery; afterward there were complications, and the recovery was slow at first. It wasn't until May that I could leave home, and my first trip out of New York was to Washington for a dinner for the Foley Foundation. Sophie Roland-Gutterman was there too.

The senior FBI official on the Fusion Cell whom I had met with in my hotel in Washington in November 2015, and a woman from the office of the Special Presidential Envoy for Hostage Affairs, a new post created with the White House new hostage policy, came over to say hello and I introduced them to Sophie, whom I had invited and who flew down after work to come to support the Foleys.

"You've been silent the past few months," said the official. I told him why and he was taken aback. "Take your time. Get well. Everything will still be there."

The official was saying that the Haqqanis were still there and so were the hostages. Susan Rice, the president's national security adviser, walked by and Sophie said hello. It was as if Sophie was my date and I was introducing her to my new world. We walked to the door to go into the dinner and I told her some of what I was involved with. I realized that I still felt closer to her than anyone. She had, after all, saved my life. She had given me a second chance.

I sat at a table in the corner. Jessica Buchanan, an aid worker who had been kidnapped and rescued in Somalia, sat across from me. Theo Padnos sat on my right. Paula Somers sat across from us. Theo and I talked about Yemen and a film that he was making in Paris about his captivity. Jessica had two children now, and her husband was next to her. Sophie chatted with Jason Rezaian, of the *Washington Post*, who was held captive in Iran for two years. His wife was held for ninety days. I went over to him, and we hugged one another. We would get together soon. Sophie told him that she had rescued me. David Rohde gave a speech and named all the former hostages who were there. "I love it when we are all together," he said.

On May 23, President Obama announced that the US killed Mullah Akhtar Muhammad Mansour, leader of the Taliban, with a drone missile in Baluchistan Province, Pakistan. The next day, "John" sent me an e-mail. "I pray for your good health. Get well soon." His cousin, Sirajuddin, was now officially military commander of the Taliban. Three weeks later John asked for my Skype address.

On June 15, for the first time, John called me. "How is your health?" he asked. "We are waiting for you to return."

I had begun a cardiac rehab program at the VA hospital. Slowly I was getting better, but I had to go slowly. A rehab program is different from training to get in shape. One day I gathered my courage and made an appointment to see a cardiologist I had known for many years.

"As you know," I said, "I've had atrial fibrillation most if not all my life." I'd been taking blood-thinning pills off and on for over twenty years.

"I know," the doctor responded. "We did a catheterization on you in 2000 and your veins were fine."

"What happened?" I asked. Why did this happen to me so much earlier than my father? He had a-fib and didn't have a bypass operation until he was eighty-four, and only then because he had a heart attack after my mother died. I told the cardiologist that I did everything I could. I started a vegetarian diet, and kept running. I had hardly any alcohol in five years. I had been in the Middle East for two years and stopped taking pills. Was that why I had to have the operation?

"No," the cardiologist said, "it had nothing to do with your a-fib." I asked about genes and she acknowledged that genes did play a role, but that was only, possibly, part of the reason. I had had this conversation with other doctors in the hospital, one of whom, from Syria, talked to me about stress. I came to the point that I had been building up to. Was it because of my kidnapping and all that had happened since then? She looked down, was quiet. She knew about the aftermath. "I'll give you some material to read on the links between heart disease and stress."

She was implying that my heart operation was probably a consequence of this. I felt so defeated at that moment. "You have no idea what the ripple effects will be," Michael Semple had said that night in Washington. I needed to lead a positive life as much as I could.

I sent an e-mail to one of the men from the Pakistani consulate who had come to see Michael at Penn Station, whom I will call Siddiqi, to see if I could get a visa. I wanted to see if what the FBI and State Department officials all said was true. Finally, after I called and sent other e-mails, Siddiqi called back and invited me to come meet with him. He asked about my life, but I was a bit more circumspect than at the consulate in 2007, and when I met with Durrani, the chargé d'affaires, at the Pakistani embassy in Kabul. We talked about his children, one working in London, the other studying at a prominent university in the US. He asked why I wanted to return to Pakistan.

I had made promises to myself in captivity, one of which was that I would always tell the truth, but I didn't dare say that I wanted to return to see the Haqqanis, that I had a book to finish, and that I wanted to help the hostages. I felt that he knew, though I wasn't certain, why I wanted to return and why I was willing to do so. I decided to say that I wanted to see Nafay. I had known her and her family for years. It was true but incomplete.

He asked me to fill out an application and to get an invitation from a friend, meaning Nafay. He didn't want me to stay in a hotel where people would see me, or to do any "professional work" that would raise suspicions. He talked about a multiple-entry visa so that I could go back and forth from Dubai. I agreed and felt that he was planning my trip. I felt further that we were talking past one another, playing a game that I didn't know how to play. I had read the transcript of Robert Gates's June 2011 deposition to the Senate Appropriations Committee, in response to a question about Pakistan, that "most governments lie to one another. That's how business gets done."[12] I couldn't break my promise to myself. I couldn't lie. It worked for other people, but not for me. I asked Siddiqi if he had a visa application. He told me to find it online, download it, and fill it out. He was clearly, at least to me, not a visa officer.

In November, I needed another operation, to repair a problem that had developed since my first one, but soon I was running again, if slowly. In mid-December I was finally ready to go back to the Pakistani consulate. I filled out the application, called Siddiqi, and went to see him. He took me to meet another diplomat and Siddiqi spoke to him intensely in Urdu. He said that they would try to work something out. I left my passport with them.

On December 19, 2016, the Haqqanis, or someone acting on their behalf, posted the video online of Joshua Boyle pleading for help with Caitlan Coleman, shrouded in an Arab-style abaya, and their two towhaired boys, born in captivity. The video was a message I felt to the Haqqanis' Arab backers, particularly in Saudi Arabia, America's and Pakistan's closest Arab ally. The Haqqanis were trying to put pressure on the US and Canada to act soon, but I didn't feel that the Haqqanis would kill them. Ibrahim didn't seem to be at war with the West, only with foreign, infidel armies in Afghanistan. He told me that they would welcome Americans in the future as visitors, but first they wanted the US military and its allies to leave, just as they had wanted the Soviet Red Army to leave a quarter century earlier. Only then could they establish Sharia.

On December 26, Michael Semple called. Siddiqi had called him. He talked about my visa. "He likes you, he is trying to help you, but he doesn't know what you want. If you are going for love"—and by this he meant if I was going to see Nafay—"then that's easy; that's a tourist visa. But if it's something else, then you must tell him." I fidgeted in my seat. Michael knew what I was doing. Siddiqi called him, I felt, to have me come clean with him. But we all knew what I was trying to do. Why did it need to be said aloud? Nobody else was declaring the totality of their intentions, after all.

"Are you still in touch with Ibrahim's son? He speaks English and is a teenager, right?"

I wouldn't lie to him. I didn't know that John was only a teenager; I thought he was in his early twenties.

"They wanted me to come back. He contacted me up until late June. He was very aggressive on the phone, anxious to talk about my return, but I couldn't return yet. Then they went to ground."

He asked me when I had last had contact with him. I said I wasn't sure, but John had recently, after months of silence, contacted me again.

"I think that Ibrahim has been arrested. That's why they posted the video of the Colemans online." It was a threat, Michael felt.

I took this in. I remembered the video of Caitlan Coleman and Joshua Boyle and their two boys playing with one another. "Are you sure about Ibrahim?" If he had been arrested by the Pakistanis I couldn't dare return. It would be a trap. Semple said that he believed so. It was hard to believe that the ISI, after all these years, would do this to the Haqqanis, but it was possible, I supposed, that Pakistan would give them up. A part of me believed that the Pakistanis must have given up bin Laden for the SEALs to be able to find him in Abbottabad. Carlotta Gall wrote that on the night of May 2, 2012, the police had received calls of explosions and shootings, but that army commanders told the police to stand down and let the army deal with this, but army and intelligence officials arrived too late. If the police had acted on the calls they would have arrived when the SEALs were there.

Hekmatyar, whom I had known from the 1980s, the most vicious of all mujahideen leaders and who had fought the US for years after 9/11, had just cut a deal with the Afghan government to come in from the cold and was now welcomed back by the Ghani government to Afghanistan.

"They're desperate," Semple continued. "I think you're being lured into a trap. 'Jere's a nice guy and all,' but they need all the American hostages they can get. They could set up an interview in a guesthouse like before, but change it at the last minute and suggest another spot." I felt cold. "You don't want to go through that again."

"No, I don't," I said softly. I had read that the Taliban had taken an American professor and an Australian professor hostage in August 2016 in their attack on the American University in Kabul.[13] I knew without proof that they would be with the Haqqanis. I wondered what to make of what Semple was telling me; perhaps he was trying to keep me away so that he could get involved in any kidnapping negotiations.

A few months before, I had written to Jefferson Dubel. Mike Mc-Garrity had left and Dubel was the interim head of the Fusion Cell. I told him that I was planning to return to Pakistan, but his response was different this time. "I will meet with you," he said, "but we don't want you to muddy the waters."

"If you could send me the date of his last e-mail then I'll be able to know with more certainty if he's been arrested," Michael Semple said. I didn't understand what difference a date would make. He would use this information for something else, but I didn't know what that was.

I didn't want to do it, but a big part of me still felt that I owed him my life, and I needed him now, because without his approval I felt that Siddiqi would not help me. I found the e-mail message and sent it, but not the address, to Semple. I sent another e-mail to Ibrahim's son. I knew that they were being read, but, again, I had nothing to hide. I asked if anything had changed and how he was doing.

He responded the next day.

> Hi dear friend.
>
> I'm sorry for not responding to your previous emails because I was out of station. Hope you are doing well and had a happy Christmas.
>
> Everything is clear and good here, you may come at any time.
> Warm regards,
> John

I liked John, but I didn't trust this e-mail. It was different from his other ones, the English better, more precise, and, therefore, threatening. I felt scared. I didn't know what was going to happen, but this was not going to be easy: a hostage negotiation among Afghanistan, Pakistan, the United States, Canada, and Australia? It would involve the Haqqanis, the Pakistani army, the civilian government, the Afghan government, and therefore the NDS, Afghan intelligence, like the ISI, operating on both sides of the border. Other Taliban groups, not all of whom were pro-Pakistan, might want to try to steal the hostages, who are commodities, after all, to be bought, sold, and traded. Even ISIS, which is in

Afghanistan and Pakistan now, could try to steal the hostages. There was also tribal politics along the border. The Haqqanis had enemies there, tribal aristocrats who were jealous that the Haqqanis had risen above them. That anyone could write an e-mail in which he claimed, "Everything is clear and good here" was hard to believe. Nafay had said, in a phone call, that it was much different now from two years before, meaning more dangerous. On the surface, nothing was happening: the hostages were languishing, and the Haqqanis were waiting for me. "We trust only you," Ibrahim had said to my face.

I knew that I was, publicly, a kidnap victim and would always be seen that way—"Afghanistan, 2008," as I came to call myself in Washington that week in June 2015, as though that was the year I graduated from an elite college. The nature of the Trade, I have learned, is that there are many people involved, subcontractors who are mostly, but not always, proxies for greater powers, and that everyone wanted to be paid. The Pearl Project identified twenty-seven people whom it said were involved with Daniel Pearl's kidnapping and murder. I had close to that number and maybe many more involved in mine.

Mirwais Yasini, whom I was told had links to the ISI, introduced me to Mullah Malang, who, Din Mohammad said, worked for everyone, meaning the CIA and the ISI, and, as two sources would tell me later, Iran. Malang introduced me to Abdullah, who was at war with Din Mohammad, my oldest friend in Afghanistan, whom two Afghans at CBS thought I was naïve to trust. Somehow involved were Professor Rahim, the former minister of education and Rosanne Klass's friend, who had close ties to Pakistan, and Sameer, the prostitute whom Bob, the FBI agent, felt was key to my kidnapping, and who introduced me to Shahwali.

Amrullah Saleh, the former head of Afghan intelligence, said I was taken by my friends—meaning people I thought were on my side. Saleh said that Semple was connected to MI6 and the ISI. Din Mohammad said that Malang and Semple were friends, and Thomas Ruttig confirmed this. But others said Ruttig was a former Stasi agent, which meant that he might work now for the BND, German intelligence. But others, it appeared, including CBS personnel, were implying, if not saying outright, that he was with the CIA. I finally called Ruttig in Berlin and asked him. "I am the cofounder and codirector of the Afghanistan Analysts Network," he stated. "As for the other, the country I come from has not existed for twenty years." By that he meant that East Germany no longer existed. I asked again about the 2004 UN kidnapping case he had worked on with Semple. "I had been with the UN in Afghanistan and later the EU and had just started with the German embassy. I asked for leave to work on the UN kidnapping and the embassy granted it to me." He never heard of a ransom payment and felt that something political between Saleh and Semple might have become personal, as he put it. "There were hints that pointed out that the kidnappers were from the north," he added. Saleh was from the north. I wondered if Saleh in some way wasn't protecting them and shifting the blame elsewhere.

I called Semple, now a visiting professor at Queens College, Belfast, and told him what Saleh, and Din Mohammad, who was the governor of Kabul then, had said about him, and Mullah Malang, and about my conversation with Ruttig. I wanted to know more about the UN kidnapping. Semple began: "I was seconded from the EU mission in Afghanistan, where I was the deputy director, back to the UN to work on this case. I had been working on kidnapping cases since the 1990s. There is a bond of comradeship that develops when you work on a kidnapping, but at the same time there are lots of organizations and institutions and egos operating in a very opaque world. You should not be surprised that there are a lot of different views on what happened." I told him that Shahmamood Meikel, the former deputy interior minister, had said that he himself was the point man on the case, and Semple laughed heartily, his energy manifesting itself on the phone. I said that many people felt I worked for intelligence agencies, which I, like other journalists, had been accused of for decades—my way of introducing this delicate subject. "I know you may not be able to talk freely about this," I said. "There are only certain parameters in which I can talk," he responded.

I said that Ruttig recalled that the kidnappers were, it appeared, linked to the north, meaning Saleh's territory.

"Thomas is spot on to say that the kidnappers were from the north," he replied quickly, "but more precisely, it was the north Kabul kidnapping industry network, overlapping with the criminal and jihadi network based in the Shomali Plains, which extends up to Kapisa, linked to the Quetta Taliban." Of these three "sets," as he called them, of kidnappers—one was from the northern part of Kabul, the Afghan capital; the second from the Shomali Plains, Tajik country, a high, flat, empty land where the Taliban poisoned the water, which extended fifty miles to the north; and the third extended from Kapisa province, to the northeast, down to Quetta, which was home of the Quetta shura, the 20-member Taliban leadership council, in Pakistan. This three-part kidnapping network was more like ruthless mafia clans or drug networks in the West. Semple was describing a criminal Taliban kidnapping industry, not unlike, it seemed, the drug trafficking world of Hajji and Qorie (the drug dealer and the Taliban commander who both used religious titles to give them a veneer of respectability), in which farmers linked with traffickers, linked with the Taliban, linked with prominent political figures, all capitalized on the destruction of Afghanistan and the chaos of nearly forty years of war, to make money. "On this case, I had specific dealings with individuals in the Quetta Taliban," Semple exclaimed, showing his sophisticated knowledge of the network. His story was almost completely different from Shahmahmood Meikel's story. It was as if they had worked in separate universes.

He wanted to talk about Mullah Malang. "In the course of the UN kidnapping quite a few prominent individuals came forward offering their assistance. On the basis of thirty years of war, and now kidnappings, there has risen up a whole colony in Afghanistan of hostage brokers. They present themselves as those who can help. They are saviors. Their pitch to hostage takers is that they can make a deal and in exchange will take a cut. It presents a fascinating contrast to the interplay of the political economy of the Anglo-Saxon-led world. In the Anglo-Saxon-led world, they have been trying to criminalize any form of dealings in a hostage situation. The West criminalizes the kind of contact that is valuable and essential. In the Western counter-terrorism world, and thousands of pages have been written about this by people who know little if anything of Afghanistan, men have been criminalized because of how the counter-terrorism regimes in the West cast their wide nets. Whereas in Afghanistan there are a whole lot of people trying to trade on their links. Some of them feel they can help while benefitting materially."

"It is the white man's colonization, over and over again," said Nafay, when I mentioned this to her. It was the West, in its wealth, and its cultural and military power, imposing itself upon the East. I thought of this later as I sat at the hotel dining room in Pakistan, where I was staying as I wrote up my notes. It was a Sunday afternoon, part of the weekend here, as it is in the West, and a pianist played "Happy Birthday," an American song, on his western instrument. I suddenly understood Semple better, a Westerner who had met a pretty Pakistani girl studying in the West while in college in Ireland, had fallen in love with her, converted to Islam, and married her. He was a man between two worlds, East and West, just as I, an American born into a separatist religious community, was part of America yet separate from the secular world all around us. "I always prefer to get a haircut in Pakistan," Semple once said to me. "I don't know why." I felt I knew why. I got haircuts everywhere, but I preferred getting them at home, in America.

"That is the big picture. In the course of this kidnapping, a lot of prominent Afghans popped up offering personally to help. I do not put Mullah Malang in this category. He was only there because I asked him to be there. He was a full-fledged member of the UN team. He worked hard, stayed late, if he even left at all many nights. Anyone who impugns his motives doesn't know what they are talking about and should be challenged to a duel." Semple stopped, caught his breath. "I mean that metaphorically."

"He entered this case honorably and can take credit for the safe return of the hostages."

Why then, I asked, would a former head of Afghan intelligence, a man close to the US, profiled on *60 Minutes*, treated with respect in Washington, talk this way? And why would Din Mohammad, a man we both knew well, from a different ethnic group than Saleh, not in contact with him but also a powerful man in Afghanistan, say the same thing?

Semple paused. "I can only say that I consider Din Mohammad and Saleh close friends, and that I love them both and intend to keep their friendship. However, it is the nature of Afghanistan that people can give strikingly different accounts of the same event from different perspectives. God is a better judge of why they do so."

I said I was trying to reach Jean Arnault, the French diplomat, head of the UN mission in Afghanistan in 2004 and one of the principals in the case. If there was any kind of ransom, he would have authorized it. Again, I asked Michael about the ransom. "My understanding of the relationship among everyone is that everything was tightly coordinated. A small amount of money was authorized, I wouldn't even call it a ransom, to help us."

This would comport with what Shahmahmood had said: that the interior ministry authorized a payment of $5,000 for proof of life, the only amount it paid. But why, I wondered, again, would Saleh say that the NDS, of which he was the head, gave Malang $5 million and that it disappeared, and why would Din Mohammad, one of the most prominent men in Afghanistan, say that €15 million disappeared? I couldn't grasp this.

"Anyone who says otherwise is doing a disservice to those who worked hard to resolve this case," Michael continued. "I acknowledge that people have different recollections of different events, and of course the event was traumatic for the hostages. In hindsight, we can say that this was one which turned out well. I don't see why there should be any recriminations."

I said that Shahmahmood Meikel had written a book about the kidnapping. "Go see [Mohammad] Akbar Agha, the Taliban commander who kidnapped the three UN employees. He wrote a book about it also. He has been rehabilitated and lives in Kabul now." Everyone had his own story to tell. I was trying to tell mine.

I was still unsure about Mullah Malang. Din Mohammad and Amrullah Saleh both said that what I was doing was dangerous and warned me. Daud Sultanzoy said "I don't think that Din Mohammad would hurt you directly." Din Mohammad? My oldest friend, who just said to me at lunch in the hotel that we were fellow mujahids in the great war against the Soviet Union. Did I have no friends here? No, I didn't believe that.

Din Mohammad wanted to accompany me if I went to see Malang. I was part of a large conspiracy here, both Din Mohammad and Yasini had said, a white man, an infidel, a Westerner, a pawn, caught in a murky byzantine struggle, lost in a labyrinth beyond my ability to navigate.

"I consider Mullah Malang an honorable person," said Semple. "That is why I gave such a robust defense of him. With your case, it was different." I pondered this statement. I asked if they were still friends. "Of course, we are friends. I have tremendous respect and love for him."

"Why did you invite those two men from the Pakistani consulate to Penn Station? You said it was because they were your friends. Is that right?"

"That's right. They're my friends."

I returned one more time to Kabul. I tried to reach Amrullah Saleh, but he had joined the new government, against which he had railed in 2014, when, sitting in his home, he had vowed emotionally to fight to the death for his side, the remnants of the Northern Alliance and its leader Abdullah Abdullah, who he said were cheated in the last election. He was again back in the highest reaches of the NDS, in the dark, seductive world of intelligence.

I was having dinner at Fazul's house, and told another Panjshari, who had been my first fixer, in December 2001, and who now lived in a small town in Canada, that I had been trying to reach Saleh. "I reached Saleh on Facebook. He is very active on social media." He advised me to send him a message. I did this. Saleh had told me to contact him when I returned and that we would work on my case together. I said now that I wanted to see him again to show him what I had written to be sure that it was accurate. He responded the next day and said "sure," he would try to find time for us to meet. I waited for a week. I sent him other notes, asking to see him, but he didn't respond.

Arifullah Pashtoon, who had introduced me to Ibrahim Haqqani, invited me to his home for dinner. "It is like bread and salt. When you have someone to your home, you become like brothers." I talked with his father, chief of the 250,000-strong Saberi tribe, about Jalaluddin Haqqani and his ties to Pakistan. Three days later, Arifullah, who wanted to take part in the negoitations with the Haqqanis as a way to ingratiate himself with the US, came to see me at my hotel. No matter how many times I told him I was a journalist, on my own, he didn't believe me. He told me that he had gone to the home of the governor of Kunar Province. "Feridoun Mohammad was there. He said, 'I want to see Mr. Jere. He is a very strong CIA agent.'"

I shook my head. Arifullah must have told him that I was here. "You must never say that," I told Pashtoon. "I am a journalist." It didn't matter what I said. I had already gone to the CIA on his behalf in 2015 in Dubai. He wanted to use me to help his star rise higher. I told him that I wanted to see Feridoun, I wanted to ask him what happened to the money. Arifullah said he did not have a phone number for him. The next night, Fazul came over to the hotel to go through the chapter I had written about him to correct the mistakes I had made in the timeline. I told him I wanted to see Feridoun. "I haven't talked to him in two years," he replied. He called him while I waited. "He is in Jalalabad, and busy with some tribal affair," he said closing his phone. Feridoun, like Saleh, didn't want to see me.

I saw Pashtoon again and told him that neither Saleh nor Feridoun appeared to want to talk to me.

"It is because they do not have eyes to see you," he replied, casting his eyes down.

He was saying that neither man could look me in the eye.

Gulob, my jailer, said that the political agent had come to see him. The police in London said that the political agent for each tribal agency knew everything. Daoud Sultanzoy, a tribal chief and friend, said that Yasini was ISI, and Yasini along with other MPs I talked to, said that Feridoun was ISI as his father had been before him. It was Gohar Zaman, a former head of intelligence with friends at MI6, who left the country and flew to Dubai to have open-heart surgery, and from the hospital ordered his brother-in-law to send the ransom to Feridoun, by-passing Abdullah and his gang completely, in Kabul.

I was not kidnapped by the Taliban. I was kidnapped by ghosts. Ahmed Shah, a CBS employee, was right to say that I could not have been kidnapped without the sanction of the ISI.

Around and around I went in a widening gyre. The truth? I didn't know what truth was. It was impossible to find.

I felt that I was standing in a large cold room with thick, translucent green walls surrounded by a dark circle of people who were walking around me all shouting in loud, aggressive, strident voices. I didn't trust any of them. They were all yelling their own version of the truth. In the Trade, there is no single truth, only lies, stories, hunches, dark alleys, and cul-de-sacs, where everyone lusts for money, hiding behind the thin veneer of religion or politics. It is not just a simple transaction of money for human beings, where the collateral is not a house or a car, but another human being. The Trade is the new cold, cruel weapon of modern warfare, like drones with no visible pilot, a barter process without official structures, a new criminal enterprise, a form of terror open to anyone. The business territory could be the borderland of a failed state, a desert, a back ally, a basement, an apartment in a large city, a cell in the mountains, or a room with a sandy floor in a hot, windy village. At the beginning, it is a crime, and then the cell in time becomes a home without comfort or rules and for some a torture chamber, for every hostage a place of constant fear. The Trade is a weapon for the poor and the weak, like suicide bombing, against the strong. It exists from the Philippines to the Sahara, and it is growing, part of the kidnap and ransom business. It coarsens everyone.

The Haqqanis said that they would find out who kidnapped me. They were waiting for me to return. I kept thinking of that cell up in the mountains, and of the other newer hostages sitting somewhere all day, every day, in darkness. I wanted to try to help them. I wanted the light still, and I still wanted redemption. I couldn't help Daniel Pearl, or Jim Foley or Steven Sotloff or Peter Kassig or Nicholas Berg or Kayla Mueller or Luke Somers. I could help their families by keeping their names alive, and I could help all of us by helping these other hostages. I understood the Trade now. It had become a part of my life.

A few days before I returned to Kabul I got a message from Shahwali asking about my health. I said I was fine and asked where he was. He was in Kabul. I asked where. He was staying with his uncle. Here was my opportunity to finally see him and forgive him.

But I was afraid of him. I waited until just before I was ready to leave. I told him to go the next day, Friday, the Muslim Sabbath, after he went to the mosque, to the lobby of the Serena Hotel at 2:30. I would see him there. It would be the first time in nine years. I was nervous, scared even, but I had to forgive him. I had to put this behind me and go on.

He gave me his phone number and told me to call him. I couldn't do that. If he got my number he would start calling me, harrassing me, maybe even tracing my call.

Shahwali asked again for my phone number and demanded that I call him. I said I would be waiting for him at the hotel. He put the thumbs up symbol on his message board. He was coming. At 2:15, I went downstairs and waited. The lobby was empty except for the security gunmen and three clerks behind the reception desk, and a Pashtoon doormen in a long robe and turban. I waited. I looked at the machine-made carpets on the floor, listened to the bland, monotonous recorded music, the same music that played day after day, washing over us, drowning us in modern boredom. Gone was the romance of old Afghanistan. Now, it was a sinister world of money and kidnappings and murder.

My phone rang. It was Fazul. "Jere, Shahwali called me. He said you had contacted him." I didn't like that he had called Fazul. "I didn't want to draw you into this," I said. "I want to forgive him. That's all. I am doing it for my health." I was doing it for my heart. I was afraid that if I kept worrying it would kill me. I survived the kidnapping but I didn't want Shahwali to get me in the end. I hated him. I felt, in my paranoia, that there was a link between Fazul and Shahwali.

"I don't know if it's a good idea to see him. He will just make you angry." I understood, but I had to do it. "He can't do anything to you in there," he added. I felt warm toward Fazul. He was protecting me again. He would to the end. I would call him that night.

An hour passed. I kept waiting. I went up a hallway to the café and stood there watching the entranceway from the side, from where I could see him before he could see me. I waited another hour, walking to the front entrance every time someone came who might be him. After two hours, I went upstairs. There was a note from Shahwali telling me to call him. I sent him a note. "I waited two hours for you." I wouldn't give him my phone number. He had already called me over a hundred times on my number in America. He said that in the future I must give him my number for security purposes. He was playing with me. Din Mohammad was right. I should let it go. It was too dangerous. Michael Semple was right. I couldn't imagine where the ripple effects would take me.

I returned to Pakistan. I talked to John on the phone. He sounded different, older, his voice deeper, more assured. I wasn't sure it was John. Nafay talked to him. "I don't believe it's John,' she said. "I am 100 percent certain it's someone else." I wasn't sure but felt that it was him. We talked some more and she made a reservation in another guest house, but she refused to go. I would go alone. Mugaddir drove Nafay and me toward the guesthouse. We stopped in front of a small shopping mall where Nafay got out. She knew where I would be. I sat alone in the backseat. We entered another courtyard and walked inside. A man in western clothes came out from behind the counter shook my hand warmly, holding my wrist. I saw a man with short hair and a moustache, in shalwar keemez, the ISI uniform, holding a cup of tea, looking down. I would be safe. A short time later, a small sedan entered the courtyard and Ibrahim Haqqani and John, smiling warmly, got out and we walked to the room.

"I talked with Din Mohammad twice," said Ibrahim. "I'm sorry, but I didn't bring up your kidnapping. If you give me the dates, I will find out who kidnapped you."

I thought that he and Din Mohammad were enemies. He refused to look at the picture of him before. Now they were talking with one another? Twice, he had seen him. I was an outsider here. I knew nothing at all.

"Don't worry," said Ibrahim, sensing that I was nervous. "If you have no other friends in the world, you can come to us. We are your friends. You were with us during Jihad. We will never forget this."

Notes

PART ONE

1. "Treaties, Engagements and Sanads relating to the Northwest Frontier Province," Area Study Center, University of Peshawar, Peshawar, Pakistan, n.d., fata.gov.pk/global.php?ild=2&pid=28&mid=13.

2. The Islamic Party.

3. Harry Burton, an Australian television cameraman with Reuters; Azizullah Haidari, an Afghan-born photographer; Julio Fuentes of Spain's *El Mundo*; and Maria Grazia Cutuli, of Italy's *Corriere della Sera*.

4. See http://www.nytimes.com/1993/07/24/world/us-increases-fund-to-outbid-terrorists-for-afghan-missiles.html.

5. See http://www.nytimes.com/2001/09/26/news/26iht-stinger_ed3_.html.

6. Peter Tomsen, *The Wars of Afghanistan* (New York, NY: PublicAffairs, 2011), 124–26.

7. Anatol Levin, *Pakistan: A Hard Country* (New York, NY: PublicAffairs, 2011), 230; Peter Tomsen, *Wars of Afghanistan*, 335, 606–7, 666.

8. This work is done by the Halo Trust. See https://www.halotrust.org/where-we-work/central-asia/afghanistan/.

9. The Uzbek city in northeast Afghanistan, in Balkh Province, where Jalaluddin Rumi, the poet, was born.

10. *Daily Telegraph* (UK), January 14, 1985.

11. Mohammad Yousaf and Mark Adkin, *Afghanistan: The Bear Trap* (Havertown, PA: Casemate, 2001), 62–63.

12. *The 9/11 Commission Report*, https://www.9-11commission.gov/report /911Report.pdf. See also Peter Tomsen, *The Wars of Afghanistan*.

13. Declan Walsh, Duncan Campbell, and Ewen MacAskill, "Three UN Workers Seized by Militants in Kabul," *The Guardian*, October 29, 2004, https:// www.theguardian.com/world/2004/oct/29/afghanistan.declanwalsh.

14. Robert Gates, *From the Shadows: The Ultimate Insider's Story of Five Presidents and How They Won the Cold War* (New York, NY: Simon and Schuster, 1996); see Brzezinski interview in *Le Nouvel Observateur*, January 1998.

15. "2 Years after Soldier's Death, Family's Battle Is with the Army," *New York Times*, March 21, 2006.

16. See http://www.nytimes.com/2007/09/05/world/asia/05iht-hostage .1.7389052.html.

17. The terms of the Mastrogiacomo release are secret, but for the Koreans, both sides admitted that a ransom was paid, the first known time that a government negotiated directly with the Taliban. See http://www.reuters.com/article/us -afghan-koreans-ransom-idUSCOL31793120070902; https://www.stratfor.com /afghanistan_latest_kidnapping_precedent; and http://www.nytimes.com/2007 /08/30/world/asia/30cnd-afghan.html?_r=0.

18. In 2014, *Profil*, an Austrian weekly news magazine, reported that Khalilzad's wife, Cheryl Bernard, who was from Vienna, was under investigation by the US Department of Justice for money laundering; see http://www.bbc.com/news /world-us-canada-29107927. Khalilzad and his wife vigorously denied the charges and called it a "gross violation of privacy"; nothing was ever proven; see http://www .theeventchronicle.com/news/north-america/former-us-ambassador-un -suspected-money-laundering/#https://www.nytimes.com/2014/09/09/world /zalmay-khalilzad-tax-evasion-investigation.html?_r=0.

19. Torkham, an ancient pass used by invaders to India, is the main border crossing east of Jalalabad on the old Grand Trunk Road between Afghanistan and Pakistan.

20. *Malik*, in Arabic, means lord, ruler, or the possessor. It is one of the 99 attributes or names of God in Islam. In Afghanistan and in the Pashtun areas in Pakistan along the Afghan border it means mostly a tribal leader. See Thomas Patrick Hughes, *The Dictionary of Islam* (Calcutta, India: Rupa & Co., 1885).

21. Although Mountstuart Elphinstone, at 29, led the first British expedition across the Indus River and into the land of the Pashtuns, he never went beyond

Peshawar, relying upon locals to provide information for his book, *An Account of the Kingdom of Caboul*. See http://www.iranicaonline.org/articles/Elphinstone.

22. See http://www.nytimes.com/2001/11/05/us/nation-challenged-resistance-leader-son-executed-afghan-rebel-leads-mourners.html?ref=topics.

23. Peter Tomsen, *The Wars of Afghanistan*, 602.

24. Ibid, 600–4.

25. Interview with US Army captain Jason Amerine, *Frontline*, PBS, http://www.pbs.org/wgbh/pages/frontline/shows/campaign/interviews/amerine.html.

26. Today, Din Mohammad, close to President Ashraf Ghani, is chief negotiator for Afghanistan with the Taliban.

27. Group for Preaching, or Society for Spreading the Faith, founded in 1927 in India. A worldwide revivalist movement considered apolitical and nonviolent, it's also seen as linked to terrorism. Gulob, my jailer, said that his father had been a Tablighi in Canada, and would be very angry at what he was doing with me.

28. The Durand Line, drawn by the British and a weakened Afghan government in 1893, is not a border, and has never been demarcated. No Afghan government has ever accepted the Durand Line as the border, first between British India or now Pakistan. The Durand Line divides the Pashtun nation between Afghanistan and Pakistan. See http://durandline.info/a-study-of-the-durand-line/chapter-1-the-birth-of-a-troubled-frontier/1-1-an-adventurous-forward-policy/.

29. *Talib* means "one who seeks;" generally a divinity student; the plural is *Taliban*.

30. Guesthouse, or guest room. Every Pashtun village, or every man of means, has a hujra.

31. As recently as 2001, the army was 71 percent Punjabi, but efforts are being made to bring in more ethnic groups; see https://www.dawn.com/news/266159/Punjab.

32. Hawala is an ancient form of Western Union, a money transfer system in which money doesn't move. Hawala originated in South Asia, and today is worldwide. A man, in, say, Peshawar with $5,000 takes the money to a hawala dealer there and gives him a password; the dealer calls another hawala dealer in Kabul, tells him the amount of money to be released, and gives him the password; the intended receiver in Kabul goes to the dealer, gives him the password, and the dealer gives him the money, minus a commission.

PART TWO

1. Sherard Cowper-Coles, *Cables from Kabuo: the Inside Story of the West's Afghanistan Campaign* (London: Harper Press, 2011), 58.

2. Carlotta Gall, *Wrong Country, Wrong Enemy* (New York, NY: Houghton Mifflin Harcourt, 2014), 218.

3. See http://www.cbsnews.com/news/ethical-dilemmas-surround-those -willing-to-sell-buy-kidneys-on-black-market/; and http://www.cbc.ca/news/ world/child-organ-trafficking-ring-busted-by-mexican-police-1.2576492.

4. "My ransom money was well spent," said Langan. See http://www.bbc.com /news/uk-30440742.

5. After being kidnapped, David Rohde and Tahir Luddin were taken at night across the border into the Tribal Areas, where they were kept by the Haqqani Network for seven months until their dramatic escape. David Rohde and Kristen Mulvihill, *A Rope and A Prayer* (New York, NY: Viking, 2010).

6. See https://www.thenation.com/article/after-david-rohdes-escape-taliban -feud/.

7. The whole story on Bergdahl's capture has yet to come out. According to the Haqqanis, he was captured by men loyal to Mullah Sangeen, a Haqqani commander, then brought from Paktika Province to Waziristan in the Tribal Areas. From there he escaped, at least once, was recaptured, and finally was exchanged for five men from Guantanamo. See http://www.foxnews.com/politics/2015/06 /15/former-cia-operative-bergdahl-was-high-when-captured-in-afghanistan .html.

8. Survival, Evasion, Resistance, and Escape, required also by the US military and by media organizations.

9. A novel by Richard Condon, published in 1959, about a son of a famous politician who is brainwashed to become a communist assassin. It was made into a movie in 1962 and remade in 2004.

10. Gracia Burnham, *In the Presence of My Enemies* (Carol Stream, IL: Tyndale House Publishers, 2002), 230.

11. Alan Moorehead, *The White Nile* (New York, NY: Perennial, 2000).

12. Anand Gopal, *No Good Men among the Living: America, the Taliban, and the War through Afghan Eyes* (New York, NY: Henry Holt and Company, 2014, Kindle edition), 148. The author claims to have met with Zaman at a hotel in Kabul where he told him—sitting by a swimming pool, drinking whiskey, with a rifle by his side—how he bilked the Americans out of millions and worked with the ISI to lead al-Qaeda down from Tora Bora to the Tribal Areas of Pakistan.

13. Ibid., 113. Gopal writes that the US supported and even paid Sherzai while in Kandahar; he was even then considered to be a notorious drug lord.

14. According to Amrullah Saleh, head of the NDS, three gunmen, at least two of whom wore suicide vests and Afghan police uniforms, attacked the hotel, considered the most secure in Kabul. The attack killed six people, including a

Norwegian reporter. The attack was traced back to the Haqqani Network. See http://www.longwarjournal.org/archives/2008/01/haqqani_network_behi.php.

15. The Trade is a growing international criminal enterprise, a new form of warfare, and it has spawned a new, unusual market—that of ransom insurance. In order to bring order to the Trade, a group of special risk insurers at Lloyd's of London cooperate to make this business insurable. See http://onlinelibrary.wiley.com /wol1/doi/10.1111/gove.12255/full.

16. William Jefferson Hague was Secretary of State for Foreign Affairs from 2010–2014.

17. Jaish-e-Muslimeen, said to be a Taliban splinter group also linked to al-Qaeda; Afghan interior minister Ahmed Ali Jalal, said that "no prisoners were released, no ransom money was paid, no demands were met." There was no mention of payment by the UN. See http://news.bbc.co.uk/2/hi/south_asia /3962707.stm; and http://www.nytimes.com/2004/11/24/washington/world /3-kidnapped-un-workers-are-released-in-kabul.html.

18. See http://www.foxnews.com/story/2004/11/23/un-hostages-released -in-afghanistan.html.

19. See http://news.bbc.co.uk/2/hi/south_asia/4045889.stm.

20. According to the *New York Times*, one of the hostages, from Kosovo, was released because of a personal appeal by Kosovo businessman Behgjet Pacoili. See http://www.nytimes.com/2004/11/24/washington/world/3-kidnapped-un -workers-are-released-in-kabul.html.

21. The rest were aid workers, contractors, construction workers, engineers, UN employees, NGO workers, teachers, and tourists; some have been killed, some ransomed, some released. See https://en.wikipedia.org/wiki/Foreign _hostages_in_Afghanistan.

22. See http://tribune.com.pk/story/320238/poland-opens-taliban-trial-over -engineers-beheading/.

23. See http://www.news18.com/news/india/polish-engineer-killed-in-pak -for-refusing-to-convert-319422.html.

24. See http://www.longwarjournal.org/archives/2009/02/taliban_feud _over_mu.php.

25. Hezb-i-Islami Khalis (the Khalis Islamic Party).

26. Peter Tomsen, *The Wars of Afghanistan* (New York, NY: PublicAffairs, 2011), 610.

27. As the Taliban surrounded Abdul Haq and his party, a call was made to Robert McFarland, Ronald Reagan's national security adviser, who called the CIA; according to McFarland, the CIA made no real effort to save Haq. McFarland blamed the CIA for its subservience to the ISI. *Wall Street Journal*, November 2, 2001.

28. US Special Envoy to the Afghan Resistance, 1989–1992.

PART THREE

1. These companies, and even nongovernmental organizations and major US universities, any institution that has a significant overseas presence, have strategic risk management plans today, which go into effect when an employee is kidnapped. See http://www.readcube.com/articles/10.1111/gove.12255.

2. A forested, mountainous province in northeastern Afghanistan, above Kunar. Its inhabitants, often said, or rumored, to be the descendants of the soldiers of Alexander the Great, did not convert to Islam until 1895.

3. Daesh stands for al-Dawla al-Islamiya fil Iraq wa'al Sham, or, the Islamic State in Iraq and Shams. *Shams* means sun, which rises in the East, in Syria, east of the Mediterranean. The plural is daw-ish, which means "bigots who force their beliefs upon others."

4. Islamic Movement of Afghanistan.

5. An article in the September 27 *Daily Telegraph* reported that the Kabul diplomatic community felt that one way to reduce Taliban potency was by splitting off less ideologically driven elements, meaning to divide and conquer the Taliban. Britain's Special Intelligence Service (MI6) felt that a major tribal revolt against the Taliban would take place. The UN said the expulsion of Patterson and Semple was "a misunderstanding." The Afghan government said they "posed a serious threat to national security." See http://www.telegraph.co.uk/news/worldnews/1573785/Expelled-Western-envoys-fly-out-of-Afghanistan.html; and http://www.longwarjournal.org/archives/2008/01divide_and_conquer_t.php.

6. Maktab is a regular primary school; madrassa, which means school in Arabic, has come in Afghanistan to mean a religious school.

7. The valley is about 100 kilometers in length.

8. See http://www.csmonitor.com/1982/0622/062233.html.

9. Badakhshan is the province in the northeast corner of Afghanistan bordering Tajikistan in Central Asia.

10. Khadamat-e Etela'at-e Dawlati (State Information Agency), the police force created by the communist Democratic Republic of Afghanistan, with strong help from the Soviet Union and East Germany, and under control of the Soviet KGB.

11. Dari is the Afghan dialect of Persian, language of the Tajiks, the main language in Kabul, and of the aristocracy.

12. The Taliban began in 1994 in Kandahar, said to be a corruption of the word "Alexander" from Alexander the Great, who founded the city.

13. About $1600.00. Today there are about 65 Afghanis to one dollar.

14. The Punjab, once in India, is today divided between India and Pakistan. Punjabis dominate the Pakistani bureaucracy and the army.

15. MSF refers to Médecins sans Frontières, or Doctors Without Borders; ICRC

means International Committee for the Red Cross; UNHCR means United Nations High Commission for Refugees; WFP means World Food Program.

16. A producer respectively, and a correspondent, for CBS News.

17. See http://www.nytimes.com/2012/04/18/world/middleeast/saudi-arabia-diplomat-kidnapped-in-yemen.html.

18. The Saudi diplomat was taken from the Saudi Arabian consulate in Aden. He was being held by al-Qaeda, which lives on land owned by tribal leaders, most if not all of whom are on the Saudi payroll. See http://www.cnn.com/2015/03/03/world/yemen-saudi-diplomat-al-qaeda/index.html.

19. The Iranian government is said to be backing the Houthis, who are Shia and live in the north, and run the Yemeni government. A Shia monarchy ruled Yemen for nearly nine hundred years until 1962. The Iranian government said that the diplomat was rescued in an intelligence operation in Yemen. The Houthi government said that he was exchanged for terrorists in an operation outside of Yemen. See http://www.reuters.com/article/us-iran-yemen-diplomat-idUSKBN0M1OI020150305.

20. See http://www.reuters.com/article/us-usa-tradecenter-rahman-aqap-idUSKBN16D2BA.

21. See http://www.readcube.com/articles/10.1111/gove.12255.

22. Part of the release agreement of US Army sergeant Bowe Bergdahl, at least that which is public, is that he would be exchanged for five Taliban prisoners in Guantanamo. By fund-raising, the US was saying that the two were soliciting funds for terrorist activities. A "transit hub" is more likely to mean Dubai than Qatar, however. See https://www.nytimes.com/2014/10/17/world/asia/haqqani-leaders-arrested-afghanistan-khost.html?_r=0.

23. Called Pashtun or Pushtun in Afghanistan, also called Pathan in Pakistan and India.

24. Rawal-pindi, or village of rawals, or yogas, meaning ascetics, there before the founding of Christianity.

25. 500 rupees was less than five dollars, 10,000 rupees less than $100.

26. For an introduction to the Mehsud and the Waziris of Waziristan, a sense of the land, and a glimpse of the current CIA-ISI relationship, see http://www.economist.com/node/15173037.

27. Sir Olaf Caroe, *The Pathans* (Oxford: Oxford University Press, 1958), 393.

28. The Mujahideen Movement.

29. Piotr Stańczak, a Polish geologist searching for oil, was kidnapped in the Punjab, and because militants felt the bridge across the Indus was heavily guarded, they sneaked Stańczak by boat across the river and took him into the Tribal Areas to exchange him for other militants in Pakistani custody. When negotiations failed, Stańczak's captors asked him, a devout Catholic, to convert or they would

kill him. He refused. See http://www.news18.com/news/india/polish-engineer
-killed-in-pak-for-refusing-to-convert-319422.html.

30. In 2009, police arrested Shah Abdul Aziz, a Pakistani politician with
links to the Taliban and a political-religious party, and an unnamed man in the
murder of Stańczak. See https://www.theguardian.com/world/2009/jul/26
/piotr-stanczak-beheading-arrests.

31. November 1990–July 1993.

32. Kroll, describing itself as the world's leading independent risk consulting company, states that by adding K&R insurance to its portfolio of offerings,
its clients will be able to benefit from insurance solutions. See https://www
.thefreelibrary.com/Aon+ASM+Relationship+Gives+Kroll+Clients+Access
+to+Lloyd's+Kidnap+%26 . . . -a0100738569.

33. II Corinthians 6:17.

34. *New York Times*, October 17, 2014, p. A6.

PART FOUR

1. KhAD, or State Information Service, a precursor to the NDS. It was said to
have been revamped after 9/11 by the CIA.

2. US military intelligence believes that Israel has been granted use of air bases
in Azerbaijan, a Muslim country bordering Iran. It appears that Mossad has also
been granted permission to operate from Azerbaijan, which is closer to Pakistan
than Israel. Israeli jets would not need to refuel in the air if they were to launch
an attack on Pakistan's nuclear arsenal from there. See http://www.israelhayom
.com/site/newsletter_article.php?id=3718.

3. "The Hostage Business," al-Jazeera English, 2016, https://www.youtube
.com/watch?v=gEKW-8W5QAI.

4. See http://www.cbsnews.com/news/us-hostage-caitlan-coleman-canadian
-husband-joshua-boyle-make-plea-in-new-video/.

5. See https://www.hulu.com/watch/1017350.

6. HostageUK is an independent charity, cofounded by Terry Waite, that sup-
ports hostages and their families during and after a kidnapping. Rachel Briggs has
since started HostageUS.

7. The Youth, a militant group based in Somalia, with links stretching to the
Tribal Areas of Pakistan.

8. Theo Padnos, a freelance writer, was taken captive by al-Nusrah, the al-
Qaeda affiliate in Syria, on October 12, 2012, and freed August 24, 2014, five
days after Jim Foley was killed, through the help of David Bradley, chairman of the
Atlantic Media Group, and his contacts in Qatar.

9. According to his wife, Paul Overby had been to Afghanistan eight times
and had studied the Qur'an. He returned in 2014 hoping to interview Sirajuddin

Haqqani. His wife said he felt close to the mujahideen. He crossed into Pakistan and has not been seen since. He is thought to be a prisoner now of the Haqqani Network. See https://www.nytimes.com/2017/01/04/us/politics/wife-of-american-man-missing-in-afghanistan-says-he-was-abducted.html?_r=0.

10. The Pentagon tasked Amerine, a rising star within the army, to do whatever it took to secure the release of Bowe Bergdahl. He and his team discovered that the Haqqani Network was also holding other hostages. He tried to help the other hostages and ran afoul of the FBI, which has traditionally been in charge of investigating the kidnappings of all Americans. See http://www.newsweek.com/2015/09/11/jason-amerine-bowe-bergdahl-fbi-taliban-afghanistan-367787.html.

11. Chairman of the Atlantic Media Group who had tried to help the Foleys, Sotloffs, Kassigs, and Muellers, and who helped Theo Padnos.

12. Gates, in testimony in 2001 before the Senate Appropriations Committee, was asked by Senator Patrick Leahy of Vermont about US relations with Pakistan "and with other nations that lie to us." See https://consortiumnews.com/2011/06/17/bob-gatess-business-of-lying/.

13. On August 7, unknown men wearing police uniforms smashed the windows of a vehicle carrying the two men, professors at the new American University of Kabul, and kidnapped them. See https://www.theguardian.com/world/2016/sep/08/us-forces-hostages-kidnapped-kabul-rescue.

Index

ARIEL KILEY

JERE VAN DYK was born in Washington State and raised in a family of Plymouth Brethren. He first went to Afghanistan in 1973 when he and his younger brother drove an old Volkswagen from Germany to Kabul. He returned in 1981 as a young reporter for the *New York Times* and lived with the mujahideen, US allies fighting the Soviet Union. There, and later when he became the director of Friends of Afghanistan, a nonprofit organization overseen by the National Security Council and the State Department, he got to know the leaders who were linked from the beginning with al-Qaeda and the Taliban.

After 9/11, he returned to Afghanistan and Pakistan for CBS News, for which he covered the kidnapping of Daniel Pearl in Karachi. In 2008, he was the next American journalist kidnapped in Pakistan. He is the author of *Captive* and *In Afghanistan*.

PublicAffairs is a publishing house founded in 1997. It is a tribute to the standards, values, and flair of three persons who have served as mentors to countless reporters, writers, editors, and book people of all kinds, including me.

I. F. Stone, proprietor of *I. F. Stone's Weekly*, combined a commitment to the First Amendment with entrepreneurial zeal and reporting skill and became one of the great independent journalists in American history. At the age of eighty, Izzy published *The Trial of Socrates*, which was a national bestseller. He wrote the book after he taught himself ancient Greek.

Benjamin C. Bradlee was for nearly thirty years the charismatic editorial leader of *The Washington Post*. It was Ben who gave the *Post* the range and courage to pursue such historic issues as Watergate. He supported his reporters with a tenacity that made them fearless and it is no accident that so many became authors of influential, best-selling books.

Robert L. Bernstein, the chief executive of Random House for more than a quarter century, guided one of the nation's premier publishing houses. Bob was personally responsible for many books of political dissent and argument that challenged tyranny around the globe. He is also the founder and longtime chair of Human Rights Watch, one of the most respected human rights organizations in the world.

·   ·   ·

For fifty years, the banner of Public Affairs Press was carried by its owner Morris B. Schnapper, who published Gandhi, Nasser, Toynbee, Truman, and about 1,500 other authors. In 1983, Schnapper was described by *The Washington Post* as "a redoubtable gadfly." His legacy will endure in the books to come.

Peter Osnos, *Founder*